"THE HIGHER CHRISTIAN LIFE"

SOURCES FOR THE STUDY OF THE HOLINESS, PENTECOSTAL, AND KESWICK MOVEMENTS

A forty-eight-volume facsimile series reprinting extremely rare documents for the study of nineteenth-century religious and social history, the rise of feminism, and the history of the Pentecostal and Charismatic movements

Edited by

Donald W. Dayton
Northern Baptist Theological Seminary

Advisory Editors

D. William Faupel, *Asbury Theological Seminary*
Cecil M. Robeck, Jr., *Fuller Theological Seminary*
Gerald T. Sheppard, *Union Theological Seminary*

A GARLAND SERIES

FORWARD MOVEMENTS OF THE LAST HALF CENTURY

Arthur T. Pierson

Garland Publishing, Inc.
New York & London
1984

For a complete list of the titles in this series
see the final pages of this volume.

Library of Congress Cataloging in Publication Data

Pierson, Arthur T. (Arthur Tappan), 1837–1911.
FORWARD MOVEMENTS OF THE LAST HALF CENTURY.

("The Higher Christian life")
Reprint. Originally published: New York :
Funk & Wagnalls, 1905.
1. Church history—19th century. 2. Missions—History
—19th century. 3. Evangelistic work—History—19th
century. 4. Church charities—History—19th century.
I. Title. II. Series.
BR477.P54 1984   270.8'1   84-18825
ISBN 0-8240-6437-2 (alk. paper)

The volumes in this series are printed on
acid-free, 250-year-life paper.

Printed in the United States of America

Forward Movements

OF THE

Last Half Century

BY

ARTHUR T. PIERSON

BEING

A glance at the more marked philanthropic,
missionary and spiritual movements
characteristic of our time

FUNK & WAGNALLS COMPANY

NEW YORK AND LONDON

1905

CONTENTS

INTRODUCTION

THE NEED OF A SOUND SPIRITUAL BASIS

It is always important to begin at the beginning. History is not only philosophy teaching by examples, but it is a constant ethical lesson to the studious and candid observer, revealing the secrets of success oftentimes through the record of failure, and constantly challenging a fresh attention to the laws which underlie the truest and largest and most enduring success.

In attempting to trace a few of the more conspicuous spiritual movements of the half century just closing, the main purpose is not so much a historical review, as a practical and spiritual result—a new incitement and inspiration in the direction of further effort, and more aggressive and progressive forms of service to God and man.

This half century has been lustrous and illustrious for the multiplied philanthropic Christian and missionary activities which have sprung up on every side, as growths of God's own planting. But, whatever has been thus far accomplished, we can only think of the poet's words about "the petty done" and "the vast undone." Modern methods, hundred handed as they are, have not yet begun to overtake the misery and poverty, want and woe of humanity. Beginnings are at best but starting points, not goals; revelations of possibilities rather than records of achievements. With the progress of the race, come new disclosures of human need, need so various, so multiplied, so extreme, as almost to paralyze effort by the measureless field of opportunity which it presents. The great question still awaits answer: How shall we cope with the destitution and distress which manifest themselves in myriad forms, all about us?

One inquiry concerns the essence of all true work for God and man, namely, the principles which constitute the base blocks upon which must be reared any enduring structure of service. If these be unsound or defective, there may be need of a reconstruction from the foundation. All serviceableness has its preparations, and to overlook or disregard them prevents even the best-intentioned work from being either effective or lasting.

In his book, " From Death into Life," Mr. Haslam tells of an elderly Cornish woman, deeply taught in the things of God, who, feeling that he was seeking to secure a higher standard of Christian activity without due care to lay right foundations in personal holiness, asked him one day as he passed by, intent on the new church edifice then in his mind, " Mr. Haslam, *are ye goin' to build your spire from the top?* " The quaint question was an arrow, not easily dislodged. He could not get the thought out of mind. " Have I begun at the beginning? Am I building from the bottom, or absurdly attempting to construct from the top down? " Such inquiries he kept asking himself until compelled to start anew and lay the broad, deep, firm foundation of all holy serving in holy praying and holy living. Such experience has been often repeated. Those who have led the way in godly enterprise have seen the radical need of a reconstruction from the base upward, and from them we may learn a divine lesson, that, to make sure first of all that the foundation is well laid on the bed rock of God's eternal plan, is to make the whole structure of our Christian activity to take on new proportions and dimensions, new solidity and beauty, and to prepare us to build into it gold, silver and precious stones, and not wood, hay and stubble. To be thus in fellowship with the great Architect and Builder gives a divine character to our whole work. It becomes in fact His work rather than ours; and, like the Temple of old, it grows up toward completion and consummation, noiselessly, symmetrically, ceaselessly, with no carnal elements built into it, with no stone or timber misplaced, and with no attempt to reshape by tools of worldly wisdom and human invention the blocks which the Divine Workman has hewn and polished in His own quarries and workshops.

It is of human nature to degenerate; and hence eternal vigilance is needful if work for God is to be kept free from worldly elements which corrupt and weaken it. If prayerful and candid disciples survey the present status of the Christian church they cannot fail to see how it is leavened by sectarianism, sacramentalism, ritualism, Romanism, rationalism and a secularism quite as fatal to spirituality as any of the rest. From such conditions a true self-sacrificing type of service is hardly to be expected. There is a serious lack of gospel preaching; reckless extravagance reigns with practical denial of stewardship; and a low level of piety prevails with its natural offspring, virtual infidelity. The church confronts the world, with its thousand million unconverted souls, scattered over fields, continental in breadth, and proves incompetent to reach them with the gospel; while at home, there is a widening gulf between the church and world, which the church cannot bridge, and meanwhile intemperance, licentiousness and anarchy become more threatening and revolutionary.

With deep affection for the brotherhood of Christ and the work of Christ, it seems of great importance to ask whether God is not leading His people to reconstruct all Christian enterprises on a firmer foundation. He seems to us by many signs to be laying new emphasis upon personal and practical holiness both in the individual, and in the collective church life. If our best forms of service are to risk no collapse but prove equal to the growing needs of mankind, some conditions are needful on our part that we may command blessing from above. The word of God must be restored to its supreme place as the inspired, infallible testimony of God; the personality and power of the Holy Spirit, the indispensableness of Christ to human salvation, the universal priesthood of believers and the need of a simple and spiritual worship, the call to separation and selfdenial for Christ, and the neglected hope of the Lord's coming,—these and like truths must be preached, taught, driven home to the conscience—until God's people are brought into more personal, living, loving sympathy with Himself.

When Rev. Dr. Alexander MacLaren, of Manchester, spoke at the Jubilee of the Free Church of Scotland, he thrilled and awed his hearers by characteristic treatment of " Spiritual Dynamics." He showed how wide reaching is the range of spiritual truth, by an illustration which had the force of a demonstration, using the image of a compass, with one foot firmly set in the true center, and the other describing a circle which, while that center was preserved, could not possibly err in width or range of circumference. Our first necessity is to get the truth center and fix there the point of our compass, and then, however wide the circle of our activity, we shall always be right, scriptural, spiritual; and, on the contrary, if we have not the true center and do not keep it, our best enterprises, by whatever name called, will be more or less failures.

Thus far, all great epochs of spiritual activity have been circles with one center: *a revival of Evangelical piety;* and, even within these, smaller circles with a uniform center: PRAYER. In other words, all wider or smaller enterprises of a true Christian character have had one center—a new

approach to God in believing supplication and intercession.
John Wesley unconsciously founded a great movement,
known as Methodism, whose results already are five and a
half million of adherents; but all this can be traced back
to a holy club of four that met in Lincoln College, Oxford,
one hundred and seventy years ago, for cultivation of holiness and prayer. The great revivals that swept over the
United States and Britain between 1830 and 1860 were all
the result of prayer that began with a few burdened souls.
The China Inland Mission leaped into life under the inspiration of one man's supplication. The Bristol Orphanages, with all the work of the Scriptural Knowledge Institution and of missions in all lands, may be traced to that
one apostle of prayer, George Müller.

If we are to sweep a wider circle of power round now
unoccupied territory, and have real progress rather than
apparent and superficial advance, the compass of all
our plans must fix its foot in the firm, pivotal center
of believing prayer and the higher holiness that
is bound up inseparably with devout and privileged
communion with God. In the brief sketches that follow,
we shall find examples of this great law of the spiritual
realm, that, in all solid advance in missions and in all other
forms of holy enterprise, there is first of all a higher type of
holy living, which is itself due to new power in supplication.

There has been no time within the memory of men now
living, which has equaled the present for critical and
pivotal interest. There is a general unrest and dissatisfaction among God's people, a common consciousness of the
need of a higher standard of holiness, and a drawing into
closer fellowship on the part of praying souls, overleaping
all previous barriers of separation and exclusion, believers
fraternizing who have been pent up within high sectarian
fences. Close limits have restrained many Baptists from

communing at the Lord's table with unimmersed believers, and many Anglicans from acknowledging as valid any ordination except that of prelatical bishops, and even from attending a dissenting place of worship; yet, even such walls have not been high enough to keep apart disciples who, in yearning for a deeper spiritual life, have found in other disciples an answering yearning, as, in water, face answereth to face.

In *this union of all disciles in common prayer and self-surrender to God for holy living and serving, is to be found the most significant sign of the times*. It suggests the one practical solution of the problem of missions, if not of all the perplexities of our Christian life. Certain it is that, wherever and so far as these movements have prevailed, the whole church has felt a new and reforming power at work. Prayer meetings have been multiplied and magnified: preaching has taken on new scriptural-tone, and new Spirit power: giving has become more spontaneous and liberal, and offers of service have been made in unprécedented numbers.

The more we study the question of the connection between piety and service, the more we are satisfied that to impart vigor and strength to spiritual life is to get down beneath all the accidental and superficial attendants of the difficulty, to its very root. If missions, for instance, languish, it is because the whole life of godliness is feeble. The command to go everywhere and preach to everybody is unobeyed, until the will is lost by self-surrender in the will of God. There is little right giving because there is little right living, and, because of the lack of sympathetic contact with God in holiness of heart, there is a lack of effectual contact with him at the Throne of Grace. Living, praying, giving and going will always be found together, and a low standard in one means a general debility in the whole spiritual being. We must come to feel and acknowledge this. And, that others may be brought into sympathetic contact with this flood-tide of spiritual sympathy and power which is now sweeping quietly over two continents, we have from the best sources possible, got accurate information on these subjects, and now spread this before our readers, together with accounts of such forms of Christian service as may help to illustrate the effctive working of the principles herein advocated.

May the God of all truth and grace add His blessing to the simple, humble effort to build up from the base a new and growing interest in the work to which our Lord gave Himself and appointed us!

FORWARD MOVEMENTS

CHAPTER I

THE INCREASE OF PERSONAL HOLINESS

'ALL real advance finds its starting-point, as also its goal, in more conformity to God. Character lies back of conduct; what we *are* ultimately shapes what we *do*. Hence the stress of the whole word of God lies upon the transformation of the man himself. His outward acts, his gifts, his prayers, his whole external life, are of little consequence if they are not the expression and exhibition of a renewed spirit, an inner self that partakes of the beauty of the Lord.

Like a bold headland at sea, with its lighthouse to guide the mariner, stand, in the survey of the past fifty years, the singularly varied attempts to raise the standard of practical godliness, sometimes called " Holiness Movements."

Under different names and from divers sources, like mingling streams merged into one flood, the current has been in one direction. Different names—" Entire Sanctification," " Second Conversion," " Higher Christian Life," have clung to these movements; some of them have been stigmatized as "Perfectionism," or mildly described as "for the deepening of spiritual life." As certain phrases have become obnoxious to criticism, linked with fanatical extremes, or calculated to mislead, others have been adopted;

but it is plain that, in all these efforts, the same Holy Spirit has been at work, showing disciples their lack of conformity to God and leading willing souls to new steps of self-surrender and appropriation of Christ. This, beneath all change of names and variety of forms, is the essential fact.

The master problem is *how to make the possible life of a disciple real?* There is an *ideal* which is to be kept before us as the model and pattern of perfection, and which we shall not reach—to reach which would leave no more progress possible. When Thorwaldsen had, for once, realized his own conception in a statue, he felt that henceforth he could accomplish nothing. But there is a *possible* life, a measure of actual approximation to the ideal, which is practically attainable, and has been attained; and it is a great mistake and mischief to count this possible and practicable life as a mere ideal, as is too often the case; but worst of all to regard it as impracticable because the level of living is so low, and the habits of living so carnal, that the possible becomes impossible, the will being too weak to resist evil, and all aspiration being stifled with the impure air we breathe.

How far is a holy life, victorious over sin and restful in God, within reach? and what are the secrets of entrance upon this Land of Promise, this present inheritance which God would have all His saints to enter and enjoy?

First, let us contrast the average life of disciples with the scriptural standard, and, at least, see what is lacking.

Socrates held his mission in Athens to be this, " to bring men from ignorance unconscious to ignorance conscious," and the first step in all attainment is to see that we have not yet attained. From at least seven points of view this contrast may be studied:

1. The Realization and Verification of things unseen and eternal.

2. The Separation and Sanctification of conduct and character.

3. The Transformation of the Inner Life of disposition and temper.

4. The Enthronement of Christ as Master and Lord of the Whole Being.

5. The Experience of the Holy Spirit's indwelling and inworking.

6. The Enjoyment of the Rest Life of Faith, and freedom from anxiety.

7. The Entrance into the Holiest of All, or the right and privilege of Intercession.

If this be not the exact order of importance and of experience, it is not widely divergent therefrom; and a few words upon each of these several points may help to impress the general theme upon our thought, and to show how natural it is that God's people should feel the kindlings of a higher and holier desire, and aspire after some much more advanced attainment.

The sense of the unseen and eternal lies at the basis of spiritual life, which, by its very term, shows its kinship with the invisible and imperishable. This world is real, and seems real because it appeals to our bodily senses; the unseen world seems vague and illusive, because it is beyond the realm of sense, and, unless faith makes it real, it will grow more distant and shadowy, till it becomes a mere phantom of fancy. The writer of the epistle to the Hebrews rebukes those who have not " by reason of use exercised their senses to discern good and evil." Obviously these are not bodily senses, but higher faculties given us of God, as channels of contact and communication with the unseen world. Reason is the sense of the true and false; conscience, of the right and wrong; sensibility, of the attractive and repulsive; imagination, of the ideal and invisible; memory is the sense of the past, and hope, of the future. If these senses are used, they become keener and more acute; if unused, duller and more blunt.

The main office of "closet" communion is the *vivid sense of God,* and hence our Lord's first lesson in the school of prayer emphasizes "thou" and "thy"—for it is necessary to shut all others out, in order to get the vivid vision of God. Far more important is it to hear Him speak to thee than to speak to Him * "Wait on the Lord"—literally, "be *silent* unto Him." This waiting for a vision prepares one for that "practice of the presence of God," which Jeremy Taylor makes the "third instrument of holy living." This vision of God makes the unseen world a verity, a reality, a certainty, as assured as the material universe, and he who thus walks with the unseen God, like Moses, endures as seeing Him who is invisible. The weekly Sabbath rest answers a similar purpose: it leaves us free to converse with celestial things. As the eye rests itself and improves its vision by occasionally looking away from nearer objects to the far horizon or the farthest stars of heaven, the whole soul rests by looking at the unseen and eternal. And he who robs God of holy time by secularizing the Sabbath, cheats himself far more.

So, also, it was expedient that Christ should go away, that henceforth He should not be known after the flesh; and that the Holy Spirit should come to dwell within, with all disciples and at all times, and school us to know Christ by that other unveiling of His personal presence through the inner sense, compelling us to walk by faith, not by sight, no longer dependent on the grosser carnal senses.

So soon as we really begin to live in this unseen realm and walk with this unseen presence, every other attainment becomes possible—in a sense natural. To be under the eye of God—consciously, constantly—to set God always before

* See very important text. Numbers vii.: 89.

us, is to have Him at our right hand, so that we can not be moved. What holy intrepidity, when He is near, and what courage in conflict with evil and in confronting barriers to service! The conduct and character become separated unto Him and sanctified, because it is impossible to sin deliberately while He is not lost sight of. It is only when we flee from His presence, like Jonah, that disobedience is habitual. To hold one's self directly under God's eye, and to stand before Him with the eye upon Him, waiting for His beck and glance, compels personal holiness—is itself the very attitude of holy obedience. In His presence sin flees as shadows before the light, for transgressions are deeds of darkness.

Even the inmost life of temper and disposition becomes transformed—transfigured—when we live as in His secret chambers. When He encompasses and enspheres us, He interposes between us and all the foes of our inward peace. Envy, jealousy, malice, anger, impatience, ungentleness, uncharitableness, unloveliness,—all these belong outside of the sphere where God and the saint meet and dwell together. It is amazing how *immediate,* and even *instantaneous,* may be the actual entrance into a new atmosphere of inward peace, when once a disciple, after many years of hopeless struggle and wrestle with that inward tormentor —a vicious temper, an unholy anger, an unsanctified disposition—suddenly enters into the conscious presence of God—feels that He is a living, present God, and that He can bring under control that wicked and unruly member, the tongue, and that even more unruly " member," the temper; so that one just gives it over into His keeping and lets Him subdue it. And then, to see Him do it! and not only conquer it, but *displace* it, and in its stead give outright its very opposite—flooding the heart with His love—so that instead of a constant war against evil, there is a new impulse, a passion for the right, so that we wonder that we ever saw any occasion for the childish impatience and fretfulness and selfishness of past years!

What a step, too, when the keys of the whole house are surrendered up to the Lord Jesus, and the whole government of the little empire within transferred to His shoulder; when the last locked room and cupboard and secret chamber of our imagery and idolatry are thrown open to Him, and He sweeps out all the vile things which the godless life has hoarded and hidden; and then turns the very hiding places of our abandoned idols into the sanctuary of His presence and communion! The enthronement of Christ in the soul—*that* is His manifestation unto the believer, as never unto the world, which is the crown of all promises. * Then it is that God " reveals His son *in* " us, and shows the vast difference between a Christ *within* and a Christ *without*—a Christ no longer knocking at the door but supping at the banquet board, He with us and we with Him.

Christ ought to be, and may be, on the throne of our inner being, Master, Lord, Sovereign. And when He is enthroned, self is dethroned. The self-life is the last inner enemy to be destroyed. It is the root of all forms of sin; and, long after every known sin and weight are put away, it survives; and when every other form of pride is brought into the dust, the subtle survival of the self-life is seen in the pride of humility. What a hydra-headed monster self is!—self-trust, self-help, self-will, self-seeking, self-pleasing, self-defense, self-glory, always intruding between the soul and its true Sovereign. To enthrone Christ in the inmost life, is to find self-distrust, self-abandonment, self-surrender, self-denial, self-renunciation, self-commitment, self-oblivion, taking the place of those hideous evils already named.

As to the Spirit's work, how few disciples even under-

* John xiv.: 23.

stand it! That sublime sentence of ten words: *He that is joined unto the Lord is one spirit* * is the summit of all revelation as to the believer's inseparable wedlock with the Lord, and it is the key which unlocks both Epistles to the Corinthians. For, inasmuch as the Holy Spirit is one with the believing human spirit, He must evince such unity by the impress of God left by Him upon the believer's inner life and outer life. And so Paul teaches that God's wisdom is reflected in the disciple's knowledge of divine things; God's ownership, in His possession of the believer as His temple; God's sovereignty, in His distribution of gifts and spheres of services; God's eternity, in the glory of the undying resurrection body; God's power, in the believer's transformation into His likeness; God's holiness, in His sanctification, and God's blessedness, in His ecstatic visions and experiences. †

But, beside the Spirit's indwelling, our privilege is to know His threefold inworking: His *sealing,* in our assurance, His *anointing,* in our illumination, His *filling,* in our gracious power for service. What a monstrous evil is that, when a child of God, who may know and feel the miracle of such indwelling, inworking and outworking of the Divine Spirit, lives a life that so grieves and quenches the Holy Ghost, that He is like a silent " voice " or a stifled and scarce burning flame!

As to the Rest Life of Faith, with its casting of all care upon God, and its perfect peace of trust, the fact that such experience is possible ought to fill every disciple with a divine unrest until it is actually his possession. This is the spiritual Canaan, the true land of promise, now to be entered, appropriated, enjoyed. Egypt with its bondage, burdens, sins, and sorrows, left behind—the desert, with its wandering, barrenness, disquiets and defeats, also left

---

* 1 Cor. vi. : 17.
  See 1 Cor. ii., vi., vii., xii., xv., and 2 Cor. iii., vi., xii.

behind, and the Jordan of a new consecration and self-surrender crossed, that He who brought us out may bring us in, into conscious fellowship with God, victory over the Anakim, possession of the promises, and fruitfulness of service. All this disciples have known, like Paul, and, thank God, thousands now know; and it is only because unbelief limits God and disobedience limits ourselves, that all who are born of God do not cross this Jordan and march through this Land of milk and honey, vineyards and orchards, forests of timber and mines of precious metal, and claim it and all its riches, as their own.

The last feature of the possible life in God is the privilege of entering within the rent veil and standing as priests and intercessors, immediately before the Mercy Seat. Prevailing prayer is so rare that it seems to be a lost art. Yet what unequivocal promises offer their crown to the suppliant believer! *"Whatsoever ye shall ask in my name"*—can anything surpass that! The only limitation to that universal " whatsoever," is " IN MY NAME," which is seven times repeated for emphasis. * The Name stands for the Person, and to ask in His name is to ask by right of oneness, identification by faith, with Him; so that, *in effect, He becomes the suppliant.* Whoever authorizes me to proffer a request in His name, *himself makes that request through me,* and the party of whom it is asked sees him back of the petitioner. This is our Lord's last lesson in the school of prayer, as closet seclusion was the first; and well it may be the last, for beyond it there is nothing more to be learned or enjoyed.

It is plain that very few, even among praying saints, do so prevail in prayer, and we all *know* it. Thousands of earnest petitions seem wasted, and, judged by results, *are* wasted. Either, therefore, God is untrue or man is unfaithful. The former supposition would be blas-

* John xiv.-xvi.

phemy; and we are driven to the conclusion that there is little real asking in Jesus' name. Here is the real core of the difficulty. Unbelief, disobedience, an alienated heart, separate the believer from Christ and the Spirit, so that the bond is practically ineffective; prayer in Jesus' name is too high a privilege and prerogative to be enjoyed without intimate union, a *sympathy* that Christ himself calls a *symphony*. * Symphony is musical accord, and implies chords, attuned to the same key and to each other and struck by an intelligent musician's hand. Even a saved soul may live a life so practically unbelieving, unloving, unsubmissive, that there is discord rather than concord— then such symphony becomes impossible, and the words " in Jesus' name " become a mere form, if not a farce.

The teaching of the word is unmistakable. James, and John, and Paul, complete Christ's lesson, and teach that it is only *holiness of life* which brings such accord with God as to make possible prayer in Jesus' name. While I continue in sin, neglect known duty, regard iniquity in my heart, the Lord can not hear me. Such a life sounds in His ear one long discord; disobedience makes even prayer a new affront to God. But, so far as we are swayed by faith, love, obedience, zeal for God's glory, the Spirit groans within and our prayers find their way into Christ's censer, and come back in answers which are mingled with the fire from the altar above. †

The believing, obedient disciple may thus enter into the Holiest of all, and take his stand as a *priest*—note the meaning of the word—*one who stands before God;* he may come to the very Mercy Seat, claim the intercessor's right and place, and, like Noah and Job, Abraham and Moses, Samuel and David, Elijah and Daniel, prevail with God. What wonder that the patriarch of Bristol, sixty-five years

* Matt. xviii.: 19. Greek.
† Rom. viii.; Rev. viii.

ago, gave himself to a life of intercession that he might prove to an unbelieving world and a half believing church that God is a present, living, faithful prayer-hearing God!

We have thus, as briefly as was possible, outlined the holiness movement of our century. It is this life of seven-fold privilege, power, and blessing, that the Holy Spirit is urging upon God's people by many forms of appeal; and the fact that extremes and errors now and then appear in connection with human advocacy of a holier life should not serve to obscure the fact that, underneath all the worthless driftwood that is borne on by this current, there is a deep, onflowing River of God.

We must at least advert to some of the conspicuous leaders of these holiness movements, if only to mention a few of them.

Charles Grandison Finney was one of the conspicuous promoters of this advance. He stands especially for the *responsible activity of the human will, versus the passivity of a fatalistic election.* He found himself living in an age of apathy, when even disciples were idly and indifferently consenting to a life, alike devoid of holiness and power, waiting for some irresistible impulse from above. And he thundered out remonstrance. He emphasized the neces-sity and liberty of the Human Will, in salvation and sanc-tification; and carried his doctrine so far, that he main-tained that all sin and holiness depend mainly on the atti-tude of the will, and hence that a *perfect choice of God* and goodness is essentially a perfect life.

Asa Mahan, and others of the same school, represent especially the definite *reception of the Holy Spirit in sanc-tification and for service.* He maintained with singular force and power that an unholy life is one which is incon-sistent with the fundamental law of salvation; that there is to be a new creation, and that the disposition is to be rad-ically renewed by the grace of God; and that this inner transfiguration may be as instantaneous as the type of it, in Christ's transfiguration.

William E. Boardman stands for a *higher Christian life* —a change, corresponding to conversion, and often known as a " second conversion "—in which the change of attitude Godward, conscious witness of God's indwelling and inworking, and power to work for human salvation, are as unmistakable as the transition from night to day.

R. Pearsall Smith, and others like him, advocated and emphasized *non-continuance in sin*, abandonment of every *weight*, even tho not positively sinful, and a definite consecration, whereby the wilderness life is left behind for the Canaan life.

The Plymouth brethren, with all their divisive, exclusive, and sometimes controversial tendencies, have with uncompromising hostility fought for the *Word of God* as the final rule of faith and practise, for a *simple apostolic worship*, and *a literal obedience to Christ's teachings*. They have done as much as any class of disciples to promote *practical separation from the world*, and must not be forgotten in the general estimate of the factors contributing to the great final result, a sanctified and peculiar people for God.

The Methodists deserve recognition, as leaders in insisting on " Sanctification," ever since the days of Wesley; but we are now particularly tracing *recent* developments without respect to denominations. The Mystics also would deserve a very prominent place in this survey, only that their history reaches back through the ages and demands separate treatment; yet it is not to be overlooked that *every great movement* in the direction of holier life is inseparable from this great current of thought that is associated with such as Jacob Böhme, St. Theresa, Catherine of Siena, Madame Guyon, Fénélon, Tauler, and William

Law. They who taught " vision by means of a higher light, and action under a higher freedom " may have run to extremes, but they got hold of two essential principles that underlie all the highest and holiest experiences, and many of them closely walked with God.

Among all the leaders of this holiness movement, we regard one, hitherto unnoticed as such, as unsurpassed in his way—the late and widely mourned Adoniram J. Gordon. Without ever talking much about it, or even thinking of himself as an example or advocate of a holy life, he *lived* what many others *taught,* and *walked* while they *talked.* Never has the writer known any man in America whose crystalline beauty and symmetry and transparency of spirit surpassed his. How far Dr. Gordon *taught* holiness is seen in his books on the " Twofold Life," the " Ministry of the Spirit," " How Christ Came to Church," etc. But how he *lived* holiness, only those know who daily enjoyed his companionship, and saw his face shine with the beauty of the Lord that was upon him.

The theme we are treating is of sublime practical importance; it is colossal, overtopping all other subjects in its magnitude as related to the triumph of Christ in this world. Only a " peculiar people " will ever be " zealous of good works." While we seek to build up missions or service to mankind, upon any other foundation than holiness unto the Lord, we are basing our work upon quicksand. All the " enthusiasm " in the world will only be like froth and foam, which overflow and leave nothing behind,—a deceptive delusive glow of sentiment, a temporary and untrustworthy excitement, followed by reaction into more hopeless apathy—unless obedience be beneath —and obedience itself based on the rock of love—a secret sympathy and affinity with God.

If God's call to a new life might lead the reader to immediate and unconditional committal to the will

of God—to a final break with the world, a final abandonment of all known sin, however seemingly trivial;
a renunciation of all doubtful indulgences, as " not of
faith " and therefore " sin "—if the hesitating and unbelieving would take the step into the overflowing Jordan,
and test God's power to bring them *in* and make the promises their own, what fulness of blessing might come to a
halting church and a revolted world!

CHAPTER II

THERE is one modern contribution both to the literature and the life of holiness which is attracting, as it deserves, wider attention than any other single development in this direction; and the whole history connected with it becomes correspondingly important. Its results have already a far wider range, and forecast a much broader future, than most of us realize. One who was as well qualified to supply the earlier records as any other, and who recently passed away from earth at an age past three score and ten, has given his calm judgment on " The genesis of the Oxford movement for the promotion of holiness." We give it a place here, for he was intimately, and from the beginning, both an actor in, and an observer of, what he here puts on record.

The spiritual history of the coming decades in England can be predicted largely from the spiritual currents among the younger men of the universities. The " High Church " or " Puseyite " tidal wave was rightly called " the Oxford movement." The " evangelical impulse," given mainly by Charles Simeon, was similarly called " the Cambridge movement." Succeeding, or parallel to this last, was a radical highly Calvinistic impulse through the unorganized body called " the Plymouth Brethren." In the well-known book, " The Fairchild Family," by Mrs. Sherwood, one may find the evangelical teaching pressed to its extreme and least attractive forms, and in the numerous and widely circulated publications of the " Plymouth

Brethren " will be found the teaching of the strongest doctrines as to implicit literal " obedience to the Word," or Scripture, combined with strictest Calvinistic statements as to the forensic condition of the believer, as an unalterable complete state of grace. The influence of this latter teaching extended through both the Established Church and most of the dissenting bodies, far beyond the limits of the unorganized Plymouth Brethren themselves, who, without formal membership or denominational system, met " to break bread," as they termed the act of communion.

In the seventies, the first generation of these three forms of revival was passing away, and the successors, who had not shared the deep spiritual crisis in which the High Church, evangelical and Brethren movements originated, found themselves with forms, either of ritual, or of doctrine, which, dulled by use, failed to meet their spiritual needs as they had supplied those of their predecessors. There was a felt lack of, and a great hungering for, a personal righteousness, which should really meet their too often starving spiritual natures. Taught that they were sacramentally complete by absolution on one hand, or judicially, forensically, perfect by forgiveness of sin on the other, they yet found themselves unsatisfied, with no well of living water within, as promised in Scripture. They lived with a high standard of holiness, yet under frequent or almost constant sense of condemnation for transgression. They exaggerated the doctrine, often expressed in the words " black but comely; " or, as they would state in prayer-meetings, they were " from the crown of the head to the sole of the foot full of bruises and putrefying sores," while yet forgiven saints, and by imputation " whiter than snow," and ready for heaven itself. Their supposed judicial standing and their lives of practical failure, were in startling contrast.

In this condition of mind numberless tender-hearted Christians found a sorrow which nothing reached. They felt that they were by their failures continually grieving the One in all the universe whom they loved best, and they suffered constantly renewed sorrow. Saved, as they believed, for eternity, from the penalty of sin, they were yet in many respects under sin's acknowledged power. They were not gross sins, but sins of pride, anger, temper, censoriousness, evil thoughts; and they even sometimes felt that some around them who made no Christian profession were more free from failure than themselves.

In 1873 a series of papers written in America appeared in a London weekly, now named *The Christian*, which called atttention to a neglected part of scriptural teaching. This teaching was that Christ came to save His people *from their sins*, and not from the consequences of them only; that in the Epistles His offering of Himself was oftener stated as for their sanctification than even for their justification; that " He gave Himself for us that He might purify unto Himself a people," etc. " Who His own self bore our sins in His own body on the tree, *that we, being dead to sin, should live unto righteousness.*" This was felt to be more than judicial pardon and imputed righteousness. One part of the Gospel had been fully preached, pardon to the sinner, forgiveness to the repentant transgressor; but its complement of a practical, continuous victory over temptation, equally provided in the Gospel, had been overlooked. A false humility, while boldly claiming pardon for sins, overlooked its correlative victory over sin.

These " views " in *The Christian* deeply affected great numbers of spiritual Christians, and when, in 1873, they were emphasized in meetings, beginning in the rooms of the London Young Men's Christian Associations, many were greatly changed by them in their attitude as to faith and personal consecration, and consequently in their lives.

What was taught was simply that a completed consecration of will and a completed trust in the Word of Christ would bring the Christian into a realization of the promises of victory over sin, and into sustained communion with God; that the only normal condition of the "believer" was that of full belief; of the "child of God," implicit obedience. That, as a bird cannot rise on one wing, so in both full trust and full obedience alone could a disciple find the promises of victory over sin a continuing reality.

What gave effect to this teaching was the steady insistence that here and now, even while this simple truth was being preached, the Christian should yield his too often divided will, give up some doubtful or consciously condemned idol or practice, and commit himself to an unreserved trust and obedience. Often it was like death itself to renounce something more or less clearly known to be evil. " I would die if I gave it up," said a popular preacher, referring to an unhallowed indulgence. The reply was, " Life to a Christian is not a necessity; obedience is. The early Christians preferred death to disobedience, and so must you." The agony almost of death was in his countenance as he said, " Then I renounce it." The battle of Waterloo is said to have depended on the possession of a small cottage as a key to the contest. It was often some small matter in which *the will* was entrenched, and till this was yielded full trust was impossible; and, conversely, often till a full trust was exercised the yielding was impossible. How near souls often were to the Rock and knew it not ! A man descending a well by a rope found himself at the end of the line, and soon his strength began to fail. He could not climb up, and to let go would be, he supposed, to be dashed to pieces. At length he could hold on no longer, and dropped. The distance to the rock was—*three inches!* How often have we seen the spiritual counterpart of this scene!

Words can but imperfectly describe the joy and spiritual power which came through the extension of these meetings to thousands of clergymen and religious teachers, and to Christians in less conspicuous conditions. By the liberal kindness of Samuel Morley, the Member of Parliament for Bristol, a leading Congregationalist, a series of breakfasts were given in London in 1874-75 for ministers, which were attended by twenty-four hundred preachers, mostly at breakfast-tables of thirty or forty in a morning. Continuous meetings of a few days at a time were held in London and the provinces and in various cities on the Continent; and, in 1874, in response to the request of a number of young men at the University of Cambridge, the late Lord Mount-Temple opened his country seat, " Broadlands," widely known as the residence of the late Lord Palmerston, for a meeting of ten days. This was by private invitation, and so great was the blessing found, that it was felt that another and larger meeting must be convened. This resulted in a meeting at Oxford of clergymen of the Establishment, as well as preachers and members of the various churches, about a thousand in number, gathered from all parts of England. At this " Convention " many pastors were also present from the Continent; and similar meetings were held later in France, Belgium, Holland, Switzerland, and Germany, which were crowded, sometimes the addresses being repeated twice in the same evening to as many as six thousand hearers. Everywhere the same remarkable results in the revival of the Christian life were realized. In France, Theodore Monod, in Switzerland, Pastor Stockmeyer, and in other countries others held similar " conventions," or " retreats " upon the same model.

In 1875 a yet larger meeting of ten days was held at Brighton, attended by about six thousand persons, among whom were about two hundred and fifty pastors from Italy, Germany, Switzerland, Sweden, Norway, Belgium, Holland, and France, and also the venerable Bishop Gobat of Jerusalem.

And now, after twenty-five years, there are still held annually in England, many such " retreats " or " conventions " on a similar plan of three-day to ten-day continuous services. The one at Keswick, established by the Rev. Canon Battersby, is widely known. The one at Guilford collects about five thousand persons annually. From many countries on the Continent continual reports come of continuous blessing still attributed to this movement. At Nancy, for twenty years a pastor has held a weekly meeting as a remembrance and continuation of the blessings received at Brighton.

This spontaneous, unorganized movement, so far as is known, never resulted in a change of the Church connection of a single individual from that in which it found him. It gave him power to work in the sphere in which he already lived. The establishment of a new denomination was confidently predicted by some, but its announced object was not a change of either doctrine or organization, but a revival of living faith in truths already accepted, and in full practical obedience within spheres already found.

All this was without public emotional expression, indication of physical excitement, not even a single Amen ! being spoken aloud. Those who led it, as it happened, did not need pecuniary support, and with little mention of needs for rents of halls and traveling expenses of Continental pastors, there was a surplus of many thousands of pounds of voluntary contributions, while no portion of a guaranty fund of twenty-five hundred pounds was required.

Seventy ushers waited on the meetings at Brighton, held in several languages, from seven o'clock in the morning almost continually till ten at night. The civic corporation gave three large halls and many rooms for the purpose, free of charge.

Among other results, a great and continuous impulse has been given the missionary movement, through the completed obedience and faith of Christians attending these " consecration meetings." Perhaps, the results were larger in Germany than in England. A German theological professor has said that, as Justification by Faith had once been established in German theology, so now sanctification by faith has likewise been largely accepted. In various quarters a great impulse was given by this wave, *to missionary work, the dedication of the will, the central thought of it all, leading to this form of service* in large numbers of cases.

When Mrs. Catherine Booth was dying she said to Mr. Edward Clifford, who was much with her, that the Oxford-Brighton movement was one of the principal means of the establishment of the work of the Salvation Army, or rather an aid to it. It brought the great number of the upper classes who have been effectually reached, into sympathy with the Salvation Army, the central power of which was the same—a completed consecration and a full faith. Curiously, therefore the " High Church " were reached at one end, and the " Free Methodists " at the other. And yet more curiously, it was the means of forwarding the agnostic " Peoples' Church " through an attendant at Brighton, who, in a joyous sense of a yielded will, and full trust, feeling the force of the historical difficulties in Christianity, tho he seemed as earnest, sincere, consecrated and true in heart as ever, felt led with the same sort of personal devotion to making a church for the large class of morally good men among the working

classes whom he found seemingly incapable of Christian
faith, in its historical sense, and he formed congregations
out of such. Many such men acknowledge that the spiritual leverage,—the power to immediately and greatly move
souls to make a choice—is wanting. In one of George Mac-
donald's novels he makes the typical " broad " doctrine cu-
rate effect only a modification of a carpenter's cynical views
of life! Sudden and effectual conversion—the ordinary
work to be wrought by evangelical preaching—is not in it,
though he had the novelist's choice.

The essence of Christianity seems to lie, not so much
in doctrine, even historical, as in the surrender of the will
and effectual realization of the real Fatherhood of God
and Brotherhood of Christ: and one burns to have these
things proclaimed in power, and souls brought out of that
misery of a conscience quickened while yet there is a
divided heart—into the joyous obedience of a realized son-
ship. This is the truth which has formed " the church
within the church " in all the ages—the inner church
which instructed Luther and the great apostles of the
faith,— even while some of them rejected the form it took.

It would not be well to close this notice of the movement
without stating what is *not* meant by the teaching above
described. Everywhere anxiety prevailed among good
Christians lest it should mean " sinless perfection." Perhaps our danger lies more in sinful imperfection, but yet
it is an honest anxiety based on occasional fanaticisms.
The wine of the Kingdom, like earthly wine, proves sometimes too much for ill-balanced souls. It was interesting
to see persons coming to these meetings full of the expectation of hearing " sinless perfection " preached, and then
to note their surprise as a speaker opened with the words,
" Perhaps no one has ever accurately defined and limited
the term *Sin*. If it be the coming short of the absolute
holiness of the Divine, I sin in every breath I draw." Such

hearers would look in surprise at one another, and the speaker would continue: " But if continuous, conscious trespass be made the necessary inevitable condition of the Christian; if he, by the law of his existence, as a follower of Christ, must continuously and inevitably grieve Him whom he loves best in all the universe; if the fence between sinners sinning and saints obeying be thrown down; if Christ did not die to redeem us all from iniquity, and purify us unto Himself, to save us from our sins, then is the Gospel a failure as regards this life, and the will of God is not our sanctification." Yet no one can claim deliverance from sin in any other sense than victory over known, discovered sin. Had we the insight of angels, we could not take one step in our confused surroundings without conscious sin. But from *known* sin, from discerned evil, one may find deliverance in Christ. And as we walk in the light and in obedience, each day shows us more of evil to be avoided. In to-day's light yesterday's sin of ignorance may become one of knowledge, to be now conquered. No wise person will boast that he has not sinned for such and such a time. But he may say, that to the utmost of his trust is his victory over known sin; and that so far as he does not trust, in so far he fails. In such a life, the moment of confession of sin is the moment of realized pardon, and also of power to avoid its repetition.

Wherein, then, does the present life of those who have found this blessing differ from former experience? It differs, first in not expecting to sin, and not making provision for the flesh to fulfil the lusts thereof; and then, in the courage of faith, that secret of victory, and the coincidence of our wish or will with what we as yet know of God's will, which makes a *habit* of victory and obedience.

You claim an undivided allegiance to your country, entire loyalty to your wife, complete affection for your children—is it impossible to have, as to the totality of your condition, equally true relations to God? Must you be partly a rebel, an adulterer, indifferent to your children? Nay, even tho there be momentary failure, the trend of your being, the habit of your life, the current of your existence, may—nay, *must*—be henceforth allegiance, loyalty, love. Then you no longer are under law—a sense of compulsion, a contest of inclination, but your will, now completely yielded, becomes henceforth that of God.

> " I worship Thee, sweet Will of God,
>   And all Thy ways adore,
>   And every day I live, I learn
>   To love Thee more and more."

CHAPTER III

KESWICK is a town of Cumberland, England, on the south bank of the Greta, some twenty-four miles from Carlisle, and having a population of from three thousand to four thousand. It has no importance commercially, tho its manufactures indicate industry and its two museums index intelligence. In this Lake District, forever famous by association with Coleridge, Southey and the poets of the Lake School, Keswick's vale is unsurpassed for picturesque beauty and fascinating scenery.

But Keswick is yet better known by the annual convention of believers already referred to, which meets there annually, during the last week in July, and during the whole year more or less radiates blessed influence through the empire and the world. More than twenty-five years ago that remarkable movement began in Britain, which in a previous chapter was traced to its beginning, and which has ever since been in progress, a sort of modern Pentecost, whose depth of meaning and breadth of influence were unknown and unsuspected at first, even by the movers of it.

An American evangelist, R. Pearsall Smith, a man whose tracts and addresses have for many years been a stimulus to holy living, was, with his wife, Hannah Whithall Smith, providentially among those who were connected with the inception of the movement.

It is a singular fact that God seldom moves only on one section of the Church, or in one locality, alone. Simultaneous quickenings commonly take place in various parts of the world, as the reinvigoration of a human body would show itself in different members and even at the opposite extremities, at the same time.

These various conventions, across the sea, were held, as we have seen, in 1874, at Broadlands, July 17-23, and at Oxford, August 8 to September 1, then at Brighton, May 29 to June 7, 1875, and the first Keswick Convention followed, from June 29 to July 2 of the same year. With the convening of the last mentioned, the lamented Canon Battersby is inseparably connected, who, as he wanted a layman to cooperate, invited Mr. Robert Wilson to join him. The first Keswick Convention was attended by between three hundred and four hundred. The Brighton gathering was for ten days, and from 6,000 to 8,000 were present.

About the time when these meetings were held in rapid succession in Britain and on the continent, there were in more than one quarter in the United States similar gatherings, as at Oberlin, Ohio, and in Maine, on the borders of Canada, where a great company assembled for purposes akin to that of the British meetings, 40,000 special railway tickets being sold in connection with the Maine conference alone.

Rev. Evan H. Hopkins, who has been closely identified with the Keswick meetings for years, has briefly written the history of this movement. * He says:

During 1873, small meetings were held in London, where great and definite blessings were realized by a few. These led to larger gatherings, and in the year 1874 special meetings for consecration, for two or three days at a time, were held at the Mildmay Conference Hall, and at the Hanover Square Rooms. These were followed by similar meetings in Dublin, Manchester, Nottingham, and Leicester. On the Continent, too, meetings for the same purpose and on exactly similar lines were held. The result was that very many of God's children, both at home and abroad, were awakened to a deep sense of need, and to an expectation of larger

---

* Life of Faith. July 22, 1896.

and more definite blessing, such as they had never conceived possible in this life. The uplifting of soul experienced by many was one of the most striking features of the movement, and the effect of their testimony upon those who came within the sphere of their influence, was one of the chief factors in arousing the Church to seek the realization of its privileges in the matter of triumph, usefulness, and power.

In the summer of 1874, the first convention at Broadlands was held. Its origin was in the desire that a number of young university men, who had found partial blessing in some meetings for consecration held at Cambridge, should have a few days of quiet meditation and prayer in some secluded spot, keeping before them the following definite aim: The Scriptural possibilities of the Christian life, as to maintained communion with the Lord and victory over all known sin. The plan was extended to the invitation of about a hundred persons for six days—July 17 to 23.

Such was the absorbing interest felt by all, that no difficulty was found in gathering the guests at seven o'clock in the morning; and it was an effort to separate when the breakfast hour of nine came. At ten o'clock conversational meetings were held, Bibles in hand, in different places through the grounds, and at eleven o'clock there was prayer, with singing and addresses. Meetings for ladies only were also held; and at three o'clock conversational meetings, followed by a general gathering at four; and after tea Bible-readings, till the regular evening meeting. The manifested presence and power of God pervaded every meeting, and many stated that the long periods of silent prayer had been to them the most solemn and helpful seasons of their spiritual life.

One wrote at the time: " We began with the negative side, renunciation of discerned evil, and even of doubtful things which are not of faith, and therefore sin. For some days the company was held under the searching light of God, to see and to remove any obstacles to a divine communion, or aught that frustrated the grace of God. We sought to have that which was true in God as to our judicial standing in a risen Christ, also true in personal appropriation and experience. Many secret sins, many a scarcely recognized reserve as to entire self-renunciation, were here brought up into the light of consciousness and put away in the presence of the Lord. We desired to make *thorough* work, so as to have no known evil or self-will unyielded; and we took the position of solemn purpose to renounce instantly everything in which we should find ourselves 'otherwise minded,' as from time to time 'God shall reveal even this unto us.'

"In the intervals of the meetings it was interesting to see groups gathered, in the more secluded places in the woods by the river, on their knees, praying, searching the Scriptures, or speaking earnestly to each other of the all-absorbing subject of our meetings. Some one had proposed to have reading at the mealtimes, so as to concentrate our minds; but no such plan was needed to keep the company, even at times of refreshment, to the one engrossing subject."

In a letter received from Pasteur Theodore Monod at the time, reference is made to this memorable occasion. He says: "The difference between those Broadlands meetings and many others that I have attended is just the difference between a flower and the name of a flower. Christians too often meet only to talk about good and precious things: peace, joy, love, and so on; but there we actually had the very things themselves. I cannot be grateful enough to God for having led me into such a soul-satisfying and God-glorifying faith. I think I may say that I got all that I expected, and more. And I begin to suspect that we always get from God everything—provided it be good for us—that we ask for, expecting to get it. Oh, for self-forgetting faith, that I may have more and more and more of it, and that the Church of Christ may cease to grieve Him, distress herself, and hinder the coming of His Kingdom, by disbelieving His Word! My French companions have all derived much benefit from the Conference. God be praised for His work! Never mind the world, nor the devil, so long as you have the sunshine of Jesus' smile in your heart."

During this Convention our brother Monod wrote the now well-known hymn, "The Altered Motto:"

> Oh! the bitter shame and sorrow
> That a time could ever be,
> When I let the Savior's pity
> Plead in vain, and proudly answered,
> "All of self and none of Thee."

It was only a short time before this hymn was written that our brother entered into the "fulness of blessing."

The account of the Broadlands Conference was read far and wide, and awakened considerable interest. Many who had never attended any meetings of the kind were led to cry to God for the fulness of the Spirit, with an expectation and earnestness of desire they had never before known. At the close of the meetings one said, " We must repeat these meetings on a larger scale, where all who desire can attend." And one of the guests volunteered £500 toward the expenses of this effort. But none of this money was found to. be necessary when the proposal was actually carried out in the conference that followed. So abundant were the offerings that large sums remained over actual expenses, to be devoted to the extension of the movement on the Continent.

It was suggested by the late beloved Sir Arthur Blackwood, who was present at Broadlands, that this proposed convention should be held at Oxford during the vacation, and it was accordingly held from August 29 to September 7, 1874. The details of the meetings were settled during a mission week in August, at Langley Park, the seat of the late Sir Thomas Beauchamp, Bart., near Norwich, who, having received great blessing himself in a similar meeting the previous year, again gathered about forty clergymen, and many others, for five days' waiting upon God for consecration and prayer. The invitation to the " Oxford Union Meetings for the Promotion of Scriptural Holiness," was issued on the 8th of August, 1874. Tho the notice was so short, a large and representative number of Christians came from all parts of the kingdom, as well as a great many pastors from the Continent.

An able review that appeared immediately after, will give some idea of the deep impression made during those ten days at Oxford :—

" ' God hath visited His people.' If any one had said a year ago that we should see, in Oxford, an assembly of Christians, very largely composed of ministers of the Establishment and various Nonconformist bodies, and including twenty or thirty Continental pastors, gathered for the purpose of seeking, by mutual counsel and united prayer and consecration, to reach a higher condition of Christian life, it would have been considered far more devoutly-to-be-wished than likely to occur. And if it had been added that we should see early morning meetings of nearly a thousand of these men and women, of all ranks in society, and of all denominations, gathered in prayer, and for the communication of their experiences in the divine life, clergymen and laymen standing up and declaring what God had done

for their souls, there would have been not a few to say, 'If the
Lord would open windows in heaven might such a thing be!'
But God *has* opened the windows of heaven, and is pouring out
a blessing that there shall not 'be room to receive it.' And not
only so, but 'God hath chosen the foolish things of the world
to confound the wise; and the weak things to confound the
things which are mighty; that no flesh should glory in His
presence.'

*   *   *   *   *

"We have attended many conferences, but in many respects
this excelled them all. It is the fruit and flower of those which
have gone before—of those at Barnet, and Mildmay, and Perth,
and other places at home, as well as of Mannheim, and Vineland
and Round Lake, in the United States. Conferences must be of
another type henceforth.

"If it be asked, What is 'the blessing?' it is the blessedness of
the man 'who maketh the Lord his trust,' 'whose strength is
in Thee;' of them who have not seen and yet have believed, who
stand by night in the house of the Lord trusting where they
cannot see Him, who present their bodies a living sacrifice, holy,
acceptable to God, their reasonable service, and who, doing this,
are not conformed to this world, but are daily being transformed,
by the renewing of their minds, that they may know what that
good and acceptable and perfect will of the Lord is."

At this Oxford Convention the late Canon Harford-Battersby
himself entered into "the rest of faith." But for this event the
now well-known Keswick Convention would never have had a beginning.*

Very soon after, similar meetings on a smaller scale, but on
the same lines, were held at Stroud, and two brethren who had
taken part at the Oxford meetings conducted this Conference,
and the Rev. Preb. Webb-Peploe was amongst the listeners. He
had not been able to attend the Oxford Conference, and we think
it was only at the Stroud Conference, or soon after, that he himself definitely entered into the blessing of the more abundant
life. The Cheltenham Conference followed the Stroud Convention, and there for the first time he actually took part in the
movement.

The next great series of meetings was the wonderful Brighton

* "Canon Harford-Battersby and the Keswick Convention," edited by
two of his sons. (Seeley & Co., London.)

Convention, held in the Pavilion at Brighton, from May 29 to June 7, 1875. There some eight thousand people, the greater part earnest, well-instructed Christians, met together for ten days in prayer, meditation, and waiting upon God. Addresses were given there during those days, which live to this day in the memories of those who heard them, and have been the means of lasting blessing to thousands. Everywhere—at home and abroad—we meet with the abiding fruits of this memorable gathering. It was at this Convention Canon Battersby arranged for the first Convention at Keswick, to take place in July of that year.

In looking back upon the years that have elapsed since then, it would be interesting to be able to note the various names of those who now take part in this great gathering at Keswick, and to record the particular year, and circumstances, when they each saw for the first time the truth of a fuller life. It canot be too clearly stated that those who are asked to speak at this and other similar conventions are those, only, who can bear testimony to a definite experience of the fulness of blessing.

Every year at the Keswick Convention numbers of God's children are brought into a realization of their resources in Christ, such as they have never before thought possible; and this has given a strength and brightness to their lives which have been felt by others around them. In this way the movement has been continually advancing and deepening, so that its influence is seen to-day in every quarter of the globe.

So writes Mr. Hopkins. In Brighton, to-day many may be found who were present at the conference held there in 1875. In a sense, the greater part knew not wherefore they were come together, except that there was a general and widespread longing and expectancy for a new and singular bestowment of Power from on high. Worldliness, formalism, apathy, selfishness in the Church, were so apparent and so alarming, that devout believers were driven to the Throne of Grace to seek help from God. Throughout the whole convention at Brighton this blessing was wonderfully realized. While engaged in prayer the Holy Spirit mysteriously laid hold on men and women, and they were swayed as by a rushing, mighty wind.

Prayer became more earnest, importunate, believing, prevailing, and some new force was manifestly controlling. The first fruits were found in a distinct entrance into newness of life on the part of many, hitherto religiously cold or conventional, hampered by forms, exclusive, uncharitable, inconsistent, and without power as witnesses. Clergymen of the Anglican Church were among the prominent parties receiving Divine enduement. At the time no one suspected the real import of this Divine visitation, and hence the early history of it has somewhat inadequate records. * It is, however, remembered by all those who had a share in it as a very unusual and quite indescribable manifestation of spiritual quickening and power. Such a meeting would of course be the mother of others, and hence the subsequent " Keswick " meetings.

These found both suggestion and warm support in the Vicar of Keswick, the late Canon Battersby, by whose influence they became connected with, and located at, that beautiful spot. While he lived, he presided, the presidency then passing by a general assent to Mr. Henry Howker, and at his death to Mr. Robert Wilson, and without any fixed committee of leadership, or definite arrangement of man, it remains with Mr. Wilson, so far as any human hand is on the helm.

Keswick stands for a peculiar type of spiritual teaching and life. Those only who understand and exhibit it are asked to take part. To a singular extent no deference is paid to men, however high their social or ecclesiastical position. The most renowned minister, evangelist or theological professor might happen in a meeting, but would be asked to speak only as he was believed to have been led out into this sort of spiritual experience and teaching.

* " Record of the Convention for the Promotion of Scriptural Holiness," held at Brighton, 1875. London, S. W. Partridge &. Co., and "Account of the Union Meeting," etc., at Oxford, 1874. F. H. Revell, Chicago.

The first Keswick Convention lasted four days, and was held in a building; but, as the meetings became more largely attended, they were transferred to a tent. The present tent holds about 3,000, but often 10,000 attend in course of the convention.

As many who are deeply interested cannot hope to attend these great gatherings, it may be well to ask and answer two questions, briefly:

What is the exact type of Keswick teaching and method?

What are the actual results reached?

The Type of Keswick Teaching.—This is definite, complete, comprehensive, and progressive. It has a beginning, middle, and culmination. Seven successive stages may perhaps be indicated, all of them important, and substantially in the following order:

1. Immediate abandonment of every known sin, doubtful indulgence, or conscious hindrance to holy living. Rom. vi. 12-14, xiii. 12-14, xiv. 21-23; Heb. xii. 1, 2.

2. Surrender of the will and the whole being to Jesus Christ as not only Savior, but Master and Lord, in loving and complete obedience. Rom. x. 9 (R. V.), xii. 1; 1 Cor. xii. 3.

3. Appropriation by faith of God's promise and power for holy living. Rom. iv. 20-25, vi. 11, vii. 24, 25, viii. 1, 2 (R. V.); 2 Pet. i. 4; Heb. viii. 10.

4. Voluntary renunciation and mortification of the self-life, that centers in self-indulgence and self-dependence, that God may be all in all. Gal. ii. 19, 20, iv. 24; Col. iii. 5; 2 Cor. v. 15.

5. Gracious renewal or transformation of the inmost temper and disposition. Rom. xii. 2; Eph. iv. 23; 1 Pet. iii. 4.

6. Separation unto God for sanctification, consecration and service. 2 Cor. vi. 14, vii. 1; 2 Tim. ii. 19-21.

7. Enduement with power and infilling with the Holy Spirit, the believer claiming his share in the Pentecostal gift. Luke xxiv. 49; Acts i. 8; Eph. v. 18.

The obvious basis of all this teaching is the conviction that the average Christian life is grievously destitute of real spiritual power and often essentially carnal; and that it is the duty and privilege of every child of God at once to enter into newness of life, and walk henceforth in the power of Christ's resurrection. A few leading teachings should be emphasized.

First, the *starting-point*—instant abandonment of sin, and of every known weight which prevents or hinders progress. Whatever is wrong or believed to be wrong in God's sight cannot be indulged for one moment with impunity; it is utterly destructive of all holy living and testimony, unnecessary because wrong, and makes impossible even the *clear assurance of salvation.* Moreover, how can we lead out others into a life we have not ourselves found? How can one help a sinner to salvation unless he knows he is saved? To continue one moment in what is felt to be sin is therefore perilous not only to holiness, but to the hope of salvation itself and to all true service.

Again, a deadly blow is aimed at self-life in its seven forms; self-dependence, self-help, self-pleasing, self-will, self-seeking, self-defense, and self-glory; in other words, a new practical *center* is sought for all the life to revolve about, and in this way a new step is taken in advance. Beyond the territory of known sin there lies another almost as dangerous, where self-indulgence is the peculiar feature. There is a large class of pleasures, amusements, occupations, which do not bear the hideous features of secret or open sin, but which all tend to give supremacy to self. In them all the real question is: What will gratify and glorify myself? For example, the pleasures of *ambition*, grasping after power and position, which feed self-glory; *avarice,* heaping up riches, which is pleasing to self-indulgence; *appetite,* eating and drinking for the sake of pleasure, which ministers to self-seeking; and other forms of selfishness, such as courting human applause by intellectual preaching, or conformity to worldly maxims.

Five or six forms of amusement bear the distinct stamp of *this world,* whatever may be contended as to their inherent innocence: the theater, the dance, the card-table, the horse-race, the opera, the wine-cup. These have been felt, for some reason, to hinder holiness and service; and some churches have distinctly made indulgence in them a matter of discipline. Whatever may be said of them, this is true: that, wherever this deeper experience of Christ's power has been known, it has always been preceded or followed by their abandonment. These matters are very seldom referred to specifically at the Keswick gatherings, as the teaching concerns great general principles of holy living and serving; yet, as a fact, those who attend are brought face to face with this question: how can you do anything primarily to *please yourself* which does not put at risk your *pleasing God?* A high type of holiness always involves two practical rules:

(*a*) I will seek in everything to please my Master as the Lord and Sovereign of my life;

(*b*) I will seek to please my neighbor for his good unto edification.

Hence one remarkable feature of this movement has been, for instance, the abandonment of tobacco, not because its use can be conclusively shown to be inherently sinful, or because of any direct pressure brought to bear by speakers; but because, where used, not as a medicine, but for indulgence of a liking, it exalts self to the throne. Paul gives by the Spirit three all-controlling principles to guide in doubtful indulgences, and in each case he carefully guards the principle by saying in advance, " all things are lawful for me;" but he adds in one case, "all things *edify not*, are not *expedient;*" and in the other case, "I will not be *brought under the power of any.*" Compare 1 Cor. x. 23 : vi. 12.

Three questions are thus to be asked after the matter of lawfulness is settled. First, is this lawful thing *expedient?* does it advance or retard holiness? second, does it *edify*—that is, help or hinder others? and, third, does it tend to *enslave* or to *emancipate* me? One whose whole heart is set on pleasing *God* will soon settle all debatable territory on such principles.

Again, the surrender of the will to God in obedience is insisted on. Christ must to every believer become not only Savior but *Lord* (Rom. x. 9, R. V.). "No man can say that Jesus is the Lord but by the Holy Ghost" (1 Cor. xii, 3.). Hundreds who accept Him as Savior from sin have no real conception of Him as the actual Master and Sovereign of the daily life. In the message to Laodicea we have a hint as to this sort of professed believers. "Behold I stand at the door and knock—." Christ, outside, knocking and appealing for admission. The keys of the house are not in His hands. He is not admitted to His own house and in control. There is a definite act of opening, welcoming, and entrusting to Him the keys, which represent government; but so long as one apartment in the house is voluntarily withheld from Him, He never practically assumes control. From the nature of the case it must be *all* or *none;* and every child of God may soon know, if he searches his own heart, whether any part of his life shuts out Jesus from practical rulership. If any part of the body shrinks and shows abnormal sensitiveness under the surgeon's touch, he begins to suspect that *there* is a lurking place of disease. And, whenever a disciple is especially sensitive as to any one or more forms of indulgence, or shrinks from the candid application of Scripture to any particular practice, he may know that at that point there lurks spiritual disease. On the other hand, if the hidden recesses be opened up to Christ and He be welcomed to the whole heart and whole life, the very chambers of previous idolatry will become the chambers of heavenly imagery and Divine communion.

Again, *the infilling of the Spirit.*—Here is perhaps the most delicate and difficult part of this teaching. But it is well not to stop on phrases; whether we agree or not on the exact form of words, we must admit facts, and a conspicuous fact is this: that thousands of professed believers, like the Ephesian disciples in Acts xix, do not practically know whether there be a Holy Ghost or not. Dr. A. J. Gordon discriminated between *sealing, filling,* and *anointing,* referring the first to assurance, the second, to power, and the third, to knowledge. The practical point is this: have you ever claimed and received as such the power of the Holy Spirit? He came down on the day of Pentecost and filled disciples. This was an experience quite apart from *conversion,* for the hundred and twenty were all disciples and some had for years followed Jesus; and yet then suddenly all received a Divine gift, whereby they had new apprehension of all spiritual truth, more assured witness borne to them as children of God, and greater power in testimony for Christ. Somehow they were filled with light, love, life, and power; their tongues were loosed, and they spake even in languages, before unknown. Now, it may be, and doubtless is, true, that such " baptism " of the Spirit was once for all, and that no further such effusion is to be expected in this age. But every disciple is at least entitled to *claim his full share in that blessing* and enter into pentecostal life and power, or rather to have it enter into him.

This is to be claimed by *faith,* quite apart from *feeling.* Nowhere in the Word of God is stress laid on feeling, for, if God made feeling a proof or test, essential to evidence or confidence, we should rest on, and trust in it, and our faith and hope would vacillate as often as our feelings do. Man is complex; he is composed of body, soul, and spirit; and body and soul have much to do with spirit. Where the body is not normal, a cloud comes over the higher faculties. What we call " feeling " is often largely at the mercy of digestion and other physical conditions which do not affect *faith* or *choice*. The will may be as unchangingly fixed on God in sickness as health, tho the feelings vary with every change of bodily mood. " According to your faith be it unto you." If you open your heart to the Spirit's infilling, claim this blessing, and rest on God's faithfulness, He will not fail you.

The ultimate result of this teaching when actually translated into experience is the enjoyment of the privileges and victories implied in this higher or deeper life, such as the rest life of faith, power over sin, passion for souls, conscious fellowship with God, growing possession of promises, and prevailing prayer and intercession. *The Revelation of Jesus Christ in the soul as an Indwelling Presence* is the climax of all. The supreme end of the Holy Spirit's indwelling and inworking is to manifest the personal Christ as consciously in our possession and in possession of us. This is the mystery: *Christ in you.* The Spirit first takes the things of Christ and *shows them* to the believer; second, he *testifies* to Christ, and, third, he *glorifies* Christ. Note the three parts of this work as laid down in John xiv-xvi: Manifesting, witnessing, glorifying. He shows Christ in all His offices and relations; He makes Him real as an actual possession; and He clothes Him in glorious charms, so that we gaze on Him, enamored of His beauty and love. It is very different to have Christ revealed *without,* as a historic personage, and *within,* as experimentally and really Master and Lord.

This latter, the Holy Spirit does, as the former is effected by the Word.

The advocates of " Keswick " teaching earnestly desire that they shall not be supposed to *advocate any new doctrine*. All the truths for which Keswick stands are as *old* as the New Testament; but it is the object of prayer and endeavor to help others to *see* what is taught in the word of God, to *claim the promises,* and *appropriate the power* of the Blessed Christ. Like the unclaimed riches in the Bank of England, there are mines of unappropriated treasure in the word of God.

One of these teachers, addressing ministers of Christ and friends in America, wrote:

" It is an unfeigned delight to find that the teaching of the Inner Life is becoming so widespread in its influence on this side the Atlantic.   Union with Christ is His death and resurrection, the reckoning oneself dead to self, the infilling of the Holy Spirit, and the Rest of Faith, Life across the Jordan in the Land of Promise, these are familiar and deeply prized truths and their wide dissemination and realization on the part of believers, together with the exposition of the Bible, as opposed to merely topical preaching seem to me the conditions of a Revival of God's work in this land, which shall reanimate the churches, and enable them to act as the cementing bond in your vast and varied population."

CHAPTER IV

KESWICK METHOD

THE New Testament reminds us that truth and error find their allies in the manner and method of conduct, as well as in formal teaching. Mute surroundings are vocal with testimony; the chosen symbols of holy influence are salt and light; the presence of a good man, and many other things beside his speech, witness to the truth; and so the personality of a wicked or worldly man has an influence of its own, quite apart from his utterances.

Keswick method, as well as teaching, has been on trial for a quarter of a century. Impartial observers, watching from without the influence exerted upon the religious thought and conduct of many thousands who have felt and acknowledged the power of this teaching, have been convinced of the Scriptural character and spiritual wholesomeness of this doctrine, and the practice everywhere found linked to it, and have given to it emphatic approval.

In April, 1897, an important convention was held in London, England, the purpose of which partly was that, in the metropolis of the world, leading Keswick teachers might give an authoritative statement of this teaching, correcting misapprehension, and bringing these vital truths into touch with many who had never been at Keswick conventions; and, it was hoped also to satisfy some whose doubts only such personal attendance at Keswick meetings could dissipate, and who perhaps had a desire " to spy out the land " and find out what weak points, if any, there were in the teaching now inseparable from the name of Keswick. The writer was at both the London and Keswick gatherings of 1897 and at smaller ones in the interval, at Dublin and other places; in fact these four months were passed in public and private contact with men and women who have been most closely linked with this movement; and the result of careful study, both of the formal teaching and the actual tendencies of the Keswick movement confirmed the previous opinion, that this class of truths furnishes a great corrective remedy for the unspiritual drift of our day, and a great educative force for lifting spiritual life to a higher level. Those who come under the influence of a Keswick convention, in a receptive spirit, feel its power, and yearn to have it essentially reproduced elsewhere, not as a mere adjunct to some already existing conference of Bible students or Christian workers, but with all its main characteristics, lest there should be lost any of the peculiar features which give it its unique power of impression, and without any one of which it would cease to be what it is.

The object of the present chapter is to give the reader a glimpse, if possible an insight, into *what it is* which makes Keswick such a force in modern spiritual life. The *teaching* is not to be accurately judged, apart from certain conspicuous surroundings which characterize the assemblies and give a unique character to the whole convention. Indeed, it may be doubted whether the verbal teaching is even the *main* feature of the Keswick movement; there are other matters at least as important, quite apart from the direct instruction given in the addresses. One may read the whole series of addresses, as reproduced *verbatim* in the " Life of Faith," and yet miss the most conspicuous charm of these assemblies—*the very aroma of the flower*. Those who have little knowledge of the matter often dismiss this teaching as a mere " school " of religious opinion akin to one of many modern types of doctrine, the tendencies of thought which differentiate one theological school from another. This is a great mistake. Keswick stands for a great deal more than the truth, orally proclaimed from its platform or promulgated through the press, and it is this other side which is needful for the comprehensive understanding of the matter, and valuable for the many instructive lessons involved.

First of all, it may be well to refer to a misconstruction or misapprehension, found in a paragraph from a prominent religious newspaper :

"The Keswick movement in some localities has run into excesses, has caused divisions in churches, has produced self-righteousness, and caused men and women to say, by their actions, to fellow-Christians, 'Stand aside, for I am holier than thou.' This does not come from the indwelling of the Spirit of God; is the exact opposite of the results of the ministry of the Holy Spirit, for the Spirit Himself has declared through an inspired Apostle that 'the fruit of the Spirit is love, joy, peace, long-suffering, gentleness, meekness.' The people who declare themselves to be of such superior spirituality that they can no longer be associated with the membership of a Christian church are misled and mistaken, and are not led by the Holy Spirit."

It is remarkable, in connection with this movement, that it has *never been found to cause " divisions in churches,"* no man or woman ever yet being known, through its influence or under its teaching, to leave one communion for another. In fact, one conspicuous result has been that those who at Keswick meetings find newness of life, rather incline to stay where they are, ecclesiastically, and seek to infuse new life into dead and formal service. If Keswick teaching " produces self-righteousness and causes men and women to say 'Stand aside, I am holier than thou,'" we have not met a single such case, for again, it is one notable fruit of this teaching that it produces *humility*, and considerate *charity* for others. As it insists that holiness is the result, not of a prolonged and persistent self-effort, but of a simple appropriation of Christ as the victor over evil, the tendency is to humble disciples by reason of the conscious inadequacy of their own endeavors, and their entire dependence on the Spirit of God. The most conspicuous exponents and examples of this teaching are, like the late Dr. A. J. Gordon, the last to assert their own sanctity, and would be shocked, should others ascribe to them holiness or perfection. They repudiate all such epithets, becoming more lowly in mind as they become the more lofty in aim and pure in heart.

There are at least a dozen matters, in regard to which Keswick is a standing protest or witness, or both, and which are entirely aside and apart from the verbal utterances of its platform, but without which those utterances would be shorn of their real effectiveness. It may be well to enumerate, tho some things evade analysis and defy description.

The methods and measures characteristic of a true Keswick convention are quite as important as the truth taught; and bear quite as distinct a stamp of peculiarity and individuality.

The *Method*, thus inseparable from the teaching, includes also seven particulars:

1. Dependence, solely and directly, upon the guidance or administration of the Holy Spirit. John xvi. 7-15; Acts viii. 29, 39, xiii. 2-4.

2. Independence of Worldly patronage, of numbers as the sign or measure of success, and of merely secular attractions. Matt. xviii. 19, 20; John xv. 18, 19; Jas. iv. 4; 1 John ii. 15-17.

3. Subordination of music, teaching, and all else to the promotion of holy living. Eph. v. 19; 1 Cor. ii. 2-5. xiv. 26.

4. Emphasis on a definite experience as indispensable to

power in testimony. John iii. 11; Gal. i. 11-16; Acts iv. 13.

5. Apostolic simplicity of worship, witness, and voluntary giving. Acts ii. 42-47; 2 Cor. ix. 5-10.

6. Unity of believers on the basis of great essentials, such as the Incarnation, Atonement, and Regeneration. John iii. 3-6; 1 Cor. xv. 1-4; 1 John iv. 2, 3.

7. Habitual waiting on God in prayer as essential both to receiving and imparting blessing. Eph. vi. 18-20; 2 Thess. iii. 1, 2.

It is refreshing to find anywhere methods so scriptural and apostolic: Direct dependence on Divine guidance, no step taken, even in minute matters, without first referring it to God to know His will; and consequent independence of human patronage; no alliance sought with great names, the rich, the nobly born, the leaders of thought, the aristocracy of intellect; to find such singular indifference to mere numbers, no emphasis being placed upon crowds as a sign of success or blessing, or as the measure of encouragement; and consequently, no catering to popularity; nothing done simply to make the meetings " draw," no savor of sensationalism, however mild. Nor is there reliance on eloquent speaking, as such. No program of speakers or subjects is ever published, and even the " speaker's program " gives no hint of *topics* to be treated.

The platform is one of *witness*, no fame, learning, or eloquence, apart from a definite experience of blessing, giving authority to bear a testimony.

A definite result is uniformly sought in the practical life of the hearer, toward which all else is directed. Hence the definite type and order of teaching, the truth being presented, not at random, but with reference to its bearing on this result. Immediate, visible, decisive action on the part of the hearer is urgently insisted upon—a surrender to God at once, carrying with it prompt renunciation of known sin and obedience to known duty. Hence, much prominence is given to after-meetings.

Sacred song is used as an aid to worship and teaching; simple, congregational singing, and always chiefly, if not solely, with reference to the impression of the Word; not as an independent *attraction,* but a subordinate *adaptation,* preparing for, and following up, the truth taught.

Confidence is felt in the Holy Spirit's presence and guidance; the pervading impression is that God has control, and hence that remarkable emphasis, laid upon public and private waiting on God in prayer, seldom found elsewhere. There is no appeal for money, even to meet expenses, save through boxes provided for voluntary offerings, it being a fundamental principle to rest on God for means to carry on His work, rather than to look to monied men and women. All disciples are recognized as " one body in Christ," and every one members one of another; only the essentials of Christian doctrine being made prominent, without regard to minor differences.

The meetings are not controlled by any one man, but by a committee and council of godly men and women, who are in hearty agreement as to the foregoing positions. While Keswick is the main center for gatherings in the end of July, during all the year, at various points in the United Kingdom, local conventions, for the deepening of spiritual life, are held under the direction of the Keswick leaders and teachers; and men and women go as missionaries both to home and foreign fields to spread the knowledge of these truths, and encourage the simple apostolic methods so blessed of God.

In all this teaching and method there is nothing new, save the new stress laid upon neglected truths. In all movements, conspicuously owned of God, there has been simply a return toward primitive apostolic models, the supreme purpose being to make real and actual to disciples the experience of the fulness of blessing offered in Christ Jesus. Because such has been the practical result of the teaching and method above outlined, God has set His seal upon it in marked blessing, tens of thousands giving proof that there has come into their lives a vital force, transforming both character and conduct.

Believing the essential conditions of blessing to be everywhere and at all times the same, the matter herein presented is commended to the prayerful consideration of fellow-believers in every place and of every name, in hope that united prayer and effort may be directed toward the establishment of conferences for the promotion of a fuller life in Christ wherever like-minded disciples are ready to meet in the name of the Lord Jesus.

The above statement of principles is necessarily condensed, and hence open to misconstruction if not interpreted according to its plain intention. It is in no sense a creed or a complete and exhaustive statement. Yet if we are to learn the lesson God would teach, it is needful to understand both the truths and the practices which have been so owned of God. However important the teaching at Keswick, these *methods of conduct are essential to the whole movement as such,* and, if there is to be a counterpart and not a counterfeit of the movement elsewhere, it must *begin* from the beginning, and upon a right basis. The methods in vogue at many existing religious gatherings, however justifiable, are certainly in marked contrast. For example, we generally find dependence on organization, numerical strength, and secular attractions; every effort made to draw the crowds, by an announced program of speakers, if not of subjects; music a studied attraction, sometimes a performance by professional artists, and singing, cultivated as a matter of art; constant effort made to get famous, prominent, eloquent and popular speakers, and the element of witness not made emphatic, or generally even essential. Whoever thinks of limiting the choice of speakers to those who have a definite experience, along a certain line of testimony? Speakers often are admitted to the platform of our summer gatherings, who are known to hold doubtful doctrine, if not to encourage questionable practice, but who are popular. No convention in America, with perhaps two exceptions, definitely aims at securing an immediate and absolute surrender to the mastership of Christ, and the entire transformation of both inner and outer life of those who attend.

Reference has been made to a *definite order* in which truth is taught at Keswick. For example, on the first day or two sin is dealt with, and its immediate abandonment, the effort being made to bring one face to face with God as a judge, and to produce conviction of guilt, sin and need. On a succeeding day, such themes as the power of Christ, and of a true, vital union with Him, of the Holy Spirit's indwelling, and the proper use of the Word of God, as preventives of sin and promotives of holiness; and on another, the Life in God with its immunities, privileges, possibilities. Then, as the convention week closes, service, its conditions, laws and qualifications, with special emphasis on the enduement and the filling of the Holy Spirit, with a final meeting on Saturday, when the mission field and its claims are urged.

This general outline is never filled in twice alike, so that it is no mechanical cast-iron model or pattern, allowing no flexibility or variation. There are many advantages in such order of teaching, which moves onward, step by step, toward definite results, and enables speakers who at any stage of the meetings make their appearance, to fall in with the purpose and purport of the teaching at that particular stage. And in arranging the speakers' program—which is only for their own guidance as to the times of their addresses—regard is had to the fitness of particular persons to deal with certain lines of truth, as shown by previous experience.

Without antagonizing methods that may elsewhere prevail, or of disputing their possible uses or advantages, one fact stands out indisputable: Keswick methods are so characteristic and so inseparable from its teaching that, if the teaching is to have its full sway, it must not be divorced from all that God has joined with it.

How can a similar type of teaching and method be given fullest scope elsewhere? Obviously there are no geographical limits to such uplifting and sanctifying influences, and disciples everywhere need such inspiration to holiness and self-surrender, as Keswick has supplied for a quarter of a century in Great Britain.

Whenever some convenient and central locality—perhaps more than one—can be chosen under God's guidance, where meetings could be annually held in some tent or tabernacle, commodious and inexpensive; if there could be a right start, with indifference to mere numbers, with careful avoidance of all men and measures not in accord with simple, scriptural and spiritual aims and methods; wherever, in a word, similar conventions could be held, starting right, and then kept within the original lines, unleavened with sensationalism and secularism, untold blessing might ensue to thousands of disciples. And we can at least devoutly pray that God would in His own way and in many other localities, lead up to such results.

But, wherever such results are sought, we must be prepared *to start with a small number of like-minded people;* where even a few are prepared to claim His promise, to the smallest number who can *meet*—two or three—He says, " I am in the midst of them." A large gathering at the outset might be fraught with risk. The greatest movements in spiritual life never do begin with large numbers. The beginnings of this great reformation in British religious life were so small as to be now hard to trace. A few people, gathering in London at noonday in a hall; then a hundred or so at a private residence, meeting by invitation; then, step by step, more and larger gatherings, until no place was found for the throngs. But more marvelous than the growth, is the way in which, for twenty-five years, the Keswick platform has been kept free from mere popular oratory, and held its position as a place of witness along a line of definite teaching. What a temptation, as the crowds grew and with the crowds divers people of diverse opinions and preferences, to cater to the popular demand for fine speakers, especially if they were Scriptural teachers, famous orators, or learned expositors! But no. The apostolic succession of *testimony* has been preserved unbroken.

Keswick teaching is definite and unmistakable. It affirms a possible and practical deliverance from continuance in known sin; a renewal of the spirit of the mind, a dominion of love, an experience of inward peace; it maintains that it is a sin to be anxious, because, where anxiety begins, faith ends, and where faith begins, anxiety ends; that it is not necessary to be under the dominion of any lust of body or mind, to live a life of doubt and despondency, or to have interrupted communion with God. Forfeited joy means broken fellowship. To every trusting, obedient soul, who dares take God at His word and count every commandment an enablement, there is an immediate deliverance from the palsied limbs that make impossible a holy walk with God; from the withered hand that prevents a holy work for God, and from the moral deformity that bows one together, so that it is impossible to lift up one's-self to spiritual uprightness and erectness. To those who are thus bound by Satan, He, who is the same yesterday, to-day, and forever, still and for evermore says, *" Thou art loosed from thine infirmity."* Divine hands are ready to be laid upon us, and make us at once straight and strong to glorify God in holy living.

Such are the real, present and practical truths, for which Keswick stands,—truths taught effectively, because taught only by those who, whatever else they lack, do not lack the personal experience of deliverance, but who can say, however humbly, boldly, " The Lord hath done great things for us, whereof we are glad ; " and the sight of those who are thus healed, as of old, stops the mouth of cavillers, and emboldens the feeble faith of the hesitating and doubtful.

Once more, let us remind ourselves that the conditions of blessing do not vary essentially with change of scene or actors. God loudly says to His people that He is waiting to bless them anywhere and everywhere, and He puts before them an example and a pattern which has had His seal for a quarter of a century. Why attempt to improve on the pattern, or to secure like blessing in neglect of the pattern? Keswick has been a fountain of spiritual life, because four great scriptural laws have there found singular exemplification: habitual prayerfulness, prominence of the Word of God, unity among all believers, and dependence on the Holy Spirit, *closely reproducing the assemblies of the primitive apostolic church.* Believers meet from day to day to magnify scripture teaching, to sing holy hymns, to know no name but that of Christ, to acknowledge no presiding or administrative power but the Holy Spirit, to exhort one another to an essentially heavenly life; they continue steadfastly in apostolic doctrine and fellowship, in breaking of bread and in prayers, and in a peculiar and sacred sense, none say that anything they possess is their own, but they have all things in common, and the Lord adds daily to the number of those who are being saved from sin unto holiness. Wherever these words reach responsive eyes and hearts, there let like-minded disciples gather, wait on God in prayer, and be content to go step by step, and God will raise up His own witnesses and helpers, if His people meet in the name of Christ, and are united in the sacred symphony of believing prayer.

CHAPTER V

THE phrase " Revival of religion " is a popular one, but a very doubtful one, and unscriptural beside. But behind the phrase lies a correct and scriptural conception and a historical and experimental fact: God does at times visit not only churches but whole communities with peculiar spiritual quickenings. One of these we select, partly because it is not widely known and familiar and partly because it teaches such valuable lessons, as to God's methods of working.

" In the beginning—God." These sublimely significant words open the Book of Books, and are the key to all real advance in human history. Every true movement forward has but one ultimate source and fountain—God; and we shall find it so, if we follow the stream far enough backward. No practical difficulty hinders true holy living and serving which is not also traceable at last, to the lack of the Divine factor. When God is not in all our thoughts; not recognized in our plans, resolves, activities; when His presence is not sought, His guidance is not real, His power is not our supreme dependence, our seeming success is but failure and our work comes to naught. And, whenever a genuine and permanent growth or increase is found, those who read its secret history are constrained to say: " The Lord hath done great things for us whereof we are glad."

It is now thirty years since, in Newport, Monmouthshire, England, a remarkable work of God began, the results of which even yet appear in a manifold form.

It was first of all noticeable how *God interposes in the extremity of His people.* Unbelief and worldliness cause serious forgetfulness of Him and departure from Him. Spiritual life declines ; and, when all our resources and dependences fail us, then, and it is sad to admit it, then alone, do we turn fully unto God. Church-life commonly sinks to its lowest ebb before the flood-tides of God sweep over a community. It was so in this instance. The narrative of this work—now out of print—records a remarkable blessing and reveals some conditions upon which such outpouring of Divine grace depends, and may elsewhere be enjoyed. *

From this account, written by Rev. J. Tinson Wrenford, we make copious extracts :

Prior to the commencement of this season of blessing was a seed-time of tears. To the inquiry, frequently made of members of different communions, " Are you prospering ? Is there much *life* amongst you ? " the humbling reply was almost always returned, " Alas ! we are not as we should be : there is much deadness of soul : we greatly need an awakening."

It pleased God (early in the year 1870) to put in the hearts of some of His children to meet together every Friday evening to pray, specially for a blessing on the services, teaching, and other means of grace on the approaching Lord's Day, and also that God would graciously pour out His Spirit on the church with which they were connected, and upon all other Christian congregations in the town. Amid various discouragements this little prayer-meeting was carried on week after week. At first only a very few assembled ; but, at last, the room became inconveniently crowded. The Lord gave them the spirit of prayer and supplication, but withheld any special or signal indication that their petitions would be abundantly answered They did certainly perceive a change in their own Minister's preaching, and remarked upon it one to another. He himself, conscious of it, was led publicly to express his gratitude to God for the sustaining intercessions of the " praying band." At length, however, a deep impression was made on the minds of some who had thus

---

* God's work at Newport. S. W. Partridge & Co. London.

continued together in prayer, that the Lord was about to commence a great work in Newport. Their faith had long been exercised: now they began to expect a gracious answer.

Just at this time the wish was expressed by members of the Young Men's Christian Association (with which several of these praying men were connected) that a meeting for *united* prayer should be held at an early date; and an earnest invitation was issued to " Christian men and women of all denominations," to meet together at the Victoria Hall, on Thursday evening, January 12th, 1871, " to call on the Lord (1.) for the descent of the Holy Spirit among them, and an increase of vital godliness; and (2.) for the conversion to God of many of their fellow-towns folk during the coming year." This united prayer-meeting was attended by a large number: a most solemn spirit pervaded the assembly: the Lord Himself was in the midst, His presence being felt by many.

There was a short season of praying and waiting again: the Lord " tarried "—but not long. The spirit of expectation continued, and, indeed, became intensified. At length came the " earnest " of the approaching " showers of blessing." On Sunday evening, February 16th, the preacher (who had himself on the previous day experienced a glorious deliverance from the buffetings of Satan, and been brought out into " a wealthy place," a place of sunshine and certainty never before experienced by him), made an earnest appeal to any who were in an anxious and inquiring condition of mind, to remain at the close of the service. Several that night found peace with God, through Jesus Christ. The work of " in-gathering " had commenced, although, as yet, but on a small scale. Several weeks passed away. Every Sunday night inquirers were led to Jesus: and every week it became more and more apparent that the Lord was preparing the minds of many for the momentous cry, " What must I do to be saved? "

About this time special " Mission Services " were held at the neighboring town of Cardiff, upon which the Divine blessing was evidently resting. Among the preachers was the venerable Robert Aitken—so long and well known in England and Scotland in connection with evangelizing labors. An invitation to come to St. Paul's, Newport, was complied with. At the foot of the handbills announcing the forthcoming special services, was printed the text from Malachi, " *Prove me now herewith, saith the Lord of Hosts, if I will not open you the windows of heaven, and pour you out a blessing, that there shall not be room enough to receive it."*

A very solemn spirit of supplication and expectancy pervaded the preparatory prayer-meeting, on Saturday night, March 25th, and on the following morning, Mr. Aitken preached, taking as his subject the incidents narrated in the eleventh chapter of John's Gospel relating to the sickness, death and resurrection of Lazarus. Mr. Aitken spoke of *realities*. The anxiety of Mary and Martha, their affliction, their grief, were real: the loving sympathy of Jesus towards His distressed disciples was also real: and so, too, His power over death and the grave. Jesus is still a *real* Savior—" the same yesterday, and to-day, and forever." His words were, that day, addressed to many of His hearers: " The Master *is come,* and *calleth for thee."*—" Take ye away *the stone."*—" Lazarus, *come forth! "*

In the evening Mr. Aitken again preached, from Heb. xii: 24. and the Spirit accompanied the word spoken. At the close an invitation was given to any who might be desirous of direction, and a large number remained, many of whom were evidently in a state of deep concern as to salvation: and that night, about seventy entered into the liberty wherewith Jesus makes His people free.

On the four evenings following, Mr. Aitken preached, to crowded congregations, " the unsearchable riches of Christ," his sermons being characterized by great simplicity and fervency. With a power of utterance at times vehement, he besought the careless, the ungodly, the mere professor, to come to Jesus for pardon and eternal life. What he contemplated was the *reality* of all that the Gospel declared,—the reality of the sinner's necessity and danger,—of the all-sufficiency of the blood of Jesus,—of the love of the Father toward the returning prodigal,—and of the power of the Son of Man to forgive sins. To him sin, the judgment, eternity, heaven, and hell too, were terribly real. Hence the " reality " of all his appeals, remonstrances, and exhortations. The Lord owned His word upon each occasion, and every night crowds of penitents came for direction. The after-services were prolonged until nearly or quite midnight: and, even then numbers lingered, as tho loth to depart without further blessing.

*   *   *   *   *

Thus were brought to the feet of Jesus the young and the old,

—hardened sinners,—mere professors of religion of many years' standing,—backsliders,—the self-righteous—persons of almost all classes and descriptions. Husbands and wives, parents and children, brothers and sisters, in some instances, whole families, were brought in—in other cases the remaining members of otherwise godly families were reached by the Word, and led to the cross.

One precious feature of these services was the *real spiritual unanimity and unity manifested by Christians of all denominations, from first to last.* It seemed as tho the Lord's prayer was fulfilled, " *That they all may be one."* His people *felt* they were " *one,"* not artificially or theoretically, but actually and truly. Distinctive titles, indicative of divisions in the family, were forgotten. Churchmen, Wesleyans, Baptists, Independents, Brethren—all met together in the house of their common Lord, not as " sectarians," but as " *Christians; "* with one heart and voice they prayed and praised; with one purpose they assisted, when occasion served, in directing the inquiring. The Spirit of the Lord was a spirit of love and fellowship to them all: and Jesus was Himself in their midst, breathing upon them, and saying to them, as to the disciples of old, " Peace be unto you."

After Mr. Aitken left Newport for his own parish, in compliance with the earnest desire of many, special services were continued during the five following days, and the Lord did not stay His hand or withhold His blessing. Every night many penitents were led to the cross, and found peace and joy in believing. Friday was a day long to be remembered. It was the commemoration of the crucifixion. A vast congregation assembled, and about five-and-thirty souls cast themselves upon the finished work of Jesus, and realized pardon and deliverance.

Thus closed the second week of the special services. Altogether six hundred souls had been brought to the Lord. Among the converts were persons connected with nearly all the congregations of the town. No attempt was made to proselytize; on the contrary, the converts were urged ordinarily to remain in connection with the communions to which they had formerly been attached. Many congregations were stirred up to pray for the outpouring of the Holy Spirit upon themselves, and a reviving work began to make itself felt among the people. Special services were commenced at several churches of the neighborhood; and the power of the Lord was present to heal and to save.

In May, Lord Radstock delivered evangelistic addresses at Newport. Two halls were secured, each accommodating at least a thousand persons. Two addresses were given daily, and each evening the hall was densely crowded. His expositions and appeals—so scriptural, clear, earnest, and persuasive—were listened to with deep attention. The Spirit of God graciously applied the word, and again the Lord brought many souls " out of darkness and the shadow of death, and brake their bands in sunder."

In June, Mr. Aitken paid a second visit to Newport, accompanied by his two sons, the Rev. R. W. Aitken, and the Rev. W. Hay Aitken. It pleased God to give His blessing to the Gospel message at each of the assemblies, conversions taking place every night.

The congregations were extremely large. On one night, nearly or quite two thousand persons were crowded into the church, while hundreds thronged the approaches, unable to obtain admission. The services were prolonged to a very late hour, in consequence of the large number of anxious ones seeking direction. The result of this second mission was that three hundred souls were brought to the Lord, in connection with St. Paul's church alone.

Surely no one can speak of an aggregate of *one thousand professed conversions* in a single parish within four months, without feelings of fervent gratitude to Him who alone can turn one sinner " from darkness to light, and from the power of Satan unto God." Many hundreds besides were awakened and led to Jesus, in connection with other communions, in the same period of time, and the work of the Lord rapidly spread to several parishes adjacent. But yet further testimony has to be borne to the goodness of God in His dealings with the people of Newport. He did not withdraw His hand, and cease to manifest His power to save, but on the contrary, proved, in the six remaining months of the memorable year 1871, that He was always ready to respond graciously to His peoples' prayers, and to own their efforts for His glory in the conversion of souls. His disciples were stirred up to multiply and extend the means heretofore employed—nothing doubting as to the results. The Young Men's Christian Association commenced a daily midday prayer-meeting at their rooms, which proved a means of spiritual refreshment and strengthening to many. They engaged the large Victoria Hall, for special Sunday evening services, the London Evangelization Society sending down, week by week, experienced evangelists. From twelve to fifteen hundred persons were thus gathered on each occasion, a large proportion being not in the habit of frequenting any place of Divine worship. The Lord caused His blessing to rest upon this additional effort, and every Sunday souls were won to Christ.

Most marked and evident was the result of God's work upon a large portion of the Newport population. The churches of Christ were revived. Christians were not contented with a bare spiritual existence. The surpassing blessedness of the " higher Christian life " was sought and realized by very many. The old condition, so far removed from that to which believers should attain, became distasteful, and from the heart—gladly, gratefully, lovingly—proceeded the cry, " *All for Jesus!* " Nor could they who had received so much at the hands of the Lord remain inactive. " Lord, what wilt thou have me to do? " was the cry of many a willing worker; and, in a variety of ways, the desire to be useful found welcome exercise. And more than, perhaps, at any time before, Christians discovered that, notwithstanding all minor differences, they could " love one another, with a pure heart, fervently."

The people of the world were, at the first, evidently perplexed by what they witnessed. The confession was again and again made, " I cannot understand it." In some instances utter incredulity was expressed; while not a few attributed it to a sort of fanatical excitement, the effects of which would soon pass away. The people of the world could not be expected to form a right judgment upon such a subject. It lay beyond them altogether; and their opinion of it could not possibly possess any value. To the unconverted, the operations of God's Spirit must ever be an enigma which they cannot explain. The Inspired Word tells us, " The natural man receiveth not the things of the Spirit of God; for they are foolishness to him; neither can he know them, because they are spiritually discerned." That is decisive.

But what a solemn season is it to a congregation—to an entire community—when God thus wondrously makes bare His arm and manifests His saving power!

In concluding this narrative of God's great work at Newport, to what shall we trace it, so far as man is concerned? Shall it not be, first, to *earnest, believing persevering prayer* " for this very thing; " and secondly, to the *real preaching of a real Gospel?*

Our Lord's words are: "If two of you shall agree on earth as touching anything that they shall ask, it shall be done for them of my Father which is in heaven." Surely, this assurance ought to be sufficient. And as to the preaching, of what avail is it unless a *real* Gospel be preached? It is to be feared there is much unreality in the preaching of the present day. If men are really sinners—perishing sinners—then away with theorizing, with speculating, with mere "opinions" and "views." Away, too, with all dead "sermonizing," be it never so correctly and artistically done. The need of men's souls is awfully real: let them hear of a God really waiting to be gracious;—of a Jesus really able to save to the uttermost and as willing as he is able;—of an all-sufficient atonement really made and accepted;—of the precious blood of Christ, that can really cleanse from all sin;—of a Holy Spirit really given to regenerate, guide, comfort, teach, and sanctify men's souls. Let them hear of a real heaven—a real hell—a real eternity; of real pardon for the guilty—real peace—real joy—real life; of a real approach of the sinner to the feet of a present Savior—of a real acceptance of Jesus, and a real surrender to Him, and then a real and most blessed discipleship. Away with mere ideas! with mere "hopes" and "trusts!" with all uncertainty and unreality!

This *reality* of praying, preaching, and hearing was at Newport, the secret of the conversion of so large a number of souls to Christ—through the power of the Holy Ghost.

Why may not such a result be brought to pass, wherever sinners are found? Doubtless, the fear of the world's frown, prejudice, routine, dead formalism, a dread of "irregularities" and of "excitement" may hinder; but should not all hindrances be surmounted for Christ's sake, and that souls may be saved?

O for *reality* in the *praying* of God's people, reality in the *preaching* of God's ministers! O for men to preach, and people to pray, who have themselves been brought into a condition of conscious acceptance—pardon—life; who themselves are "*in Christ,*" and who know, in their own daily experience, the sweetness of that "peace of God" which "passeth all understanding," and of that "joy" which is "unspeakable and full of glory." O for *reality!* A real lifting up of Jesus in the midst of perishing sinners—not that "doctrines" or "views" (be they ever so correct) may be set forth, discussed, demonstrated,—but that the guilty may draw near—may look—may live! O for the

"real presence" of Jesus in our assemblies,—the real coming
of the sin-burdened to Him there and then,—and the real reception from His willing hands of a most real salvation!

So wrote in substance, the original narrator of God's
work at Newport; and we seek to perpetuate and extend
this testimony to one of the most deep-reaching and remarkable spiritual movements of the last half century, because we are confident that God means the whole church
to learn a lesson from it.

That lesson is manifold in instruction altho it all bears
in one direction. This solemn story of Divine dealing
lays peculiar stress upon *united prayer, a pure Gospel,
hand to hand contact with souls, and simple faith in God's
present power to save.* Here was no grand array of
agencies, no unusual and striking combinations—no far-
famed evangelist sent for to inaugurate a revival, no appeal to novelty, nothing dramatic, spectacular, sensational.
The whole work began in the prayers of a few fervent
believers for the church with which they were connected,
and particularly their own minister. Their prayers first
brought to him new blessing and new power in preaching; then, as souls were won, the work spread to other
congregations; the circle of prayer expanded and became
more inclusive; differences of doctrine and polity were
forgotten in the bond of unity; variety of congregational
life was merged into community of work for souls. As
aid was needed, the most spirit-filled helpers were sought
—and dependence was never transferred from God to
man, but the power of a God-given Gospel and of a God-
given Spirit constantly and reverently recognized.

Contrast all this with modern efforts to secure revival.
A private pamphlet, prepared by a certain evangelist as a
guide to committees who were making ready for his coming, proved to be shockingly full of dependence on "busi-

ness methods," such as advertising striking announcements, big posters, etc., etc.—he would have everything done to create a public *furore* in advance. This is the way of the world, and it is now fast becoming the way of the church. Boston wanted a revival; and Mr. Moody must be at Tremont Temple, and Sam. Jones and Francis Murphy at other " temples "—men whom the people will flock to hear must be got—so said an acute observer, as he contrasted the revivals of fifty years ago with those of to-day. We design no reflection on either of the above-named evangelists, while we would emphasize the fact, that, for a true revival whose results are to be lasting, dependence must be first of all on God, not on man; we must magnify the messenger less, and the message and the Spirit, more. The most wide-reaching revivals of this century have been associated with the most unexpected times, methods and men—a surprise often to those through whom they were wrought. They have been preceded by fasting and prayer, beginning often in a union of prayer between two or three burdened souls. For instance, a few young men, who could find no better place to meet, went into a church belfry, unwarmed, tho in winter, and there sought blessing for the congregation; their numbers slowly increased until the unfinished room was too strait for them; and while as yet their meeting was scarce known to the congregation, a mighty flood of blessing was already outpoured. In another case a very ordinary preacher, speaking to his own people about parental duty and responsibility, felt moved to call on parents, impressed with their own unfaithfulness, to come from their seats and stand in the aisle in token of repentance and earnest seeking for blessing. Out of the pews moved fathers and mothers, until the aisles were filled and they crowded about the communion table—and the place was turned in a Bochim.

We are getting away from *dependence on ordinary means of grace,* whenever we do not expect any widespread blessing on the preaching of the simple Gospel and on prayer, and on personal contact with souls. We must have several churches united, and great meetings with distinguished evangelists and great choirs with far-famed Gospel singers, or we look for no divine outpourings. All this is unscriptural, unspiritual, abnormal. The Gospel would be a failure if it were not. And because our churches, and pastors, and the people at large lose confidence in the ordinary use of God-appointed means, and depend on extraordinary efforts alone, every interest of the churches is in peril. Even for missions we must have colossal meetings—some president, ex-president, governor, or other celebrity must preside—a great crowd got together in some way; it matters little if the speakers are not spirit-filled men, if they are only attractive—or if the assemblies be not composed of the more devout, provided the numbers are large and the *élite* are there! Such are the unspoken sentiments which too often guide the arrangements, repel the Spirit of God and forfeit blessing. If the church wants greater prosperity in the life of her members, and in the abundance and constancy of her benevolent offerings, there must be more honor put upon the Holy Spirit, more believing prayer and faith in God's promises. God's arm is not shortened nor His ear heavy, but there are modes of doing and attitudes of being which He will never own with the sanction of His blessing.

Let any pastor undertake in his own congregation and parish work to follow a few simple rules, and see the result:

1. Get himself thoroughly *right with God,* by abandoning every known sin or doubtful indulgence, and seeking first of all for himself the very type of life and character which he craves for his people.

2. Trust himself absolutely to the Gospel as the power of God and the wisdom of God unto salvation, and expect that God's word, faithfully preached, will not return to Him void, in a single instance.

3. Give himself to prayer—giving time enough to get the sense of God in the closet; and never leaving the place of supplication until he gets a divine vision—a new impartation of life and power.

4. Go himself to seek individuals—not depending on mere pulpit exhortations—but remembering that souls are won by individual approach, and that all such contact will make his preaching more personal and effective.

5. Keep himself from all direct or indirect dependence on man; avoid seeking men's applause, or looking to man's patronage for support and encouragement. Let him study the Acts of the Apostles and aim at an apostolic church life.

6. Live himself a life of faith, depending on God for his support, daring to cut loose from the pew system and take his support from voluntary offerings; and sedulously cultivate in his people the same spirit of direct leaning upon God.

7. Yearn himself over a lost world—cherishing a missionary spirit, and claiming the entrance into the holiest as the intercessor's place and privilege; and educating his people to regard missions as the indispensable proof and fruit of all spiritual life.

No man could follow seven such simple rules and patiently wait, without seeing a mighty work of God in his own life and sphere of labor. And it is only in such a new level of spiritual life and character and conduct of God's work that the permanent revival of missions is to be found. The stream needs a source more abundant and elevated—then the channel will be full and the current rapid. God is speaking, and it is not in this case, out of the cloud—no mystery attends His utterance. All the great spiritual movements of the century have hinged on supernatural interposition in answer to believing prayer. If we are to have other such divine interpositions, other intercessors must be found, mighty through the same means which were used by Job and Samuel, Elijah and Daniel.

CHAPTER VI

THE pivot of piety is prayer. A pivot is of double use: it acts as a fastener and as a center; it holds in place, and it is the axis of revolution. Prayer is also the double secret: it keeps steadfast in faith, and it helps to all holy activity. Hence, as surely as God is lifting His people in these latter times to a higher level of spirituality, and moving them to a more unselfish and self-denying service, there will be new emphasis laid upon supplication, and especially upon intercession.

This revival of the praying-spirit, if not first in order of development, is first in order of importance, for without it there is no advance. Generally, if not uniformly, prayer is both starting-point and goal to every movement in which are the elements of permanent progress. Whenever the church is aroused and the world's wickedness arrested, somebody has been praying. If the secret history of all true *spiritual* advance could be written and read, there would be found some intercessors who, like Job, Samuel, Daniel, Elijah, Paul and James, like Jonathan Edwards, William Carey, George Müller and Hudson Taylor, have been led to shut themselves in the secret place with God, and have labored fervently in prayers. And, as the starting-point is thus found in supplication and intercession, so the final outcome must be that God's people shall have learned to pray; otherwise there will be rapid reaction and disastrous relapse from the better conditions secured.

Patient and long continued study of the religious history of the race confirms the conviction that no seal of permanence is stamped upon any movement, however spiritual in appearance and tendency, which does not sooner or later show a decided revival of the praying spirit.

There is a divine philosophy behind this fact. The greatest need is to keep in *close touch with God;* the greatest risk is the loss of the sense of the divine. In a world where every appeal is to the physical senses and through them, reality is in direct proportion to the power of contact. What we see, hear, taste, touch, or smell—what is material and sensible—we can not doubt. The present and material absorbs attention and appears solid, substantial: but the future, the immaterial, the invisible, the spiritual, seem vague, distant, illusive, imaginary. Practically the unseen has no reality and no influence with the vast majority of mankind. Even the unseen God is to them less a verity than the commonest object of vision; to many He, the highest verity, is really vanity, while the world's vanities are practically the highest verities.

God's great corrective for this most disastrous inversion and perversion of the true relation of things, is prayer. " Enter into thy closet." There all is silence, secrecy, solitude, seclusion. Within that shut door, the disciple is left alone—all others shut out, that the suppliant may be shut in—*with God.* The silence is in order to the hearing of the still, small voice that is drowned in worldly clamor, and which even a human voice may cause to be unheard or indistinct. The secrecy is in order to a meeting with Him who seeth in secret and is best seen in secret. The solitude is for the purpose of being alone with One who can fully impress with His presence only when there is no other presence to divert thought. The place of seclusion with God is the one school where we learn that He is, and is the rewarder of those that diligently seek Him. The closet is " not only the oratory, it is the *observatory,"* not for prayer only but for prospect—the wide-reaching, clear-seeing outlook upon the eternal! The decline of prayer is the decay of piety; for prayer to cease altogether, would be spiritual death, for it is to every child of God the breath of life.

To keep in close touch with God in the secret chamber of His presence, is the great underlying purpose of prayer. To speak with God is a priceless privilege; but what shall be said of having and hearing Him speak with us! We can tell Him nothing He does not know; but He can tell us what no imagination has ever conceived, no research ever unveiled. The highest of all possible attainments is the knowledge of God, and this is the practical mode of His revelation of Himself. Even His holy word needs to be read in the light of the closet, if it is understood. " And when Moses was gone into the tabernacle of the congregation to speak with Him, then he heard the voice of one speaking unto him from off the mercy seat that *was* upon the ark of testimony,—from between the two cherubim, and he spoke unto him." Numbers vii., 89.

And, where there is this close touch with God, and this clear insight into His name which is His nature, and into His word which is His will made known, there will be a new power to walk with Him in holiness and work with Him in service. " He made known His *ways* unto Moses, His *acts* unto the children of Israel." The mass of the people stood afar off and saw His deeds, like the overthrowing of Pharaoh's hosts in the Red Sea; but Moses drew near into the thick darkness where God was, and in that thick darkness he found a light such as never shone elsewhere, and in that light he read God's secret plans and purposes and interpreted His wondrous ways of working.

All practical power over sin and over men depends on maintaining closet communion. Those who abide in the secret place with God show themselves mighty to conquer evil, and strong to work and to war for God. They are the seers who read His secrets; they know His will; they are the meek whom He guides in judgment and teaches His way. They are His prophets, who speak for Him to others, and even forecast things to come. They watch the signs of the times and discern His tokens and read His signals. We sometimes count as mystics those who, like Savonarola and Catharine of Siena, claim to have communications from God; to have revelations of a definite plan of God for His Church, or for themselves as individuals, like the reformer of Erfurt, the founder of the Bristol orphanages, or the leader of the China Inland Mission. But may it not be that we stumble at these experiences because we do not have them ourselves? Have not many of these men and women proved by their lives that they were not mistaken, and that God has led them by a way that no other eye could trace?

But, for close contact with the living God in prayer, there is another reason that rises perhaps to a still higher level. Prayer not only puts us in touch with God, and gives knowledge of Him and His ways, but it imparts to us His power. It is the touch which brings virtue out of Him. It is the hand upon the pole of a celestial battery, which charges us with His secret life, energy, efficiency. Things which are impossible with man are possible with God, and with a man in whom God is. Prayer is the secret of imparted power from God, and nothing else can take its place. Absolute weakness follows the neglect of secret communion with God—and the weakness is the more deplorable, because it is often unsuspected, especially when one has never yet known what true power is. We see men of prayer quietly achieving results of the most surprising character. They have the calm of God, no hurry, or worry, or flurry; no anxiety or care, no excitement or bustle—they do great things for God, yet they are little in their own eyes; they carry great loads, and yet are not weary nor faint; they face great crises, and yet are not troubled. And those who know not what treasures of wisdom and strength and courage and power are hidden in God's pavilion, wonder how it is. They try to account for all this by something in the man, or his talent, or tact, or favoring circumstances. Perhaps they try to imitate such a career by securing the patronage of the rich and mighty, or by dependence on organization, or fleshly energy—or what men call " determination to succeed "— they bustle about, labor incessantly, appeal for money and cooperation, and work out an apparent success, but there is none of that Power of God in it which can not be imitated. They compass themselves about with sparks, but there is no fire of God; they build up a great structure, but it is wood, hay, stubble; they make a great noise, but God is not in the clamor. Like a certain preacher who confessed that, when he felt no kindling of inspired thought and feeling, he walked up and down the pulpit, and shouted with all his might—they make up for the lack of divine unction and spiritual action by carnal confidence and vehemence. There is a show of energy, resolution, endeavor, and often of results, but behind all this a lamentable and nameless deficiency.

Nothing is at once so undisputable and so overawing as the way in which a few men of God live in Him and He in them. The fact is, that, in the disciple's life, the fundamental law is " not I but Christ in me." In a grandly true sense there is but one *Worker,* one Agent, and He divine; and all other so-called " workers " are instruments and instruments only, in His hands. The first quality of a true instrument is *passivity.* An *active* instrument would defeat its own purpose; all its activity must be dependent upon the man who uses it. Sometimes a machine becomes uncontrollable, and then it not only becomes use-less, but it works damage and disaster. What would a man do with a plane, a knife, an axe, a bow, that had any will of its own and moved of itself? Does it mean nothing when, in the Word of God, we meet so frequently the symbols of passive service—the rod, the staff, the saw, the hammer, the sword, the spear, the threshing instrument, the flail, and, in the New Testament, the vessel? Does it not mean that a *willful* man God can not use; that the first condition of service is that the will is to be so lost in God's as that it presents no *resistance* to His, no *persistence* beyond or apart from His, and no *assistance* to His? George Müller well taught that we are to wait to know whether a certain work is *God's;* then whether it is *ours,* as being committed to us; but even then we need to wait for God's *way* and God's *time* to do His own work, otherwise we rush precipitately into that which He means us to do, but only at His signal, or we go on doing when He calls a halt. Many a true servant of God has, like Moses, begun before his Master was ready, or kept on working when his Master's time was past.

There is one aspect of prayer to which particular attention needs to be called, because it is strongly emphasized in the Word, and because it is least used in our daily life, namely, *intercession.*

This word, and what underlies it, has a very unique use and meaning in Scripture. It differs from supplication, first in this, that supplication has mainly reference to the suppliant and his own supply; and again because intercession not only *concerns others,* but largely implies the need of *direct divine interposition.* There are many prayers that allow our cooperation in their answer, and imply our activity. When we pray, " Give us this day our daily bread," we go to work to *earn* the bread for which we *pray.* That is God's law. When we ask God to deliver us from the evil one, we expect to be sober and vigilant, and resist the adversary. This is right; but our activity in many matters hinders the full display of God's power, and hence also our impression of His working. And the deepest convictions of God's prayer-answering are wrought in cases where in the nature of things we are precluded from all activity in promoting the result.

It will, therefore, be seen that the *objection* which often hinders our praying, or praying in confidence of results— namely, that we are in that particular case entirely helpless to effect any result—is the grand reason for praying; and when such praying is answered, the evidence of God's working is irresistible. It is when we are in trouble and refuge fails us, when we are at our wits' end, that it becomes plain that *He* saves us out of our distresses. Unbelief is always ready to suggest that it is not a strange thing if a prayer for the conversion of another is answered, when we have been bending every energy toward the winning of that soul; and we find it very hard to say how far the result is traceable to God and how far to man. But when one can do nothing but cry to God, and yet He works mightily to save, unbelief is silenced, or compelled to confess, this is the finger of God.

The Word of God teaches us that intercession with God is most necessary in cases where man is powerless. Elijah is held before us as a great intercessor and the one example given is his prayer for rain. Yet in this case he could *only pray;* there was nothing else he could do to unlock the heavens after three years and a half of drought. And is there not a touch of divine poetry in the form in which the answer came? The rising cloud took the shape of "a *man's hand*," as though to assure the prophet how God saw and heeded the suppliant hand raised to Him in prayer! Daniel was powerless to move the king or reverse his decree; all he could do was to "desire mercies of the God of heaven concerning the secret;" and it was because he could do nothing else, could not even *guess* at the interpretation when he knew not even the dream—that it was absolutely sure that *God* had interposed, and so even the heathen king himself saw, felt and confessed.

All through history certain crises have arisen when the help of man was vain. To the formal Christian, the carnal disciple, the unbelieving soul, this fact, that there is nothing that man could do, makes prayer seem almost a folly, perhaps a farce, a waste of breath. But, to those who best know God, man's extremity is God's opportunity, and human helplessness is the argument for praying. Invariably those whose faith in prayer is supernaturally strong, are those who have most proved that *God has* wrought by their own conscious compulsory cessation of all their own effort as vain and hopeless.

George Müller set out to prove to a half-believing church and an unbelieving world that God does directly answer prayer; and to do this he purposely abstained from all the ordinary methods of appeal, or of active effort to secure the housing, clothing, and feeding of thousands of orphans. Rev. J. Hudson Taylor undertook to put missionaries into Inland China, by dependence solely upon God, not only asking no collections, but refusing them in connection with public meetings. He and his co-workers are accustomed to lay all wants before the Lord, whether of men or money, and expect the answer, and it comes. The study of missionary history reveals the fact that, at the very times when, in utter despair of any help but God's, there has been believing prayer, the interposition of God has been most conspicuously seen—how could it be most conspicuous except amid such conditions?

One of the most encouraging tokens of God's moving in our days is, therefore, the revival of the prayer-spirit,

which is noticeable in the numerous " prayer circles " and
" prayer covenants," formed within ten years past.   In
Great Britain particularly, intercession has been unusually
emphasized of late.   The Keswick movement has been
more conspicuous for prayer than for anything else.   The
whole atmosphere of the convention has been laden with
its fragrance, and the intervals between the meetings are
very largely filled up with private supplication, or with
smaller gatherings of two or three or more who seek
further converse with God.   There are organizations for
prayer alone—some whose members do not know each
other, or meet in common assemblies, but whose only bond
is a covenant of daily supplication for one another and for
objects of mutual interest.   Any one who will read the
two volumes in which is told that wonderful story of the
China Inland Mission, will find that beyond all else, believing prayer is brought to the front, as *the* condition of
all success.   At the Mission Home, in London, from morning till night there is one sacrifice of praise and prayer;
and, at least once a week, with the map of China in full
sight, the various missionaries and stations are mentioned
by name, individually, the peculiar circumstances being
made known, which incite to earnest, sympathetic supplication.   And thus, both in larger and smaller circles of
prayer, the spirit of intercession has a marked revival.

This is doubtless the most hopeful sign as yet apparent
above the horizon, and it is a *signal,* calling God's people
to a new life of unselfish and believing prayer. *Every
church ought to be a prayer circle;* but this will not be,
while we are waiting for the whole body to move together.
The mass of professing Christians have too little hold on
God to enter into such holy agreement.   To all who yearn
for a revival of the prayer-spirit, we suggest that, in every
church a prayer circle be formed, without regard to *numbers.*   Let the pastor unite with himself any man or

woman in whom he discerns peculiar spiritual life and power, and, without publicity or any effort to enlarge the little company, begin to lay before God any matter demanding special divine guidance and help. Without any public invitation—which might only draw unprepared people into a formal association—it will be found that the Holy Spirit will enlarge the circle as He fits others, or finds others fit, to enter it—and thus quietly and without observation the little company of praying souls will grow as fast as God means it shall. Let a record be kept of every definite petition laid before God—for such a prayer circle should be only with reference to very definite matters—and as God interposes, let the record of his interposition be carefully kept, and become a new inspiration to believing prayer. Such a resort to united intercession would transform a whole church, remove dissensions, rectify errors, secure harmony and unity, and promote Holy Ghost administration and spiritual life and growth, beyond all other possible devices. If in any church the pastor is not a man who could or would lead in such a movement, let two or three, who feel the need, meet and begin by prayer for *him*. In this matter there should be no waiting for *anybody else;* if there be but *one* believer who has power with God, let such an one begin intercessory prayer. God will bring to the side of such an intercessor others whom He has made ready to act as supplicators.

Not long since, in a church in Scotland, a minister suddenly began to preach with unprecedented power. The whole congregation was aroused and sinners marvelously saved. He himself did not understand the new enduement. In a dream of the night it was strangely suggested to him that the whole blessing was traceable to one poor old woman who was *stone deaf,* but who came regularly to church, and being unable to hear a word, *spent all the time in prayer* for the preacher and individual hearers. In the

biography of C. G. Finney similar facts are recorded of
" Father Nash," Abel Cleary, and others. In Newport,
England, is a praying circle of twelve men, who have met
for thirty years every Saturday night to pray for definite
blessings. Not one death occurred in their number during
a whole quarter century. The first impulse leading to this
weekly meeting was interest in Mr. Spurgeon's ministry.
They felt that with his great access to men he had need of
peculiar power from above, and on the Sabbath following
their first meeting, he began to preach with such increased
unction as attracted general notice.

Examples might be multiplied indefinitely. But the one
thing we would make prominent is this: that above all else,
God is calling His people to new prayer. He wills that
" men pray everywhere, lifting up holy hands without
wrath and doubting;" that, *first of all*, supplication,
prayers, intercessions, and giving of thanks be made for all
men. * And if this be done, first of all, every other most
blessed result will follow. *God waits to be asked.* He has
the fountains of blessing which He puts at the disposal of
His praying saints. They are sealed fountains to the ungodly and the unbelieving. But there is one Key that unlocks even heaven's gates; one secret that puts connecting
channels between those eternal fountains and ourselves,
that key, that secret, is prevailing prayer.

In London an enterprising newspaper has a private wire
connecting with Edinburgh, in order to command the latest
freshest news from the Scottish Athens. One night the
clerk, who was out to collect local items, returned late and
could not get in—he had forgotten to take his night-key.
He thought a moment. It was of no use to knock at the
door—the only fellow-clerk in the building was too far
away to hear him. He stepped to a neighboring telegraph
office and sent a message to Edinburgh: " Tell —— that

* 1 Tim. ii, 1, 8.

I am at the street door and can not get in." In twenty minutes the door was unfastened and he was at his desk in the office. *The shortest way to get at the man in the fourth story was by Edinburgh.* How long will it take us to learn that our shortest route to the man next door is by way of God's throne! God has no greater controversy with His people to-day than this, that, with boundless promises to believing prayer, there are so few who actually give themselves unto intercession.

" And there is none that calleth upon Thy name,
   That stirreth up himself to take hold of Thee."—Isa. lxiv, 7.

CHAPTER VII

It is of the highest consequence to recognize that the work of missions has, as its central encouragement and inspiration, the promise of a supernatural presence and power. "Lo, I am with you always, even unto the end of the age," means nothing less than that, in a special sense, an exceptional manner, the omnipresent One will accompany the march of the missionary band.

This is the most emphatic of all the arguments for missions, and the all-sufficient compensation for the self-sacrifices which a true missionary life always and necessarily implies and involves. It is, however, a truth that belongs to the highest altitude both of divine teaching and human experience, that *the one way for man to command the supernatural lies through the closet.* Real prayer is a divine inbreathing and therefore has a divine outreaching; it is of the essence of the miraculous and works essentially supernatural results.

The power of prayer is the perpetual sign of God's working in the human soul and among men, the standing miracle of the ages. Upon no one thing does the word of God so frequently and heavily lay the stress of both injunction and invitation; to no one agency or instrumentality are effects so marvelous both assured and attributed. Nothing marks the decline from primitive piety, and the virtual apostasy of the church, more than the secondary place assigned to prayer both in the individual life and in public worship, and the formalism that substitutes liturgical, or, still worse, mechanically tame, stale, lifeless saying for prayers, for true prayers found first of all in the suppliant's heart.

Prayer can be interpreted only by conceding a superhuman element. While much of the benefit and blessing that comes to praying souls may doubtless be traced to natural and secondary causes, in numberless other cases we are compelled either to deny the fact of the answer or else to admit a supernatural factor. If we deny divine interposition, there are events and experiences in the actual history of every praying soul which, without that interposition, remain as inexplicable as the deliverance of the three holy children from the furnace, or of Daniel from the den of lions.

Jonathan Edwards lived on the verge of the unseen world, and was in peculiar contact and communication with it. From ten years of age, his prayers were astonishing, alike for the faith they exhibited and the effects they wrought or secured. The intellect of Edwards reminds of a cherub, and his heart, of a seraph; and, therefore, we can distrust neither his self-knowledge nor his candor. His communion with God was neither a dream of an excited fancy nor an invention of an impostor. Yet it was so rapt and rapturous, that the extraordinary views which he obtained of the glory, love and grace of the Son of God so overcame him that for an hour he would be flooded with tears, weeping aloud. Such prayer brought power not less wonderful than that of Peter at Pentecost. Edwards's sermon at Enfield, on " Sinners in the hands of an angry God," terrible as it was, and delivered without a gesture, was clothed with such unction that it produced unparalleled effects. Hearers leaped to their feet and clasped the pillars of the meeting-house, as if they literally felt their feet sliding into ruin.

God chose that devout man, in the midst of an apostasy

from God that was well-nigh a wreck of religious faith in England and America, to turn, by his prayers, the entire tide of church-life from channels of worldliness and wickedness into a new course of evangelistic and missionary activity. In 1747, Jonathan Edwards pealed out his trumpet call, summoning the whole Christian Church to prayer. In his remarkable tract in which he pleads for a " visible union of God's people in an extraordinary prayer," he refers to the day of fasting and prayer observed the year previous at Northampton, and which was followed *that same night* by the utter dispersion of the French Armada, under the Duke d'Anville; and Edwards adds, " This is the nearest parallel with God's wonderful works of old in times of Moses, Joshua and Hezekiah, of any that have been in these latter ages of the world."

That trumpet peal to universal prayer, one hundred and fifty-three years ago, marks a turning point especially in modern missions. Edwards felt that only direct divine interposition would meet the emergency, and his whole tract shows that he expected such divine working in answer to believing prayer. The results that followed reveal anew beyond a doubt, that, if the Church of God will but pray as she ought, every other needed blessing and enlargement will come to her missionary work. To emphasize this truth and get an intelligent survey of the state of the world and the church as it was then; this only would reveal the desperate darkness that drove disciples to the mountain tops for communion with God and kept them on their knees till the light broke forth as the morning.

At the opening of the eighteenth century spiritual desolation was so widespread, that a prospect more hopelessly dreary has not alarmed true disciples since the dark ages. Hume, Gibbon, Bolingbroke, the giants of infidelity, were acknowledged leaders in English society. In France, Voltaire, Rousseau and Madame de Pompadour ruled at the royal court, and at the tribune of the people. In Germany, Frederick the Great, the friend and companion of Voltaire, flaunted his deistic opinions and dealt out to his antagonists kicks with his thick boots. " Flippancy and frivolity in the church, deism in theology, lasciviousness in the novel and the drama," these were the conditions that prevailed in England, which Isaac Taylor declared was " in a condition of virtual heathenism," while Samuel Blair affirmed that in America " religion lay a-dying."

And what was the pulpit of those days doing to offset this awful condition of apostasy? Nothing! Natural theology without a single distinctive doctrine of Christianity; cold, formal morality or barren orthodoxy constituted the staple teaching both in the established church and the dissenting chapel. The best sermons, so-called, were only ethical essays, a thousand of which held not enough gospel truth to guide one soul to the Savior of sinners. There seemed to be a tacit agreement to let the devil alone; instead of Satan being chained so that he could work no damage, it was the church that was in bonds so that she could work no deliverance. The grand and weighty truths for whose sake Hooper and Latimer dared the stake, and Baxter and Bunyan went to jail, seemed like the relics of a remote past, curiosities of archæology and paleontology. A flood of irreligion, immorality, infidelity, flooded the very domain of Christendom. Collins and Tindall stigmatized Christianity as a system of priestcraft. Woolston declared the miracles of the Bible to be allegories and myths, and Whiston denounced them as impositions and frauds. By Clark and Priestly Arianism and Socinianism were openly taught, and to heresy was thus given the currency of fashionable sanction. Blackstone, the legal commentator, went the rounds from church to church till he had heard every clergyman of note in London; and his melancholy testimony was that not one discourse had he heard among them all which had in it more Christianity than the writings of Cicero, or from which he could gather whether the preacher were a disciple of Confucius or Zoroaster, Mahomet or Christ!

Archbishop Secker in one phrase gave as "the characteristic of the age" an "open disregard of religion." The bishops themselves led the van in the hosts of the worldly and gay; Archbishop Cornwallis gave at Lambeth Palace balls and routs so scandalous that even the king interfered. It was jocosely said that the best way to stop Whitefield in his work of reform was to put on his head the bishop's miter.

It was such a state of religion and morals, of corrupted doctrine and perverted practice, that bowed true disciples in great humiliation and drove them to God in sheer despair of human help. They felt as David did when he wrote the twelfth Psalm:

> "Help, Lord! for the godly man ceaseth,
> For the faithful fail from among the children of men."

Over the entire extent of the Christian Church there began to be little praying circles of devout souls who entreated God once more to pluck His hand out of His bosom and show Himself mighty to deliver.

Of such a character was that little gathering which, eighteen years before Edwards blew that clarion blast, began to meet in Lincoln College, Oxford; when John Wesley and his brother Charles, Mr. Morgan and Mr. Kirkham, burdened with the awful condition of an apostate church, conferred and prayed together for such a reviving as could come only from the breath of God. Six years after these meetings began, there were only fourteen who came together; but, out of that humble meeting where prayer to God was the entire dependence, was born *Methodism*, the mightiest movement of modern times, save only the Moravian, in the direction of evangelical faith and evangelistic work.

The God of prayer heard these suppliant voices, and Whitefield and the Wesley brothers began to preach with tongues burning with pentecostal flames. They were resisted by a rigid, frigid church; but driven into the open fields and commons, they so reached the masses of the people as they could never have reached them within chapel walls.

At this precise juncture, Jonathan Edwards, in America, profoundly impressed with the dreadful condition of both the world and the church, urged upon the churches of this country concerted prayer; and across the seas another trumpet peal echoed his own, summoning all disciples to unite in special prayer " for the effusion of God's spirit upon all the churches, and upon the whole habitable earth." The era of prayer was now fairly inaugurated. In England, Scotland, Ireland and Wales, and throughout New England and the Middle States, believers began to pray for a specific blessing and to come together for united supplication.

We have not space to trace minutely the remarkable interpositions of God; but a few salient facts stand boldly out in the historic page. In 1780, under the influence of the Haldanes, Andrew. Fuller, Rowland Hill, Sutcliffe and others like them, there came pulsing over the church the mighty tidal wave of genuine revival. William Grimshaw, William Romaine, Daniel Rowlands, John Berridge, Henry Venn, Walker of Truro, James Hervey, Toplady, Fletcher of Madeley—these are some of the men that belonged in this grand apostolical succession that during this period of reformation kept feeding and fanning these revival fires. How was it that, in such numbers and at such a crisis, they were raised up to stem the tide that with resistless momentum threatened to sweep away every landmark of religion and morality? But one answer can be given; *Jehovah of Hosts was conspicuously answering prayer.* The full significance of those concerted prayers can never be fully known until eternity opens its august doors and unfolds its sealed books. But we can even now trace to those prayers, at the darkest hour of modern church history, *the inauguration of the new era of universal missions.* Out of these prayers came the establishment of the monthly concert of prayer in 1784, the founding of the first distinctively foreign missionary society of England in 1792, the consecration of William Carey to Oriental missions in 1793, with all the wonderful work of that pioneer who, with his co-laborers, secured the translation of the Word of God into 40 different tongues, and the circulation of 200,000 copies, providing vernacular Bibles for 500,000,000 souls, within the space of a half-century!

These are only the results of those prayers traced in one direction. All that modern missions have wrought on four continents and the isles of the sea; all the doors that have opened into every new land of pagan, papal, heathen or Moslem peoples; all the hundreds of organizations, formed to cover the earth with this golden network of love and labor; all the hundreds of translations of the Bible into the tongues and dialects of mankind; all the planting of churches, mission stations, Christian homes, schools, colleges, hospitals, printing-presses and the vast machinery of gospel effort; all the thousands of laborers who have offered to go and have gone to the far-off fields; all the Christian literature created to supply the demand of awakening minds hitherto sleeping the sleep of intellectual stagnation; who shall say what is not to be attributed to those prayers that from Lincoln College, Paulerspury and Northampton went up to God a century and a half ago!

To those prayers even the details of missionary history

are closely linked. For example, Asia was a continent, to be evangelized. To reach its teeming populations the strategy of the gospel struck at the heart of the continent and sought to pierce its vital, working center, India. England was already there in the East India Company, but that company was virtually the implacable foe to missions, for the unselfish and uncompromising morality of the gospel interfered with a lawless greed that subordinated everything to trade; and so India was practically closed to the gospel. The presence there of representatives of an enlightened Christian government had erected new barriers more insurmountable than any that existed before Elizabeth signed that primitive Trading Company's charter!

But prayer for the " whole habitable globe " included India. And God had heard those prayers and was moving. He had given Britain territorial possessions and political rights in India, and a scepter over 200,000,000 people. Time was close at hand when in this central stronghold of Brahminism, this central field of Oriental missions, Christianity, through that sordid East India Company, was to get a firm foothold. England had an incipient empire in the Indies; this made necessary an open line of communication with the home government in order to maintain an open highway of travel, traffic and transportation between London and Calcutta. Hence, in the providence of God came that political necessity which ultimately determined the attitude of every nation along that highway that was opened through the Mediterranean and the Red Sea. All along that roadway, through great waters, the bordering nations must, if not favorable to Christian missions, at least be neutral.

Those who care to look more minutely into the providential process by which a highway for the gospel was prepared will note how, within ten years after that trumpet call of Edwards, the battle of Plassey occurred, which deserves to rank among the decisive battles of the world. Robert Clive, the scourge of God, in that conflict settled it that Protestantism, and not Buddha nor the Pope, was to rule in India. Then just one hundred years later the Sepoy rebellion swung the great English power in India to the side of Christian missions and put the great heart of Asia under control of the foremost Protestant and missionary nation of Europe, if not of the world. We have given this one instance with some fullness of detail, as one example of prayer, swaying the balance of national history and a world's destiny. But even yet only the bare outlines have been indicated of that grand march of events which is even now in progress, and whose magnificent movement, if not originated, was marvelously accelerated, by the bugle call of the angel of the Lord in response to prevailing prayer!

The whole basis of successful missionary work is to be found in believing and importunate prayer. Whatever enthusiastic appeals are made to human ears, however compact and business-like our Missionary Boards and organizations, however thorough and systematic our methods of gathering offerings, it depends primarily and ultimately on prayer, whether the appeals really move men, whether the organizations prove effective, whether the offerings are cheerful and ample. The men, means and measures for a world's evangelization have always been hopelessly inadequate and disproportionate to a world's extent and needs; they always will be, while selfishness is lord of even nominal disciples. But what we need is supernatural power; then one shall chase a thousand and two put ten thousand to flight. And this divine working comes only in answer to united prayer. No time is lost in waiting for the Holy Spirit and the tongues of fire. Fire means light and heat for the believer, so that he shall no longer walk in the darkness of doubt or the chill of indifference. Fire means a consuming force that burns away, melts, subdues, all obstacles to human souls. Better, therefore, than any new standard of living and giving is a new experience of praying. As surely as believers take their stand on the promises and plead with God as Jacob did, they shall become like him, princes of God, and shall prevail. For a praying church a dying world is waiting.

Missionary history shows the value of the prayer for laborers.

"*Pray ye* therefore the Lord of the Harvest that He would thrust forth laborers into His Harvest."

The grand inspiration to all missions, the world over, and to all missionary spirit and sacrifice in the Church, is PRAYER? not appeal to men, but appeal to God.

This is but one of those injunctions and promises which fix our eyes upon *Prayer* as the great motor in the kingdom of God. Again we affirm it: *Prayer has turned every great crisis in the kingdom.* It can bring men, it can furnish money, it can supply all the means and *material* of war. Yet this, the grandest of all the springs of missionary activity, is that on which the least practical dependence is placed in our missionary machinery.

Let us look at the bearing of believing supplication upon our supply of laborers for the harvest field.

The fascination about all true Christian work is that, first of all, it is *God's work*. The true child of God longs to find his place and sphere in that grander sphere of divine activity where he is permitted to share *co-operation with God*. Now all true adaptation to our work depends on a higher plan than ours. God's work reaches through the ages and spans even the eternities. Every workman must have his *fitness for his particular work*, and that fitness must be of God, for the workman cannot know what peculiar demands that work will make upon him until he gets at work, and then it is too late to prepare. Preparation must be carried on earlier, and, because no man can tell with certainty what he is to be called to do, or where he is to be placed, the only hope and faith that can solve the perplexity must fasten on the Providence of God. He who foresees and foreknows what the work is to be must predestine and prepare the worker to do it.

Does He not? Who that studies history—which is the mere record of God's dealings with humanity—can not see that a divine plan is at work? that in the great crisis of affairs He brings forth some man or woman singularly prepared, unconsciously prepared, often unwillingly prepared, for the work and the sphere? so that, as in the building of the temple, no sound of axe, hammer or tool of iron was heard while it was in building, so again there is no need of any adaptation after the man and his work meet—they mutually fit as stone does stone, or timber does timber, where the work has been properly done in the quarry and in the shops.

Many a man has no chance or need to adapt himself to his " environment." One of the great objections to " evolution " is found in the frequent examples of preadaptation with which nature abounds. A caterpillar that lives on the earth, crawls on its own belly, eats leaves and refuse,— at a certain stage of its history enters the chrysalis state. It is to emerge from its cocoon a winged butterfly, henceforth to soar, not creep or crawl, to sip the honey from the dainty nectaries of flowers. Here is a wholly new experience, of which the life of the worm furnished no earnest. Now if you run a sharp blade down the length of the cocoon, and cut through the cuticle of the animal while yet in the chrysalis state, you will find *all the peculiar organs* of the future butterfly or moth mysteriously enfolded beneath that skin. How are they to be accounted for? That caterpillar no more knew its future state and needs than the unborn infant knew its coming wants. It could not be said to adapt its organs to its new life *after* its emergence from the cocoon, for those organs were all there, long before the moment of that new birth. And so the reverent Christian scientist accounts for the preadaptation by a higher evolution in the plan of a Creator.

Just so we discern in history preadaptations that defy any explanation without faith in the providence of God. Men themselves have been undergoing a peculiar training for ten, twenty, thirty, forty years, which has found its explanation only when God has brought them and their preordained work together! Moses, in the palace and court of Pharaoh, from the hour when he was taken out of the basket of bulrushes, was unconsciously preparing to become God's great agent in Israel's deliverance and organization: the fitness of that man as leader and law giver, poet and prophet, organizer and administrator, is so exact and marvelous that it compels belief in God. Luther at Erfurt and Wurtemberg, Knox in Scotland, Calvin in Switzerland, John Wesley and Charles Wesley in England, Jonathan Edwards in New England, William Carey at Hackleton, Adoniram Judson in Williamstown, John Hunt at Hykeham Moor, John E. Clough studying civil engineering, David Livingstone poring over Dick's " Siderial Heavens," Henry M. Stanley reporting for the New York *Herald*—these are examples of men whom God was unconsciously making ready for a special work of which they had no conception, and for which they could make no intelligent preparation.

Who was it that not only raised up those six remarkable men and missionaries—Schwartz, Carey, Judson, Morrison, Wilson and Duff—but raised them up in the same age and epoch of missions? All of them from humble life, but of varied nationalities, of different denominations, Lutheran, Baptist, Independent, Presbyterian; who was it gave to all of them essentially the tastes and the training of scholars, tho their early surroundings in several cases specially forbade; who was it that singularly fitted them to be theologians, translators, philologists, scientists and teachers? Who was it that so singularly adjusted the plan of these several lives that each spent some forty years among the natives of India, Burmah or China; passed the advanced limit of three-score years and ten, and died rejoicing not only in their labors but in the fruit of their labors? *

Sometimes, indeed, it suddenly appears to the man himself that the adaptation somehow exists; but it is only the consciousness of a pre-fitness. John Hunt has been compared to the forest bird, which, hatched in the nest of some common domestic fowl, moves about restless among the pullets and ducks in the barnyard, until some day, finding its pinions grown long and strong, and instinctively conscious that the air, not the earth or the water, is its native element, suddenly soars from the ground and makes straight and swift flight toward the freedom of the woods and the higher realms of the atmosphere! Of how many of God's workmen might similar words be written? And what new hope does it impart to missions as the enterprise of the Church to know that while God buries the workmen He carries on the work! No gap ever occurs that He cannot fill. How often a desponding spirit cries, when such a man falls as John Williams of Erromanga, or Mackay of Uganda, or Livingstone at Lake Bangweolo, or Keith Falconer at Aden, "How shall that man's place be filled?" But God has another man ready, and sometimes two to take the place of one. And so the work goes on.

The subject will bear indefinite expansion; but our object is only to sound once again the grand key-note of all missions: *Believing Prayer.* The field is wide—world

---

*See Dr. George Smith.

wide. The Harvest is great, but the laborers are few. How are they to be supplied? There is but one way authorized in Scripture: " PRAY ye therefore the Lord of the Harvest that HE would send forth laborers into His Harvest." Nothing else can fill these vacant fields with an adequate supply of workmen. Education cannot do it. A great deal of our education is leading young men and women away from mission fields. " The spectacles of the intellect," says Dr. David Brown, " are binocular." There is a tendency in all intellectual culture, as in the gathering of earthly riches, to make us practically Godless. Men become purse-proud by accumulating wealth, and brain-proud by accumulating learning. If God does not hear prayer and give learning and culture a divine direction, a heavenly anointing, our colleges will only raise up a generation of sceptics. Our appeals and arguments will not give the Church missionaries; unless the demonstration of the Spirit is added to the demonstration of logic, no conviction will result that leads to consecration—that higher logic of life.

And, when workmen are *on the field,* it is the same prayer that must secure to the word they preach " free course," so that it is glorified. When the Church at Antioch, praying and fasting, sent forth Barnabas and Saul on that first missionary tour, the Church kept praying; and, in answer to prayer, doors, great and effectual, opened before them, and repentance unto life was granted unto the Gentiles, and mighty signs and wonders were wrought by the hands of those primitive pioneer missionaries.

We have heard many things said in depreciation of J. Hudson Taylor and the China Inland Mission. We have heard his whole work stigmatized as " without a foundation," a " wild scheme," " impracticable," " lacking all elements of stability and permanence; " we have heard said of it, that it " gets men and women into Inland China, and then leaves them there to starve," etc. One thing is very remarkable about it: it sets us all an example of *faith in God* and *power in prayer.* The history of the China Inland Mission is a wonderful story; it sounds like new chapters in the Acts of the Apostles. Mr. Taylor was at the little Conferences of Believers at Niagara-on-the-Lake in July, 1888 and 1889. At the first, he made a precious address, fragrant with the anointing of God—unpretentious, modest, simple, childlike. It took us all captive by a divine fascination. He simply unfolded the word of God, made no appeal, and would, in fact, have no " collection." But that little company of believers, mostly poor, constrained him to accept a freewill offering of some $2,500. To their surprise he was rather anxious than pleased. And in 1889 he told the source of his perplexity. He said:

" When that money was put into my hands, I felt burdened; when the Lord sends me workers I feel no anxiety, for I know that He who provides laborers for His harvest-field will provide the means to put them into the field. But when the Lord gives me money and not the workmen to use the money, I know not what to do with it. When from the Conference of 1888 *thirteen volunteers* subsequently offered themselves for the great field of China, I said, ' Now the Lord has solved my perplexity.' But, you see, we sometimes reckon too fast. And so it was with me. For when I went to the places from which these beloved laborers were to go forth to the harvest-field, the churches to which they belonged insisted on paying all the expenses of their outfit and journey; and so I *had this money still on hand,* and my perplexity was increased. Now, dear friends, *don't give me any more money unless you give me the men and women to use it!* "

Here was the head of a great missionary movement whose *main care is not money at all,* and who is *more anxious to have workmen than funds;* who, in fact, begs us not to give him *any more money* until we first *provide the workers to use it.* The ordinary conditions seem somehow reversed. We hear on all sides frantic appeals for *money.* A few years ago scores of young men and women were offering to go, but there was no money to send them; appeals for workmen were more enthusiastically responded to than the Church responded to the needs of an over-taxed treasury!

Have we not, in missionary work, fallen into the snare of worldly care? Do not missions stand in our thought too much as an enterprise of the *Church,* and too little as the work of *God,* of which the Church is the commissioned agent? Back of all other causes of the present perplexity in mission work; behind all the apathy of individuals and the inactivity of churches, all lack of enthusiasm and of funds, all deficiency of men and means, of intelligence and of consecration, of readiness to *send* and of alacrity to *go,* there lies one lack deeper, more radical, more fundamental —*viz.:* THE LACK OF BELIEVING PRAYER. Until that lack is supplied the doors now opened will not be entered, and the doors now shut will not be opened; laborers of the right sort will not be forthcoming, nor the money forthcoming to put them at work and sustain them in it; until that lack is supplied the churches in the mission field will not be largely blessed with conversions, nor the churches in the home field largely blessed with outpourings and anointings of zeal for God and passion for souls.

The first necessity for the Church and the world is also the first central petition of the Lord's Prayer: *Thy Kingdom Come!* of which the hallowing of God's name is the preparation and the doing of God's will is the consequence. And that Kingdom comes only in answer to expectant prayer. We need, first of all, a revival of the praying spirit which moved Jonathan Edwards to publish his appeal in 1747, and led William Carey and John Sutcliffe to

republish it in 1787. Modern missions had their birth in
prayer; all their progress is due to prayer. A few souls
that have close access to the Mercy Seat have kept up the
apostolic succession of supplication; and because of this,
alone, doors have been opened, workmen thrust forth, and
money provided. But suppose the *whole Church* would
get down before God! What if, where one now prays, a
hundred were bowed on their faces like Elijah on Carmel!
What if, in place of the naturalism that is eating at the
vitals of spiritual life, there might be a revival of faith in
the supernatural, a new and universal awakening to the
fact that God is a present, living, faithful, prayer-hearing
God; that the closet is his ante-room, nay, his audience-
chamber, where, to the suppliant soul, he extends his
sceptre and says, " Ask what thou wilt in Jesus name, and
it shall be given unto thee! "

The late Mr. Neesima, of Japan, said to his fellow-
countrymen when planning an evangelistic tour—*" Advance on your knees! "* To work without praying is practical atheism; to pray without working is idle presumption. But to pray and work together, to baptize all work
with prayer and to follow all prayer with work—that is an
ideal life. Of such a life we may reverently say, *laborare
est orare*—work is worship and worship is work.

In the vision of Isaiah (vi.) the seraphim have six
wings, and four of them are used in the office of humble
and reverent worship, while only two are reserved for fly-
ing. As Dr. Gordon beautifully says, " Let us learn a lesson
on the proportion to be observed between supplication and
service." Better twice as much devout preparation as
work, than a hurried and superficial communion with God,
and an unprepared and hasty dash and rush into activity.
Let us linger before God until we get power, and then life
becomes grand. It shines with the glory of His Face, and
it moves with the might of His omnipotence.

CHAPTER VIII

THE GROWTH OF " FAITH-WORK "

" FAITH MISSIONS " is a very imperfect term to describe a movement which needs some descriptive, definitive title, as one of the conspicuous developments of the century.

Johannes Evangelista Gossner, born at Hausen, near Augsburg, in 1773, and dying in Berlin in 1858, at the age of eighty-five, has been called " the father of faith-missions." With his name we must associate the names of August Herman Francke, of Halle, George Müller, of Bristol, J. Hudson Taylor, the founder of the China Inland Mission, and many others who have, in a peculiar sense, become coworkers with God under the inspiration of faith and prayer and with sole dependence upon Him.

To some the term " Faith Missions " seems invidious, as though other missions were not carried on upon the principle of faith. Yet, to learn God's lessons from history, we must neither be too jealous concerning mere phrases, nor too proud, self-willed, or sensitive, to admit our errors or deficiencies. There are two classes of activities among disciples. In one class what are called good " business methods and principles " are adopted as the basis. The church, local or general, takes up an enterprise, calls to its aid strong and wise counselors, and forms a Board ; then goes about its proposed work after the method of worldly prudence—it will cost so much to carry it on, and so much must be raised by contribution. The most vigorous appeals are made for money and for men—the main dependence being upon thorough organization and wise administration. If funds fail, there must be new appeal. No forward step must be taken without a sufficient guaranty, better still if in advance the supply of material is such as assures success. God's blessing will be sought by true disciples, who carry into the Lord's work the principles practically found to assure to worldly enterprises the greatest prosperity and progress. Why, then, are not all such church activities scriptural and apostolic? And is it not Pharisaic and pretentious to describe other enterprises as Faith Work, as tho nobody else had any faith?

To such questions we offer a humble and candid answer. It is possible in work for God to give undue emphasis to its human side, or, rather *too little emphasis to the divine side*. We may do really Christian work in the energy of the flesh rather than in the energy of the Spirit; we may practically trust more to human wisdom than to divine direction; we may put prayer behind our activity rather than before it, thus reversing the true order which puts prayer always first, and we may depend more on appeals to men than on appeals to God. And, if we read God's lesson rightly, here is precisely the providential meaning of these faith movements. They are designed by God to make more vivid and prominent to our faith the *Presence and Power of a Prayer-Hearing God*—to make more real the actual providential administration of the Lord Jesus in the affairs of His Kingdom, and the actual gracious administration of the Holy Spirit in applying the truth to human souls and enlisting believers in a true cooperation with God and each other.

It is a great help to get a view of missions, for example, as The Enterprise of God, for which He is supremely responsible; to feel that He alone can select and separate and send forth His chosen laborers; that He alone can open wide and effectual doors, and meet and drive back the many adversaries; that He alone can move the people to give themselves, their sons and daughters, or their money; that He alone can lift believers to the high level of prevailing prayer, and stir them to loving, passionate sympathy with lost souls; and that consequently it is of first consequence to keep in living, loving contact with God, that our prayers be not hindered; to use only scriptural and spiritual methods in appealing to men, or in raising funds; and that there are times and matters in which we may safely, trusting in His leadership, take bold steps in advance, where, at the time, no human guaranty is furnished for success; as when, at Jesus' command, twelve disciples undertook to feed with five loaves and two fishes five thousand men, beside women and children. Faith counts on God as the Invisible Administrator, who can do things impossible with men, can open doors with a word or a will, thrust forth laborers, put the right man in the right field, supply all the money needful at the moment of need, and, in a word, do exceeding abundantly above all we ask or think. Faith sees that God is honored by being trusted, that believing is not presuming, that the audacity of confidence is sometimes really the humility of dependence and the courage of obedience.

The genuine Faith Work of our day is one of the great inspirations in service to God and man. We may thank God even for the rebuke it has often administered to hesitating unbelief, secular methods and unscriptural appeals, dependence on man and resorts to worldly methods for raising money, and for the example it has furnished of confidence in God in great straits. God has shown us, by many examples, that He is more jealous and zealous for His work than are any of His workmen; that He holds the keys of the situation, and that the government is upon His shoulder.

These lessons can best be understood by studying the

men and the methods themselves, and letting philosophy teach us by examples. The miracles in apostolic days were not more real manifestations of the power of a present God than some modern triumphs of faith which are a sort of addition to the eleventh chapter of Hebrews.

George Müller always comes to mind when we refer to faith work. His history was one long record of blessing received in answer to prayer. He started more than seventy years ago, to demonstrate how much might be accomplished by believing prayer, that the weak faith of disciples might be strengthened. This was his one great desire and design. And what is the result? The various schools, from the beginning, have had over 120,000 pupils, with constant conversions, sometimes over 100 in one school in one year. But only believers are allowed to teach, and only believers who are known as having power in prayer. It is computed that at least 10,000 of these pupils have been led to Christ. During this same period there have been circulated in various parts of the world nearly 2,000,-000 copies of the Bible, or portions thereof, and over 108,000,000 of books, pamphlets, and tracts. Missionary operations have been carried on or aided in twenty-five different lands and countries, and hundreds of missionaries aided in their work, through whom tens of thousands of souls have been brought to Christ, and from the one church organized by Mr. Müller in Bristol, sixty brethren and sisters, forty of whom are yet engaged in labor, have gone forth.

All this is beside the orphan work, in which during the thirty years over 3,000 orphans were converted while in the institution, beside hundreds who found Christ after they had left its walls. And the total amount of money disbursed for all purposes during these sixty-three years was about *seven and a half millions of dollars.* Here is an annual present expenditure for the orphan houses alone of

£22,000, or about $110,000. And all this money has come, with all other supplies, directly in answer to believing prayer. Beyond the annual report, no statement of the financial condition of the institutions was ever made to the public, and even the Report never appeals directly for aid. Never, even in the greatest straits, was one penny asked of any man, or any method resorted to, whatever, of obtaining money or other supplies, except believing prayer. Even the helpers, who meet daily for united supplication, are cautioned not to mention, outside, the wants of the orphans, lest it should seem like looking to other aid than the Divine. And yet supplies have never once failed. The first donation for the orphan work was *a shilling;* in 1896 23,500 pounds! and Mr. Müller learned to ask God as confidently for twenty thousand pounds as, when he began, for a shilling.

Those who would find the principles of faith work expounded by Mr. Müller himself, must read " The Lord's Dealings with George Müller."

There he gives six reasons why a *new* institution was founded by himself and Mr. Craik, instead of working through institutions already founded. Let this faith-worker briefly define his own position. He writes:

1. The *end* which these religious societies propose to themselves, and which is constantly put before their members, is that the whole world will gradually become better, and at last be converted; whereas Scripture teaching is that in the present dispensation, things will not become spiritually better, but rather worse, and that it is not the whole world that will be converted, but only a people gathered out from among the Gentiles for the Lord. As it is unscriptural to expect the conversion of the whole world, we could not propose to ourselves such an end in the service of our Lord.

2. That which is worse, is the connection of those re-

ligious societies with the world, which is completely contrary to the Word of God. In temporal things, the children of God need, whilst they remain on earth, to make use of this world; but when the work to be done requires that those who attend to it should be possessed of spiritual life, the children of God are bound, by their loyalty to their Lord, entirely to refrain from association with the unregenerate.

3. The means made use of in these religious societies to obtain money for the work of the Lord are also, in other respects, unscriptural; for it is a most common case to *ask the unconverted* for money, which even Abraham would not have done.

4. It is not a rare thing for even committee members (the individuals who manage the affairs of the societies) to be manifestly unconverted persons, if not open enemies, of the truth; and this is suffered because they are rich or have influence.

5. It is a common thing to endeavor to obtain for patrons or presidents of these societies, and for chairmen at public meetings, persons of rank and wealth to attract the public. Never once have I known a case of a *poor*, but very devoted, wise, and experienced servant of Christ being invited to fill the chair at such public meetings.

6. Almost all of these societies contract debts, so that it is a comparatively rare case to read a report of any of them without finding that they have expended more than they have received, which is contrary both to the spirit and letter of the New Testament.

7. Another law, is that God only is acknowledged as the patron of the work, and all appeals for help are to be addressed to Him in believing prayer—that success is to be gauged, not by the amount of money given, but by the Lord's blessing; and, while desirous to avoid needless

singularity, the one aim will be to go on simply according to Scripture, without compromising truth. *

Gossner, the humble pastor of the little Bethlehem church in Berlin, had no thought of being a leader in a new movement, or, above all, a "missionary founder." He simply walked, a step at a time, after the Divine leader, venturing to put faith in the words of God, and not discount his promises by unbelief, or by limiting them to the apostolic period, or some remoter time. The story is fascinating in its successive steps, showing how marvelously God leads a willing soul who is courageous enough to follow. Three or four artizans sought him for advice, when they felt the burning fire shut up in their bones, and were weary with forbearing; they felt that they must preach the Gospel in the regions beyond. But when he would not give them aid or approval, they begged, at least, what he could not withhold—a partnership in prayer that God would guide them. He consented, but it was perilous for unbelief, for he found himself praying sympathetically and, at last, fervently, until the symphony of prayer became a sympathy of service. Then he went another step, and began to give them positive help. They came to him when their day's work was over, and Gossner became to them an educator, training them in such knowledge of the Word of God, and the truth according to godliness, as he found lacking. He had suddenly and unconsciously established a training-school.

Then followed the next step. To encourage men to go forth to the world-field without first running the round of the regular curriculum of classical and theological training, was an ecclesiastical heresy which subjected Gossner to a fire of criticism. Yet he was so sure that he had followed, tho at first reluctantly, the leading of God,

* The Lord's Dealings with George Müller. I. 107-112.

that the assaults of his accusers only confirmed him in his course. He shut himself in with God for prolonged prayer, and he found the shield of faith still able to quench the fiery darts hurled at him as an innovator, introducing customs not lawful for his brethren to receive neither to observe—being Germans. He could not act independently of the approval of his brethren, without also cutting loose from their pecuniary aid. And so Gossner thrust his self-trained workmen forth in sole and simple *dependence on God for all needful supplies.* This was the distinctive characteristic of the Gossner Mission, and it was this which God ordained should be an example to others who should afterward dare to trust Him after the same sort. Gossner remembered our Lord's solitary injunction when he showed His disciples the fields that were white for the sickle: " PRAY YE, therefore, the LORD of the Harvest that HE will THRUST forth laborers into His harvest," and he remembered the singular illustration of the working of this principle in the Antiochan Church, when the Holy Ghost called by name and sent forth Barnabas and Saul. * Such precept and practice were to him sufficient warrant for both looking directly to the Lord for such laborers, and for asking for such money, as were needed.

Gossner was already sixty-three years old when he broke off connection with the Berlin Missionary Society, and began to work on independent lines. At that age, few men think of becoming pioneers, rather beginning to withdraw from active labors. Yet Gossner was permitted to put into the field two hundred men and women, and for the outfit and support of this mission band he was simply in partnership with God. And so sacred did he consider this divine partnership, that it became an act of unbelief to ask of men any longer, since he was permitted and authorized to ask of God in faith, nothing wavering. Faith made

* Acts xiii, 1-5.

him bold, and, as he quaintly phrased it, he counted it his business to be employed in "ringing God's prayer-bell rather than the beggar's door-bell." Did God honor the partnership of faith? Let the sufficient witness be the words spoken over Gossner's open grave: "he prayed mission stations into being, and missionaries into faith; he prayed open the hearts of the rich, and gold from the most distant lands."

As Dr. A. J. Gordon says, "Gossner believed in the Holy Ghost, whom he regarded as the administrator of missions. Therefore he relied on prayer more than on organization." Having done all in his power, he would sit in his little room and commit the distant work to this Divine Executor, and "Beg Him to direct it all and order it after His own will." Instead of an elaborate manual of instructions, this was the simple and stirring commission which he put into the hands of his missionaries: *"Believe, hope, love, pray, burn, waken the dead! Hold fast by prayer; wrestle like Jacob! Up, up, my brethren! The Lord is coming, and to every one he will say, 'where hast thou left the souls of these heathens? With the devil?' O, swiftly seek these souls, and enter not without them into the presence of the Lord."* *

It would be a long chapter that should trace the apostolic succession from this missionary founder and trainer. Louis Harms is one example—in Hermannsburgh, daring to undertake missions on a scale unparalleled in history. Think of this pastor, who over fifty years ago inaugurated in his own church—a church of poor farmers, artizans, peasants, and mechanics—a missionary society, which came to have shortly not only its missions and missionaries, but its own ship, its own magazine, its own training college, its own complete equipment. At the end of thirty-one years, Louis Harms had put into the field and kept there,

---

* "The Holy Spirit in Missions," by Dr. A. J. Gordon. 68, 69.

over 350 missionaries, and in ten years more, could praise
God for 13,000 converts in the mission churches, while the
church at home had grown to unprecedented proportions,
and was the largest in the world. Let us look into his
simple diary. " I prayed to the Lord Jesus that He would
provide the needed sum of ——." " Last year, 1857, I
needed 1,500 crowns, and the Lord gave me sixty over.
This year I needed double, and He has given me double,
and one hundred and forty over."

Other, and more recent enterprises—founded and conducted on the same essential basis as Francke's, Müller's, Gossner's, Harms'—need separate treatment. Their
one essential principle is that they treat the work as God's,
and Him as the responsible founder and administrator;
and they lay great stress on two subordinate laws of conduct: First that, as the Scriptures are the express revelation of His will, no methods or measures should be admitted or permitted in His work that are not according to
His word; and secondly, that, as the throne of grace is the
eternal storehouse of supplies, all appeal for help is to be
primarily to God; and that all dependence on man for aid,
and especially on direct appeal to man, is practically a departure from the simple, divinely ordained channel of supplies. Such principles as these, vindicated by such practical illustrations, demand, and should receive, careful
study by all who seek to work with God.

The last few years have furnished two quite apposite
examples of successful work for God, on two quite different lines—The work founded and fostered by George
Müller in Bristol, and that founded and developed under
Dwight L. Moody in America. Both grew to giant dimensions; both had God's Glory in view and both were educational and philanthropic. George Müller died March 10,
1898, and left behind him the Scriptural Knowledge Institution with its five branches; of one only we need to take

notice—the school and orphan work, as most nearly resembling Mr. Moody's, altho the vast colportage work, in distributing Bibles and tracts in various languages closely resembles Mr. Moody's latest effort, the sending forth of the printed page to bless the prisoner in his solitude. Dwight Moody died on December 22, 1899. Here, then, after an interval of less than two years, this second departure took place, and each man left behind him a colossal enterprise which he had been led to inaugurate and carry forward. It is a peculiar parallel also that to carry on the work in each case demands annually an income of about $125,000. Mr. Moody, from the time, in 1879, when he began the school work, up to the day of his death, in 1899, when he left behind these great collegiate schools in Mt. Hermon and Northfield, and the Training School at Chicago, with this increasing colportage work—had conducted all on the most approved Christian business principles. He kept the names of all the best available men and women of the United States and Britain who had money and were givers, and were known to him, and unhesitatingly appealed to them for aid. Sometimes he would write a hundred letters, with his usual tact and with a certain authority born of unselfishness, and tell them he needed aid and how much he wanted them to give. Those to whom he appealed believed in him and his work and usually responded to his call. In this way mainly he raised all the money represented in the school property, and needed in the annual outlay which was but half covered by charges for board and tuition. When Mr. Moody died, there was no man of like large acquaintance and influence and tact to step into his place, and a crisis inevitably arose. Unless, by permanent endowment of $3,000,000 or by annual collection of $120,000, money were supplied, the work must decrease if not decline, and organized effort became necessary to press this matter on the attention of the public, and secure permanence to the noble institutions which he had taken twenty years to build up.

Now let us go back about two years. Suddenly George Müller died, much more without premonition than Mr. Moody. A similar sum of money was needed to carry on the work he left behind; even if it be restricted to the orphan work only. There was no crisis, and there has been no appeal to the public for money, beyond the indirect challenge to liberality found in the work itself and the yearly report of its progress. Everything goes on just as before. There is the daily meeting for prayer, and God is asked in faith, to feed, clothe and provide for the 1600 orphans housed on Ashley Down. Not one word has been spoken or written, revealing any crisis incident to the death of the founder of the orphanages, or suggesting any lack of supplies incident to, or consequent on, his departure. For over threescore years George Müller made but one direct appeal for aid—to God. His successor and son-in-law, Mr. Wright, does the same, and Mr. Bergin and his helpers are in full sympathy. It was the writer's precious privilege to pass several months of the years 1898 and 1900 in Bristol in constant fellowship with Mr. Wright and Mr. Bergin, coming into close touch with the staff of helpers at the orphanage, and mingling with them in prayer for all needs of those hundreds of poor orphan children. It was also his privilege to watch for months the daily supply meeting the daily need, without one public meeting, one word in the public press, or even a private and confidential statement to a few close friends, of any emergency to be met. Yet with the very unique personality of Mr. Müller withdrawn, and whatever personal influence he had in getting money, no longer available, not a child was sent from the orphan houses, not a meal lacked food, and not a want went unsupplied. For sixty years the God of Heaven had been solely appealed to and He is not dead. The same Divine hand still supplies in answer to the prayer of faith every possible need, out of His riches in glory by Christ Jesus. Day by day, without any machinery of collectors, any asking for help save of God, money and other gifts pour in unceasingly. Mr. Müller's departure left no gap to be filled save in the love and yearning hearts of those who loved him. The same principles of faith and prayer which he laid as the cornerstone of the work, remain to sustain it.

Now the contrast compels us candidly to ask, which is the more scriptural and spiritual method of carrying on work for God, and which brings the work into least peril when the workman dies? These are questions which are not idle or useless but intensely practical, and there is one consideration which reaches beyond even this question of the permanency of the work. *The response of God's people* to the calls of God depends largely on their education in giving. If for example a pastor habituates his people to give only under his personal and stirring and urgent appeals, then when he is gone or fails to present the case with power the gifts drop off; or it may be that the person who would otherwise give is not present when the appeal is made and so does not feel its urgency. On the other hand, suppose a congregation thoroughly trained to think of themselves as God's stewards—to consider every cause of God in its inherent worth and claim, and seek of God to know duty and privilege—then gifts come in with the regularity of an overflowing stream. The Word of God distinctly teaches us that the basis of Christian giving must be found in prayer to God and the culture of individual responsibility as in trust with God's property. This principle faith missions seek to emphasize.

J. Hudson Taylor on one occasion made a strong presentation of China's needs, but declined to take any collection on the occasion, asking the hearers to go and consider prayerfully what their duty was. The chairman happened to be also Mr. Taylor's host and he remonstrated that he had lost an opportunity. But the next morning handing Mr. Taylor a check for a large amount he remarked that he was now persuaded of the propriety of his course, acknowledging that, had he given at the time he would have given a very small amount, but that after prayerful weighing of the matter he had seen his whole duty.

CHAPTER IX

THE CULTURE OF THE GRACE OF GIVING

PAUL has apparently rescued from oblivion a *logion* of the Lord Jesus, more valuable than any of those over which Egyptologists have lately made so much ado: "Remember the words of the Lord Jesus, how He said, 'IT IS MORE BLESSED TO GIVE THAN TO RECEIVE.'" This priceless oracle seems to be one of those sayings, handed down by tradition, but not embodied in the Gospel narratives. Its unique value largely consists in this, that it lifts giving to its highest plane, and crowns it as the true secret of the most exalted blessing to the giver himself.

Nothing needs reconstruction more than modern giving; in fact, the reconstruction must be a revolution, for the whole basis is wrong. A great German, in a clever epigram, contrasts Socialism and Christianity thus: the former says, "What is thine is mine"; the latter, "What is mine is thine." But as the late Dr. R. W. Dale said, "The epigram itself needs correction. Christianity really teaches us to say, 'What seems thine is not thine, what seems mine is not mine. Whatever thou or I have belongs to God; and you and I must use what we have according to His will.'"

This is the essence of that sublime truth everywhere taught in Scripture: God's inalienable *ownership;* man's undeniable *stewardship.* This is the one corner-stone of the whole Biblical system of giving; and because it is practically denied or virtually obsolete, we need to begin at the beginning, if we are to have a new and a true system in the Christian use of money.

So fundamental is this grace, that, whenever and wherever there is spiritual advance, the standard of giving becomes more worthy of God's people. When Carey sounded the bugle call for a new crusade of missions a century ago, one of the first signs of a response was found in the thirteen pounds two shillings and sixpence, laid on God's altar in Widow Wallis' parlor at Kettering on that memorable October day in 1792. And "Carey's penny," the systematic weekly offering, was the recognition of the need of a regular, stated, habitual setting apart of the Lord's portion.

From that day to this the matter of giving has been one of the three perplexing problems to be solved in our church life: *praying, going, giving.* Many have been the attempts at solution. Most prominent, perhaps, has been the restoration of the *tithe system,* which has the advantage of being originally God's own appointment. This, with all its merits, is much misunderstood; it belongs to law rather than grace, and it fails to answer the demands of Christian equity. Commonly, the tithe, or tenth, is supposed to have satisfied God's claims and man's needs, while, in fact, the Jewish tithe represented not the maximum but the minimum, and, in some years, the proportion given to the Lord's purposes reached *two-fifths,* if not *three-fifths,* of the faithful believer's income. Again, under a dispensation of grace we become sensible of a new ownership of ourselves by God, as redeemed, regenerated, Spirit-filled saints, including all we have and are. Under this new order, the Sabbath is not less God's time, but all days become Sabbatic; the tithe is not less His, but all money is in trust for His uses; all things and all work become part of a consecrated life for His glory. Moreover, while the tithe may be a fair proportion for a poor saint, it is manifestly out of all proportion for the rich, for our giving is, in equity, to be estimated not by what is given, but by what is *kept*.

Another prominent plan has been the apostolic way of laying by in store, weekly, or at stated times, according as God has prospered, not a fixed sum or proportion, but a variable amount, depending on ability at the time. This has advantages, most obviously the tendency conscientiously to weigh and prayerfully to consider what duty is, and how the measure of obligation varies with increasing prosperity. Its obvious defect is the lack of uniform supplies for the work of God, and the risk of too flexible a conscience in the estimate of real ability.

In some quarters much stress has been laid on a stated season of special restraint upon appetite and other indulgences, as in the " self-denial week," which has yielded large returns to various benevolent enterprises. But there is no Scripture warrant for a method so spasmodic and sentimental. The risk is, that, after the special " lenten " season is over, indulgence may run riot, as tho there were some new right acquired to pleasure-seeking, by the previous self-imposed restraints.

The various individual schemes for promoting true giving need only a mention, since they have so limited a range of experiment. Some few devote to the Lord's purposes, pound for pound, or dollar for dollar, an equal amount to that expended for self. Equitable indeed it seems, to make God the partner who shares alike with ourselves in all the outgo of property. But does not this imply, at least, that the half we spend on ourselves is not His, and that the moiety we hand over to Him equalizes all claims? A few Christians *limit* their accumulations or expenditures to what they deem a reasonable sum, and put the whole remainder at the Lord's disposal—a high example of giving, indeed, in contrast with the low level of most saints.

But of these and all such methods, more or less current, the question still arises, and claims a candid answer, *What is God's standard of giving?* This grave matter should be looked at solely in the searching light of the will and word of God. We have come to accept *methods*—and, still worse, *notions*, of giving, which *begin in an issue with the universal Owner.* We count what we have *our own, not His,* and think of ourselves as owners and proprietors, not stewards and trustees. We satisfy ourselves with setting aside the Lord's portion, and consider ourselves entitled to determine what that portion is, and treat the rest as our own, to do with it as we will. Hence come avaricious hoarding and self-indulgent spending, which are supposed to be legitimate; and hence comes also that tardy atonement of " munificent bequests," of which Shaftsbury was wont to speak with such contempt, as tho there could be any real munificence in giving away what one can no longer use or even keep. Rightly viewed, it is questionable whether there be even such things as " munificent *donations,*" since a " debtor," a " trustee," a " steward "— which are God's own terms for His human creatures—can not make a *donation,* but can only discharge a *debt,* fulfil a trust, execute a commission.

This truth is drastic, but it is God's medicine for the deadly disease of greed, and the fatal selfishness of which greed is only a symptom. The teaching of the blessed Word is unmistakable, and may be briefly stated under the following seven " theses," to borrow Luther's word:

1. God owns all things and all creatures, and never alienates or transfers His ownership.

2. God claims us, with all we are and have, as His by creation, preservation, redemption, and endowment.

3. God teaches us that the one goal of our lives, in every detail, is to be not our own pleasure or profit, but His glory.

4. Every man is a debtor to all other men, to love and further their well-being even as he loves and furthers his own.

5. All we possess, being held in trust, is to be used so as to serve the highest, largest, and most lasting ends for God's glory and man's good.

6. Hence the one supreme life of light and love, duty and privilege, honor and blessing, is to lose oneself in the will of God.

7. Giving belongs to this highest plane of privilege. We multiply ourselves in our gifts, as one spring may fill many streams. No miser can be happy, for the very end of reception is impartation.

These laws of giving belong to a code, practically obsolete with man, yet eternally in force with God, immutable as Himself. And not only missions, but every other form of work for man's uplifting and salvation, will find its chariot wheels drag heavily, until the divine idea of giving holds the throne and shrine in our conviction, and sways our lives. Every cry of retrenchment is an assault on God and an insult to His claims. Even were there no more than the faithful bringing in of the tithes, there would always be meat in His house and blessing on His people. But could His Church once be roused from lethargy and apathy, feel her debt to a dying world, and see her apostasy in the matter of withholding what is her's only as held in trust for the payment of that debt, a river of beneficence would flow into the various channels of Christian service, which would overleap all present banks, and demand new and more adequate modes of distribution—a river to swim in.

The *ministry of money* has never yet been appreciated by disciples. The vast power, latent in hallowed riches, is one of the great dormant forces of the moral universe. Wealth belongs to the material world, but, once consecrated, it becomes a moral and spiritual motor—a motive power in the realm of the unseen. Out of the mammon of unrighteousness we may make friends, coining money into saved souls and good works done for God. Money is a lever for all good enterprises, and represents values of all sorts. It not only provides home comforts and drives the wheels of industry, but it relieves poverty and misery, promotes education and art, is a great civilizing force, and the handmaid of evangelism. But its abuse is as mighty for evil as its use is for good; indeed, the best, perverted, always becomes the worst.

What colossal fortunes are held by single owners! When a well-known New Yorker died, he left behind, it is said, two hundred millions of dollars. If that amount were piled up in standard silver dollars, one on top of another, it would represent a column over three hundred miles high. Yet the whisky money of this nation would represent a similar column over three thousand miles high! The *annual income* of the Duke of Westminster would itself support four thousand married missionaries with their families in the costliest fields of the Orient! And yet, what do such giant fortunes amount to, in the retrospect of a selfish life? The vast treasure of A. T. Stewart was all gone, within a decade of years after his decease. His body was stolen and his splendid mausoleum is empty. How few to-day rise up and call him blessed! The inventor of the fire-extinguishing apparatus, called by his name, died in a California almshouse at seventy years of age, after having received $10,000 a month for royalty on his machines.

Extravagance saps the very foundation of honesty and virtue, and removes all the base-blocks of individual and family life. Decline of marriages, which was one of the chief causes of the fall of the Roman Empire, was due to the *cost of living* which forbade a Roman young man to marry. Thus the middle classes were crushed out—which to every nation are its backbone. The same causes are now conspiring to ruin two of the foremost so-called Christian nations of the earth!

Modern extravagance seems to outstrip even ancient waste. The wedding ceremony itself often involves enormous outlay. While China was appealing to the world to help her starving millions in famine, the Emperor's wedding festivities wasted millions of dollars. An eccentric millionaire was buried not long ago in a casket which cost $10,000, the funeral, as a whole, costing thrice that amount. A banker's wife, in a party at the Capital, is said to have worn a dress covered with one-hundred and five-hundred dollar bills, so as to make it appear one pattern, the waist and sleeves being thousand dollar bonds sewed in; her fingers were ablaze with diamonds, and she wore a tiara worth $80,000, the total value of her costume being about $300,000! In recent art sales in London, $10,000 were spent for a dessert service, and $50,000 for two rose-tinted vases. Nearly fifty million smokers are now in the United States and Britain, and the cost of this indulgence is one hundred times what the whole Church of Christ spends on missions.

The churches—alas! lead the way in setting up a wrong standard of expenditure. One well-known church spends $3,000 a year on the choir, and averages $150 a year for foreign missions! Bishop Coxe found a man in his diocese who put five cents a Sunday into the church box, and $800 a season into the opera box; another millionaire could be named who gives a dollar a Sunday, but stops even this payment when he takes his annual winter excursion to the South, where he spends thousands for his own enjoyment!

Where is zeal for God? The men of this world do not hesitate to embark on an enterprise whose profits are uncertain, and to risk vast sums on an experiment. The ship canal projected from Bordeaux on the Atlantic, to Narbonne on the Mediterranean, would cost $130,000,000. When a few years ago a new fleet of ninety-two vessels was planned for the navy of the United States, it was expected to call for $20,000,000 a year, for fourteen years! What a work it was to build the pyramids, employing one thousand men at a time, and occupying twenty years! The Russian war cost England alone $500,000,000. Consider what might have been done in the field of missions with that last sum, which represents *all that has been given in the last seventy-five years for world-wide evangelization, by the whole Church!*

It is a shame that we should find the most munificent givers *outside* of the Church of Christ. Baron Hirsch, of Paris, recently dead, gave to the poor Russian Jews, and their fellow Hebrews in Poland, Hungary, and Austria, $10,000,000; and shortly after as much more to other charities. His benefactions are yet without a parallel in history. And this famous financier and railroad king, besides giving ten millions to *Christian* schools and hospitals in Europe, gave $40,000,000 to build commercial schools in the waste lands of the continent for the Jews.

One awful fact is that there has been a decline and decay of liberality in the churches: While the membership increased in thirty years three and a half times, there was a decided falling off in the rate of giving, so that while the total of gifts increased, the amount given, reckoned by the average, went down to about one-half.

God wants *self-denying* giving. The wealth of church members in Protestant communions is, by the census, at least $10,000,000,000. Their contributions average one-sixteenth of a cent for every dollar, or one dollar in about $1,600. Who can look at the Japanese temple, with its coil of rope,—larger than a ship's hawser, and weighing a ton and a half, made from the hair of Buddha's worshipers, and used to lift timbers and stones to their places in the temple building,—without feeling the rebuke implied to our self-sparing gifts?

What a sacrifice of vanity was that when the women of Israel gave their metal mirrors to be melted down and recast for the laver of the holy court. As surely as the barnacles eat their way into the oak timbers of a ship and sink her, selfishness eats into and destroys Christian character. Mr. Spurgeon had a contempt for all parsimony, and occasionally thundered anathemas against it, or again pelted it with ridicule. One morning he said of some unwilling givers that they squeezed each shilling until the queen's head was well nigh obliterated. The Abbé Roux keenly remarked, that " It is not as far from the heart to the mouth as from the mouth to the hand," meaning that many who talk generously give stingily.

On the other side of the sea are found examples of disproportionate giving very rare in America—giving which would be thought by most people quite out of proportion to their selfish indulgence. For example: *First case*—A governess, who out of the £100 earned, keeps £50 and gives the other £50 away; like Zaccheus, she says: " Behold, Lord, *the half* of my goods I give to the poor." *Second case*—" One whose income is £2,000, lives on £200 and gives £1,800 away," thus parting with not only *one-tenth,* but with *nine-tenths* of what is received. *Third case*—" Another, who earns £1,500 a year, lives on £100 and gives £1,400 away," and thus £14 out of every £15 are devoted to the claims of religion and charity. *Fourth case*—" Another, whose income is £8,000, lives on £250 and gives the balance away." What a balance to part with: £31 given back to God out of every £32 received from Him! Mr. Gladstone's brief eulogy of Mr. Peabody was: " One who taught us the most needful of all lessons:

how a man may be a master of his fortune and not its slave." There is one lesson even more needful—namely, that we should learn that no man can assume to be the "master of a fortune" without virtually disputing the fact of stewardship.

God wants *consecrated* capital for consecrated work. When Theresa felt the need of a hospital, she had but three farthings, but she began to build, for while "Theresa and three farthings were nothing, God and three farthings were incalculable." He wants *conscientious* and *systematic* giving. Stonewall Jackson, on the day after the second battle of Bull's Run, in the midst of all the feverish excitement of the war, inclosed his contribution for missions due on the Sabbath. Tho he could not be present, he could not neglect the offering.

He who appropriates a certain *proportion* to benevolent work, should increase the proportion as wealth accumulates. More than half a century ago, Nathaniel Cobb sat down in his counting-house in Boston, and wrote the following solemn covenant:

"By the grace of God, I will never be worth more than fifty thousand dollars. By the grace of God, I will give one-fourth of the net profits of my business to charitable and religious uses. If I am ever worth *twenty thousand dollars,* I will give *one-half* of my net profits; if I am worth *thirty thousand dollars,* I will give *three-fourths;* and the *whole* after fifty thousand dollars. So help me God, or give to a more faithful steward, and set me aside."

This covenant he subscribed and adhered to with conscientious fidelity as long as he lived. On his death-bed he said to a friend, "By the grace of God, nothing else, I have been enabled, under the influence of these resolutions, to give away more than *forty thousand dollars.* How good the Lord has been to me!"

The ministry of money should begin when we have but little. As the Persian proverb says:

> " Do the little things now;
> So the big things shall by and by
> Come asking to be done."

Scriptural giving is *worship,* and so every worshiper of God must be one of God's givers, whether rich or poor. Dr. Howard Crosby used to say, " The poor man should no more omit giving, on account of his poverty, than the illiterate his praying because of his bad grammar." The mites God values as much as the millions, if they mean prayerful, and devout, and worshipful giving, but God has as much contempt for the mites of a miser as he has respect for the mites of the poor widow.

It *is* more blessed to give than to receive. When disciples learn the true ministry of money, the privilege of giving will swallow up the obligation.

When we understand our stewardship, we shall see that every dollar belongs to God. Dr. William Kincaid says : " A friend of mine was receiving some money at the hands of a bank officer the other day, when he noticed, depending from one of the bills, a little scarlet thread. He tried to pull it out, but found that it was woven into the very texture of the note, and could not be withdrawn. ' Ah ! ' said the banker, ' you will find that all the government bills are made so now. It is an expedient to prevent counterfeiting.' Just so Christ has woven the scarlet thread of his blood into every dollar that the Christian owns. It can not be withdrawn; it marks it as His. When you take out a government note to expend it for some needless luxury, notice the scarlet thread therein, and reflect that it belongs to Christ. How can we trifle with the price of blood?"

Beautiful is the myth of Elizabeth of Hungary, the

pioneer saint and martyr. When carrying, in her robe, supplies of food for the poor, her husband pressed her to know what was the burden she was bearing, and, opening her robe, he saw only heaven's red and white roses, and was dazzled by the supernal glory of her face. In God's eyes how many of our simplest gifts for His poor are really celestial blooms, full of a holy fragrance as the sweet smell of incense!

Were we brought into such vital and habitual sympathy with God as to see this lost world through His eyes, that would solve every problem. We should then learn to *pray*, for we should share in the travail of the Son of God; we should yearn to *go*, for the want and woe of mankind would draw us as it drew Him; and we should find it easy to *give*, and correspondingly hard to keep. Each soul in harmony with God will say, as Christ said: " Lo, I COME TO DO THY WILL, O GOD! "

To ask unbelievers for gifts to carry on God's work, or even to urge believers to give, is not God's way, and neither will be done by a church that is devout and truly consecrated. Nor will a few large givers be permitted to do all the giving, as tho it were by the *amount* given that the total is to be estimated.

These are truths that are sadly obscured in our day, and need a new emphasis. Malachi records how God's own people robbed Him, and adds a representative promise:

> " Bring ye ALL THE TITHES into the storehouse,
>   That there may be MEAT IN MINE HOUSE;
> And prove me now herewith,
>   Saith the Lord of Hosts,
> If I will not open you the windows of Heaven
>   And POUR YOU OUT A BLESSING
> TILL FAILURE OF ENOUGH! "—Mal. iii: 10.

Certain words here are put in capitals to show the symmetric parallelism. The one command and condition is, *a full rendering to the Lord of His own;* the grand result is *a full supply for all the needs of His work;* and the grand reward is, *a full blessing from above,* until there is *none left to pour out!*

When God gives His own solution to a problem, we need look no further. He here calls our attention to the ministry of money in His kingdom. Observe, not the ministry of *wealth.* The poverty of the poorest as well as the affluence of the richest has a ministry to fulfill, and the only encomiums bestowed by the Lord on givers have been on those the abundance of whose poverty abounded unto the riches of their liberality.

The scriptural principles upon the subject of giving are now-a-days receiving new study.

The law of the consecration of the first-born and of the first-fruits sets a sort of keynote to the Scripture teaching on giving. In Exodus xiii.: 14, 15, and parallel passages, the law of these first offerings is inseparably linked with the Exodus and the Passover. When, for the sake of the blood, the Lord passed over the houses of Israel and spared their first-born, He decreed that henceforth *all that opened the matrix* should be holy to Himself. Even the earth itself was embraced within the application of this law: regarded as each year anew becoming a mother and opening her womb to give birth to harvests. Nay, more than this, each fresh yield of orchard and meadow, of vineyard and oliveyard, was regarded as the offspring of a maiden earth coming for the first time to maternity, and from her matrix giving forth unto the Lord her first-born. There was poetry as well as piety in the Jewish system of offerings to the Lord!

The Bible teaches throughout that God asks, and in the highest sense accepts, for the purposes of His Kingdom, *only consecrated money.* It may be a small minority, who boldly hold and advocate this view, but it is the only scrip-

tural and spiritual view; and the church will never have
the highest blessing in her work for God till she dares to
stand on this elevated platform with Him.

As far back as Leviticus ii.: 13 we read these significant
words:

> " And every oblation of thy meat offering
> Shalt thou season with salt;
> Neither shalt thou suffer the salt
> Of the Covenant of thy God
> To be lacking from thy meat offering.
> With all thine offerings shalt thou offer salt."

Here is another unmistakable parallelism. A divine principle is laid down not only for meat or food offerings
where salt is naturally added for the sake of savor, but to
be applied to all offerings. Salt represents *covenant relation with God,* and hence is used symbolically to express
the truth that offerings to God have the savor of accept-
ableness only when salted with a covenant relationship.

This is remarkable as the only certain reference to salt
in the ceremonial law, * and yet so emphatic is the command that from this point increasing importance is ascribed to it. †

This was the one symbol never absent from the altar
of burnt offering. What was its significance? Some
carelessly interpret it as the unfailing sign of the imperishable love of Jehovah for His people. But is this the
natural interpretation of the command concerning salt?
In its unalterable nature it is the contrary of leaven, which
is held up as an evil and corrupting principle to be avoided
as rendering offerings unacceptable. Salt is not only
capable of imparting *savor;* it *saves* as well as savors and
seasons; it has a cleansing power and is antiseptic, ow-

---

* Exodus xxx.: 35, margin.

† Compare Numb. xviii : 19, 2 Chron. xiii : 5, Ezek. xliii : 24. Mark ix :
49, 50.

ing to the presence of chlorine. It is the opposite of leaven.
As leaven made offerings corrupt and offensive and gave
them the savor of death, salt made them pure, acceptable,
and imparted the savor of life. Hence, in order to an offering being acceptable to God, the offerer must *salt it
with a covenant spirit and relation.* God has no need of
unconsecrated and unsanctified offerings, and will not
accept them. He demands first self-surrender, then as a
logical consequence—nay, part of that self-surrender and
involved in it—the surrender of what we have, or, as we
say, " possess."

Of this law or principle the Fiftieth Psalm is the fullest
exhibition in the word of God. That Psalm is simply
Leviticus ii: 13 expanded into a sublime poem of twenty-
three verses. Its keynote is in the fourth, fifth and sixth
verses, which close the introductory stanza. Then follows God's first address to His people, verses 7-16, and a
second address to the wicked, verses 17-23, both being on
the subject of sacrifices or offerings, and setting forth
fundamental principles.

First comes the keynote of the Psalm:

> " He shall call the heavens from above
> And to the earth
> That He may judge His people.
> ' Gather my saints together unto me;
> *Those that have made a covenant with me by sacrifice,'*
> And the heavens shall declare His righteousness,
> For God Himself is Judge."

Here two things are plain: God for some reason takes
the judgment seat, as if for an important decision, and
calls before Him His own saints, who have made a covenant with Him by sacrifice,—literally "those that *set more
by the covenant than by any mere offering*" (Cf. Exod.
xxiv: 7, 8), or who " ratify my covenant with sacrifice."
In other words, Jehovah solemnly summons to His pres-

ence those who have been offering sacrifices and have not
properly understood the relation of sacrifice and covenant.
And now what has the Judge to say? First to His people:

> I will not reprove thee on account of thy sacrifices,
> For thy burnt offerings are continually before me.

He was not now, as afterward, through Malachi, re-
proving His people for the lack of offerings, but for the
wrong spirit that lay behind their formal obedience. To
Asaph himself, a chief among the Levites, whose whole
life was devoted to temple service, it was given to set forth
in this psalm, in Jehovah's name the truth that all outward offerings, however costly and ample, without the
prior offering of the heart and life are rejected. All godless or unsanctified giving proceeds on the principle that
God has need of money, which is here especially dis-
claimed.

> " For every beast of the forest is mine,
> And the cattle upon a thousand hills.
> If I were hungry I would not tell thee;
> For the world is mine and the fatness thereof.
> Will I eat the flesh of bulls
> Or drink the blood of goats? "

God is neither hungry nor in want. If He were, He
would not need to appeal to man, for His resources are
infinite. Offerings, therefore, made to supply a need in
God or His work, are a mistake! Hence the conclusion:

> " Offer unto God thanksgiving,"

literally, " Sacrifice thanksgiving; " Instead of peace-of-
ferings for a thanksgiving or vow, in a legal spirit, the
acceptable offerer must bring that which the sacrifice represents, viz.: praise from a loving, loyal, grateful heart.
In other words, the salt of the covenant must not be lack-

ing. Outer offerings are worthless that do not express
first of all genuine devotion and obedience to the will of
God.

Here, then, is the great lesson. Our offerings are not
primarily intended to relieve or supply any want of God
or His work, but to express obedience and gratitude on
the part of the offerer. Hence they imply the salt of
the covenant, the previous *offering of self*.

The same lesson is taught in the second part of this
judicial address. God now turns to the wicked, and in
the plainest words spurns his offering:

> "What hast thou to do to declare my statutes,
>   Or that thou shouldest take my covenant in thy mouth:
>   Seeing thou hatest instruction
>   And castest my words behind thee."

Willful transgressors bring offerings, while living in
sin and disobedience. The salt of the covenant being lacking, their formal sacrifices God indignantly rejects, and
warns them that, instead of accepting their offerings, He
may tear them in pieces and none can deliver.

Then the lesson of the psalm is reiterated in a closing
stanza:

> "Whoso offereth praise glorifieth me.
>   And to him that ordereth his way of life aright
>   Will I show the salvation to God."

Here then is a solemn setting forth of the fact that the
primary condition of acceptable offering is that the offerer
be in covenant relation with God. God is not a beggar or a
beneficiary in any sense whatever. He is not dependent
upon the help of any man for carrying on His work. He
admits us to a double privilege; first, of giving expression and expansion to our best impulses; and secondly, of
taking part with Him in a holy ministry of benevolence
and beneficence. Hence the two conclusions follow:

First, no unconverted man can offer an acceptable gift to the Lord. While he hates instruction and casts His words behind him, the conditions are lacking which make a gift acceptable. Instead of being salted, it is leavened; the corruption of unforgiven sin and an unreconciled heart spreads itself through the offering and challenges God not only to reject the gift but to destroy the giver!

Secondly, for believers to depend upon unconsecrated money to carry on God's work is contrary to the expressed will of God. Appeals to unconverted men for pecuniary aid in such work are both inconsistent and harmful. We remember a rich but godless man who was approached with a request that he would give $500 to relieve a pressure of debt in a Foreign Missionary Board. His answer was: "You ministers say from the pulpit that we unconverted rich men are idolaters; but you come to us idolaters for our money to carry on what you call the Lord's work!" To such deserved rebuke the Church of God lays herself open by indiscriminate appeals for money.

Great as is the need of money, it is not so great as to justify an unscriptural plan for raising it. God calls us to rise to the plane of faith; to remember that He owns all, that the hearts of men are in His hand; that He can unlock the treasuries of the rich and make the abundance of poverty to abound unto the riches of liberality. All frantic appeals for miscellaneous collections; all eagerness to get large gifts without regard to the character of the donors; all representation of the pressing needs of God's cause, as though He were a pauper and a beggar; all flattery of godless givers which encourages them to think they have put God under obligation by their gifts, while living in rebellion; all slavish dependence upon others than disciples for funds for work that only disciples can either conduct or appreciate; all this is in violation of Bible principles and causes blessing to be withheld.

Great efforts to raise funds, with a trumpet flourish over success, to be followed by a reaction, a proportionate decline in giving, depletion of treasuries, and a minor strain of complaint and despondency,—surely this is not God's way of carrying on His work. Raising money according to a worldly fashion is walking by sight, not by faith, as also is using pressure of appeal more than the prayer that prevails, depending on importunity with man more than on importunity with God. We must not forget Who opens human hearts and sends forth laborers into His harvest, and bestows the spirit of liberality; nor must we look to human patronage in a work that by its nature disdains any patron but the Lord himself.

CHAPTER X

THE Anglican Church, conspicuously, is in the throes of a great convulsion. Like an earthquake for which pent-up fires have long been preparing, and of which lesser up-heavings have been the premonitory symptoms and signals, this modern outbreak has for more than a quarter of a century given increasing indications that the coming conflict was inevitable, and a meeting for protest convened in Albert Memorial Hall in London, in January, 1899, under the chairmanship of Baron Kinnaird, ten thousand Protestants assembling to give their grievances a voice.

The crisis has been hastened, partly by the bold, alarming, and flagrant practices of the Ritualists and Romanists in the English Church, and partly by that astonishing exposure of the facts found in Walter Walsh's " Secret History of the Oxford Movement," which had so rapid a sale that it was at one time difficult to get a copy, notwithstanding large and repeated editions. That book ought to be read by every lover of the Protestant and Reformed faith, and of a simple apostolic worship. No such volume has been published for half a century, and it can be understood only by a careful and candid reading. It exhibits the candor that it challenges in others, and at the same time is marked by a courtesy, rare in controversy. Mr. Walsh claims to have reluctantly undertaken the work, under pressure of duty to open the eyes of loyal

* " The Secret History of the Oxford Movement," By Walter Walsh, published by the Church Association, London.

churchmen to what is going on beneath the surface; and being reluctantly compelled to his task of unearthing church secrets, he boldly drags forth into the daylight a hideous brood of monsters that have been rapidly and insidiously undermining the foundations of the Anglican Church as a Protestant, reformed, and anti-Romanist body.

One conspicuous feature of this volume is that these secret and subtle plotters, who seem Jesuits in disguise, are *made to tell their story in their own words.* Full references and proofs are given for all statements made, and the confirmation is drawn from the writings of the Ritualists themselves, almost all authorities quoted and appealed to being ritualistic.

The book thus appears to be an unanswerable array of facts, and a fair arraignment of the parties and the practices which it exposes. Secrecy has been the veil behind which these objectionable movements have been carried on. Ritualistic societies of this secret character have been annually increasing in number and growing in membership and influence for years, until the Church of England is honeycombed with them, and the ultimate object appears unmistakably to be corporate reunion with the Church of Rome.

One feature of Mr. Walsh's volume is that it gathers together the scattered evidence found in various biographies and letters of those who have been the head plotters and actors in this apostasy from Protestantism, and masses the testimony so as to give it force and weight. Much that in the earlier history of affairs was successfully concealed has been revealed, including the secret or private documents of the Ritualists, with reports of speeches actually made in the secret meetings, where freedom was naturally given to the real expression of the intent and purpose of the actors.

The secret history of the *Priest of Absolution* is here for the first time brought to light. The exposure, made twelve years ago in the House of Lords, by Lord Redesdale, of the indecencies of the manual used by ritualistic father confessors, roused throughout Britain a great excitement, and so alarmed the brethren of the secret Society of the Holy Cross (S. S. C.), that they met to consult as to their course, and the full reports of their conferences, printed for members only, are here open to inspection.

The exposure has come none too soon, and it is none too bold. For the Church of Rome, even Protestants may have some respect and forbearance, which it presents itself in its proper garb and without any false pretenses: but not for a movement, which, in the guise of Protestantism, is poisoning the very fountains of the reformed faith and worship? This is an act of ecclesiastical treason which has no more claim to either concealment or forbearance than the acts of a traitor in the state.

Mr. Walsh's four hundred pages ought to open the eyes of all lovers of pure faith and church life. Here the veil of estheticism and elaborate ceremony is rent asunder from top to bottom, showing the real intent and tendency of artistic musical services, spectacular display, imposing ceremonial, gorgeous man-millinery, and the importations of papal notions and customs, such as the confessional, the mass, prayers for the dead, etc.; and, behind all this outward pomp and grandeur, we catch a glimpse of the real doctrines and practices which Protestants abhor and denounce.

Mr. Walsh's book is not, however, the only expositor of this occult Jesuitism in the English Church. One has only to put patent facts together to see that the tendencies of things are by no means latent only. Ritualism has been getting bolder and more defiant until there is little hesitation as to open collision with the bishops, as well as with all remonstrants. Not only confusion, but anarchy prevails, and some diocesans confess, as did Dr. Ryle, the late evangelical bishop of Liverpool, their practical helplessness to contend with the sons of Anak that have their stronghold in the very " city of priests; " and, alas! in too many cases the bishops themselves are either ritualists, or connive at what they ought to suppress.

¶No one disputes the right of men in a land of liberty to follow conviction, or even tastes and preferences. But no man has a right to stay in a church after he is not in vital sympathy with its doctrine and polity; and, above all, do common honesty and decency demand that there shall be obedience to law, regard for order, and a still more sacred respect for the personal obligations assumed and implied in the ministry of a church. For any man, while yet in a church or denomination, secretly or openly to defy its constitutional law and constituted authority, is a first-class offense against the common law of conscience.

The saddest part of this volume is perhaps the unveiling of the downright disingenuousness and sometimes deliberate deception and hypocrisy of men who have at least been credited with sincerity of conviction and loyalty to conscience. One feels a moral shudder at the atrocious frauds and unblushing lies of leading men in the Tractarian and ritualistic developments of the last seventy years. Ever since 1833, which Cardinal Newman marked as the starting point of the Tractarian movement, there has been the forging of a chain of deceptions, to which link after link has been added. The *Disciplina Arcani,* or secret teaching of the early centuries of corruption, seems to have been revived; and the so-called *" Economical "* mode of teaching and arguing has been one of the prominent links in this chain. Cardinal Newman himself defines these two—one as " withholding the truth," the other, as " setting it out to advantage," quoting with approval the advice of Clement of Alexandria, who gives rules to guide the Christian in " speaking and writing *economically.*"

> He both thinks and speaks the truth; *except when careful treatment is necessary,* and then, as a physician for the good of his patients, *he will* LIE, or rather utter a lie, as the sophists say. *He gives himself up for the church.**

Mr. Walsh's book traces the history of the development of this Oxford movement, and any one can see how natural the steps are from secret doctrines, learned not from the Word of God but from the church, to the erection of tradition as of coordinate value and authority with Scripture, and so on to the sanctioning of customs, not only extrascriptural, but antiscriptural.

From the Ritualists themselves it is made plain that the secret societies within the Church of England were for " the dissemination of High Church principles," and that because the open declaration of this purpose would involve risk to its success, privacy and secrecy and subtlety were resorted to in place of publicity and straightforwardness. The names of the instigators of this movement were, so far and so long as possible, concealed. For fifteen years no list of brethren of the S. S. C. found its way into Protestant hands, and the printed lists had no dates or places of issue by which to be traced to their source and time of publication. It seems difficult to believe that such men as Cardinal Newman, Cardinal Manning, Dr. Pusey, Joshua Watson, Harrell Froude, Prof. Mozley, F. W. Faber, and even Mr. Gladstone could have winked at such methods. A letter from Newman has been published, in which he confesses, " I expect to be called a papist when my opinions are known." Mr. Froude acknowledges that he is doing what he can " *to proselytize in an underhand way,*" and it becomes too plain that many

* Secret History, etc., p. .

who have in public professed to be evangelicals, have in private made quite other professions, and belonged to secret societies, whose object was unmistakably Romish. Among the doctrines held back in reserve for the initiated only, were such as the atonement, free grace, etc., which Protestants reckon fundamental and for universal acceptance. To conceal their real intent, some of these Tractarians were " crypto-papists," and actually *wrote against popery while seeking to promote it*, " teaching people Catholicism without their suspecting it," so " that they might find themselves Catholics before they were aware."*

Newman is thus shown to have abused and denounced the Church of Rome to cover his real aims, and afterward, when his temporary purpose was answered, withdrawing all these charges.

A letter is published from Rev. Wm. G. Ward, who was Newman's successor in leading the Tractarians, in which he confessed that he no longer believed the English Church to be a part of the true Church at all, but " felt bound to retain his external communion with her members, *because he believed that he was bringing many of them toward Rome*" (p. 15). We are not surprised that such a man upheld equivocation, and said, " Make yourself clear that you are *justified in deception,* and *then* LIE LIKE A TROOPER " (p. 16).

Newman's " Cœnobitium " at Littlemore, was ostensibly a " hall " for students, in reality a monastery, as he acknowledged to a friend. Yet he elaborately and in terms denied this to the bishop of Oxford. We can understand his *Apologia,* in the light of such conduct, when he says: " There is some kind or other of verbal misleading which is not sin; " but we fail to see that such use of words is " *not* sin."

Mr. Walsh brings to the light of noonday not only the

* *Ibid,* page 10.

secret history of the Oxford movement, but the Society of the Holy Cross, the secrecy of the ritualistic confessional, and the Priest in absolution, the Order of Corporate Reunion, the ritualistic sisterhoods, the Confraternity of the Blessed Sacrament, etc.

As to Ritualism, a careful study of the Old Testament will reveal similar snares, exposed long ago, in the golden calf of Aaron, the brazen serpent of Moses, the ephod of Gideon, Micah's house of gods, the carved altar of Ahaz, etc., all of which are recorded for our admonition.

And now, in view of all this, and much more that can not here be written, the solemn crisis is now before the whole Church of God, to be met fairly and squarely and promptly, viz.: What are Protestants going to do about the ritualizing and Romanizing tendencies so patent, especially in prelatical churches?

There is much talk about ritualism which does not touch the core and root of the evil, which is *sacerdotalism,* or priestly pretension. A priest is something foreign to New Testament ideas, since all believers are in Christ priests, having priestly access and prerogatives. The word *priest* is justified as an abbreviation of *presbyter;* but practically it is a corruption of the Scriptural term, and represents one who (*pre-sto*) *stands before* God in place of the believer—assuming the mediatorial place and function.

Whatever be the etymology, modern sacerdotalism is a subtle system of imposture which *puts a human being between the believer and Christ.* It establishes a merely human and arbitrary medium of approach, thus preventing immediate access to and fellowship with God. It renders every believer or inquirer liable to forfeit all true blessing by the fallible and even false nature of that mediation which alike perverts his conceptions of Divine things, and misleads him in his supposed conformity to the Divine will. It is an unwarranted *priestly intrusion between a human soul and God.*

To see this clearly we need only to put these pretensions together. To consider the confessional, prayers for the dead, etc., apart from this system, is to lose their main significance. These are not *disjecta membra,* but members in a body to which they belong, and in which, with singular skill, they are fitted to their place. There are at least seven parts of this body of doctrine: 1. Priestly *ordination.* 2. Priestly *regeneration.* 3. Priestly *indoctrination.* 4. Priestly *absolution.* 5. Priestly *confirmation.* 6. Priestly *administration.* 7. Priestly *intercession.* In other words, ordination, baptismal regeneration, tradition, confession, confirmation, the real presence, and prayers for the dead.

1. The basis of all the rest is *Priestly Ordination,* which puts priestly intervention between a believer and his right to act as a minister of Christ, and is supposed to confer, by a sort of succession in grace, the Divine authority to preach and administer sacraments. In the primitive days all believers preached (Acts viii: 1-4, xi: 19, 20), and Philip baptized, tho he was set apart for a *temporal* office, and was, therefore, a " layman," and one case breaks the sacred line. Priestly ordination is the *head* of the whole system of sacerdotalism, and, if granted, it carries the rest with it by making a human authority necessary for all ministry, so that one is dependent for all else upon such priestly intervention.

2. Then follows *Baptismal Regeneration,* which puts the ordained priest between the infant child and the church. Infant baptism becomes the means of regenerating the infant with the Holy Spirit and engrafting the child upon the body of Christ.

3. Next follows *Priestly Interpretation* or indoctrina-

tion, which puts the priest between the baptized child and the Word of God. The priest becomes the teacher of the child, and churchly tradition the practical source of authority. Wherever the testimony of Scripture is considered doubtful, tradition interprets it; and wherever the two conflict, tradition takes precedence. Hence the Bible is not a safe book to be put into the hands of any but priests.

4. *Priestly Absolution* naturally follows. The child is supposed to err, fall short, commit sin, and the only way to get clear of it is by the way of the confessional. This puts the priestly intervention between the sinner and Divine forgiveness.

5. Next follows *Priestly Confirmation*, in which is supposed to be found the channel of grace to the believer, as in ordination to the priestly candidate. This puts priestly intervention between the " child of the church " and the Holy Spirit.

6. Then comes *Priestly Administration* of the Eucharist, whereby some mysterious change—transubstantiation, consubstantiation, or whatever it be called—takes place, in priestly hands, in the " bread and cup," so that they become the body and blood of the Lord. Hence the Lord's table becomes an altar, and the Supper a sacrifice. This puts priestly intervention between the child of the church and Christ's atoning death and sustaining life.

7. Finally come *Prayers for the Dead*. The soul departing lingers in some intermediate state of more or less imperfect and disciplinary suffering, until priestly intercession relieves it of disabilities, and promotes fuller entrance into the heavenly estate. This puts priestly intervention between the human spirit and final entrance into glory. What must the dying thief have done with no priest to baptize, instruct, confirm, absolve, administer the " real presence," or pray for the repose of his soul!

To put all this together is to see the singular and subtle completeness of the whole system. If priestly ordination is the head of this body of sacerdotal pretension, we may compare baptismal regeneration to the breath which gives life; priestly interpretation, to the brain which supplies thought; priestly absolution, to the hands which apply cleansing water; priestly Eucharistic administration, to the mouth which receives food; priestly confirmation, to the blood which affords vigor; and prayers for the dead to the feet whereby all final advance within the doors of heaven is secured.

It is not necessary to contend that for none of these features of modern sacerdotalism there is any Scriptural foundation. All most subtle error is at bottom a half truth, and herein lies its fatal character; but whenever even a Scriptural truth or practise is lifted into unscriptural prominence, or is linked with other unscriptural teachings and practises, *it becomes error*. Truth is wholly such only while it holds its true position and true relation. The most sacred teaching, if made to uphold error, becomes practically erroneous.

The question is whether any permanent and thorough cure of the existing malady in the church can be found until disciples renounce the *whole system of sacerdotalism* as such, and return to the simple New Testament faith and life. A system of idolatry is the inevitable outcome of the present growth of the sacerdotal pretensions which too many meet with practical apathy. The priest is virtually assuming Divine prerogatives; in the eyes of the victims of sacerdotal superstition, the water of baptism is becoming holy water, the bread of the Lord's Supper an adorable " host," the confessional a throne of grace, the priest a Divine teacher and intercessor, and the church, instead of a mere helper in drawing nigh to God, a hopeless barrier —not a means to an end, but itself the end.

There seems to be no alternative but to " worship the Lord in the beauty of holiness," and disregard the claims of mere artistic and esthetic beauty. Under the guise of symbolism and sacramentarianism and sacerdotalism, we are in danger of creating new Nehushtans, and erecting new houses of idols under the name of Christian churches. A sagacious Christian philosopher said thirty years ago, as he watched the tendencies already too apparent in Protestant churches, that the only safety would be found in " excluding any practises *not* enjoined or encouraged in the New Testament."

CHAPTER XI

THE crowning external revelation of the Word of God is the doctrine of the Holy Spirit, and the corresponding internal revelation of the Spirit in and to the believer is the crowning experience of the Divine life and love.

Of all the important spiritual movements of the half century not one compares in importance with the revival of interest in the person, functions, and offices, the in-working and out-working of the Spirit of God. Without this there could be no other truly *spiritual* movement or development; this gives character, genuineness, spiritual quality, and permanent stability to all other godly growths in knowledge, usefulness, and power.

This may be called the Pentecostal Movement, since the bestowment of the Spirit for fuller activity in and through the believer, dates from Pentecost. But by this name is now meant the general movement, peculiar to our day, in the direction of new emphasis upon the work of the Spirit of God, in three aspects—*sanctifying, enduing, and filling.* If any regard these latter terms, enduing and filling, as equivalent, we do not care to defend the distinction, but only to lay heavy stress upon one all-important fact and need; the *fact* that most disciples practically have never yet known the Holy Spirit as a presiding and controlling power, and the corresponding *need,* which, of all deficiencies in Christian experience, is the most lamentable and deplorable.

---

* See " Pilkington of Uganda," by C. F. Harford-Battersby, published by Marshall Bros., London, and Fleming H. Revell Co., New York.

First of all, we call attention to the Scripture teaching, and to the progress of doctrine, so conspicuous when the great leading texts are set in order as they occur in the New Testament.

Our Lord, as Matthew reports, says, in that first great discourse which held the germs of all His subsequent teaching:

If ye then, being evil, know how to give good gifts unto your children, how much more shall your Father which is in Heaven give good things to them that ask Him? Matt. vii: 11.

Luke, in his report of the same discourse, specifies a particular good gift:

How much more shall your Heavenly Father give *the Holy Spirit* to them that ask Him? Luke xi: 13.

Upon a comparison of the Gospel narratives this appears to be the earliest statement, in the order of time, found in the New Testament, as to the *gift of the Spirit of God to the believer in answer to prayer.* Up to this point there had been no mention of the Spirit, except in His relation to the person of Christ, or as connected with the gift of prophecy, as in Zacharias, Elizabeth, Simeon, etc., or by way of teaching the new birth, etc. But, from this point on, it becomes clearer, that believing prayer can claim of the Father a special gift of the Spirit, and a few texts bearing upon the development of this doctrine should ever be written large in the memory. Conspicuous among these are the following:

In the last day, that great day of the feast, Jesus stood and cried: If any man thirst, let him come unto Me and drink. He that believeth on Me, as the Scripture hath said, out of his belly (*i. e.*, the inner man) shall flow rivers of living water. But this spake He of the Spirit which they that believe on Him should receive. For the Holy

Ghost was not yet *given;* because Jesus was not yet glorified.   John vii: 37-39.

At this stage of progress in the unfolding of the truth, we learn that this gift of the Holy Spirit will make the disciples' inner life a fountain of life to others, so that from him shall flow spiritual rivers of Spirit power and influence; and that such gift of the Spirit waits for Christ's glorification as the condition of its bestowment.

Next, we meet that inspiring passage in Mark, so unique in its teaching as to the condition of a proper asking:

And Jesus answering saith unto them, Have faith in God (or reckon on God's good faith).   Therefore I say unto you, What things soever ye desire when ye pray, believe that ye receive them and ye shall have them.   Mark xi: 22-24.

Here we rise to another sublime height of teaching. The first passage quoted revealed God's fatherly readiness to give the Holy Spirit to them that ask Him; the second showed the effect of such gift in making the recipient a reservoir of living spiritual power and blessing; and now we are taught that, in asking for such a supremely good gift, we must reckon on the faithfulness of God to His promise; not only desiring and praying for the Spirit, but trusting our Heavenly Father to do as He says.   We are not to depend upon our consciousness of some new force within, or on our own inward frames of feeling.   It is a question, not of *perceiving,* but of *receiving.*   If we come and desire and ask, having no doubt that God will keep good faith with us, we shall have this good gift.

One other stage in this progressive teaching is the last discourse of our Lord, recorded in John xiv-xvi, where there is more teaching about the Spirit than in all the previous narratives of the four Gospels combined; out of this

wonderful talk of our Master, we select *two* very significant sentences:

He dwelleth with you and shall be in you. John
xiv: 17.

Here there appears to be a declaration of a present fact
and an intimation of a fact yet future. (παρ' υμιν μενει,
και εν υμιν εσται.) There was a sense in which the Holy
Spirit was already *with* them, but there was another sense
in which He was yet to be revealed as *in* them.

The other text is John xvi: 7:

Nevertheless, I tell you the truth: It is expedient for
you that I go away, for if I go not away, the Comforter
will not come unto you; but, if I depart, I will send Him
unto you.

What mysterious elevations of truth! So important
was this gift that to receive it would repay for Christ's
withdrawal! How few have ever reflected on that fact and
realized its awe-inspiring grandeur! To have the personal companionship of the Lord Jesus, but lose the fulness
of the Spirit's revelation within, would be a calamity—so
Christ himself teaches.

How immeasurably important then, that every disciple
should know his own need of the Spirit, should feel the impossibility of any compensation for such a lack, should understand how ready God is to give the Spirit, and should
pray in faith for the gift!

There is one ditch into which many believers practically
fall, so that they never get to the firm resting-place of actual reception of this crowning gift of God. They say the
Spirit of God was on the day of Pentecost given, fully,
finally, and to all believers, and hence is not to be sought
or asked in prayer as an unbestowed boon. In one sense
this is true, but in another sense it is a snare. There was
on the day of Pentecost an outpouring of the Spirit on all

believers. The new dispensation of the Holy Spirit was then inaugurated, and we are not, therefore, to look for any such bestowment of the Spirit. But, individually, we find disciples filled with the Spirit subsequently, and in Ephesians v: 18, we find a distinct command, " Be filled with the Spirit." There must therefore be some true sense in which disciples are to claim, receive, and avail themselves of this last and greatest gift of God. Christ was once offered for all, a sacrifice for sin, but every new believer takes Christ as a Savior, and so makes practically available the work of Christ for sinners; and so the Holy Spirit was once for all given, but every believing child of God accepts and receives the fulness of this gift by faith, so that practically it is as tho the Spirit had been specially given to him.

For the philosophy of the matter we are not jealous, but for the practical realization of the fact we well may be; and it is perhaps best to drop all mere punctilious criticism of terminology and verbal expression, in the intense desire that all disciples may know and make real their experimental share in the Pentecostal gift.

One fact knocks over all hostile theories: Men and women are in our day *coming into an entirely new experience by the enduement of the Holy Spirit.*

The case of George L. Pilkington, of Uganda, presents an instance in point.

Referring to his own need of the Spirit he says:

If it had not been that God enabled me after three years in the mission field to accept by faith the gift of the Holy Spirit, I should have given up the work. I could not have gone on as I was then. A book by David, the Tamil evangelist, showed me that my life was not right, that I had not the power of the Holy Ghost. I had consecrated myself hundreds of times, but I had not accepted God's gift. I saw now that God commanded me to be filled with the Spirit. Then I read: " All things whatsoever ye pray and ask for, believe that ye have received them and ye shall have them" (Mark xi: 24, R. V.), and claiming this promise I received the Holy Spirit. (P. 222.)

I distinguished between the presence of the Holy Spirit *with* us and *in* us; our blessed Lord said to His disciples, "He abideth *with* you and shall be *in* you." John xiv: 17. (P. 224.)

"He that believeth on me, out of his belly *shall* flow rivers (not a stream or a simple river) of living water. Greater works than these shall ye do because I go unto the Father." What are these rivers and where are these mighty works? We must ask rather, where is "he that believeth on Him? Surely, He is not unfaithful to a single line of His promise. What wonder that infidelity abounds when the worst infidelity of all is in our hearts! What wonder if popery increases, when we have dethroned the Holy Spirit from our hearts!" (P. 223.)

About this same time a great desire arose for mission services to be held in Uganda. In the absence of special missioners from abroad, it occurred to the missionaries that God wanted to use them, and all in prayer newly dedicated themselves to Him, and asked Him to baptize them anew. This was December 8, 1893.

That very morning they began. They had not told the people, but went up after prayer, at the usual time, believing for a blessing. Mr. Pilkington conducted the meeting. They sang

Have you been to Jesus for the cleansing power?

and Mr. Pilkington prayed, and then spoke of a very sad case which had indirectly led to the conviction of the need of such meetings, and of a new power from God coming on the native church and even on the missionaries. A certain Musa Yakuganda had asked to have his name given out as having *returned to the state of a heathen,* and his reason was startling: "I get no profit from your religion." Being asked if he knew what he was saying, he replied: "Do you think I have been reading seven years and do not understand? Your religion does not profit me at all. I have done with it." Pilkington pointed out what a cause of shame and reproach such a case was to the missionaries. The need of the deeper and fuller life and power of the Spirit took strong hold on the missionary preachers and teachers, and first of all humbled them before God. Then blessing came to the whole native church, until hundreds were all praying for forgiveness, while others were in the simplest language praising God.

Each morning fully five hundred were present, and they found themselves in the midst of a great spiritual revival, and their joy was beyond expression. The after meetings saw two hundred waiting for individual dealing. Among other fruits of this work was that same Musa who had announced his return to heathenism. Great chiefs boldly confessed their wish to accept Christ, and one chief, who had been a leading teacher but suspended for misconduct, acknowledged, in the presence of the king and his pages, that he had not before accepted the Lord Jesus as his Savior, but did so then. The missionaries appointed the week following the mission services as a time for special meetings for the deepening of the spiritual life.

Those wonderful three days, Dec. 8-10, 1893, will never be forgotten. They were the signal for years of blessing, pentecostal in character and wonderful in results. First of all God had brought the missionaries to humble themselves, feel their need, and seek larger blessing—to be filled with the Spirit. Then they were led to confess to the native church their previous lack of faith, of power, and of prayer, and to ask God for forgiveness. Then came similar humiliations and confessions among the Christians of Uganda. Many who had been looked upon as leading disciples began to see their lack also, and to realize a new force and power in their Christian experience. In fact, such a spirit of confession and humiliation was poured out on the native church, and such secret sins came to light in this great upturning and uncovering of hidden things, that the missionaries felt called on to restrain these public confessions, lest they should bring too great reproach on the name of Christ, and the awakened backsliders were counseled to seek the brethren for private confession and prayer before God.

The conversions and reclamations were almost invariably connected with *knowledge of the Word of God.* At the Liverpool Conference in 1896, Mr. Pilkington said:

" The power to read the Bible is the key to the kingdom of God. With the exception of one case, I have never in Uganda known *any to profess Christ who could not read.*"

Throughout this great revival God put special and very remarkable emphasis upon the Holy Scriptures as the means both of the new birth and the new quickening in spiritual life. *Reading houses,* or, as the people called them, " synagogi," were built where native teachers could instruct the people under the supervision of more experienced workers. This system became a *leading feature* of the work in Uganda, and was the means of causing the revival which started in the capital to spread that same year far and wide through the various outlying stations.

By April 1, 1894, between thirty and forty teachers had offered themselves for such service in the country districts, and thirteen were solemnly sent out in one Sunday, and seven more the next week. Shortly word came from the islands of an enormous increase of " reading." A spirit of new inquiry was found, even among Roman Catholics and Moslems. In the autumn of 1894, before the church at Mengo fell in a great storm, at least 2,000 were assembling every weekday morning, and in the 200 country churches some 7,000 more, and on Sundays, 20,000 in the various places of meeting. Of these, 6,000 were in classes, under regular instruction ; and this great work, reaching out over a circle of territory three hundred miles in diameter, and nearly one thousand in circumference, had to be directed by only twelve Europeans, who worked with the double hindrance of an imperfect knowledge of the language and constant liability to fever. Yet with all these disadvantages, the work so rapidly extended that, when in December, 1894, the year was reviewed, some such results as the following were obvious as signs of God's moving:

When the year began the number of country churches, reading rooms, or synagogi, did not exceed twenty; at the close of the year there were ten times that number, and the ten largest would hold 4,500 persons. Exclusive of the capital, there were on week days not less than 4,000, and on Sundays, 20,000 hearers of the Gospel. The first teachers, paid by the native church, went forth in April, and in December there were 131 of these, in 85 stations, twenty of which, being outside Uganda proper, were in a sense foreign mission stations. Even these figures can not represent the whole work, nor does this number embrace all the teachers, twenty of whom not reckoned in the above number were at work at Jungo. At Bu'si also, an island near Jungo, there were three churches, and 2,000 people under instruction. The " readers " ordinarily became catechumens, and the catechumens candidates for baptism In 1893 the catechumens numbered 170, during the year 1894 some 800 were baptized, and 1,500 catechumens remained. The movement, so far from having expended its force, seemed not yet to have reached its height, and there was every evidence that an enormous accession would yet come, as was the case.

Mr. Pilkington, being in England on furlough, in 1895-6, electrified his audiences by his stirring account of the dealings of God with the Uganda mission. Emphasis was laid on this fact, that the *first step* in this vivification of the church in Uganda was this, that *the missionaries and teachers themselves were led to just views of their own deep need;* they saw the absolute necessity for personal consecration, and the experience of a direct and supreme work of the Holy Spirit in themselves.

Here, then, is another mighty argument for seeking, with a desperate sense of helplessness, and with a confident faith in God's promise, Holy Ghost power. Not to Mr. Pilkington and his fellow-workers only, was this indispensable, but the whole native church of Uganda owes the almost unparalleled movement of that decade of years to the new enduements of power which proved even to these missionaries such a divine equipment for their work, and to the native evangelists also.

A few examples of the efficiency of these Waganda evangelists will suffice.

A missionary visiting a small island in the lake two or three years ago, found but one person who could read at all. Two teachers were sent, and, after nine months, sixty were reading the Gospel. Two teachers were sent to another island, and in a year one very rude church building, that even when uncomfortably full could hold but one hundred, had multiplied into four, one of which would hold seven hundred; the congregation of a hundred had multiplied tenfold, and fifty or more had been baptized.

On the large island of Sese all the chiefs are Roman Catholics. Yet there are some three hundred and twenty Protestants, nicknamed " The people of the Holy Ghost," which, like the nickname " Christians " at Antioch, is an honor, not a reproach ; and these disciples, ignorant as they are, evince a like readiness with the early Christians to face opposition and persecution for His name, and nowhere has a greater desire for " reading " been shown.

The *educational* value of the reading of God's Word has been very noticeable in Uganda. The very physiognomy of the people seems to have been modified by it, so that it is almost possible to distinguish a reader by his outward appearance. The *reality of God* seems to impress itself on the native mind more forcibly by this daily poring over the pages of the New Testament, at first mechanically and almost blindly, then with eyes partially opened to catch a glimpse or a glimmering of the meaning, until, with another illumining touch of God, the Divine message of love is intelligently grasped. Sometimes the impression is like a driven nail clinched and fastened by a sermon, or a prayer service, or the faithful words of a friend. What a lesson God is thus teaching us all as to the honor and value He sets on His own Word, and this at a time when, more than ever before, even professed Christian teachers in Christian lands seem bent on lowering in the public mind the sense of the dignity and majesty of the Heavenly message.

At first those of the Baganda who hear these words find them unintelligible; such terms as sin and salvation, love and faith, convey little meaning to minds that have been cast in the narrow and cramped mold of heathenism. But, as they hear and read, Scripture interprets itself, and under the light of the Spirit they get totally new ideas of Divine mysteries.

The outcome of this Holy Spirit revival in Uganda can not be measured; only from the Spirit comes the clear vision of Divine truth, as well as the inward experience of Divine life, and in the native preachers have been developed remarkable spiritual discernment and power in presenting truth.

A preacher at Mengo said in his sermon that "to form a judgment of man's deserts, *man's* way is to put into one scale his evil deeds and vices, and into the other his virtues and religious observances; but that *God's* way in such a case would be to put *both these into the same debit scale.*" This native preacher had learned that rudimental truth, hidden from many of the wise and prudent, that "all our righteousnesses are as filthy rags," and that the only hope of justification is that the perfect obedience of our adorable Lord, Jesus Christ, shall be placed in the credit scale, and so overbalance and outweigh our evil and selfish deeds.

Another preacher, discriminating between inward heart piety on one hand and outward religious observances on the other, used the following apt and original simile:

Religion may be compared to a banana (the natural food of the Baganda). The real heart religion is the juicy pulp; the forms and ceremonies are the skin. While the two are united and undivided the banana keeps good until it is used. And so it is with religion. Separate the forms from the spirit, and the one will be of no more value than the banana husk, while the latter will speedily decay and become corrupt, apart from the outward expression. Observances have their value in protecting the holy germ within, and fostering the feelings of the heart. (P. 248.)

This discourse had its suggestion in a certain spirit of insubordination, which sought to rebel against the ordinances of the church. But, as Mr. Pilkington asks, " What European teacher could have used such a simile."

Another native preacher, referring to Romish teaching, said:

No poisoner gives poison meat if he would remain undiscovered. The devil knows that. He has two devices; he will do one of two things; first try to deprive you of food, and if he can not, he will corrupt it. (P. 248.)

Pilkington before British hearers pleaded earnestly for a sufficient force to take possession of this great opportunity in Uganda, for a hundred additional missionaries, men and women filled with the Holy Ghost, as organizers and leaders for native workers, at least ten of whom could master, and then translate into, the native tongues; and with rare insight into the true philosophy of missions he urged a *new policy of occupation*. He contended that the only true method of distributing missionary workers is to send a large force where *a desire for instruction* and an *aggressive missionary spirit have been strongly developed among the native converts,* instead of sending the bulk of missionary force to places where there is neither desire for teachers nor a missionary spirit. And his argument is that the ultimate outcome of the former method will be far the greater in good. For instance, he says, after ten years little or no impression will have been made on the indifferent and hostile community, and this begets depression among the workers and in the church at home. Whereas, if the work, at the field where God's Spirit has been outpoured, were reenforced, it will so progress that it becomes a source of wide influence; a strong native church is developed with a large force of native evangelists, and thus the fire God has kindled is carried to the other field and transferred to this other center. The result is encouragement both among the missionary band and the supporters at home.

So moving was this plea that the missionaries of the Church Missionary Society in India asked the society, when it could be done, to send candidates, offering to go to India, to Uganda, for the time being, instead, to avail themselves of the exceptional opening in that field, the growing conviction being that God's singular blessing in any particular field is a signal for a special reenforcement at that time of the force at work there.

Mr. Pilkington gave, in Britain, a vivid picture of the Uganda work in the shape of four consecutive scenes, afterward issued in pamphlet form, and called " The Gospel in Uganda."

A hundred thousand souls brought into close contact with the Gospel, half of them able to read for themselves; two hundred buildings raised by native Christians, in which to worship and read the Word of God; two hundred native evangelists and teachers wholly supported by the native church; ten thousand New Testaments in circulation; six thousand souls seeking instruction daily; numbers of candidates for baptism, confirmation; adherents and teachers more than doubling each year for six or seven years, and God's power shown by their changed lives— and all these results in the very center of the world's thickest spiritual darkness and death shade!

This was in 1896, and the later reports eclipse even this.

The changes wrought by the Gospel in Uganda can be appreciated only by setting in sharp contrast the state of things in 1880 and in 1895.

Old Isaiah, "the good-natured giant," will tell you how three hundred brothers and cousins of the king were penned within the narrow limits of the dike, still visible by the roadside, two or three miles north of Mengo, and by his orders left there to starve to death! A boy of fifteen lost sight of a goat he was herding, and his master cut off his ear. For a trifling misdemeanor both eyes were gouged out. An unfortunate courtier accidentally trod on the king's mat, and paid the penalty with his life. The king, simply to support his royal dignity, ordered the promiscuous slaughter of all who happened to be standing on his right and left hand, or all who might be met on the streets at a certain time, by a band sent out for the purpose of such slaughter. Should a remonstrance be made against killing the innocent, the answer would be, "If I only kill the guilty, the innocent will not respect me." Women and children were sold into helpless slavery and misery. Spirits were believed in, feared, propitiated, and worshiped. Charms were worn; woman was a beast of burden, etc. Christ and his Gospel has changed all this. Domestic slavery no longer has any legal status, and any slave may claim freedom, and this claim will be honored. Woman takes her place by man's side. Conversion has brought victory over vicious habits; cruelty is seen to be cruelty, and around the Lord's table gather from time to time those who were once darkness, but now light in the Lord, " washed, sanctified, justified, in the name of the Lord Jesus, and by the Spirit of our God.

CHAPTER XII

THE commentator, Ewald, holding up a Greek New Testament, declared to his students, that that one little book had in it more than all the wisdom of the ages,—putting in one sentence the sublime secret of its hold on the mind, as well as the heart, of intelligent believers. This also explains the fact that, exactly in proportion to the actual prominence of the Bible in our faith and life, will holy living and holy serving most truly develop.

The unique position of the Word of God lies in this, that it claims to be, and justifies the claim to be, the One Book which God has given to man as a revelation of His will. Its plenary inspiration and complete adaptation to man's wants make it at once, as James teaches, the perfect *mirror* of character; as David teaches, the perfect *medicine* for the soul; as Paul teaches, the perfect *mold* of holy manhood (Rom. vi, 17. Greek); and, as all inspired writers agree, the *miracle-worker* which transforms the heart and life.

There is a reason, and a very special one, for giving to this authoritative Word of God an exaltation in our present daily life of study, which had been in previous centuries impossible. Few of us appreciate the difference between ancient and modern times, in the facilities for individual Bible reading and searching. In the remote days of Ezra, copies of the sacred books were so rare that all the multitude could hope to do would be to *hear* passages read and expounded, and such privileges brought overwhelm-

ing joy. (Nehemiah viii.) In Luther's days, only three
and a half centuries since, the Bible was found only in
convents and public sanctuaries, and even there chained to
a pillar as a rare and costly treasure.

Ruskin reminds us how books introduce to the company
of the wise, and great, and good, at whose doors we otherwise so often wait vainly for admittance. What shall we
then say of the supreme honor and privilege of Bible study,
since this is the " open sesame "—the mystic watchword
which opens the door to the true King's treasuries! By
this devout search into the Word of God we actually unlock the secret chambers of God, and find that " where the
Word of a King is, there is power." (Eccl. viii: 4.)
Here the most marvelous wonders burst on our astonished
eyes. The Bible is God's palace, and it has palatial apart-
ments, indeed. There is one—the very sanctuary of the
Word—where the living oracles are heard; another, where
the complex mirrors reflect all our past and present, and
even forecast our future history; yet others which are
chambers of peace, whose windows look out on the
heavenly hills, and the very atmosphere of which is rest.
The Bible has its picture galleries, with portraits of holy
men and women, and, above all, the very image of the
Son of God; it has its museum with the unfolding mysteries of God, and the curious relics of antiquity for instruction and admonition; there is also a banquet-hall for
the refreshment of all believers, where babes may find
milk, and the strong man, meat and honey. And in one of
these glorious rooms we may find the crown jewels, which
are there in store for God's crowned kings in the day of
Christ's coming.

Neglect of the Scriptures is in a sense a sin that hath no
forgiveness; for it implies irreparable damage to spiritual
life and forfeiture of spiritual blessing. No repentance
and reformation can ever restore the years which this can-

kerworm of indifference to the Word of God has eaten. What an insult to the royal Author, who puts in our hand the key to His treasure chambers! What a sign of apathy and lethargy of soul, when the carnal ambition to be wise and great, and move in the society of the wise and great, actuates us more than the aspiration to be wise and great in God's eyes, and abide in His companionship! Do Bible possessors realize that they have a chance to enjoy a university education in the school of God? That the Word of God is itself life and light, a passport to heavenly society, free to all alike, as children of the King?

Believing and perceiving, as we do, that God has been by various voices calling His people to a new life of holy living and serving, it would be natural to expect that *Bible study* would form an inseparable condition of such advance. And what is more conspicuous than the fact that during the last half century the facilities for such search into the King's treasuries have been indefinitely multiplied, so that every man and woman may now possess a first-class copy of the Word, with the best helps, bound in the one cover, and all the material so well put together as to last with ordinary care for a lifetime.

If the facilities for Bible study have so increased, Bible study itself has kept pace with them, for never were there so many careful and habitual searchers into the Word of God, nor so many new methods of helpful study. That devout and lamented Irishman, Harry Morehouse, first introduced into America, " Bible Readings "—a new way of comparing Scripture with Scripture—when he distributed little slips of paper, each containing a text, illustrative of some great theme, like " Forgiveness," " Salvation," " Grace," " Eternal Life ; " and then, calling for the reading of them in succession, with a few words interposed as explanatory, or connecting links, the subject grew before the assembled company as a buiiding rises from cornerstone to capstone, till the climax of impression was reached.

This and a multitude of other methods have brought the Bible itself to the front, as never before. And, tho some so-called Bible readings have been travesties, evincing no thorough search, and attracting derision as examples of "grasshopper exegesis" or "kangaroo exegesis," from the monstrous leaps taken without regard to contextual difficulties, grand advance is due to these methods in promoting acquaintance with God's book. We thank Him for the Bible in a portable form; for the era of the Bagster and Oxford presses; for the Sunday-school lessons, and the varied expositions of them; for the Bible-schools and conventions—and scores of other means whereby the great mass of believers, rich and poor, learned and ignorant, old and young, may be henceforth without excuse if they do not know what rich mines of wealth are in the blessed Word, waiting to be dug into and explored.

For a number of years now there have been held, especially in summer, Bible-schools, or conferences, for the study of Scripture with the best aid that man can supply. The conference at Northfield, Mass., now so famous, and linked with that lover of Scripture, Dwight L. Moody, is perhaps the most conspicuous of all; but that smaller conference known as the Niagara Conference, attended by about 300 believers, is perhaps second in spiritual power to no other, and is *exclusively* for biblical study and prayer. At the "Thousand Islands," "Geneva Lake," "Round Lake," "De Funiak Springs," etc., similar schools are held—indeed, the number is too large to enumerate them. It will suffice to call attention to the one first mentioned, as an example.

Every place has its atmosphere. Better sanitary conditions insure a delicious fragrance in place of unsavory odors, and healthful inspirations instead of malarial exhalations. In the higher realm of mind, intellectually and socially, morally and spiritually, every community has its atmosphere, and what is more needful than to improve the conditions on which depend a purer, holier influence?

Northfield, Mass., has become known as the " Home of Conventions," a New England Jerusalem, whither the tribes of the Lord go up annually, to keep solemn feasts and joyful festivals. There is literally a yearly Feast of Tabernacles—for many are compelled to dwell in tents if not in booths; and a feast of Pentecost—for hundreds get a blessing from above.

These conferences originated with Mr. Moody, who loved Northfield as his birthplace and home. His later career as an evangelist was conspicuous for quickening disciples as well as for arousing and converting sinners. As he went from place to place, he found many believers anxiously longing for a fuller salvation, a higher knowledge of God's Word, a deeper draught of the fullness of the Spirit; and it occurred to him to call together at Northfield, for a few weeks, such as yearned for closer fellowship with God, and greater power in service. Now that such convocations have a world-wide reputation and influence, we gather up some historic fragments and give them a permanent form.

The August Conference of 1900 was the eighteenth of its kind. The first was in 1880, and the second in 1881; then, Mr. Moody's campaigns in Great Britain caused an interval of three years; but since 1885 they have been annual.

In 1880 the call was mainly for " A CONVOCATION FOR PRAYER." It read thus:

"Feeling deeply this great need, and believing that it is in reserve for all who honestly seek it, a gathering is hereby called to meet in Northfield, Mass., from Sept. 1st to 10th inclusive, the object of which is not so much to study the Bible (tho the Scriptures will be searched daily for instruction and promises), as for solemn self-consecration, and to plead God's promises, and to wait upon Him for a fresh anointing of power from on high.

" Not a few of God's chosen servants from our own land and from over the sea will be present to join with us in prayer and counsel.

" All ministers and laymen, and those women who are fellow-helpers and laborers together with us in the kingdom and patience of our Lord Jesus Christ—and, indeed, all Christians who are hungering for intimate fellowship with God and for power to do His work—are most cordially invited to assemble with us.

" It is also hoped that those Christians whose hearts are united with us in desire for this new enduement of power, but who can not be present in the body, will send us salutation and greeting by letter, that there may be concert of prayer with them throughout the land during these days of waiting."

This conference in September, 1880, was attended by some three hundred persons, among whom was a delegation from Britain. East Hall, being then built, served in part to lodge visitors, but tents, garrets,—every available place—was in requisition, and the quiet village waked up to a new sensation—the dawn of a new era. The Congregational church was scarce large enough for a meeting place, and a large tent became needful. The predominant idea of that first conference was *Spiritual Power;* the doctrine of the Holy Spirit was dwelt upon, and prayer pervaded the meetings for a new effusion of power. Mr. Moody presided; and the meetings, devotional and heart-searching, left a deep and permanent impression.

The convention of 1881 occupied the whole of August. The conspicuous figure was Dr. Andrew A. Bonar, of Glasgow, whose accuracy, precision, unction, can never be forgotten. He combined deep insight into truth with characteristic quaintness of manner and a strongly marked individuality; and, besides Mr. Moody, Dr. Pentecost, A. J. Gordon, J. H. Brookes, E. P. Goodwin, Evangelists Whittle, Needham, and Hammond, and Editors R. C.

Morgan and H. L. Wayland, were among the speakers. The leading feature was *Bible Study*. Every afternoon in the Congregational church one leading address, followed by briefer ones, treated in a somewhat connected presentation leading Christian doctrines. Morning and evening worship, and various side meetings of a devotional character, filled up the time. In the course of the month from eight hundred to nine hundred persons were in attendance. The school buildings, and every house that had spare rooms, was full, and a large delegation was present from across the sea.

The convention of 1885 occupied ten days in August. Perhaps the prominent figure in this gathering was J. E. K. Studd, Esq., of London, who told the story of the movement among the English university students, and of the Cambridge band who went to China, among whom were Mr. Charles T. Studd and Mr. Stanley Smith. From Northfield Mr. Studd went to visit American colleges and carry the sacred coals. Two famous temperance reformers were heard that summer, William Noble, of London, and John B. Gough. Dr. A. J. Gordon spoke with great power on " Christian Life," and Dr. L. W. Munhall, Rev. W. W. Clark, and the writer, gave aid. " Marquand " and " Stone " halls being now built, became temporary hotels, the latter supplying the main auditorium, a tent near the road serving for additional and occasional gatherings. The predominant idea of *this* convention was *Life and Service.* Great prominence was given to foreign missions, and the interest culminated in a " call " issued by the convention, and signed by representatives of each Christian denomination, summoning a *World's Conference on Missions,* which call was one of the first steps which led to the great World's Conference of 1888, in Exeter Hall, London.

In the 1886 convocation, Rev. Marcus Rainsford, of

London, was conspicuous. His unfoldings of Bible truth were remarkable, but scarcely more so than the narratives by which they were illumined, drawn from his pastoral life. Drs. Nathaniel West, W. J. Erdman, H. M. Parsons, and Mr. William E. Blackstone were heard, in addition to the neighing of the usual "war horses." Perhaps the prominent idea of this convention was *Dispensational Truth,* especially the Lord's Second Coming.

This year was marked also by a convention—the first of its sort—of college representatives of the International Y. M. C. A., held at Mount Hermon, Mass., in the boys' school buildings, beginning July 7th, and continuing for twenty-six days. It owed its origin to a suggestion of Mr. L. D. Wishard, that these students should be called together for *"a summer school of Bible Study."* Invitations were sent to two hundred and twenty-seven college associations, and a total of about two hundred and fifty students responded, representing ninety institutions. Mr. Moody and Major Whittle, Drs. Gordon, Brookes, West, Prof. W. G. Moorehead, Rev. W. Walton Clark, and A. T. Pierson, with Messrs. Wishard and C. K. Ober, addressed and taught the students. The first morning hours were given to "Association work;" from 10 to 12, to systematic teaching on Christian Evidences, Prophecy, Bible Analysis, etc. If any one idea was pre-eminent, it was *God's Word and Work.* Great Missionary meetings were held, at one of which ten young men, representing as many different peoples,—Siam, China, India, Persia, Armenia, Japan, Norway, Denmark, Germany, and the Indians of America,—made short addresses, and, at the close, repeated, in their various tongues, *"God is Love."* It was like a new Pentecost, and proved the source of one of the greatest movements of our day. Some twenty-three had come to Mount Hermon pledged to the foreign field—the number rose to a full hundred before the students dispersed, and so hot did the missionary fires burn that two of their number were sent on a visiting campaign through the colleges. This was the origin of " The New Crusade," whose motto is " The Evangelization of the World in this Generation."*

Two annual conventions were henceforth to move side by side. The year 1887 saw four hundred delegates, from some eighty-two colleges, assembled at Northfield from July 3 to 12. Perhaps the conspicuous personality was the late Prof. Henry Drummond, who then first spoke in America. Beside Drs. Gordon, Pierson, etc., Profs. John A. Broadus and L. T. Townsend, Rev. Jos. Cook and H. L. Hastings, and Dr. Jacob Chamberlain, of India, spoke. If any one thought ruled this convention, it was *Preparation for Service.*

The August convention of 1887, which surpassed all that preceded, held up a *High Ideal of Character.* Prof. Drummond, Prof. W. H. Green, of Princeton, Dr. Josiah Strong, author of " Our Country," Francis Murphy, the temperance agitator, as well as Drs. Gordon, Pierson, Pentecost, and Clark, were among the speakers.

The students' conference of 1888 reached again four hundred, from ninety institutions; twelve delegates were from Europe, representing Oxford and Cambridge, Edinburgh, and Utrecht. Dr. Broadus again taught, as did Dr. H. Clay Trumbull, Bishop Hendricks, Dr. Alex. MacKenzie, and Prof. W. R. Harper; Rev. Geo. W. Chamberlain, of Brazil, Messrs. Wilder and Forman and Rev. J. Hudson Taylor fanned the missionary fires.

The August convocation of the same year magnified *Spiritual power.* More foreign missionaries than at any previous gathering were there, and J. Hudson Taylor's deeply spiritual addresses swayed the great throng.

* This motto was suggested by the writer, who has often been asked where he himself found it. Any one who will carefully examine Acts. xiii : 22 and 36, will find its suggestion there.

In the convention of 1889, among the new features were the addresses of Rev. I. D. Driver, from Portland, Oregon, a vigorous, forcible, original speaker, and of Bishops M. E. Baldwin, of Huron, and Cyrus D. Foss; Robert E. Speer, John G. Woolley, the temperance orator, and Pastor Charles Spurgeon, son of the metropolitan preacher, also gave addresses. Four hundred and seventy-three students were present at the college gathering, and fully the usual attendance was observed at the later conference.

In 1890, three hundred and eighty students appeared from one hundred and twenty-one institutions. Prof. W. W. Moore, Pastor Adolph Monod, of Paris, Rev. H. G. Mowll, of London, Bishop Thoburn, of India, Rev. W. P. Prague, of China, Dr. R. S. MacArthur, of New York, and Dr. Charles Parkhurst will be remembered in connection with this gathering.

At the August conference the central thought was *Christ, Consecration, the Holy Spirit,* and again Rev. Marcus Rainsford gave grand help, and David Baron, a true prince of the house of David, opened up the Messianic prophecies, as only a converted Jew could.

In 1891 four hundred students again gathered, and Rev. John Smith, of Edinburgh, and John McNeill, the Scottish Spurgeon, were among the speakers.

In August, Rev. F. B. Meyer, of London, made as deep an impression as any man who had ever spoken there. He struck the keynote, *Holiness,* which was maintained throughout. Dr. Edward Judson, Dr. J. E. Clough, of the Telugu station in India, Dr. J. R. Hykes, of China, Dr. H. C. Mabie, and Dr. Eddy, of Syria, all spoke.

In 1892 Mr. Moody was in Britain, but Dr. A. J. Gordon proved equal to the emergency and nobly led the August convention, at which Dr. J. T. Gracey, Dr. J. L. Nevius, Dr. Arthur Mitchell, and Dr. S. L. Baldwin spoke on missions. Mr. J. R. Mott guided the students' conference.

In 1893 Mr. Moody was again absent, during a part of the time, engaged in work in Chicago during the World's Fair, but Dr. Gordon once more took his place. Dr. Geo. E. Post, W. M. Upcraft, Dr. Lyman Jewett, and Dr. A. C. Dixon were among the speakers. This year inaugurated the *young women's* conferences—over two hundred college women being present from thirty-one educational institutions, societies, and associations. They came to study the Word of Life as the sword of the Spirit, and to confer as to practical Christian work. This year, therefore, a third annual conference took its place beside the other two.

These conferences have gone on from year to year, each new series of conferences presenting one or more unique features, The group of teachers from America and Britain that have been on the platform at Northfield would probably find no equal for variety of ability, and teaching power on the platform of any other annual conference. Keswick alone would suggest a comparison, but the platform of Keswick conferences is purposely restricted to those who by their doctrinal teaching and practical experience are identified with that particular movement. Mr. Moody's effort at Northfield was to secure any man from any quarter that could speak to edification, and some men were invited who would not be regarded by all evangelical believers as perfectly safe teachers, and whose presence on the conference platform created no little opposition. The fact is Northfield does not stand for any distinct form of belief or practice, provided there be a general acquiescence in what is known as Bible truth. There has been some teaching there not often surpassed, as when Rev. Webb Peploe and Rev. Andrew Murray, Rev. G. H. C.

Macgregor and Campbell Morgan led the conferences. And now that Mr. Moody is no more, the question arises, will the conventions go on without their great originator and conductor, and will any one be found qualified to give them the hold they had in Mr. Moody's day on the popular mind and heart; for there is no doubt that Mr. Moody's personality was the center of attraction after all.

As we review the history of these twenty years, a few general facts seem essential to the full annals we now record.

First, the original purpose of these conventions has been permanently controlling. *Bible study, mutual conference, devout praying, waiting for enduement,* have been the conspicuous features; and, of late years, there has been much comparison of methods of Christian work. As the conventions have multiplied, and their influence has been enlarged, this little New England village has been taxed to its utmost to lodge and feed the gathering throngs, and in view of the large inflow of guests, addresses and Bible readings fill up the intervals between the convocations. As early as the first of May, parties seeking accommodations can with difficulty obtain them, tho the accommodations are at least fivefold what they were when that first assembly was convened in 1880!

This " Saints' Rest," which unites many charms of Keswick, Mildmay, and Exeter Hall, affords a rare opportunity to see, hear, and come in contact with some of the men and women of the church universal, who, like John the Baptist, are " great in the eyes of the Lord." Taking the whole list of speakers since 1880, it may be doubted whether an equally varied and illustrious grouping of ministers and evangelists, theological professors and college presidents, bishops and benefactors of humanity, foreign missionaries and home workers, has been found on any other convention platform.

Noble free-will offerings have here been made from a few hundred dollars up to three thousand, which on two occasions was given to Bishop Thoburn's work in India, and ten thousand for the evangelization work in Chicago, and toward fifty thousand for the new auditorium opened in 1894, and holding twenty-five hundred persons.

We have given the Northfield Conventions prominence merely as a type of similar gatherings. The original purpose of them has somewhat expanded, until Northfield now stands for a sort of Ecumenical Council, annually meeting to consider the truths of the word and the claims of the work of God. Perhaps its present keynote is full as much *aggressive activity for Christ,* as anything; but this is largely owing to the strong personality of Mr. Moody himself, who was a born leader in active evangelism.

What grand occasions are these Bible Conventions for stimulating all that is good in thought, in love, in life-giving aims! Harrison Gray Otis, perceiving that Daniel Webster, while speaking in Faneuil Hall, had lost the thread of his thought and broken the continuity of his utterance, sagaciously asked him a question, which touched the very quick of his being and at once roused to their full exercise all his giant powers. In such gatherings, somehow, a new impulse is constantly furnished, rousing to fullest exercise and exertion all the best that there is in the hearers; so that for the sake of such living impulses to new consecration and activity, such new inspiration in Bible study and incentive to prayer, many go far, and stay long, at no little cost. They feel as J. Lothrop Motley did, in college, that they can spare the " necessities of life, but not its luxuries." Here is illustrated Arthur Hallam's famous aphorism, that the " Bible is God's book because it is man's book, fitting at every turn and curve the windings of the human heart; " and many there are who at Northfield and Keswick have learned so to love this Word, that they feel toward it some such devotion as Michael Angelo did for the famous Torso of Hercules, when he not only went to the Vatican museum to sketch it from every point of view, but, when sight failed, begged to be led where through the touch of his fingers he might experience delight in contact with its symmetry.

Here believers get into touch with the men and women who move the world, and with God's Holy ones, some of whom are like Burke, whom you could not have met under a porch, while waiting for a shower to pass by, without the conviction that you had met an extraordinary person.

The visits of Rev. F. B. Meyer, and notably of Prebendary H. W. Webb-Peploe, of London, and Andrew Murray, of Wellington, S. Africa (who were at Northfield in 1895), and the late G. H. C. McGregor introduced into Northfield conferences the grand teaching of Keswick. Indeed, since their visit it has been felt that what America most needs now is an annual gathering where the specific truths, so magnified in the English Lake district, and so blessed to thousands of believers, shall receive prayerful attention. During the visit of Messrs. Murray and Webb-Peploe, the truth already taught in part by Mr. Meyer was so expressed, impressed, illustrated and enforced, that impressions were made which never can be forgotten; but, what is of far more consequence, believers actually did so appropriate divine promises as to enter upon a new career of victory over sin and rest life by faith. The Jordan of a new Consecration was crossed, and the Land of Promise entered. " Keswick " is having its " clouds of witnesses " now in America also.

The Niagara Conference holds tenaciously to the study of the Word, and prayer, and there is felt to be a certain advantage in the restriction and limitation of its purpose. There is no encouragement given to those who have a " speech " to make or a " cause " to present, and who are sometimes the bane of spiritual gatherings.

Pastor Archibald G. Brown, lately visiting Boston, was asked to give some account of his work in London, and his narrative was thrilling. He attributed any success he had then enjoyed to two things: *dependence on the Word and the Spirit of God;* on Sunday mornings he gave a Bible reading, and on Sunday evenings, a simple Gospel sermon, and yet he baptized 6,000 believers in thirty years! There were no meretricious attractions of art, music, sensational oratory, or secular festivity. Pastor Brown might have added, if his modesty had not forbidden, that through the East London Tabernacle, thus educated and edified by Bible teaching, a work was done for London and for far off lands, that any congregation might envy.

CHAPTER XIII

WOMAN'S WORK AT HOME AND ABROAD

The "Diamond Jubilee" of the accession of Queen Victoria naturally suggested the marvelous development of Christian womanhood during the half century in all the manifold forms and phases of missionary and philanthropic activity. Among all the achievements of the Victorian era, none is perhaps more conspicuous than what may be called *The Epiphany of Women—i. e.,* her emergence out of the obscurity of centuries into something like her true position and relation as to the work of God. It is also a curious coincidence that such emergence should so exactly correspond with the period during which a woman has occupied the throne of the most prominent of Protestant kingdoms, and, during sixty years—the *longest reign of a woman* on record—has challenged admiration by her unblemished personal character and Christian influence! Victoria may well stand as the historic type of the era of woman's development as a distinct and separate factor in the Kingdom of God.

In the Old Testament seven women stand out with singular and unique distinctness, namely, Eve, the universal mother; Sarah, the mother of the faithful; Miriam, the minstrel prophetess; Deborah, the ruler and judge; Esther, the interceding Persian Queen; the Queen of Sheba, and the Queen of Massa who seems to have been the mother of Agur and Lemuel whose wise words are the fruit of her teaching (Prov. xxx, xxxi). These seven women seem typical of the new era which Christianity was to inaugurate, when womanhood was to be associated with holy minstrelsy and teaching, with Christian government and counsel, with consecrated courage and intercession in critical emergencies, with adoring gifts to the King of Kings, and with the imperial power of home influence whereby to train a household of princely characters to wield the scepter of social life.

Surely, among the most remarkable movements, guided by God's hand, in our times, has been this singular and steady forward march of Christian womanhood towards the front rank of consecrated service. While God was opening new doors and removing old barriers to heathen peoples, He was preparing new workers and agencies to enter the doors and occupy the accessible fields. The story of the organization of women, in boards of missions, especially in zenana work; and of their entrance upon every other form of Christian service, to promote total abstinence, social purity, systematic giving and united prayer, to disseminate intelligence and educate a new generation of givers and workers,—this is one of the greatest of the modern chapters in the new acts of the apostles. The importance and significance of this series of developments, and the obvious leadership of a divine hand in them all, entitle them to a special and permanent memorial among the marked spiritual movements of our time.

We must go back to the beginning. It is sixty-six years ago since David Abeel, returning from China, told the women of Britain about the women of the far East, who, shut up in zenanas, harems, seraglios, were inaccessible to all holy influences, unless *their own sex* could be induced to undertake work in their behalf. That moving, melting plea was the parent of zenana missions, which marvelously synchronize with the accession of this Christian Queen to the British throne! At the very time when God was lifting to the seat of an empire that reaches round the world, a young Christian woman, He was revealing to woman throughout the world the throne of her predestined influence, and putting in her hands a hitherto undreamed of scepter of imperial power! The Victorian era is woman's era. When Victoria was crowned, the diadem was placed upon the head of her sex, and woman's true epoch began, as we behold it in our day. We can do no more than briefly trace the outlines in this sixty-year history.

The project of carrying the Gospel to women in their oriental seclusion and exclusion, seemed at first the wild visionary scheme of unbalanced enthusiasts; and wise men and even sagacious women shook their heads in doubt, if not derision. How impracticable, nay, how impossible! It was like forcing gates of steel in walls of stone, to seek to get access to the harems of Turkey and the zenanas of India. But something must be done. The condition of womankind in the East was so destitute and desolate that it had long drawn toward the wives, mothers, daughters of the Orient the attention and sympathy of the whole civilized world. And there seemed to be neither hope nor help for woman, unless it should come through woman herself. No activity or generosity in sending and supporting male missionaries would solve the problem; for no man could without risk to life enter these sealed doors even in the capacity of a physician. Such facts seemed to *compel woman's ministry.* God was saying to woman as from heaven: " Thou art come to the Kingdom for such a time as this;" and to those who had ears to hear and heart to heed, there seemed no alternative. Christian women must undertake the work of carrying the Gospel within zenana gates.

The facts are appalling. In India alone it is estimated that there are one hundred and forty millions of women and girls. These were found sunk in such depths of degraded ignorance, that one-third of them could neither read nor write; one-tenth of them were widows, and of these widows fourteen thousand were under four years of age, twenty-two thousand were under ten, and one hundred and seventy-five thousand under fourteen. Think of such a host of women, twelve million of girls under fourteen, and half of them wives! and all of them absolutely unreached and unreachable by any existing influence that could elevate, educate, or evangelize them! What words could fitly portray so low an estate for nearly half the population of oriental empires!

The work was undertaken, at first, by British women. Reason opposed, but faith proposed and disposed. It is an old familiar, pathetic story, how in the days of Rev. Dr. Thomas Smith, then of Rev. John Fordyce and Alexander Duff, the first systematic efforts were made to get access to the zenanas of India. * Then the deft needle of a missionary's wife, Mrs. Mullens, was used further to unlock the doors. A simple piece of embroidery, wrought by her skillful fingers, attracted the attention of the secluded inmates of one of these household prisons; they argued, that if a woman could do such work as that,

---

* This history has been carefully outlined elsewhere ("Crisis of Missions," Chap. XIX, " New Acts of Apostles," Part II., Chap. 3) but we here rehearse the main facts. Rev. Dr. Thos. Smith, March 1840, urged on the *Calcutta Missionary Observer*, the question of zenana teaching. But it was fifteen years later before his sensible plans took such root as to have practical and lasting growth. Rev. Jno. Fordyce and others secured the services of two or three lady visitors, and got access to some native families. Then Mrs. Mullens, Mrs. Eliz. Sale, Miss Briton and others enlarged the work. But in 1851 the work had as yet no importance sufficient to give it any statistics. In 1871, twenty years after, 1,300 houses were found to be under visitation and there were about 2,000 pupils, and twenty years later, the homes found accessible had multiplied more than thirtyfold, to over 40,500. In 1896 the following are the figures for the work *outside this field of India*.

Foreign and European female teachers	711
Native teachers	3,661
Day-schools	1,507
Scholars	62,414

See MISSIONARY REVIEW. April 1897, p. 273-279.

other women might learn how, and so, with the cordial consent of the lord of the zenana, this Christian woman was welcomed within the veiled chamber, and encouraged to teach his wives the woman's art of embroidery; and, as she wrought on a pair of slippers the beautiful pattern, she was quietly working into the very fabric of their hearts and lives scarlet threads dyed in the blood, and golden threads shining with the glory of the Lamb.

It is a poetic and pathetic fact, that, under the gentle touch of a woman's hand, the long-locked gates have been flung wide open, and the barriers of ages are no more! Christian women go, almost without restraint, sometimes with urgent entreaty, into the homes of women in Turkey, Syria, China, India, and the Orient generally. The girls are gathered by hundreds of thousands into Christian schools; and the increase in the number of female pupils has been so rapid, that it doubled in ten years between 1876 and 1886, and multiplied much more rapidly in the next decade. As long ago as 1884, one hundred and sixty women missionaries had been enrolled in the work of that one London mission; pupils numbered thousands within the zenanas, and tens of thousands in their day-schools. Ten years later, Bible women entered the richest homes freely, and Hindu husbands actually clamored to have their wives and daughters taught. Fourteen years ago, the Church of England society alone had under visitation eighteen hundred zenanas with four thousand pupils; and both visitors and schools have steadily grown in numbers and influence.

Thus suddenly the women of Christendom discovered a new world, with limitless possibilities of work for the Master. Leupolt, contemplating the fact that, not only to the houses of the lower classes of natives, but to the zenanas in cities like Benares, Lucknow, Agra, Delhi, Amritsi, Lahore, etc., European women with their native assistants were admitted freely, to teach the word of God, exclaimed: " If any one had hinted twenty-five years before that this would be, I would have replied, ' All things are possible to God, but I do not expect such a glorious event in my day.' But what has God wrought! more than we asked or thought, expected or prayed for! His name be praised." And, when Leupolt thus wrote, already to more than twelve hundred such seraglios the agents of the Female Normal School and Instruction Society had access; and even this was many years ago, when the work was at its inception comparatively, and referred only to the success of one organization! An intelligent Hindu says: " If these women reach the *hearts* of the women of our country, they will soon get at the *heads* of the men."

It was about sixteen years since, that the Indian Education Commission officially reported to the government that the most successful efforts at woman's education, after leaving school, had been conducted by missionaries; that in every province of India, Christian women had devoted themselves to teaching in native homes; and recommended grants for zenana work to be recognized as a proper charge on public funds, etc. Soon after, a Mohammedan paper of Lahore urged those who would propagate Islam, to see to it that zenana women were taught the Koran, lest by the Christian teaching that was making such inroads the very foundations of Allah's empire should be demolished.

Shaftesbury, at the jubilee of the Society for Promoting Female Education in the East, in 1884, said: " The time is at hand when you will see the great dimensions of the work you are now doing, not only in India but throughout the East. Great changes are in the future." His words were prophetic of what is already taking place. Ten years ago this society had missions not only in India and Ceylon, but in Japan, Persia, and Africa, etc. One instance may be cited as a representative example of how in individual cases this zenana movement proves far-reaching and mighty, namely this: at the girls' central school in the capital of Madagascar, Miss Bliss taught the young princess who at the crisis came to the throne in that great island.

While God was thus opening the door of approach and access to Gentile women, behold Him moving Christian women to organize for the great Woman's Crusade of modern history! And so was written that new chapter of history which records the rapid growth of Women's Boards of Missions, marking the next grand epoch of woman's epiphany and activity.

Much pains have been taken to trace the facts, the early records of which were destroyed by fire, and to correct the general misapprehension as to the origin of the parent society. Rev. L. A. Gould, in a letter to the writer, says: " The exact facts are as follows: Mrs. Ellen B. Mason, wife of Rev. Francis Mason, D.D., a Baptist missionary from Burmah, stopped in Calcutta on her way to America, and learned the story of Mrs. Mullens' zenana slippers. Mrs. Mason, with two ladies, still living, Mrs. J. D. Richardson and Mrs. H. C. Gould, my mother, visited influential families in Boston; and the first society, consisting of nine ladies, whose names I have, was formed in Boston, November, 1860, Miss M. V. Ball, President. Subsequently, in 1861, societies were formed in New York, Brooklyn, and Philadelphia; and the New York society, by reason of its strength, was allowed to become the general society. These facts are not vital, only advantageous for accuracy."

Thus, then, was organized, forty years ago, in America, the Woman's Union Missionary Society, which, under the leadership of the loved and lamented Mrs. T. C. Doremus, became the pioneer society of America, with *The Missionary Link* as its organ. This was an undenominational society, and led the way, as the parent of the various denominational Women's Boards now found connected with all the great Christian bodies. Of all these societies the one originating cause was the inaccessibility of heathen women save to their own sex; and the one aim was to organize women, in cooperation with the existing foreign missionary societies, for sending out and supporting unmarried women as missionaries and teachers to their neglected heathen sisters.

The rallying cry, heard in Britain over sixty years ago, and loudly echoed in America about twenty years later, brought Christian women boldly to the front in all the leading denominations. Early in 1868, was formed in Boston the New England Women's Foreign Missionary Society, with Mrs. Albert Bowker for President, and Mrs. Homer Bartlett for Treasurer. The previous year the American Board had sent into the field ten single women, appropriating for this end $25,000. Christian women felt called of God to this special work, and the following were the dominant reasons:

1. Women abroad were inaccessible except to women.

2. Christian womanhood would naturally both prompt and help work for woman.

3. Woman owes a special debt to Christ for what He has done to uplift her socially and domestically.

4. Woman naturally sympathizes with her own sex, and can appreciate woman's degradation and elevation.

5. Woman abroad needs the practical illustration of what the Gospel can do, and has done, for women.

6. In all education woman is God's ordained pioneer. As wife, mother, sister, daughter, she is the heart of the home and sways its scepter.

7. This work provides a legitimate sphere in which all that is best in woman can thus be amply exercised and developed.

The results are correspondent with what might be expected. Christian women became, for the first time in all history, thoroughly united in organized work for souls. Their interest in the spiritual uplifting of their own sex was quickened; larger means for supporting women as missionaries and teachers were forthcoming; intelligence was more widely spread, partly by cheap mission leaflets and booklets; offerings were systematically gathered in small sums, like "Carey's weekly pennies"; direct correspondence with women workers, stated meetings, for prayer, and hearing of news from the field—these were the results, which became in turn causes of new and larger results.

The collections of the first month enabled this early New England society to assume the support of a missionary to South Africa. At the end of three months, three women became living links with the foreign field, Miss Edwards in Africa and Miss Andrews and Miss Parmelee in Turkey; and ten native Bible women were to be maintained by the society. By October 8th, 1868, at Norwich, Conn., this society was already the parent of auxiliaries everywhere forming, and changed its name to "The Women's Board of Missions."

In the same month of the same year, a similar society was formed in the great West, "The Women's Board of Missions *for the Interior,*" and the next year this new society assumed the support of Mrs. Tyler of the Madura mission, and Miss Dean of Oroomiah, and issued its quarterly, *Life and Light for Heathen Women.* During its first year about $4,000 were gathered.

So rapidly grew the women's societies, that in 1884

there were twenty-two Women's Boards, representing twelve denominations, and an aggregate of about $1,000,-000 receipts! In 1897, the total number of women's societies had reached upwards of one hundred.

One example of the rapid *increase of gifts* ought to be added to show the power of many little sums, systematically gathered. One Board, the Presbyterian, that reported in 1871 $7,000, reported $224,000 in 1886—thirty-twofold increase in fifteen years! And the increase still goes on.

No wonder Thos. Chalmers should have declared that he had found in benevolent work, that one woman was equal to seven and a half men!

Zenana work was only one direction in which Christian women have organized for holy activity during this Victorian era—the first trumpet-blast that rallied this vast reserve force of the Lord's army. Then came the Women's Boards, both of Home and Foreign Missions. But since then, there are many and various forms of holy enterprise upon which the Christian sisterhood have entered. Four or five stand out conspicuous, tho far from exhausting the long list.

The Women's *Temperance Crusade* is one of the most memorable for its desperate daring. Aroused by the cruelties inflicted by strong drink, and hopeless of human intervention, Christian women in the United States took the kingdom of Satan by violence, and went into the drink-shops to protest with dram-sellers, knelt on the floors of bar-rooms, and with prayers and tears besought God to curse the drink traffic and stop its awful ravages. When turned into the street, they knelt on the pavements, interposing their bodies between the door of gin palaces and those who would enter. The haunts of the drunkard were turned into places of prayer, rum-sellers changed to evangelists, and sots into saints. The Women's Christian Temperance Union, baptized in tears and prayers and blood, has a holy martyr history.

The Woman's League for *Social Purity* attempted to do with the brothel and all its accessories what the Temperance Crusade undertook with the drink-shop. Obscene books, prints, exhibitions, houses of ill-fame, the uses of the post for immoral purposes, and the perversion of law to impure ends,—these and other helpers and abettors of prostitution and corruption occupied their attention. It was a mighty movement, and has still an increasing momentum, directed toward the purity of our homes, as its sister movement, toward their sobriety. It required great heroism and courage of conviction, for women to cast off the trammels of a mock modesty and a refined sensibility, call things by their right names, and in public as well as in private, before men as well as women, and sometimes in courts and legislatures, grapple with an evil that even men had found it difficult to discuss. But they have done it, and challenged universal admiration for their intrepid fidelity.

The Young Women's *Christian Association* has done grand work for young women, as the Y. M. C. A. has for young men. It is making itself felt in all our great cities, in throwing a loving shelter about young girls who come to the great centers of population to find employment and who have no proper home-life. These associations have erected suitable buildings where young women find board, lodging, companionship, employment, libraries, prayer-meetings, Bible classes, and every aid to temporal and spiritual advancement. If there is any more beneficial institution of its sort in existence, we do not know of such; and the writer can speak with confidence and from personal knowledge of the immense benefit accruing, having himself a daughter who is the secretary of one of these city organizations. Just now this work is expanding and becoming a power in foreign lands, gathering native young women, as in India, into the embrace of a consecrated Christian sisterhood.

Women's *Medical Mission* Work is one of the latest born of the organized movements of women in Christian lands. To have women going forth into all parts of the world, not simply as nurses but as fully qualified physicians; and commending themselves even to imperial governments as competent to practise medicine and surgery side by side with the most skillful male practitioners, is certainly a very marked advance. Here is especially a new feature of the zenana movement. Women penetrate the seclusion of oriental homes with the balm of Gilead in one hand and the balm of the apothecary in the other; they go to heal the body and to heal the soul, to preach and to cure; and in true apostolic fashion to commend themselves to the heart, by skill in ministering to the ills and ailments of the body. There is an eminent fitness in woman's medical ministry to woman, and upon it God is setting His seal and sanction.

In the Young People's Society of Christian Endeavor, and the Student Volunteer Missionary Union, women are perhaps as prominent leaders, if not as numerous members, as men. But our object is to call attention mainly to organizations solely composed of and officered by women, and those which have been selected out of many, suffice to illustrate how in every direction the female factor in the Church of Christ is making itself felt as never before in the various forms of Christian activity. There is not one department of service to Christ and a lost humanity, in which women's gentle hand is not found conspicuous, not only in association with men, but in independent methods of organized action.

What the church and the world have gained hereby, it would be difficult to estimate. One example might be given out of many thousands as a typical instance. Somewhat over forty years ago, Mrs. Murrilla B. Ingalls, widow of Rev. Lovell Ingalls, a missionary to Arakan, after a visit to America, returned to Burma, and went at once to Thongze, where she remained and had entire control, without help from any male missionary, except a native ordained preacher and a few other native assistants. Often alone, with marked capacity and sagacity she carried on the mission with conspicuous blessing. Without transgressing the limits of propriety, or assuming ecclesiastical functions, she became a sort of acknowledged bishop of a vast diocese. In all that has to do with Christian doctrine and church organization and administration, she taught both women and men. She chose and then trained native evangelists, overseeing the schools and discovering the aptitude in pupils for teachers, and then training them for educational work. She maintained strict discipline, guided the church in appointing pastors, and then humbly trained pastors in Bible truth, homiletic studies, and pastoral theology. She established *Zayat* preaching, organized a circulating library, and distributed Bibles and tracts over a wide district. Seeing the great destitution about her, she went with her Bible women on tours into the country, and her tent became the resort of multitudes who sought instruction. She reminds us of another woman, who, being accused of " preaching " by those who were jealous of her influence, and defending her course as justifiable from New Testament examples, was asked, " Were you ever ordained? " " No," she answered, *" but I was foreordained."* Mrs. Ingalls is a bright example of what woman has done and is doing in all lands, and those who would pursue the study of the theme have only to read the story of such heroic women as the three wives of Dr. Judson, the second Mrs. Carey, Mrs. Krapf, Mrs. Judith Grant, Fidelia Fiske, Eliza Agnew, Mrs. Mc-

All, Mrs. Moffat and Mrs. Livingstone, Mary Whately, Matilda Rankin, Mary Graybell, Clara Cushman, Hannah Mullens, Rebecca Wakefield, Sarah B. Capron, Mary Williams, Dorothy Jones, Anna Hinderer, and a host of others who have adorned the annals of missions. And who needs to be told that the names of Florence Nightingale and Clara Barton are inseparable from the ministry to wounded and sick soldiers and victims of famine and persecution and pestilence the world over?

Surely, when God lifted a Christian woman to the British throne He was saying to her whole sisterhood in all Christian lands, " Let woman appreciate her opportunity, for it is the golden age of her reign, and she holds a scepter that sways empires. Let her prove herself to be a power ordained of God to fulfil a holy mission!"

CHAPTER XIV

RAMABAI AND THE WOMEN OF INDIA [*]

THE most prominent figure among the women of the Orient in our day is Pundita Ramabai, whose work in India is becoming so well known, and awakening such deep interest the world over.

The census of 1891 showed 280,000,000 people in India, with 600,000 more men than women, owing to the low status of woman and the murder of female infants. Those who are not starved to death or otherwise disposed of in infancy, find life so miserable that many become suicides. The men rank as " golden vessels," however defiled the vessel may be, but it is a crime to be a woman; she is but an earthen vessel, and a very unclean one. Especially is a widow despised, for her husband's death is supposed to be due to her sin. The suttee is, therefore, deemed a fit penalty. Cattle have had hospitals, but not until fifteen years ago was a woman treated with as much consideration as a cow. Everything about that animal is sacred, even to her dung, but now only where Christ has taught the new theology of womanhood is woman respected. Widows are plenty, for every fifth woman is a widow; and altho despised, they are considered good enough for servile work. When no longer able to serve, they are allowed to die like other beasts of burden. As the nightingale's eyes must be put out if it is expected to sing in its cage, educa-

---

[*] This article, already incorporated in the " Miracles of Missions, 3d series, is here added to complete the survey of these movements of the half-century and especially the movements for woman's elevation.—A. T. P.

tion is denied to woman, and the eyes of her understanding are blinded lest she rebel against her lot. Not one in fifty can read, not to say write. Volumes have been written upon woman in India, * for in no one country, perhaps, is woman so bound down by chains wrought of combined custom and law, caste and religion. Womanhood is crushed out because hope is abandoned by all those who enter woman's estate. Even the sacred books sanction this horrible degradation. According to these, she has no legal or social status, no rights which a man is bound to respect. She is not capable of any acts of devotion; is to obey her husband, however immoral his commands, and worship him if she would have salvation. She is an incarnation of sin and lying, and can not be believed under oath. The results of such a system of society are, *of course,* not only child marriage and polygamy, but infanticide, slavery, prostitution, and the suttee.

CHILD WIVES AND WIDOWS

The last census taken in the presidency of Madras throws a lurid light on the terrible evils of the accursed system of child marriage in this great eastern empire. It showed 23,938 girls under four years of age, and 142,606 between the ages of five and nine married; 988 baby widows under four years of age, and 4,147 girl widows between five and nine years of age. There are two ceremonies in connection with an Indian marriage. Should the bridegroom die between the first and second of these ceremonies, the little bride becomes a widow, doomed to lifelong wretchedness and ignominy. Many little girls are married to old men tottering on the verge of the grave,

---

* The following authorities may be consulted: Bainbridge, "Round the World Tour;" Woodside, "Woman in India;" Stewart, "Life and Work in India;" Wilkins, "Daily Life and Work in India;" Storrow, "Our Sisters in India;" "Wrongs of Indian Womanhood," *The Bombay Guardian,* etc., etc.

and this again aggravates the evil. In the Madras presidency alone are some 60,000 Brahman widows, widowed in childhood, and doomed for life to the coarse white cloak and shaven head of the woman who is cursed by the gods.

The unhappy lot of Indian widows is partially described in the following native editorial extract quoted from the *Arya Messenger*. This paper devotes much time and thought to the glorification of everything indigenous, and its testimony regarding the sad lot of its womankind is, therefore, particularly valuable. Were a missionary to use the language of this extract, he would at once be accused of mendacious exaggeration, or something equally terrible. The extract reads thus:

There are at present out of 6,016,759 married girls between *five* and *nine* years of age, 174,000 widows in India. These unfortunate creatures are condemned to a life of perpetual widowhood, for no fault of their own. These infants, what could they have possibly done to deserve so cruel a fate? They could have absolutely no idea of the moment when they were betrothed, and most of them could have no idea of the time when they were married. They had no hand in the choice of husbands for themselves, their parents bestowed them on whomsoever they chose, and now, before they have fairly learned to talk, they are husbandless, doomed never to know the joys of a home. It is impossible to imagine anything more heartless, anything more savage and barbarous than the treatment which has been accorded to these unhappy girls by their misguided parents. Why should they have been betrothed and wedded when mere infants, and on what grounds can it be justified that their future shall be dark and dreary—a succession of miseries and sufferings? No law, human or Divine, can justify such a thing, and since it is an outrage upon Divine teaching and upon man's own sense of justice, it is but natural that we should suffer for it. And we do suffer for it in a thousand ways, and we know it. What can be more ridiculous, more monstrous than that while a decrepit, spent-out old man, with one foot in the grave, can marry a young girl at any time, a virgin, who is in the prime of life, who has not as yet lived in the world one-fifth the time the old man has, should be absolutely denied the right of taking some young man as husband! The *father* of a widow of eight or nine years old may marry again when he chooses, but the poor girl herself must never! This is a state of things which exists nowhere else under the sun.

There is no real family life in India. There could not be when Hindu philosophy teaches that, " He is a fool who considers his wife his friend." A few extracts from a Hindu catechism give some idea of the basis for the ill-treatment of Indian women:

> *What is the chief gate to hell?* Woman.
> *What is cruel?* The heart of a viper.
> *What is more cruel?* The heart of a woman.
> *What is most cruel of all?* The heart of a soulless, penni-less widow.
> *What poison is that which appears like a nectar?* Woman.

The marriage of girls to *Khandoba* is a custom which, like sodomy, can not be treated in plain words, as it belongs among the things of which it is " a shame to speak." Suffice it to say that it implies a devotement to a life of vice as a *murli,* and reminds one of the similar customs connected with the rites of Venus and Bacchus. Parents lend themselves to these nameless horrors, and additions to the Indian penal code have been directed to the mitigation, if not abolition, of these enormities.

THE STORY OF RAMABAI

Ramabai is a middle-aged woman, with black hair; she is slightly deaf, and a quiet atmosphere of power invests her. She talks with intelligence, and is heard everywhere with profound interest—the more so as the facts of her life are known.

This woman has a romantic history. Her mother was herself a child-bride, wedded to a widower at nine years of age, and taken to a home nine hundred miles away.

Ramabai learned many lessons from her mother's lips, who would not marry her in infancy, and so " throw her into the well of ignorance." Her father, who was an educated Brahman priest, had her taught Sanskrit and trained her well. He lost all his property, and, after enduring fearful suffering with his wife and elder daughter, fell a victim to the awful famine of twenty-five years ago—1874-77. Everything of value was sold for bread, and then even the necessities of life had to yield before its extremities; and the day came when the last handful of coarse rice was gone, and death stared them in the face. They went into the forest to die there, and for eleven days and nights subsisted on water and leaves and wild dates, until the father, who wanted to drown himself in the sacred tank, died of fever, as also the mother and sister. The father's dying prayers for Ramabai were, indeed, addressed to the unknown God, but have been answered by the true God, who heard the supplications of a sincere but misguided parent. Then the brother and Ramabai found their way to Calcutta, where they were scarcely better off, being still half starved, and for four years longer endured scarcity. There this brother also died—a very strange preparation for the life-work to which God called Ramabai. When twenty-two years old, her parents being dead, in a period of famine, during which she suffered both for lack of food and clothing, as well as shelter, she learned a lesson which prepared her to sympathize with others who suffered. Life's sorrows and privations became a reality.

Left thus alone, her beauty and culture won her the coveted title, *saravasti,* and attracted to her friends and admirers. Finally she married a Bengali gentleman, and for about eighteen months was happy in her new home, a baby girl being given her. But her husband's death introduced a new experience of sorrow. The world was before her and her child, and two grave questions confronted her:

First, how shall I get a living? and second, what shall I do for others?

Ramabai, being thus early left a widow, began to know the real horror of a Hindu widow's lot, and resolved to undertake, as her life mission, to relieve this misery and poverty. Her heart kindled with love for these 25,000,000 child widows and deserted wives, who know no happiness; who are often half starved, are doomed to perpetual widowhood, and to whom their departed husbands are practically gods to be worshipped.

At the age of twenty Ramabai went to England, where she heard the Voice that called Abraham to go out, not knowing whither, and like him she obeyed. There she was converted to Christ, and baptized in 1883. She taught Sanskrit in the ladies' college at Cheltenham, her purposes for life meanwhile taking definite shape.

About twelve years ago she visited America, where she found friends disposed to help her start her school for high-caste widows in Bombay. She began with two pupils, but, despite opposition and ridicule, she went on with her God-appointed mission, and now has over 400 pupils and a property worth $60,000, embracing a hundred acres, cultivated by them. About 225 girls have been brought to Christ, and many have been trained for useful work, happily married, or otherwise profitably employed. In nine years Pundita Ramabai received upward of $91,-000 for the work. For a time her attitude was negative and neutral as regards Christianity, but her work is now distinctly evangelical and Christian. Love is its atmosphere, and unselfish labor for those who are in need, as is shown by the opening of her doors lately to welcome 300 famine orphans. Through help obtained in England and the United States she built at Poona a building, and opened a school called Sharada Sadan (Abode of Wisdom).

In 1896, hearing of the famine desolating the central provinces, she made arrangements for the fifty or more widows to be cared for at Poona, and went to the famine districts resolved to rescue at least 300 girls from death; and these became her own, under her control, to be brought up as she pleased. Within two years nearly one-third of this number had accepted Christ. These were placed on the farm at Kedgaum, about thirty-four miles from Poona.

One must have lived in India and gone through a famine experience to understand the facts. Government poorhouses and relief camps she found to be inadequate; even where the bodies were sheltered and fed, the soul was in danger from the character of those who were employed as mukadams, managers, etc. She found young girls " kept " for immoral purposes in these government shelters where virtue was presumably also in shelter; and when the deputy commissioner was told of the facts, like Gallio, he " cared for none of these things." Ramabai says that young women had to sell their virtue to save themselves from starvation. British soldiers often oppose missionary labor because it breaks up this infernal traffic in virtue. Dr. Kate Bushnell and Mrs. Andrew exposed the doings of high military officers, and further exposures are feared where godly women have freedom to work.

During the late famine, when Poona was abandoned, Ramabai was supporting 372 girls, of whom 337 were in Kedgaum, at the farm, while the rest were at different places. When this farm was bought, embracing 100 acres, the government would not allow dormitories to be put up. Ramabai's reply was, " I will build a barn for bullocks and grain." She went on and put up a large building, and by the time it was completed, she had permission to put girls in it instead of cattle. Thus she stored it with " grain for the Lord." That "cattle-shed" became a shelter for 200 famine widows, and later served as school-house, chapel, dormitory, etc. Temporary shelters were also erected and the new settlement was called Mukti (Salvation).

The work at Mukti is constantly growing, and has the growing confidence of intelligent and Christian people. The new buildings now completed are already insufficient to accommodate the inmates, and new buildings will be put up as fast as the Lord sends means. The heart of this godly woman travails for souls, and she can not see the misery and poverty about her without yearning to relieve it. A few poor women, ruined by vice and terribly diseased, are housed for the time in separate *chuppee* huts, until a home for such can be provided.

This home is not a place of idleness, but a hive of industry. Education for the mind, salvation for the soul, and occupation for the body is the threefold law; washing and weaving, cooking and sweeping, growing grain and grinding it, flower culture and fruit raising—these are some of the industries in which the girls are trained, and which contribute toward their self-support.

The teachers are *exclusively Christian,* and the settlement is a truly missionary center. Miss Abrams, who superintended the work in Ramabai's absence, gives her whole time to it, giving Bible instruction in the school, and supervising the village work. She had only to suggest to students a pledge like that of the student volunteers, and *thirty-five* at once offered to follow any leading of God into mission work. A score of neighboring villages are already accessible to the Gospel, and crowds gather around Miss Abrams and her Gospel women.

The Holy Spirit works with Ramabai. The girls show real sorrow for sin, and hunger after salvation. Then when they are saved, they become witnesses, and in their own simple way tell of forgiveness and cleansing. In the hospital there are also frequent manifestations of God's healing power.

When she set up her school in Poona, Ramabai made no efforts at proselyting the inmates but some five or six years ago twelve or thirteen of them, won to Christ by her unselfish love, renounced heathenism, and were baptized into Christ. Poona was greatly aroused by such an event, and for a time it seemed as tho the home itself would be reduced to a ruin. Ramabai called a public meeting, and undertook to explain why these widows had accepted Christ. The streets were thronged with people, and a crowd of young men filled the hall where she was to speak. Without a sign of anxiety, Ramabai stood up to address them. She spoke of the moral and spiritual slavery of the Hindus; how incapable they are of helping themselves, while they are asking for political freedom; how unhappy their family life is, and especially how miserable is the lot of their women. Then, holding up the Marathi Bible she said:

" I will read to you now what is the reason of all your misery, degradation, and helplessness; it is your separation from the living God!" It was growing dark, and she asked one of the excited Hindu youths to bring a lamp that she might read. Without a moment's hesitation he obeyed. After reading some passages, she began to speak of the conversions of the widows, and then said: "Your view of my actions cannot influence me in the least, nor can your threatenings frighten me. You like to be slaves; I am free! Christ, the truth, has made me free." The excitement was tremendous, and the Brahmans only restrained themselves with difficulty; but they heard her out to the end in dead silence, and allowed her to walk uninjured through their ranks to her home.

The storm passed away, and the home remained undisturbed—sheltering some sixty women, and training them for lives of usefulness. The Sharada Sadan is still a secular school, but Mukti is distinctly Christian, tho unsectarian.

Pundita Ramabai has made two visits to this country. Once ten or eleven years ago, when she came to ask aid, and again, more recently, when she came to give account of her stewardship. During this decade of years, the Ramabai circles had sent her upward of 80,000 dollars. Fifty thousand dollars of this she had invested in property, free from debt, and over 350 high-caste widows have already enjoyed the benefits of her school, and are now filling various places of self-support and service.

CHAPTER XV

EVER since the Reformation there have been going forward two exactly opposite movements, due to as many opposite tendencies—the movement toward sectarian division, and the movement toward denominational union.

That two so opposite tendencies should be in operation at the same time seems, at first glance, contradictory and inexplicable; but a moment's careful consideration will show not only that it is a fact, but that there is a reasonable philosophy behind the fact. The Reformation broke the shackles of religious thought by releasing men from bondage to papal superstition and prelatical authority. It must be remembered that Rome holds that heresy is to be suppressed, not only in its expression, but in its conception; and hence the Inquisition dealt with parties suspected of heretical opinion, and sought, by the rack, to compel the disclosure of individual and secret sentiment. The immediate effect of the dawn of religious liberty was that men began to *think* freely, then to *speak* freely; and thus they disclosed divergencies of opinion, which, being positively held and expressed with impunity, led to controversies, and controversies to separations for opinion's sake, until even minor matters of differing opinion became the watchwords of ecclesiastical parties, and sects multiplied until we have now about as many nominally Christian bodies, large and small, as there are days in the year.

This result was natural. The only way to keep men from such separations is to keep them in ignorance, and in dependent slavery to authority. Liberty always leads to individualism and independence. Men can be kept on a level only by the despot's method—cutting off any head that rises above the common plane. The instant that a dead level of equality and subordination is no longer enforced by violence done to manhood, differences begin to assert themselves and to become increasingly manifest and manifold.

On the other hand, hearts are drawn together by a common *faith* and a common love and a common service. True disciples can not but feel that all believers are essentially one—one in agreement upon fundamentals—and it requires but little candid consideration to perceive that the things in which we agree are of infinitely more consequence than those upon which we differ. After all these wars in words, however bitter the controversial spirit may have been, when true believers get on their knees together, they pray the same theology, and the purest hymnology of all the ages shows no traces of rancorous strife over lesser matters of divergent opinion. Prayers and praises never betray sectarian shibboleths.

And, as there is a common faith down beneath all denominational creeds so there is a common *love* down beneath all external alienations and separations. Those who love the unseen God respond with affection toward His image wherever found in man. The unseen God appears manifested in the seen likeness of God in the disciple. There may be different tongues on earth, but Abba, Jehovah, Hallelujah, are the same in all tongues, and tell of a common heavenly dialect. Whenever the Spirit works in common, common fruits appear, and the first of them all is *love*.

Again, common *service* brings disciples together. They leave the atmosphere of denominational variance behind when they come face to face with the desperate needs of a lost race. Where, as in India, woman has no rights, which a man is bound to respect, while everything about a cow is sacred, even to animal excrement, the differences that divide evangelical Christians at home seem ludicrously little. Where, as in Africa, mud from a river, molded into a rude resemblance to a human form, is set up for worship; or a snake's poison fang, an elephant's tooth, or a bit of parchment, is looked upon as a charm more potent than prayer to the infinite God, missionaries forget their Calvinism and Arminianism, their differences in church polity and doctrinal standards, and come close to each other in the effort to lift men out of the awful slough of fetish worship and animalism. *

And so, at home, the more Christians know of each other, and the more frequently they meet for common worship or in common work, the more they forget that, in any respect, they are not one. They misjudge each other while they see each other from a distance; but, when they come nigh, each sees in the other the countenance of a friend, a brother, a sister. They feel ashamed of what has kept apart those who are redeemed by the same blood and indwelt by the same Spirit, and are on their way to the same home.

Of late years, after denominational and sectarian divergencies had spent their force, and the centrifugal tendencies had so long and so sadly prevailed, the centripetal —the power of one faith, love, and work—began to be more manifest and to claim recognition. One of the first of these counter-movements was what is known as the Evangelical Alliance—a happy name to express an alliance whose basis is evangelical truth held by all alike. This movement is a little over fifty years

---

* See also the "Declaration of Unity," issued by the Protestant missionaries in China printed in the January number of the *Missionary Review*, 1899, p. 52.

old, having been organized in London in 1846. In its public meetings, brethren have met on a common platform, uttered harmonious testimony, and evinced mutual sympathy; and, in face of common perils, or the invasion of Christian privilege and right, have stood by each other in a united and effective remonstrance. It is to be lamented that in America the Evangelical Alliance is far less effective as an organization, in some respects, than in Britain, tho, under the lead of Dr. Josiah Strong, there were ten years of most efficient work done in one direction, namely, that of reaching the non-churchgoers in our great cities. In more recent years the free churches of Britain have been drawn closer in an annual church congress, which is now becoming a confederation. This latter is, perhaps, the most conspicuous form of church unity in our day, and, in some respects, the most promising, tho not perhaps without its difficulties and dangers.

Those who have watched the signs of the times have noticed, with more than a passing interest, the development of this unifying tendency. For example, in 1890, representatives of various bodies met in England—ministers and members of the Established Church and of the Congregational churches—and held a series of twelve conferences, seeking a platform on which they could agree, and which might serve as a doctrinal basis on which to unite and become one church. * Among those composing

---

* We here condense an account of the Free Church Federation, from a recent English periodical: "In 1890, Dr. Guinness Rogers suggested the holding of a congress of all denominations. Wesleyans, Presbyterians, Baptists, Congregationalists, meeting on the same platform, not for an interchange of compliments and courtesies, but for true Christian fellowship in devotional service, and for counsel on common Christian work, would be a striking illustration of a Catholic Church including various sections, each with its own form of development, and with its distinctive features of doctrine and ritual, but all one in Christ Jesus."

Invitations were sent out to a first congress in Manchester, England, in 1892. Two years later a second congress was held at Leeds, where a more formal organization of the movement was commenced, and by 1896 ten thousand churches, with a membership of a million, were represented. By

the conference, were seven Episcopalians, including Canon Westcott and the dean of Worcester, and six Congregational ministers, including Rev. Dr. Henry Allon, H. R. Reynolds, president of Chestnut College, and Rev. Dr. J. P. Paton.

The conference was able to agree upon a statement of the essential doctrines of Christianity, as revealed in the Bible; the divine authority of the Scriptures, the Apostles' and Nicene creeds, the Trinity, the Incarnation, the Atonement, the Resurrection, the need of saving faith in Christ, being held by all, universally accepted by Christians, and already expressed in terms unobjectionable to all evangelical denominations, as in the doctrinal basis of the Evangelical Alliance. But the main obstacles to a union of all the churches lie in the denominational peculiarities. The use of a liturgical service might be made optional; but immersion, the form of church organization and government, the doctrine of priesthood, are matters on which such difference of opinion and conviction exists, that little advance has been made toward reconciling or eliminating them.

Here the English conference split in 1890. The Angli-

---

the end of 1898 some five hundred local councils had been formed, divided amongst twenty-five district federations.

The objects of the movement have been defined thus: (a) To facilitate fraternal intercourse and cooperation among the Evangelical Free Churches. (b) To assist in the organization of local councils. (c) To encourage devotional fellowship and mutual counsel concerning the spiritual life and religious activities of the churches. (d) To advocate the New Testament doctrine of the Church, and to defend the rights of the associated churches. (e) To promote the application of the law of Christ in every relation of human life.

The methods adopted to attain these objects have been many and various; one of the most important being the holding of united missions.

Another important phase of the work is the arranging for systematic visitation, with free distribution of good literature, and invitations to attend places of worship. This is greatly facilitated by dividing the neighborhood covered by the local council into "parishes," special maps having been prepared in many cases showing the streets allotted to each of the churches. The growth of Evangelical Protestantism, the increase of the social well-being of the people, and the deepening of the spiritual life of the churches have already been the result.

cans held fast to the priestly order, to ordination by the laying on of Episcopal hands, as qualifying to duly administer the sacraments " in all those things that of necessity are requisite to the same," and to a participation in the sacraments, so administered, as essential to membership in the holy Catholic Church. Congregationalists and other believers, outside of the Anglican and Roman churches, were not ready to accept such opinions or bow to such claims. We quote:

"It is well to be frank. It is best to declare at the outset that we positively reject the priestly order of ministers, as contrary to Revelation and history. There was no such order in the Apostolic Church. It was one of the innovations which led to the formation of the papal hierarchy. The churches of the Reformation with entire propriety, excluded every trace of hierarchical office and power from their organizations. From this the Church of England is the chief dissenting body. It adopted the hierarchy, man made, as it found it, simply cutting off the pope and his council. It, and not the Congregational or Presbyterian body, is the non-conforming church. The churches of the Reformation held, as they were taught by the New Testament, that the entire body of Christian believers constitutes 'a royal priesthood,' and that no minister is or can be a priest in any sense differing from the priesthood of believers.

"It should be distinctly understood that the large majority of Christians conscientiously, decisively, and absolutely rejects the doctrine that a minister is a priest in any special sense, in a sense differing in any degree from the priesthood of every believer; that the necessity for Episcopal ordination is as distinctly and absolutely rejected by the same majority; that the dependence of the sacraments for efficacy on a priestly order is no less absolutely rejected. This rejection of a priestly order, and all it includes, is conscientious, and rests upon faith in the Scriptures. No union is possible between the majority of Christian denominations and the Episcopal Church, if it involves an acceptance of a priestly order of clergymen.

"Not a few question if it be wise to bring all Christians together in one church organization. Would not such a body be exposed to mighty temptations, involving great perils? There is a great deal of old Adam left in the best of us. Position and power are very attractive. There are ambitious men in the Church, who are also good men, who seek for places of influence and control. Such an organization would have great political importance, and aspiring politicians, just as was the case with the Papal Church for many years, would strive to secure the support of the one great holy Catholic Church. Their schemes would be invented and applied with consummate skill, and the leaders of the Church would be exposed to temptations tremendous in power and persistence. Is it wise to enter upon such risks?"

A federation of denominations is, however, another matter altogether, and seems desirable. Every desirable end that an organic union could secure, could be as well obtained, perhaps, through a federation of churches, without incurring many of the risks otherwise involved.

The following basis of agreement was reached at this conference. It would be difficult to improve upon it, perhaps, as an acceptable ground for common agreement:

THE CHRISTIAN FAITH.

I. In recognizing the Bible as of Divine authority, and as the sole ultimate test of doctrine in matters of faith, as is expressed in the sixth article of the Church of England.

II. In accepting the general teaching of the Apostles' Creed and the Nicene Creed, including, of necessity, the doctrines of the Holy Trinity, the Incarnation, and the Atonement.

III. In recognizing a substantial connection between the resurrection body and the present "body of humiliation."

IV. That saving faith in Christ is that self-surrender to Him which leads a man to believe what he teaches, and to do what He bids, so far as he has opportunities of knowledge.

THE CHRISTIAN MORALITY.

I. In the conviction that it is the duty of the Christian society to consider, in the light of the principles, motives, and promises of the faith, the problems of domestic, social, and national morality, with a view to concerted action.

II. That progressive sanctification is essential to the Christian life; so that without it neither professed faith, nor conversion, nor sacraments, nor worship, can avail for the salvation of the soul.

CHRISTIAN DISCIPLINE.

I. That the divisions among Christians render the due administration of discipline, in the case of those who openly deny the fundamental truths of Christianity, or offend against Christian morality, extremely difficult; and that greater caution should be used in admitting to the privileges of membership those who leave, or are expelled from, the Christian community to which they have belonged.

II. That while it is most desirable that this caution should be exercised in all cases of members of one Christian society seeking admission into another, by careful inquiry being made, and adequate testimony being required, as to their Christian character, this is especially important in regard to those who desire to exercise the ministerial office.

CHRISTIAN WORSHIP.

I. That Congregationalists can accept and use the treasures of devotion—hymns, collects, liturgies, etc.—accumulated by the Church during the Christian ages; and many Nonconformists think that in certain circumstances it is desirable to do so.

II. That Churchmen can accept the use of extempore prayer in public worship; and many Churchmen think that in certain circumstances it is desirable to do so.

III. That rigid uniformity in public worship is undesirable, and that to enforce it by civil penalties is a mistake.

THE CHRISTIAN SACRAMENTS.

That altho it is desirable that every one should seek to know the true doctrine of the sacraments, yet their efficacy does not depend upon such knowledge, but lies, on the one hand, in the due administration of the sacraments " in all those things that of necessity are requisite to the same," and, on the other, in the use of them with a true desire to fulfill the ordinance of Christ.

THE CHRISTIAN CHURCH AND MINISTRY.

I.

1. That the Catholic Church is a society founded by Christ, the members of which are united in Him, and to each other, by

spiritual ties, which are over and above those that attach to them simply as men.

2. That these ties depend upon a special union with the Person of the One Mediator, and a special indwelling of the One Spirit.

The Nonconformist members of the conference are unable to admit:

1. That the reception of visible sacraments is essential, in ordinary cases, to the establishment of these ties.

2. That through the reception of the visible sacraments these ties may subsist, tho not forever, in those who are not believing and living as Christian people should.

Both agree:

II.

1. That Christ has established a perpetual ministry in the Catholic Church.

2. That no one can rightly exercise this ministry unless he be ordained to it by Christ Himself.

3. That there is a divinely appointed distinction of office in this ministry.

The Nonconformist members of the conference are unable to admit:

1. That there is a divinely appointed threefold distinction of orders in this ministry.

2. That external ordination by the laying on of Episcopal hands is necessary for its rightful exercise.

The objections to organic union, above stated, are not the only ones urged by those who doubt the wisdom or expediency of such union. There are those who are exceedingly jealous of the simplicity of worship, and who fear the rapid encroachments of modern ritualism; and they apprehend danger from the contagion and infection of closer contact with all this formalism and sacerdotalism. For example: Protestant clergy were indignant at the celebration at an Anglican church, at a Church Congress service, of what was practically high mass. On behalf of a number of members of the congress, Mr. Harry Miller sent a protest to Archdeacon Emery, the permanent secretary, mentioning among illegal practices introduced—a procession in the church with banners, crucifix, lighted candles, and thurifer; the use of chasuble, alb, etc., the bishop (of Argyll and the Isles) wearing miter and cope; the use of wafer bread; the elevation of, and kneeling before, the consecrated elements; ceremonial mixing water with the wine during service; ceremonial lighting of twenty candles immediately before the prayers of consecration; the frequent use of incense and the censing of the communion table, celebrant, choir, and congregation; the use of sacring bells; the celebrant standing with back to the people during the prayer of consecration, so as to hide the manual acts; the use of "altar" cards; procession with bishop to the pulpit, with lighted candles and crucifix, etc., etc.

If church union means mingling of a radical Protestant sentiment and practice with such "rags of Romanism," there will be not a few "dissenters" from such union, and "absenters" from such services.

A very conspicuous peril besetting all these modern efforts toward organic union, lies in the tendency to *undue breadth* of platform. Charity may only be another name for laxity. In the desire to make room for all disciples there is a subtle temptation to add another plank which extends the basis a little beyond the strictly evangelical limits. Implied forbearance with individual peculiarities of teaching and practise may easily pass into express toleration of serious errors and unscriptural practises. Loose views of inspiration, Socinianism, Pelagianism, Justification by works, notions of the Holy Spirit which rob Him of all proper personality, and the various evasions of future retribution, may all easily demand a recognition, at least the recognition of silence which is practical consent. Here we must all recognize a rock of risk of which disciples in drawing near to each other must steer clear. Practically this is a present risk in the movement toward unity in Britain and causes many to withhold their presence and co-operation.

The question naturally arises, how far may we safely go in reference to federating evangelical disciples in closer external bonds? To this inquiry we give such answers as we may, glad to have our readers suggest any modification.

1. Hearty and formal recognition of the essential and vital truths of Christianity, as the common basis of all intimate fellowship, such as the plenary inspiration of Scripture, the Divinity of our Lord Jesus Christ, His vicarious Atonement, Justification by faith, the personality and indwelling of the Spirit, the resurrection of the dead, and future judgment.

2. Voluntary avoidance and suppression of all sectarian controversy whether with tongue or pen. If, in addition to this, there could be an interchange of pulpits, and the barriers which fence off the Lord's table could be broken down, so that there might be a recognition of all true preachers, and a fellowship of all true believers in the breaking of bread, some of the most conspicuous hindrances to practical and visible unity would be removed.

3. Devotional conferences and meetings for fellowship might be most helpfully multiplied. In Britain the external barriers to unity are very exclusive. The Anglican Church is an establishment, and the non-conformists are not only ecclesiastically but socially under the ban. The assumptions of Anglican episcopacy seem to many the more monstrous, because bolstered up by governmental patronage. And yet it is remarkable that the most conspicuous and effective unifying forces for bringing disciples into line are found in Britain. The annual Keswick conference takes for its motto, " All one in Christ Jesus; " and, altho that movement originated with, and is still mainly supported by, Anglicans, it is for all practical purposes one

body of evangelical believers. Presbyterians, like Dr. Elder Cumming and the late Mr. McGregor, Methodists like Gregory Mantle and Charles Inwood, Episcopalians, like Webb-Peploe and Evan H. Hopkins, Baptists, like F. B. Meyer—all are equally at home, there, and teach with equal acceptance and authority. Here is a union of believers where charity does not degenerate into laxity. Besides Episcopalians, Presbyterians, Methodists, Baptists, Congregationalists, Quakers, there are a few nondescripts; it might be difficult to define just Robert Wilson's or J. Hudson Taylor's denominational position—so far do they seem above all these narrow landmarks. But, because they so conspicuously exhibit the fruits of the Spirit, they are leaders in the Keswick movement. But not *one teacher,* connected with this broad fellowship of disciples, is an unsound man in any of the great essentials to which we have already adverted.

4. In no one respect is church unity so desirable as in *mission fields and mission work.* The foes of Christ, whatever their differences, stand together in their opposition to the Christian faith. There is no break in their ranks. They mass their forces to break down and defeat all efforts at a world's evangelization and redemption. What a lamentable blunder, if not a crime, that Christian disciples should show a divided front, and often a dissentient spirit, even in missionary operations!

This subject has never as yet been considered as it ought to be. After the Hawaiian islands had been wonderfully brought into the fellowship of Christian peoples, a new denomination entered the islands in October, 1862—over forty-three years after the brig Thaddeus sailed from Boston with the memorable seventeen representatives of the American board, and after the Presbyterians and Congregationalists of America had been for nearly half a century at work in evangelizing and Christianizing this people—

Bishop Staley, with his two presbyters arriving as representatives of an English mission to be known as the " Reformed Catholic." That movement has ever been regarded by unprejudiced observers as one of the most unseemly and intrusive violations of denominational comity in the history of missions. One has only to read Dr. Anderson's temperate treatment of the matter in his book on " The Hawaiian Islands," to see the exact position of affairs.

Here was a land, just lifted by Christian effort out of the slough of a barbarous paganism, and taking its place,—the first example in the history of modern missions—as a newly converted nation in the family of Christian peoples. The whole unevangelized world, with its thousand millions of unsaved souls, was waiting for the Gospel. Was there not room enough for missionary effort without introducing a rival sect into a peaceful Christian community? The members of this mission came, not to introduce Christianity to ignorant and barbarous savages, but to inoculate denominational controversy upon a tree of God's own planting. They came to a people, taught Christianity in its simplest evangelical faith and forms, to inaugurate a new style of worship, encumbered with the conventionalities of the High Church. The Protestant clergy of Honolulu—embracing missionaries and others—extended a fraternal hand, and took early opportunity to invite to a monthly union meeting for prayer, one of the newly arrived brethren, who, after consulting his bishop, made a reply which was like an apple of discord thrown into the circle of believers:

" He (the bishop) strengthened my own opinion, viz: that it would be inconsistent in a clergyman of our church to attend a prayer meeting in a place of worship belonging to a denomination of Christians who do not regard episcopacy of divine appointment."

Here was the keynote of the new mission: a refusal to

meet Christian brethren; even in a union prayer meeting, and this in face of a recently converted heathen people, suggesting to them irreconcilable differences between believers, on points not affecting salvation. Moreover, as these newcomers held to baptismal regeneration, they thought it right, if not duty, to baptize infants wherever they could, without regard to existing relations of the parents to the Protestant churches or missionary pastors. Confirmation, by a bishop of the Holy Catholic Church, was taught as necessary for all true believers, and as the only proper qualification for " the blessed sacrament of the altar."

The story of this new mission is a sad story and a stain on the history of modern missions. It introduced an element both of division and dissension never before known, and put a stumbling block before newly converted natives. The whole mission was a breach of the courtesy due from one Christian body to another, and above all, in the mission field. Here was, after over forty years of battle with paganism, an hour of conquest; and just as those to whom the victory belonged were taking measures to secure the spoils of battle for the Lord of the whole Church, a small body of professed allies enter the field, carrying a new banner, and, declining practical fellowship with those whose self-sacrifice has won the day, undertake to rally the converts under their standard! When a like movement began, whose object was to send a bishop and six presbyters to that crown of the London Missionary Society, Madagascar, it led to a great remonstrance in London, over which the Earl of Shaftesbury presided, uttering words which deserve to be pondered by every true disciple.*

We have no disposition to override the conscientious scruples of brethren, however inexplicable they may be to

* See Anderson's Hawaiian Islands, 358-9.

us. We assert for ourselves and accede to others fullest liberty to follow conviction. But the field is world-wide, and Christian unity should exhibit itself in Christian courtesy and comity. Where any body of disciples are already successfully at work, let other Christian bodies not intrude, unless there is room and need for other workers without interference or overlapping. To meddle with the splendid work of the United Presbyterians in the Valley of the Nile, the Baptists in the Karen country, the Congregationalists in Turkey, the Episcopalians in Tinnevelly, would be alike needless and harmful. And in entering new fields like Cuba and the Philippines, the Sudan and the Upper Kongo basin, can there not be amicable conference beforehand so as to divide up the territory and work side by side, instead of setting up rival missions in the same narrow district?

While there is much ardent talk about unity here is a practical way of living out Christian charity and of exemplifying and exhibiting love's holy law. And if we may venture an individual opinion, one such example of the actual unity of love is worth far more for God's glory and man's good than a Church, organically one, whose unity is at the price of a concession of one fundamental truth, or is the cloak to cover internal alienation and strife. So far as we hold the same vital truth we are one; so far as we work together without friction, our unity reaches its highest practical result.

CHAPTER XVI

HUMAN progress is neither rapid nor regular, potent nor permanent for good, when it does not, in some way, educate and elevate *the youth of the race*. The salt that heals the waters must be cast in the springs where the rills rise and whence the rivers flow.

Childhood is a mirror, catching and reflecting the images of whatever surrounds it—a reflector as sensitive to impression and injury as the metallic mirrors of the ancients. It would be as irrational carelessly to spray water, or, worse still, a corrosive acid, on a polished steel surface, expecting to efface the rust which no scouring will remove, as to expose childhood to needless contact with evil, and expect to find no lasting injury left upon the delicate susceptible nature. Youth is the time for making deep and wholesome impressions, as well as for guarding character from injury! What a golden age of opportunity for teaching—for engrafting lessons from that best of books, that unique *child's* book—the Bible! The German proverb quaintly says that " what *Johnnie* does not learn, *John* never learns." The mind of youth " receives like wax, but retains like marble."

The youth of a country should be made familiar with the highest, noblest ideals, to inspire what Schopenhauer would call *the will to live*, and what Nietzsche would call *the will to be a power*. To will to live unto God, and to be a power for God and good, is the mainspring of a great, grand, heroic soul. We can excuse an excess of zeal and jealousy for God, but not vicious excesses or even apathy toward goodness. Better a violent torrent than a stagnant pool, for the torrent, once controlled, is made a force for good, but a pool is always and only a breeder of poisonous malaria. David Brainerd was expelled from college for telling a tutor that he had no more grace than the chair he sat in, but the impetuous Brainerd became one of the saintliest missionary heroes of his country. It is obvious that, without some work of God, especially among the young, we should not have had the existing state of intelligence and earnestness in any departments of service to God.

A recent writer* says: " With reluctance and sorrow it must be confessed that the majority of Oxford and Cambridge undergraduates are without, or profess to be without, any religious beliefs at all. There are, of course, many exceptions. Exceptions, however, they remain; certainly the greater number are Gallios so far as the Church is concerned." Do these two facts— that modern university life is so largely tinctured with German rationalism, and that so many skeptics and agnostics are issuing from university halls—stand related as cause and effect? If so, then the influence of German thought on our educational life is deplorable. But, bless God, there have been educators that have been men of faith, and they have raised up children of faith, a faith larger, more intelligent, and more manly than that which was before it. The Scudders, Dwights, Hodges, Uphams, Waylands, Judsons, Osgoods, Stevensons, Spurgeons, Cairns, Flints, Wattses, Storrs, Christliebs, Candlishes, Bernards, Liddons, have not been headmasters of schools of sickly skepticism. " We correctly test the soundness of a system of thought by its unforced tendencies in the

* The *Nineteenth Century*, October, 1895, "The Religion of Undergraduates."

minds of studious young men, for a teacher is better known by the beliefs and lives of his pupils than by the manner of man that he himself seems to be. A tree is known by its fruits."

Family life also, before the public-school and college touch the young man or woman, must look well to the child-life and its development. It has been well said that the feeling with which one administers punishment will generally excite in the child a corresponding experience. If the parent be moved by anger, anger will be excited; if, by affection and sorrow, the child will respond in sorrowful feelings; if by moral convictions, the child's conscience will answer back again. In the household, first impressions for good or evil are received. The absence of discipline is criminal, for it implies an unformed character; but the spirit in which discipline is admonished may go far to determine the benefit resulting.

And woe be to the *church* that has no warm bosom for the young! The statistics of conversion have frequently been gathered, and these are the approximate results as taken from one careful report. Out of a thousand Christian people, the following is the classification as to the age at which they were converted:

20 years and under......	695
Over 20 and up to 30...	208
Over 30 and up to 40...	69
Over 40 and up to 50...	19
Over 50 and up to 60...	6
Over 60 and up to 70...	2
Over 70 and up to 75...	1

These figures show that only 305 of the 1,000 were converted after the age of 20; only 97 after the age of 30; only 28 after the age of 40; only 9 after the age of 50, and only 3 after the age of 60. According to this writer's knowledge, the earliest age at which conversion occurred was four years, as was the case with a minister well known over all the world, and the most advanced age at which conversion took place was 75, and the longest time spent in the Christian life was 80 years. The average age at conversion is 19 1-2 in this list of a thousand. What an argument against procrastination and in favor of remembering the Creator in the days of youth.

In view of such facts and considerations, it is quite inconceivable that God could be controlling the stupendous movements of modern history, and yet no arousing and arising of the young men and women of Christian lands be included in His plan.

What do we find? A development and organization of the forces of youth, never before known or imagined in history. It seems as tho God, foreseeing the last great Armageddon at hand, had brought forward His reserves —the immense battalion of young men and women, never before massed on the battlefield of the ages! And this amazing development has mostly been the product of the last fifty years.

Some of the facts, however familiar, demand a rehearsal as a part of this striking history.

We begin with the *Young Men's Christian Association,* whose records are fresh in mind from the recent Jubilee celebration in 1894. Sir George Williams, its founder and father, still lives, and tells the simple story of its humble beginning. A little more than fifty years ago, he, a young man of about twenty-one, spoke to another young man about his soul; this conversation led to other like approaches; then to a meeting for mutual edification, Bible study, and united prayer; then to an organization of young men for these purposes in what is now the great mercantile house of Hitchcock, Williams & Co., in London; then to similar organization in neighboring mercantile houses, and finally to a meeting of their representatives, and the formation of a Y. M. C. A. for the city of London. A thought so manifestly of God could not be hid or confined within narrow bounds. It proved contagious—it spread across the sea, it became the seed thought of such associations over all the English-speaking world; it reached out to the continent of Europe; it sent out its branches round the globe, until now the aggregate membership of the Y. M. C. A. is numbered by millions, and there is not a prominent land or nation, Christian or heathen, which has not a representative organization of young men belonging to the world-wide fellowship. Its conventions have passed city, state, and national limits, and have become international and cosmopolitan.

Here is an astounding modern development. Never before had young men been thus brought to the front, united in Bible study and Christian work, magnifying the essentials of Christian faith, fraternizing in forgetfulness of lesser divergencies, and aiming specifically at the reclamation of young men.

To this organization may be directly traced the origin of the Young Women's Christian Association, the United States Christian Commission, so active in the late war for American unity, and especially that college association work which has already given us the Student Volunteer Missionary Union, and started the new crusade in missions. All this and more within the half century! Well may we exclaim, What hath God wrought!

This Student Volunteer movement, which, beginning at Cambridge in 1885 and at Mt. Hermon, Mass., in 1886, is now but about fifteen years old, has enrolled probably nearly 10,000 young men and women in its ranks from the beginning until now, and has sent nearly one-tenth of its recruits to the field. In 1897, the membership in Great Britain had reached about 1,400 and between 300 and 400 were already engaged in mission work.

A memorial from this body of students was then before the missionary secretaries and the ministers of Christ in Britain, praying them to unite in supplication to God that the lack of gifts might not be suffered to hinder their going forth to the field! Surely this was a new development, when young men and women, offering for missionary service, entreated the church not to embarrass their work for the lost race of man by withholding money from the treasuries of God.

Rapid as has been the spread of the Y. M. C. A. the *Young People's Society of Christian Endeavor* outruns it. This latest form of the great organizations of youth outstrips all competitors in the race and encircles the world.

Let Rev. F. E. Clark, D. D., the President of the United Society, tell his own story of the origin of this movement, now twenty years old.

In the winter of 1880-81 a revival spirit visited the Williston Church, of Portland, Maine, and many young people gave their hearts to God. The pastor and older church members, naturally anxious concerning these young disciples, felt that great wisdom and care were necessary to keep them true to the Savior during the first critical years of their discipleship. The problem weighed heavily upon their minds, for they felt that neither the Sunday School, nor the church prayer-meeting, nor the young people's prayer-meeting. tho all well-sustained, admirable in their way, were sufficient to hold and mold the Christian character of these young converts. There was a gap between conversion and church membership to be filled, and all these young souls were to be *trained and set at work.* How should these things be done? These were the pressing problems. After much prayer and thought. the pastor invited the recent converts and young church members to his house, February 2, 1881, and after an hour of social intercourse. presented a constitution, previously drawn up, of the "Williston Young People's Society of Christian Endeavor." This is essentially the same as that adopted by the great majority of Societies of Christian Endeavor at the present day.

Some three years later, at the request of one of the national conventions, with the aid of Rev. S. W. Adriance, the originator revised the constitution and framed the by-laws, adding various committees as they now appear in the "Model Constitution." But the *essential* features of the work were in the first constitution: the definition of the object, the two classes of members, the "prayer-meeting pledge" (the most important part of the constitution), the consecration or experience meeting, the roll-call, the provision for dropping members, and the three main committees, are provisions which are all found in the first constitution.

Thus the Society of Christian Endeavor, born of a revival, was the outcome of a real, felt necessity of training and guiding aright the young Christians who might otherwise stray away. It was a mere experiment, in the first place, and little credit is due to the originator, except for an effort to train his own young people in the Christian life, an effort always made by every true pastor. To his delight, and somewhat also to his surprise, nearly all the young people who assembled at his house, on the 2d of February, signed the constitution containing the stringent prayer-meeting clause, and *they lived up to it.* The young people's meeting took a fresh start; the spiritual life of the members was intensified; their activities were very greatly enlarged; and, so far as they were concerned, the problem of leading them to confess Christ with their lips, of setting them at work and keeping them at work, seemed to be solved. When that pastor also found that in many other churches the same efforts accomplished the same results, he began to feel that the hand of the Lord was in it.

The first knowledge of this experiment given to the world was contained in an article published in the *Congregationalist,* of Boston, in August, 1881, entitled " How One Church Cares for its Young People." This article, and others which followed it, at once brought letters from pastors and Christian workers in all parts of the country. First they came singly, then in pairs, and then in scores, almost every day, and they have kept coming, in constantly increasing numbers, ever since. One of the first pastors to introduce this system of Christian nurture among his young people was Rev. C. A. Dickinson, then pastor of the Second Parish Church of Portland, and no small share of the success of the movement has been due ever to his wisdom and counsel. The first society in Massachusetts was established in Newburyport, Mass., by Rev. C. P. Mills, in the same year that the movement originated. He has also ever since been one of the staunch friends of the cause; while another gentleman, who soon threw himself into the movement with characteristic energy, was Rev. James L. Hill, then of Lynn. The first President of the United Society, Mr. W. J. Van Patten, of Burlington, Vt., was one of the first to recognize the potency of the movement. The first man who signed the constitution, at his pastor's house, on that winter evening in 1881, was Mr. W. H. Pennell, teacher in the Williston Sunday-school of a large class of young men. He took this step, perhaps, as much to help his boys as for any other reason. The national convention honored his early devotion to the work by choosing him for three successive years its President.

So far as careful search reveals, the distinctive features of the Christian Endeavor Movement, the strict prayer-meeting pledge, the consecration meeting, the roll-call, the variety of committee work, and the duties of these committees, are characteristic of this organization alone.

Thus, at first, the Society of Christian Endeavor grew apparently as it were by chance. Wherever one of the winged seeds of information was wafted, it usually " struck " and took root, and a little Christian Endeavor plant was the result; or, as some one wittily expressed it, " The Society was contagious, like the measles; if one church had it, the church next to it was pretty sure to catch it also."

For some years little was done in a systematic or organized way to establish societies. One of the first developments of the new work was naturally in the line of annual conventions. Those interested were not content to work out the problem for themselves, they must come together and tell each other what great things the Lord had done for them. The first of these conferences was held June 2d, 1882, in the Williston Church, Portland, Maine. But six societies were recorded then. In these were 481 members, the Williston Society leading off with 168.

The Second Annual Conference was held in Portland, June 7, 1883. A large growth over the preceding year was noted, tho statistics were obtained from only fifty-three societies with 2,630 members. Of these fifty-three societies the report says five were organized in 1881, twenty-one in 1882, and twenty-seven in the first five months of 1883, showing what an impetus to the work was given by the little convention of the year before. Seventeen of these societies were found in Maine, eleven in Massachusetts, forty-one in all New England; while of the other twelve, five were in New York, and the rest scattered throughout the West, a very large one being found in Oakland, Cal. After this convention the society grew rapidly and steadily, but did not call another national convention until October 22, 1884, when it convened in Lowell. This was a two days' session. and a large, enthusiastic meeting.

By the time the national convention of 1885 met, July 9th and 10th, at Ocean Park, Maine, the society had grown to embrace 253 similar societies, with 14,892 members in all parts of the country. They had begun to be reported in foreign lands also, even in Foochow, Honolulu, and other mission fields. From this convention the work received a marvellous impulse, and everywhere the churches began to establish societies. In 1887, at the Saratoga convention, Dr. Clark was chosen President of the United Society, and editor of Christian Endeavor literature; he, in the following autumn, resigning the pastorate of Phillips Church, Boston, to accept the position.

Unions existed, by the year 1888, in nearly all the States of the Union, and local unions in hundreds of places; and under the blessing of God, the one society of 1881 has grown to the myriads of the present time, with their hundreds of thousands of members in America, and many added thousands in Great Britain and all missionary lands.

In his letter of acceptance the President of the United Society formulated certain principles which he presented to the societies as conditions on which he accepted their call. These principles, adopted by many influential State conventions and local unions, may fairly be considered the platform on which the society stands, and are therefore here embodied:

PLATFORM OF PRINCIPLES.

"1st. The Society of Christian Endeavor is not, and is not to be, an organization independent of the church. It is the CHURCH at work for and with the young, and the young people at work for and with the CHURCH. In all that we do and say let us bear this in mind, and seek for the fullest cooperation of pastors and church officers and members in carrying on our work. The Society of Christian Endeavor can always afford to wait rather than force itself upon an unwilling church.

"2nd. Since the societies exist in every evangelical denomination, the basis of the union of the societies is one of common loyalty to Christ, common methods of service for Him, and mutual Christian affection, rather than a doctrinal and ecclesiastical basis. In such a union all evangelical Christians can unite without repudiating or being disloyal to any denominational custom or tenet.

" 3d. The purely RELIGIOUS features of the organization shall always be PARAMOUNT. The Society of Christian Endeavor centers about the prayer-meeting. The strict 'prayer-meeting pledge,' honestly interpreted, as experience has proved, is essential to the CONTINUED success of a Society of Christian Endeavor.

" 4th. The Society of Christian Endeavor sympathizes with temperance and all true moral reforms, with wise philanthropic measures, and especially with missions at home and abroad; yet it is not to be used as a convenience by any organization to further other ends than its own.

" 5th. The finances of the Society shall be managed economically, in acordance with the past policy of the Board of Trustees, and the raising of funds to support a large number of paid agents or Christian Endeavor missionaries, either in connection with the United Society or the State Unions, is not contemplated. In winning our way, we can best depend in the future, as in the past, upon the abundant dissemination of our literature, and on the voluntary and freely given labors of our friends, rather than upon the paid services of local agents.

" The expenses of the central office will be largely for the publication of literature and for the expenses of our General Secretary in the field. In raising very large sums, and employing many agents for whose work the United Society will be responsible, and yet which it cannot to any great extent control, we shall run the risk of losing the sympathy of the churches. There is little danger that the society will not grow with sufficient rapidity, if every member does his best to make known our principles. Let it be our chief concern that our growth shall be as strong and substantial as it is rapid. In all State and local work the society can best rely upon the zeal and generosity of its friends, hundreds of whom, both laymen and ministers, are willing freely to lend their aid to our cause.

" 6th. The State and local unions and the individual societies and members will heartily uphold the United Society, its officers and trustees, with their sympathies and prayers (and their material support so far as necessary), and hampering and destructive criticism of well-meant efforts are not deemed accordant with Christian Endeavor principles."

That this historic review should bring the story of this remarkable movement down to present date, we add a few brief items.

In 1884, the first *Junior* Endeavor Society was formed. In 1888, Dr. Clark's journey to England greatly stimulated the progress of Christian Endeavor there. "Christian Endeavor Day," the society's anniversary, first became a fixture during this year. In 1892, the convention was held in New York City, and attended by 35,000, with a large representation from foreign lands, Hindus, Chinese, and native Africans being among the speakers. Within a few weeks after this convention, Dr. Clark, with his wife and son, set out on a round-the-world journey, both to organize the work, and to study the conditions to which the Endeavor Society must adapt itself, and its capacity and adaptability to them. This journey covered nearly 40,000 miles. Over 350 addresses were made by Dr. and Mrs. Clark before aggregate audiences of 100,000. Twelve nations were visited, and, through interpreters, addresses were made in upwards of twenty different tongues. This journey was conspicuous, especially for its incidental connection with the foreign mission interest, which it naturally served to create or quicken. It emphasized fellowship among the nations, and the brotherhood of the race in sin, need, and redemption, and ever since then the Christian Endeavor Society has been linked with the world-field in sympathy, prayer, and giving. At Boston, in 1895, 56,000 delegates registered, and about 650,000 attended the 825 different meetings of the convention. Thirteen different countries or peoples of the world, from England to Japan, and Alaska to Africa, were represented

and a *World's* Christian Endeavor Union formed, and a
" prayer chain " now merged into the " quiet hour."

On Jan. 1, 1900, the following is the official enrollment,
worth preserving and comparing with the records of nineteen years before:

The total number of societies is 48,305, of which 7,172
are in foreign lands, and a total membership of 2,800,000.

Surely God has some great mission for this vast host of
united young men and women. If we might venture to
suggest to this great army of Christian Endeavorers seven
grand things to be kept in the very foreground as secrets
of success, we should unhesitatingly say:

1. First of all, *Set the Lord always before you.* All life
of holiness or power absolutely depends on the supremacy
of God in the character and conduct—a real elevation of
Him to the first place. Matt. vi, 33. All else is idolatry.

2. *Beware of pride of numbers.* Power is not dependent on multitude or even organization. God often works
mightily by the few, who do not forget individual duty and
responsibility, and depend on the Holy Spirit.

3. *Guard the habit of closet prayer.* Matt. vi, 6.
Nothing else so determines the true character as the vision
of God in the secret place (Numbers vii, 89) and in His
Word.

4. *Regard yourselves as stewards of God,* in trust with
time, talents, money, and opportunity. Use all for him.
Aim at a Scriptural standard of giving.   2 Cor. viii, 9.

5. *Abide in your calling with God.* Every honest and
honorable work is a divine calling, a sphere of Christian
Endeavor. Take God as your partner. 1 Cor. vii, 20, 24.

6. *Lose your own will in the will of God.* Ps. xl, 8.
This is the soul of all true Christian Endeavor. Be content to be simply His instruments.

7. *Serve your own generation* by the will of God. Acts

xiii, 36.   Wherever you are, be a missionary, and set before you to do your utmost to bring the Gospel into contact with every human soul.

CHAPTER XVII

WORLD-WIDE UPRISING OF CHRISTIAN STUDENTS

WE have already noticed the rapidity of movement, noticeable in modern civilization, which invades the realm of mind as well as of matter. Every enterprise seems to go on wheels, or if steam or electricity were harnessed to it. There is something abnormal in the tremendous pace at which men are moving. Haste is waste. Hurry implies worry. There is risk of losing deliberation; of doing things precipitately, and superficially; the calm of God can not be known in the excitement inseparable from such driving energy. A swift-sailing steamer, plowing through the waves at twenty-five knots an hour, creates a commotion in air and sea as it goes—it *makes* a storm if it *meets* none.

One modern development has outrun almost any other, and yet so real has been its progress, that we marvel whether its apparent sagacity and success are not due to a special divine supervision, and its momentum, to Him to whom one day is as a thousand years. We refer to the remarkable onward and upward movement of the Christian young men of our higher educational institutions, the advance of which has been so rapid and yet so regular, so swift and yet so sure, so sudden and yet so permanent; and, while under the guidance of the young, so exhibiting the wisdom associated with age and experience, that we are compelled to look upon it as a *spiritual* movement—a marshaling of human forces under divine generalship; and to look behind it to the Divine force that alone can account for much that is taking place before our eyes.

In this uprising of Christian students several distinct stages are noticeable: First of all, the introduction of the Young Men's Christian Association into the universities and colleges of Christian lands; then the organization of these associations into a national and international alliance; then the extension of such associations in the higher educational centers of foreign and heathen lands. Simultaneously with these came the era of conventions, summer schools, etc., bringing these young men together, and cementing the bonds of personal fellowship. Then The Student Volunteer Movement, appearing in the Cambridge Band of 1885 and the Mt. Hermon Band of 1886, and exerting immense influence in the direction of the foreign field. Then followed the grand scheme of coöperation —whereby the Christian students in mission countries are to act as a home missionary contingent, for the uplifting of their own countrymen, under the lead, or with the help, of Christian students from America and Europe.* And now comes the last of these great strides—the " World's Student Christian Federation." †

As the first Y. M. C. A. was organized in 1844, this whole history reaches over only about a half century; and it may be doubted whether another movement so varied, vast, far reaching, and important, has marked any half-century of history before.

To look carefully at the latest feature of this great enterprise—the federating of the young men of the world into one great organization, and marshaling them under the Banner of the Cross, will be to survey the whole movement from its loftiest summit.

In August, 1895, on the shores of Lake Wettern,

---

* " New Program of Missions."
† " Strategic Points in the World's Conquest."

and within the old Swedish Castle of Vadstena, a gathering of students was held, which has well been compared
to that famous Haystack prayer meeting on Williams' College Hill, near the beginning of the century, which was
the starting point of organized missionary work on this
side of the sea.

This Scandinavian Congress met to consider the expediency of uniting the national intercollegiate movements
of the whole world in one great federation, for three great
ends: first, to associate Christian students of all lands more
closely; second, to enable them more deeply to impress national as well as social and university life; and third, to
influence fellow students to take up definite mission work
at home and abroad.

At this conference the five great intercollegiate organizations had their representatives: The American Intercollegiate Y. M. C. A.; the British College Christian
Union; the German Christian Students' Alliance; the
Scandinavian University Christian Movement; and the
Student Christian Movement in Mission Lands. After
days of prayer and holy conference, the constitution was
unanimously adopted, by which the World's Student
Christian Federation came to be a historic fact. The
momentous importance attached to this new step may be
inferred from the fact that no other student convention
ever had been held in which delegates from all the great
Protestant powers were present, and of this the impressive
grouping of the respective flags of all these nations was the
outward symbol and expression.

The name adopted is itself a history. It tells of a *student*
movement, distinctly *Christian* and *world-embracing* in
membership and aim. It is a *federation* rather than a
union, each previously existing organization keeping in
the federal bond its own individual and independent character. The great comprehensive object is to combine all

the available forces of the universities and colleges of the world in the many-sided work of winning educated young men for Christ, building them up in Him, and sending them out as workers for Him.

The Federation being formed, other organizations joined it: The Intercollegiate Y. M. C. A. of India and Ceylon; the Australian Student Christian Union; the Students' Christian Association of South Africa; the College Y. M. C. A. of China, the Student Y. M. C. A. Union of Japan, etc.

Certain ends must be directly promoted, such as:

1. The full investigation of the exact moral and religious status of students in every part of the world.

2. The gradual and rapid improvement and development of all that is best in young manhood.

3. The introduction into new and different fields, of organized Christian activity under favorable conditions.

4. The promotion of a living bond of sympathy among all educated Christian young men.

5. The cultivation of a spirit of united prayer and systematic Bible study.

6. The study and development of that important science of comparative humanity—or young manhood in various conditions.

7. The penetration and permeation of college life with an evangelical and missionary spirit.

Gladstone remarked that in the middle ages the universities " established a telegraph for the mind, and all the elements of intellectual culture scattered throughout Europe were brought by them into near communion. They established a great brotherhood of the understanding." This federation establishes " a telegraph in things spiritual —a great student brotherhood in Jesus Christ."

No one can watch this work without feeling God to be

behind it, and rejoicing in its unifying power. Not only does it both simplify and unify methods of work among students, but brings Christian young men everywhere to recognize that oneness in Christ Jesus which must ever exist between true disciples, and will be seen and felt whenever the accidents of external separation and division are no longer allowed to have prominence. National and denominational barriers will be forgotten, as young men who belong to Christ in different lands and churches come together, federated into unity, to magnify only essentials and remand nonessentials to their true place. True Christians need only to know each other to love each other; and the devil triumphs whenever by any of his devices he can keep them from mutual and sympathetic contact. Already so far as relates to Christian educated young men, there is " no more sea; " the barriers of language do not divide, and the national names are forgotten in the Christian name. Christ is in these days anew slaying the old enmity by his cross, and of Himself making one new man, not of twain only, but of a multitude of hitherto alienated and estranged bodies.

The student's federation already blends into organized unity students belonging to over seventy branches of Christ's church, thus approaching the fulfillment of our Lord's prayer, " that they all may be one, that the world may believe that thou hast sent me? " This federation is destined perhaps to be a grand means of promoting world-wide faith in the messiahship of the Lord Jesus.

The ultimate object which the Lord has in view in this unifying process is thus a world's evangelization. Never since apostolic days have the duty, privilege, possibility, and feasibility of actually carrying to the whole world the message of salvation within the lifetime of one generation, been obvious to so many disciples. The work of evangelization is a campaign, and the universities and colleges are the strategic points which must be seized and held as commanding the field, and determining the "line of communication."

The young men in our educational institutions are to be, and that very soon, the leaders of the nations. Our schools are the cradles of the coming princes, and whether they are to rule for God or for Satan, must soon be determined. If the Japanese maxim, telegraphed to the Northfield Conference of young men in the summer of 1899, "MAKE JESUS KING!" becomes the motto of the leading educational centers of the world, with what unexampled rapidity will the earth be encompassed with the network of missions, and every creature reached with the good news!

All these movements are the visible working of an invisible power. What has taken place between the organization of young men for Christian service in 1844, and the Federation of Christian Students fifty years later, shows a supernatural hand. When less than twenty-five years ago the American Intercollegiate Y. M. C. A. was inaugurated, less than thirty college associations were to be found in the United States and Canada. Twenty-three years later, in about six hundred and forty higher educational institutions within the same territory, these Christian associations are rooted, and embrace over thirty-three thousand students and professors, and nearly as many students have been led to Christ by this means; so that instead of one in three, there are about one-half of the students confessing Christ. Twelve thousand students are enrolled in the voluntary Bible classes of these associations, having multiplied fourfold in ten years. About five thousand young men have been led into the ministry; a still larger number having given their lives to foreign missions, over sixteen hundred of whom are on the foreign field. Dr. Roswell D. Hitchcock had already recognized, before his death some years since, that the great fact in the religious life of the college was the "omnipresence," and he felt half inclined to add, the "omnipotence," of the Intercollegiate Y. M. C. A.

Only six or seven years ago the *British* College Christian Union began its real work. At first seventeen universities and colleges were united in it. Three or four years later it embraced one hundred other organizations, and every considerable institution in the United Kingdom of Great Britain and Ireland was identified with it. Not only has there been this rapid increase in quantity, but the quality of the work done has been correspondingly enriched. Bible circles, private Bible study, aggressive work among students at the outset of their college career, personal and faithful dealing with the young men, and the actual winning of multitudes to Christ—these are among the marked signs of genuineness in the activity, and spirituality in the methods employed.

There has been a missionary spirit at work—the infallible token of God's Spirit. The Student Foreign Missionary Union has become the mother of the Student Volunteer Missionary Union. When this latter organization was formed, there were about three hundred expectant missionaries among the British college students; in 1897 that number had been multiplied over fourfold, and out of these twelve hundred over one-fourth were already in the foreign field. The Student Missionary Convention, held in Liverpool in January 1896, was unsurpassed in spiritual power by any missionary meeting of our century. A thousand young men and women met for the purpose of organized effort to evangelize the world in their generation, and the meeting was presided over and conducted wholly by young men. Cambridge and Oxford—the very *ganglia* of the educational system and life of the British Empire—are now embraced in this·missionary uprising, as well as the great university centers of Scotland, Wales, and Ireland, and thus the molds of the future leaders of the Church and State are becoming God's own matrices of character.

Germany has exercised a mighty and dangerous influence on modern religious thinking. The German mind is masculine, original and profound and persistent in research, but secular and sceptical in tendency, often not only rationalistic but materialistic. Germany has been the seedsower of religious, as France has been of scientific, scepticism. What a triumph for Christ, when the German students form a Christian alliance, form Bible circles, seek to promote personal purity and evangelical faith among young men, and do in a large and pervasive way among students at large, what the lamented Christlieb did at Bonn—infuse the spirit of simple faith. The Liverpool Convention sent home delegates, anointed with spiritual power and thoroughly convinced of the danger and deadness of mere religious formalism, to kindle God's fires on the altars of Germany, and sow the seeds of missionary consecration. A year or two later there were over thirty student volunteers in German institutions, the influence daily spreading. In the twenty-one universities of that great European empire there are over thirty thousand students, with twenty-five hundred instructors, and this university army ranks next to the military force in influence and power. Can we afford to neglect the opportunity of turning this vast host of educators and educated into the defense of the faith which otherwise they may undermine and assault? All great spiritual movements, like all great sceptical influences, are ultimately traceable to these thought-centers; and here at the springs the salt must be cast in if the waters are to be healed.

This movement, which embraced Britain and Germany, has also penetrated Scandinavia. In August, 1895, Norway and Sweden, Denmark and Finland, united in an inter-university organization. The Scandinavian universities rank very high in popular favor, and are open to all classes. They are the higher schools for the masses; and yet their standards are very high, as is shown by the fact that a full medical course consumes a decade of years. These students are physically and intellectually worthy of their Norsemen ancestors, and to turn such strong men into sturdy disciples is worth any amount of effort and sacrifice.

Then there is the student body of papal lands. A population of thirty millions in Italy, with about sixty thousand Protestants; about eighty educational institutions with twenty-five thousand students, and not one Christian organization! Is not this appalling? The first Christian association was formed at Torre Pellice, the historic center of the Waldensian Church that for six centuries has stood out firmly against Romish intrigue and persecution. France, Austria, Hungary, Spain and Portugal, and Belgium are included in the scheme of the Students' Christian Federation, and the one hundred and thirteen thousand young men of the seven papal lands of the Continent are to be saved, if possible, from the drift of scepticism, and agnosticism, and materialism, and sensualism, to which they are terribly exposed.

The earnest spirit of those who are at the head of this world movement, can not be restrained within the bounds of one continent or two. They are reaching out the hand of help to the remoter East. Turkey is not forgotten, where Robert College furnishes so admirable a center of operations. This Christian institution on the shores of the Bosphorus has sent forth three hundred and twenty-five graduates. It has furnished teachers for Bulgaria and Armenia; it has drawn students from fourteen nationalities, and sent many of them back as missionaries to their own people; and it has been happily compared with the noble Syrian College at Beirut, the Duff College at Calcutta, and the earlier days of the Doshisha at Japan.

Greece, with its historic Athens and its thirty-five hundred students is included; Syria, with its sacred sites; Nazareth and Jerusalem are to be Y. M. C. A. centers; and Beirut, whose college has practically created the medical profession in the Levant, and supplied the educated class for the whole territory round about Palestine, and whose printing press to-day sends its unrivaled Arabic Bibles throughout the Arabic-speaking world, with its hundred and fifty million people. Is it of no consequence to bring the young men of these countries into living contact with holy fruits of Christian culture in the Occident, and lead them to a pure faith and a dedicated life?

Look again at the Nile Valley. One theological college, founded by the United Presbyterians at Cairo, has supplied all the ordained native ministers of Egypt. The training college at Asyut has four hundred students, and has educated five times as many, and most of its graduates have become teachers or preachers of the Gospel. So high do these Christian schools stand in even the government's esteem that its own schools have been largely modeled thereby. Here a Y. M. C. A. has been organized. Is not this a true strategic center for the world campaign? The followers of Mohammed think so, as the great University of El Azhar, with its seven thousand students from all parts of the realm, swayed by the green flag of the crescent, sufficiently proves. It has a nine years' course of study, and is, on the whole, the greatest propaganda in the world.

The new century is to reveal Christian work among the students of all lands. Especially will India have a strategic value as a center both of activity and influence. Here meetings have been held by scores by Mr. Mott, the proceedings all in the English tongue, and the tide of spiritual awakening rising steadily to the last. One hundred and twenty educational institutions were represented, and the total number of students registered was seven hundred and fifty-nine, or, including Ceylon, over one thousand. Three hundred and eleven missionaries, representing nearly all the sixty societies at work in India, were in attendance. Seventy-six students accepted Christ as Savior and Lord, in face of terrible obstacles, and one hundred and twenty-seven delegates volunteered for mission-service in India. Five hundred and seventy-seven covenanted to keep the morning watch of Bible study and prayer.

China had its series of conferences, at which over twelve hundred of the educated class of students or teachers were present. All but two of the higher institutions sent delegates. Four hundred and eleven missionaries were present, and thirty-seven missionary societies were represented. The total number of regular delegates at the four conferences,—Chefoo, Peking, Shanghai, and Foochow—reached three thousand, and came from the ends of the empire. The meetings revealed a constantly rising tide of interest and power. Eight hundred pledged to keep the morning watch; over one hundred serious inquirers, seventy-seven volunteers for Christian work, and general tokens of a great spiritual awakening were among the notable signs of God's hand. The number of Y. M. C. A. was multiplied fivefold; steps were taken towards a national organization, and the college Y. M. C. A. of China was formed in November, 1896, and at once admitted to the Federation; and thus the great land—the Gibraltar of the Orient, where the population embraces one-fourth of the whole race of man now living, where the combination of difficulties is the most appallingly formidable, where the possibilities are correspondingly great, the great land of which

Napoleon said, " When China is moved it will change the face of the globe,"—was visited by Mr. Mott, with most cheering tokens of God's presence and power.

We add a comprehensive résumé of the whole work as presented in Mr. Mott's Round the World Tour.

During twenty months 60,000 miles were included, and twenty-two countries, and one hundred and forty-four educational institutions. Twenty-one conferences were held, with fifty-five hundred delegates, of whom thirty-three hundred were representatives of three hundred and eight institutions of learning; seventy students' Christian associations were organized, and many more reorganized or reinvigorated. Five national student Christian movements were promoted, and much other work was done incidental to the creation of a literature of devotion and habits of holy living and praying. Over five hundred young men were led to acceptance of the Savior, including students who had been Buddhists, Brahmans, Confucianists, and Mohammedans, Agnostics, and Sceptics. Some twenty-two hundred pledged themselves to the " morning watch," and about three hundred gave their lives to definite work for Christ. The greatest result of all is one that can not be put on paper, or tabulated in statistics. A great world-wide volume of interest, sympathy, prayer, was created, which, like ocean tides and trade winds, has a strange power of far-reaching communication and influence, and is likely to be a permanent and increasing factor in both the unification of disciples and the evangelization of the world.

CHAPTER XVIII

THE PROBLEM OF CITY EVANGELIZATION

THE familiar phrase, " The Church and the masses," suggests, perhaps, the most perplexing question of the home field : What can be done to get hold of the great bulk of our city population who now attend no church? The late Dr. John Hall quaintly observed that " in Britain the population is divided between churchmen and dissenters ; in America between church-goers and *absenters.*"

Pope, angling for a compliment, after he had published his " Essay on Man," asked Mallet what new things there were in literature, and the reply was, " O, nothing worth notice—only a poor thing called an ' Essay on Man,' made up of shocking poetry and insufferable philosophy." " I wrote it," cried Pope, stung with rage, and Mallet darted out of the room, abashed at his blunder in thus offending its author unawares.

The Church is practically writing an " essay on man " which, it is to be feared, is not very honoring to the Master or His disciples. It is a patent fact that for half a century there has been a constantly widening gulf between the Church and the mass of the people. Candor compels the admission that there has been little systematic effort to gather in the non-church-goers, or even to provide accommodations for them, for not more than one-fifth of our city population attend church, and not more than one-third could find sittings, if they wanted them. Candor likewise compels the concession that the responsibility for church neglect lies largely at the door of Christian disciples. Church buildings are transferred to fashionable localities, and if any work is carried on in the deserted quarters, it is done in mission chapels, which suggest an invidious distinction, and foster a caste spirit. Churches that were once greatly blessed of God in gathering in the people, are even now consolidating and moving "up town," both decreasing the number of church buildings in proportion to the population, and removing from the quarters where the greatest need exists. The fashionable church, with its rich surroundings, large-salaried pastor, costly choir, etc., is not intended for the poor, and they know it, and do not feel at ease, and will not come.

In former days a large part of the ministers in New England had small salaries, and eked out a subsistence by farming. If they were not so learned or eloquent as the ministers of our day, they were linked closely with the people, and the churches were full, and revivals were frequent. Have not our modern churches too much taken on the cast of the religious club, their buildings becoming the resort of those who can afford the luxuries of the club-house? Can we blame the poverty-stricken multitude for having the impression that they are outcasts, in the very nature of things, from these elaborate temples with their elegant garniture and furniture?

There are many more things that might in honesty be added as to the actual and undeniable causes of the present estrangement between the churches and the common folk. The Gospel, the Spirit of God, the love of souls, are just as mighty to-day as ever, and, if these were really depended on, and practically operative, the churches would regain and retain hold on the people.

Our present purpose is to call attention to *three* practical examples of actual success in reaching the common folk— three examples, each of which presents the subject from a different point of view: Thomas Chalmers in Glasgow,

Charles H. Spurgeon in London, and John Wanamaker in Philadelphia.

Chalmers may be called the *parish evangelist*. He is especially worthy of a permanent record, as one of the men who led the way in the practical solution of that great problem of our civilization: " *How to deal with the masses in our great cities.*" At his sixty-fifth year we find this greatest of Scotchmen on fire with all his youthful ardor, in this mission to the masses in Edinburgh, where, as in Ephesus, the gold, silver, and precious stones of the sacred fanes and palaces were in strong contrast to the wood, hay, stubble of the huts and hovels of the poor. With sublime devotion Chalmers at this advanced age, when most men retire from active and arduous toil, entered upon the most difficult experiment of his life, that he might demonstrate by a practical example what can be done for the poor and neglected districts in a great metropolis.

The West Port, in the " old town " of Edinburgh, was the home of a population whose condition may be described by two words, *poverty* and *misery*. He undertook to redeem this heathen district by the Gospel, planting in it schools and a church for the people, and organizing Christian disciples into a band of voluntary visitors. The name " territorial system " was attached to the plan as he worked it, and has passed into history under that sonorous title. In St. John's Parish, Glasgow, he had already proved the power of visitation and organization. Within his parochial limits he found two thousand one hundred and sixty-one families, eight hundred and forty-five of them without any seats in a place of worship. He assigned to each visitor about fifty families. Applications for relief were dealt with systematically, and so carefully, yet thoroughly, that not a case either of scandalous *allowance* or scandalous *neglect* was ever made known against him and his visitors. There was a severe scrutiny to find out the *fact* and the *causes* of poverty, to remove necessary want, and remedy unnecessary want by removing its cause. The bureau of intelligence made imposture and trickery hopeless, especially on a second attempt. And not only was poverty relieved, but at a cost which is amazingly small. While in other parishes of Glasgow it averaged two hundred to every thousand of the population, and in many parishes of England it averaged *a pound for every inhabitant;* in St. John's it was but *thirty pounds for one thousand people.*

It was an illustration of heroism, in these modern times, when a man, past threescore years, whose public career, both with his pen and tongue, had made him everywhere famous, gave up his latter days to elevate the physical, mental, moral and spiritual condition of a squalid population in an obscure part of the modern Athens. His theory was that about four hundred families constitute a manageable town parish, and that for every such territorial district there ought to be a church and a school, as near as may be, free to all. This district in West Port contained about this number of families, which were sub-divided into twenty " proportions," each containing some twenty families.

A careful census, taken by visiting, revealed that, of four hundred and eleven families, forty-five were attached to some Protestant church, seventy were Roman Catholics, and two hundred and ninety-six had no church connection. Out of a gross population of two thousand, one thousand five hundred went to no place of worship, and of four hundred and eleven children of school age, two hundred and ninety were growing up entirely in ignorance. It is a curious fact that these four hundred and eleven families averaged one child each of appropriate age for school, and that of these four hundred and eleven children there were about as many growing up untaught as there were families without church connection. This careful compilation of statistics revealed that the *proportions of ignorance and non-attendance at church correspond almost exactly;* in other words, families that attend a place of worship commonly send children to school, and the reverse.

Another fact unveiled by this effort at city evangelization was that about one-fourth of the inhabitants of this territory were paupers, receiving out-door relief, and one-fourth were habitual, professional beggars, tramps, thieves, and *riffraff.*

Here was a field, indeed, for an experiment as to what the church could do in her mission among the masses. Chalmers was hungry for such an opportunity; it stirred all his Scotch blood. So he set his visitors at work. But he did not himself stand aloof. Down into the "wynds," and alleys, and "closes" of West Port he went; he presided at their meetings, counseled the people sympathetically, identified himself with the whole plan in its formation and execution, while his own contagious enthusiasm and infectious energy gave stimulus to the most faint-hearted. He loved to preach to these people, not less than to the most elegant audiences of the capital, or the elect students of the university. He would mount into a loft to meet a hundred of the poorest as gladly as ascend the pulpit of the most fashionable cathedral church, crowded with the élite of the world's metropolis. And those ragged boys and girls hung on his words with characteristic admiration.

Two years of toil, with the aid of Rev. W. Tasker, enabled Dr. Chalmers to open a new free church in this district; the Lord's Supper was administered, and out of one hundred and thirty-two communicants, one hundred were trophies of the work done by him and his helpers in that obscure district. With a prophetic forecast Chalmers saw in this success the presage of greater possibilities, and a practical solution of the problem of city evangelization, and hence he confessed it was the joy of his life and the answer to many prayers.

The plan pursued by Dr. Chalmers was not at all like the modern evangelistic services—an effort spasmodic, if not sporadic; preaching for a few weeks in some church edifice or public hall or tabernacle, and then passing into some other locality, leaving to others to gather up results and make them permanent. From the most promising beginnings of this sort, how often have we been compelled to mourn that so small harvests have been ultimately gleaned! He organized systematic work that looked to lasting results. The plowman and the sower of seed also bore his sickle, and watched for the signs of harvest. And whenever the germs of a Divine life appeared they were nurtured, cherished, guarded, and converts were added to the church, set at work, kept under fostering care, and not left to scatter, wander at will, or relapse into neglect.

As to his mode of dealing with pauperism, the sagacious Chalmers saw that, while a ministry of love to the poor, sick, helpless was a first necessity, it would be unwise and hurtful to their best interests to encourage them to depend on charity. The church must not be an asylum in which indolence and incompetence and improvidence should take refuge. The poorest must be educated to maintain, rather than to sacrifice, self-respect, and *compelled* to form and maintain habits of self-help, industry, economy, thrift. Instead of clothing the poor with the half-worn garments of the better class, he would have them taught to save money worse than wasted on tobacco, drink, and vicious indulgence, and buy their own garments. And the results of this wise policy were seen in the gradual and rapid improvement in appearance of the attendants at church—rags gave way to respectable raiment, which was not the cast-off clothing of their betters.

Chalmers had no less ambition than to *ameliorate* and *finally abolish* pauperism, and his success in St. John's Parish, Glasgow, had proven that he was master of the situation; and no one can tell what results might have followed but for the Poor Law, enacted in 1845, which, by the admission of a statutory right to public relief, encourages improvidence, weakens family ties among the poor, conduces to a morbid satisfaction with a state of dependence, and thus sows the seed of the very pauperism it professes to relieve and reduce.

Charles H. Spurgeon met with the greatest success of any man of our century in gathering the common people about him and holding them for over forty years. His methods were totally diverse from those of Chalmers. He was too busy with his pen, and too remote in residence from the mass of his adherents, and too frail in bodily health, to do a work of parish visitation, or go himself among the people. Spurgeon's power lay in the preaching of a plain, searching, rousing Gospel message. He was less the teacher than the preacher. Others have excelled him in pulpit exposition and systematic exegesis, as did Adolph Saphir, and as Alexander McLaren does to-day. But few men ever excelled him in the power to preach the Gospel so as to lay hold of mind, heart, conscience, and will. Some attribute his success to his humor, or his mimicry, or his dramatic power, or his simplicity of character; but the real secret was deeper: Spurgeon preached as a man who believed his message and meant to make others believe it; as one who loved Christ and rejoiced in Him, and meant to constrain others to love and rejoice in Him. And all the rest was but accessory to this, his main method. He practised no art but the divine art of earnestness, and his whole soul was on fire with his message. The conspicuous absence of all studied artistic aid was most undeniable.

The Metropolitan Tabernacle building was immense,

but there was no decoration. It was built simply to hold the people and enable everybody to see and hear with comfort, and from four thousand to six thousand assembled there every Lord's Day, morning and evening. There was nothing but congregational singing led by a precentor, and not even a pretense to fine music, no organ or choir, not even modern popular hymns and songs. But the people went and kept going, and they were the common folk —the rich were comparatively the few, and so were the cultivated; the bulk of Spurgeon's congregation was composed of the poor, the unlettered, the humble folk of the great metropolis.

We turn now to John Wanamaker, whom, being still living, it would be indelicate to compliment or praise. Bethany Church in Philadelphia, whoever may have been its pastors, owes mainly to Mr. Wanamaker whatever it is as a church of the people, and we know of no instance so conspicuous in America of success, carried on for over forty years, in reaching the masses of the common people. The secret here is somewhat unlike that of either Chalmers or Spurgeon. The origin of this work was peculiar, and it has stamped the whole history with its likeness. There has never been an essential deviation from the primary and original purpose, which was *to reach people who had no church home.*

At the twentieth anniversary of the organization of Bethany Church, in 1885, Mr. Wanamaker himself told the history of the enterprise, reluctantly because he was necessarily so conspicuous in it. But it was a thrilling story.

On a February afternoon in 1858, he, with Mr. Toland, a missionary of the Sunday-school Union, began a mission-school in a second story back room on Pine street. Driven out of this first room by the rowdies of the neighborhood, they tried again on South street, and at the first session gathered twenty-seven children and two women, besides Mr. Wanamaker and Mr. Toland. To-day in that huge Sunday-school building between two thousand and three thousand children and adults gather every Sunday afternoon, while Mr. Wanamaker's own Bible-class fills the spacious adjoining church. Bethany has a membership of over three thousand, and the people never tire of going there. The Gospel is preached; but there is another secret: the people are loved and sought and made at home. They are taught that the whole of this great institutional church is for them, their home, and that everybody is there made welcome for his own sake, and not for the sake of his money, his learning, his social status, his business influence, his ability to help, or his external surroundings. Here is a model institutional church, and its history and methods are well worthy of study.

For over forty years Bethany Church has demonstrated that the common people, and in great multitudes, can be got hold of and kept hold of, and that success is not spasmodic and uncertain, but permanent and uniform. In February, 1899, the writer, a former pastor, went there to speak at an anniversary of the Bible Union, spending a Sabbath with his former flock. He attended and addressed *nine* meetings, which filled the day from an early hour of the morning until the close of the evening service. It was a day of hard rain, and most church buildings would have been two-thirds empty. Bethany was well filled. There were little children's meetings, and services for all ages and classes. Bible study was the one marked employment and enjoyment. There were fellowship and brotherhood meetings, all bright, cheery, sunny, helpful. Mr. Wanamaker was ubiquitous—he was everybody's friend, cordial and hearty, simple and accessible to all. No one would suppose that he was an ex-postmaster-general and a millionaire, conducting business on a scale almost unparalleled.

He was as thoroughly free from airs or assumptions, as tho he were the common workingman from the carpenter's bench or the shoemaker's shop. Forty years of unique success in his own business and the Lord's business, which he seeks to make practically one, have not made him any less the man of the people, and the humble believer in the Christ. All his genius for organization has been turned into the Lord's work at Bethany. His great Bible class numbers well on to 2,000, and it is divided into centuries of one hundred each, with a centurion at the head, and these into companies of ten, with a titheman at the head. The tithemen keep track of attendance, collect the offerings, and take oversight of the physical and spiritual well-being of the little bands under their care. If there be sickness, the sick are cared for, and if in any one band there is more illness than that band can manage, other bands come to their help. By this simple system of diversion, everybody is kept track of, and feels the influence of oversight. Men, women, and children feel themselves to be somebody because somebody else takes interest in their welfare.

There is scarce a night in the week when something is not going on at Bethany. The people learn to associate church life with everything that is helpful and attractive. The channel is always open to the popular current, and the current flows that way. Prayer meetings are thronged; and so is every other sort of service. And around Bethany gather lay college savings bank, deaconesses' house, bookroom, and whatever encourages frugality, charity, and service. The neighborhood is transformed. Mr. Wanamaker obtained control of blocks of buildings that he might build homes for the people and displace whisky-shops by cheap and neat houses. The church is in the midst of a settlement, where peace and order reign.

Nothing will explain Bethany but Bethany itself. It is not a place or an institution to be photographed or described. It must be seen and heard and felt. There is nothing dry, stale, perfunctory about it—no dead orthodoxy nor cold refrigerating propriety. There is life and love, warmth and motion. And while this great church stands, and is faithful to the truth and the Christ, it can not be said truthfully that the people can not be drawn to places of worship, or kept within the embrace of the Church of God. A kid glove is a non-conductor; but the open hand and the warm heart can be made mighty by God's Spirit to lay hold of the neglected and indifferent, and make them members of Christ's mystical body.

Of late Bethany church-building has undergone extensive repair and enlargement, greatly adding to its fitness for its great mission, and it is now the most complete edifice for church purposes in the world. It richly repays the trouble of a visit, especially on the Lord's Day.

It may be interesting to add a little information about the men and women's guild at Bethany, known as the Superintendent's Bible-Class. We reprint the circular of the guild in the appendix.

CHAPTER XIX

THE best products are of slow growth. Dr. Morgan, of Oberlin, warned a young man, who was rushing into the sacred calling without due time for training, that God takes long years to grow an oak, but, if it be only a squash, a few weeks suffice. Time is needed to think thoroughly and plan wisely; but the restless spirit invades all departments of life, and the modern motto seems to be " push and rush." Even sacred activities are subject to this insane hurry. Sermons must be short, prayer-meetings brief, closet devotion timed by the clock; there is no leisure so much as to eat with moderation.

At this fast pace there can be no proper acquisition and assimilation of knowledge. Cramming takes the place of learning; to pass an examination depends more on memory than on understanding, and implies no lasting impression. True information is in-form-ation, knowledge crystallized into a structure within the mind.

The main hindrances to a true zeal for missions are selfishness and innate hostility to divine things, and these must first be broken down. But true zeal for God is inseparable from knowledge, and knowledge takes time. To learn facts demands pains and patience; but nothing save holiness commands such homage as a thorough mastery of facts, which is the rarest and costliest product in the mental market. When Daniel Webster heard Prof. Silliman talk for an hour about the application of chemistry to agriculture, his great intellect bowed before the scientist,

and, with a child's docility, he said to Mrs. Silliman:
"Were I rich, I would pay your husband $20,000 to come
and sit down by me and teach me, for I know nothing."
This was in 1852, the year of Webster's death, when his
knowledge was ripest.

Various efforts have been made during the last half
century to awaken more zeal for a world's evangelization.
It has been combat with the giants. A *colossal ignorance*
of the whole matter, and a *colossal indifference* largely due
to that—a son of the other giant—have confronted the advocates of missions; and success has been only in proportion as these have been driven from their strongholds.
If, even yet, the average disciple knows so little of the
real condition of the world-wide field, fifty years ago
the ignorance was appalling. With here and there an exception, even intelligent Christians had then so little idea
of the extent, destitution, and degradation of pagan, papal,
and moslem fields, that the rudiments of a missionary education seemed lacking, and many could not even pray intelligently. Ignorance was not so culpable while there
were few facilities for getting information; but cheap,
varied, attractive, and effective means now are at hand,
whereby all may inform themselves as to the exact condition of the world's need and of the Church's work.

Of all the means, used for the stimulation of missionary
zeal, one takes the first rank—*the creation of a rich and
abundant missionary literature.* This is a little world in
itself, and consists mainly of three classes of books and
other printed matter: first, historical and biographical;
second, topical and philosophical; third, descriptive and
pictorial. Beside the statelier volumes are periodical is-
sues, whose name is legion, more evanescent in character,
designed to keep track of the march of the Lord's hosts—
they are the bulletins of the war of the ages. The women's
boards have done great service in supplying missionary

leaflets, brief, telling, cheap, available for gratuitous distribution, and fitted to win their way to even the hasty and careless reader. As to the half-century's aggregate product in the literature of missions, they cover every field from Japan to Alaska, and from Greenland to Patagonia; they span all the centuries from Christ's advent to the present day; they embrace geography, philology, sociology, religious belief and customs, dress, diet, habits of life, art, science, medical work—every variety of topic within the range of the great theme. Of the religious products of the press in the last ten years alone, considered as to quantity, probably *one-fourth* have to do with missions either directly or indirectly, and as to quality the class of books produced would do honor to any author or theme. Many of them are superbly gotten up and illustrated, written by the foremost writers of the day, deserving careful reading and study. Surely, so far as missionary zeal depends on information, there is no apology for ignorance and apathy. As Rev. F. B. Meyer says, " There is no sense in always telegraphing to heaven for God to send a cargo of blessing, unless we are at the wharf to unload the vessel when it comes." There is, nowadays, the guilt of wilful ignorance, if there be no real knowledge of God's work in this world. If all may not go abroad, all may help those who do go, by intelligent sympathy and cooperating prayers. As Godet says, one thing is greater than working miracles, and that is to confer the power of miracle working. And one thing is as great as to be a missionary, and that is to foster the missionary spirit that makes missionaries of others by the contagion of our zeal. This latter is possible to every man and woman, and finds its field anywhere and everywhere where our lot is cast.

One method of stimulating missionary zeal is mainly the outcome of the last ten years, and may be called *the exposition of missions,* borrowing from the French the term associated in our minds with an exhibit of those products of human invention and industry which serve as exponents of progress.

More than ten years ago, under the caption, " An Exposition of Missions," the writer advocated some such exhibit of the history and progress of missionary work in a form which might appeal to the eye, vividly presenting the contrast between the original and present conditions of the various peoples among whom the Gospel has had a fair chance to work. Some such exhibit was urged in connection with the Columbian Exposition, and steps were taken toward it, but stopped short of the goal. Some such seed-thought found lodgment and bore fruit, however, in the Missionary Literature Exhibits at the Student Volunteer Conventions, and across the sea the Church Missionary Society has for years been holding a series of such exhibits on a larger scale and with great success. In halls arranged for such purposes, collections of costumes, implements, models, etc., have been made, illustrative of the daily life of foreign missionaries in various lands, and of the habits and customs of the people among whom they labor, retired or returned missionaries being in charge, who assist by explanations, adding thus a verbal exposition of what is exhibited to the eye. Thus both by eye-gate and ear-gate the city of Mansoul is approached. Such success has crowned this scheme that in Birmingham alone 100,-000 visitors were admitted by ticket.

A similar method of exhibiting facts, arousing zeal, and raising funds for mission work was exemplified in the exhibit in connection with the Ecumenical conference in New York city in May, 1900; and in hopes to promote such, elsewhere, we here present some details of the actual working of such schemes for practical education in missions.

The " Missionary Loan Exhibition " is the name by

which these exhibits have been known in Britain. For example, such a Loan Exhibition was held in the Dome and Corn Exchange, Brighton, for three days, and the following " hints about loans " were published for the information of such as would assist.

1. The date fixed for the opening of the exhibition is Wednesday, November 29th, and it would be well if all articles from a distance lent for the occasion should reach Brighton on Saturday, November 25th, and local contributions not later than Monday, November 27th.

2. All packages should be addressed Missionary Exhibition, The Dome, Brighton. The committee will gladly pay carriage both ways, if desired. Address-labels are inclosed herewith, and, if insufficient, a further supply will be sent on application.

3. The dispatch of such packages should be advised to the Honorary Secretaries, The Dome, Brighton.

4. A full description of each article sent for exhibition will very greatly add to the interest and usefulness of the contribution. This information should be given in as concise form as possible, suitable for publication in a catalogue. It is recommended that a duplicate copy be kept of the list supplied, and that each article bear some private mark by which it can easily be identified.

5. *Packing*. The committee will undertake on their part to repack everything with the greatest care, so as to insure safe transit, and hope their friends will kindly take equal care.

6. The exhibition is intended to include objects of interest of every description from any of the following countries :—Africa (East, West, and Central), Palestine, India (North, West, and South), Ceylon, China, Japan, N. W. America, and New Zealand. Articles of clothing, or food, all works of art, books, writing materials, models, pictures, photographs of native buildings, especially when illustrative of missionary progress, objects of worship, etc., will be acceptable.

An illustrated prospectus was published in connection with the Bristol exhibits, the prospectus itself being a valuable pictorial pamphlet. Four thousand curios from all parts of the heathen and Mohammedan world were there to be seen, a unique collection, not easily brought together again. There were illustrated lectures, and luncheons provided for visitors. Season tickets for one person, available during the whole time, were purchasable for about fifty cents, and the hall was divided into courts: African, Indian, Chinese, Syrian, Egyptian, Canadian, Japanese, etc.

The Zenana department contained a full-sized model room in a Bengali zenana, fully furnished; and ladies connected with zenana work gave there explanation of the life and customs of women in India, illustrated with native costumes, the mode of cooking, etc., being also shown. Missionaries from Japan similarly expounded Japanese manners; and models of idols, temples, private houses, suits of armor, jinrikshas, prayer charms, bronzes and bamboo work, ancestral tablets and shrines, embroidery and wearing apparel, etc., were to be seen.

Donations of provisions and money relieved the committee of expense, and promoted the success of the exhibit. Circulars were issued with instructions to stewards, which made all mistakes avoidable and promoted efficient service. While the exhibit was dependent largely upon *local* aid for its material and success, many of the articles used were, of course, available also for use in other localities—such as the models of buildings, etc.

No success can be assured without painstaking preparation. And the " official hand-book and guide," issued in connection with the Bristol exhibit—a book of 170 pages—attests the care taken to make it a grand triumph. It was a rare chance to study missions, for an observer who went through the seven courts or sections of the exhibit, would feel as tho he had made a tour of the countries represented, with intelligent guides to the interpretation of what he saw, and all at a trifling cost of time and money.

The projectors of the Bristol exhibit say, in review of the whole enterprise:

The work was not one which was hastily undertaken. An executive and sub-committees were formed; the various departments of preparatory work gradually took shape; from the first, it was felt that *without prayer* no real success could be attained, and so in private, and in all the regular meetings of the various committees, the subject was continually commended to God; and all interested in the work of foreign missions were specially asked to cooperate. Thus by prayer and persistent effort linked together, the work was carried forward, and, as a consequence, perfect unanimity of feeling and a gathering enthusiasm were increasingly manifest as the time approached, and everything was done to make the effort as far as possible worthy of the object we had in view, and those who had the privilege of visiting the exhibition, must at least have felt that the efforts put forth were not in vain, but had been graciously accepted of God, and that he was using it as an effective means of diffusing a deeper and wider interest among us in the great work of the evangelization of the heathen. The primary idea which was constantly present to the minds of the promoters, was not to make it a means of collecting money, but rather to spread information, awaken sympathy, and to elicit self-denying effort in the cause of foreign missions, and this idea of subordinating all attempts at pecuniary profit to the fostering of the missionary spirit, was kept conspicuously prominent throughout, and was, we believe, one of the reasons why God has deigned to use the effort for His glory.

The organization, which was gradually called into existence, rendered the effort of making the public acquainted with our intentions specially effective; we rested not so much on newspaper advertisements, tho these were not neglected, as upon the ramifications of parochial endeavor, and the personal influence of many friends; means were found by which even parishes which did not specially sympathize with the C. M. S. were not left in the dark as to the nature and objects of the approaching exhibition, and so, when at length the opening day arrived, the public were prepared to take advantage of what had been provided, and crowds thronged the building from the very first, and in this the case of Bristol differed from other localities where similar exhibitions were held, for while in these it often happened that several days were required before the full interest of the people was awakened, with us that interest was apparent from the commencement, and this was mainly due to the laborious and persistent use of every legitimate means within our reach.

It was especially pleasing to note the continuous attendance of the visitors at the different courts, even when there was no special exposition going on ; the people seemed patiently to listen, from hour to hour, to the instruction given by the stewards, and on the second day the crowds surrounding each court became so large that it was found needful to have a steward placed upon a chair, at a little distance from the court, where he or she, holding up successive exhibits, explained them to a still larger circle.

The model zenana was an object of special attraction, and was in every respect admirably worked. It was said that the proceeds from this source amounted, for a time, to nearly a shilling a minute, and what was far more important, a vivid description was there given, to a continuous stream of eager inquirers, of the degraded condition of women in India and the East, and the terrible need of increased efforts for their Christian instruction and social elevation.

Short, spirited addresses were delivered from time to time, illustrated by several ingenious devices, by which were set forth the extent of the heathen world still unevangelized, the comparatively small impressions modern missions had yet made, the inadequacy of the means which are being employed and the small amount contributed to foreign missions, when compared with the enormous sums spent yearly upon luxuries of various kinds. It was scarcely possible to listen to these expositions without feeling that something more ought to be done for the extension of the Redeemer's Kingdom, and the gifts which were put in the scale were a kind of pledge that it would be soon.

The admirable way in which the Free Missionary Literature had been previously sorted, so that it might be given with intelligent purpose and discrimination, was, we believe, a unique feature in our exhibition, and the patient way in which that literature was disseminated, so that there could scarcely have been a single visitor who left the building without some printed missionary information, can not be without some fruit in future. It is also to be noted that the arrangements made for the reception of the children of the various elementary schools of Bristol, and the neighborhood, worked without a hitch. Every morning some 2,000 children, or more, streamed into the building, and from nine to eleven o'clock they were instructed by persons specially apointed for that purpose, and as they passed from court to court they were shown objects of interest and attraction, illustrating the habits and customs and the religions which exist in different parts of the heathen world, and the urgent need that there is to give to them the bright and blessed message of the Savior's love was pressed home.

The medical court, with its practical illustrations of what can be done in this direction for the heathen, must have come with surprise to many, and must have given a more comprehensive view than is generally taken of the complete work of delivering the Gospel message, which includes within its scope not merely the salvation of the soul, but the emancipation of man's body from needless pain and suffering, and from the misery of preventable disease.

The Japanese receptions were especially popular, and very strikingly showed the tact and patience which are needed by the missionary in dealing with a polite and gifted people, who, with all their versatility and attractiveness, are still strangers to the light of God's love in Jesus Christ.

The lime-light lectures, upon different parts of the mission-field, were full of instructive matter, and were largely attended, and the sacred concerts helped to release a little the tension of feeling which the exhibition as a whole was calculated to produce. But the picture would be incomplete without some reference to the well-organized Sale of Work, which was conducted in an adjoining room; fourteen stalls, tastefully draped, exhibited the industry and energy of the various parishes throughout Bristol and the neighborhood. For months previously, many hands and brains had been steadily at work, and to all these parishes, together with their friends and workers, and specially to some of the poorer parishes of our city, the thanks of every well-wisher of the missionary cause are due. Such quiet, unobstructive, sustained and united work, cannot be without its reflex blessing on all concerned. Nor should we forget the ability and energy with which the refreshment department was administered, meeting as it did with a surprising elasticity the ceaseless demands which were made upon it.

Our only source of regret has been that the exhibition was of such short duration. Had it been possible to have prolonged it, we might have reaped still richer results, and we might have avoided the disappointment which we are sure some of our friends must have experienced by the over-crowding of the rooms, but this could not have been anticipated, and if it had, with the limited space at our disposal it could scarcely have been avoided.

But the great lesson of our exhibition is undoubtedly this: Bristol, and the neighborhood, has received an immense amount of additional information upon the present condition and needs of foreign missions; with this information there is inseparably connected a weighty responsibility; we can no longer plead ignorance, the veil has been lifted! and we know something of the cruelty, the degradation, the corruption, and the hopeless despair which exists in the heathen world.

The suggestions, made years ago, having thus been proven feasible and practicable by experiment, may again be urged with deeper conviction of their importance. What is there to hinder such a series of Missionary Loan Exhibits in America, wherever a fit place may be secured? A *permanent* MISSIONARY INSTITUTE is about to be established in the city of New York, open at all hours of the day and evening, where parents may take their children and find both recreation and instruction in that greatest of enterprises—a world's transformation. Many devoted friends of missions have missionary curiosities and relics which they would gladly lend for occasional exhibits, or better still, contribute to such a permanent missionary institute. We know of one man who has a considerable and valuable collection of curios, illustrative of life in Japan, India, China, Palestine, Africa, etc., which he would place in a missionary museum as part of its equipment. In connection with such an exhibit there might be at stated hours stereopticon exhibitions of slides, carefully selected, and constituting a most attractive educative aid, with addresses and lectures on missionary topics. The best and most recent maps, charts, and other aids to knowledge would naturally find a place in such an exhibit; and a building permanently used for these ends, would come to be a place of habitual resort, and to the young especially a sort of missionary college.

Anything is worth attempting if we may increase knowledge of facts. The field of missions is still a *terra incognita*. A leading philanthropist of Britain confessed himself to have been ignorant of the great leading facts of missionary history, and the bulk of disciples have yet to embark on their first voyage of discovery. But to those who will set out to explore, a new world waits to unveil itself.

In the Indian department of the Glasgow exposition were not merely pictures and photographs, but models of native habitations and dress, Hindoo temples, the car of Juggernaut, the Suttee pile, and various modes of torture, etc. Such methods of reproducing or representing facts to the eye have the effect of actual travel in making observers familiar with the fields of mission labor. And the materials are so abundant!

The Foreign Missionary Conference, similar in aim and character to the World's Missionary Conference of 1888, was held in New York in the month of April, 1900, and furnished a most fitting opportunity for such an exposition of missions especially as the nineteenth century, now drawing to a close, has been marked by such a triumphant career of missionary evangelism.

Let us imagine a building suitable for a grand permanent exposition of missions. In the Burma section, there might be represented the Schway Mote Tau Pagoda, with its idol shrines and superstitious wild men as it was in 1825, and confronting it, the Kho-Thah-Byu Memorial Hall with its reverent service of worship, its intelligent classes of pupils, and its various accessories for Christian service—the memorial of fifty thousand Karen converts, living or dead. In the department of the islands of the Sea, the thousand cannibal ovens of the Fijians—the chiefs' huts built on piles around which human beings were buried alive—the chiefs' canoes launched over living human bodies as rollers

—on the one side; on the other the thousand Christian churches, and still more numerous Christian homes where the voice of family worship may be daily heard, and the floating bethels where seamen learn of Him who came not to destroy men's lives but to save them. In the African department might be exhibited the refuse from slave ships, gathered at Sierra Leone, as found by W. A. B. Johnson in 1816, with no communication but that of vice and no cooperation but that of crime; and that same community as organized into a model Christian state within seven years after. Madagascar might be contrasted, as at the coronation of Ravanalona I. and of Ravanalona II. The first Malagasy who ever learned the alphabet of his own native tongue died less than twenty years ago, aged seventy-two. He had lived to see fifty thousand of his countrymen taught to read, and over seventy thousand profess their faith in Christ.

Tahiti might be represented, as during the " long night of toil," the missionary amid a group of savage cannibals seeking to get a lodgment for that sacred little Gospel, John iii, 16; and Tahiti, after the love of God had taken hold on the people, and that first convert of 1814 became leader of a host now numbering a million! and, of hundreds who have gone forth as evangelists, not one has yet proved recreant or faithless!

Zululand might be exhibited, as when the naked savage comes to the mission house to trade for a calico shirt, or, worse still, when the cruel Dingaan slaughtered a hundred girls as the equivalent for the penalty exacted from a hostile tribe, one thousand head of cattle; and Zululand with its Christian households, its eloquent native preachers, its self-denying weekly offerings to send the good news far and wide, and its self-governing, self-supporting, and self-propagating churches.

What a department might the Bible societies themselves

stock with their more than four hundred translations! Think of these great missionary agencies, avera-
ging over three new translations for each year of the century! For nearly each year one new language without
alphabet, grammar, or lexicon, has been reduced to writing,
and a literature created out of nothing! " Walk about
Zion, tell the *towers* thereof, mark well her *bulwarks*, consider her *palaces*." What cathedral towers are those societies that lift the word of God in all these tongues to such
a lofty height! What bulwarks these aggressive activities,
whose offensive warfare against the powers of darkness are
the best defensive measures for the church at home!
What palaces are those praying assemblies, where the
King Himself abides, and where the spirit of missions
constitutes a court of Christ!

Of course, the greater proportion of Gospel triumphs
defy tabulation or visual demonstration. The aggregate
number of converts from heathen lands, during the century
is not far from ten to fifteen million at the least, and probably would reach thirty million if complete statistics could
be gathered. Who shall ever write out that secret history
of self-denying love, exemplified in thousands like the obscure Chinese convert who sold himself as a coolie in New
Guinea for the sake of close contact with his unsaved countrymen, and who shortly led over two hundred of them to
Jesus? The reflex influences of missions can not be exhibited. When irreligion and infidelity seemed folding the
Church in the fatal embrace of an arctic winter, it was the
new missionary era that broke the charm of this deadly
stagnation and congelation.

But if some results cannot be exhibited, there is no reason why we should not avail ourselves of what may be
shown vividly to the eye. In the Crystal Palace at Syden-
ham, modern enterprise built, on a scale of one-third the
actual size, Assyrian palaces, Egyptian rock tombs, Greek

and Roman temples, Alhambran and Pompeian halls and chambers, medieval cathedrals, so that the visitor might in a walk of half an hour actually see three thousand years of successive civilizations reproducing their marvels. In the Egyptian museum at London, vast galleries and corridors are assigned to the huge tablets, sculptures, sarcophagi, vases, papyri, etc., gathered from the buried cities of the East. And in Paris a few years ago, in the " Nouvelle Bastile," the old demolished fortress prison was re-erected, tho only for a season, to gratify transient visitors.

In connection with the International Exposition in Glasgow, in 1888, was a vast building, a quarter of a mile long, filled with twenty-five classes of industrial products. Agriculture and horticulture, mining and engineering, both civil and naval; machinery of the most colossal and complicate, as well as of the most minute and delicate character; cutlery and arms, carriages and other wheeled vehicles; the most recent and improved methods and devices for illumination by oil, gas, and electricity; textile fabrics of wonderful variety and delicacy; food and cooking utensils; paper, printing, and book-making; furniture and decoration; fishery, pottery, and glass; jewelry and plated ware; shipbuilding, with a profuse display of exquisite models; nay, even the subtler sciences and fine arts—physical training and education, chemistry, and philosophy, music and painting, and sculpture and architecture—all these and much more besides found there exhibition and exposition. A new world was unveiled in the single department of woman's work, the arts and industries at which she presides. The field, represented in this garner of abundant harvests, was well-nigh world-wide. England, Scotland, Wales, and Ireland, Canada, France, India, and Ceylon—all helped to make this International Exposition one of the world's wonders.

It is high time that Christian believers showed some

such spirit of enterprise in behalf of the cause of God. Those who are familiar with the history and literature of missions, feel themselves to be walking through the corridors of a colossal exposition. They see a lamp more wonderful than that of Aladdin banishing the death shade and transforming the whole aspect of heathen communities,— the simple Gospel displacing rags with robes, vice with virtue, filth with cleanliness, ignorance with intelligence, cruelty with charity,—the magician's enchantments outdone by the miracles of the Holy Spirit. Facts, properly exhibited, will outshine the fables of Oriental fancy. There is an architecture that is sublimer than " frozen music ; " the structures which missionary heroism has built up are the temples of God, their timbers more fragrant than cedar, and within and without they are overlaid with the gold of the upper sanctuary.

CHAPTER XX

GOD's working, like His works, bears the stamp of infinite variety and versatility. His Spirit can not be confined within narrow limits or arbitrary restraints, but, like the mighty wind, bloweth whencesoever and whithersoever He will, and no man can say or do aught to control His sovereign and majestic movements. God's working obeys law, but it is a higher law than that which man's methods prescribe, and a holy humility becomes us as we study the spiritual history of the race; for the true criterion of judgment is not whether a measure is conformed to human notions, ancient customs, or established precedents, but whether it is of God, whether it bears the mark of His leadership and sanction. For if it be of God, man can not overthrow it, and in opposing it may haply be found even to fight against God.

For a half century there has been a steady increase of Individual and Independent Missions—enterprises undertaken outside of the denominational channels, sometimes starting with an individual, or a few like-minded disciples, but generally in some sense a new departure, and in contrast with the older, commonly accepted, and approved ways of carrying on mission work. As might be expected, many of these have exhibited no grace of continuance, and have soon died a natural death. But others have proved so vital, so energetic, so successful as to compel recognition, and some of them have threatened to revolutionize existing methods by the conspicuous signs that they are conformed to God's mind.

Independent enterprises are not necessarily *antagonistic* to the older and more prevalent methods, but they may be only *supplementary*. The ball and socket in a perfect joint are exactly opposite to one another, but that is a condition of their mutual adaptation: they are counterparts. There is not only room for all sorts of methods in a world-wide work, but all sorts of methods are needed for all sorts of men. The round peg needs the round hole and the triangular peg needs a hole as angular as itself. It is simple folly to contend with people who would like to work in their own way, and to condemn their way as peculiar. It was a great monarch who, after trying to make a dozen watches run exactly alike, gave it up in despair, but it did not need a great man to reach this sensible conclusion that, if machines can not be made to move precisely in unison, the human machine is far less likely to be subject to such uniformity.

God made no two men exactly alike, and the beauty of His work is, that it has a particular place and sphere for every worker, into which that worker fits with predestined precision. If there be unity in essentials, there not only may be diversity in non-essentials, but such diversity is a help and not a hinderance to the final result, for it allows every human instrument full play for its perfect and peculiar adaptation to the working out of the will of God.

There are advantages, undoubtedly, in the older established forms of mission enterprise. Antiquity is not always a sign of excellence—for, as Cyprian says, it may be *vetustas erroris*—the old age of error. But commonly in Christian service there is a survival of the fittest, and what lasts and outlasts, has usually some secret of vitality. The common way of doing mission work is by " Boards of the Church," with their " secretaries " and other machinery. Representative men, clerical or lay, or both, are chosen to represent denominational interests, and secretaries to be the direct channels of correspondence with the field. This is a wise business arrangement, with two classes of helpers—administrators and agents—those who on the one hand undertake the general work of administration, and others who on the other hand come into closer contact with the field and the laborers, study their mutual adaptation, and superintend the work directly. Thus the wisdom of wise men in counsel and the energy of practical men in action are combined happily and effectively. And, when the wise men are not too cautious, or the practical men too energetic, so that the boards and the secretaries do not pull together, this is probably as safe an arrangement as human sagacity can dictate. Sometimes boards have proven so conservative that they put on the brakes even when the road was all up hill, or secretaries so progressive that they used the whip even when the grade was down hill. But allowing for such exceptions, the denominational method has proved on the whole very effective in carrying on missions.

And yet, there are some serious drawbacks, even where boards do not hamper secretaries and secretaries do not harass boards. Let us grant all the advantages of a large denominational backing, of long existing and approved methods, and of the promise of permanence. Let us freely concede that, when a great Christian denomination undertakes mission work as a body, the work is likely to be more thorough, more lasting, more far-reaching; likely to command more general support, to be kept within safer lines, to be conducted with more denominational comity, so as not to collide with other branches of the Church; likely also to put in the field workers, better trained, more scholarly, more fitted to grapple with the problem of missions and to furnish more competent translators, educators, leaders of the host. But are there no manifest risks run in the " Board " System?

There is no doubt that denominational societies are often " hide-bound " by conservatism and ecclesiasticism—timidly over-cautious, and hesitating and vacillating in cases where a holy boldness and goaheadativeness is the only hope of success. Boards and committees often lack audacity. Mr. Spurgeon once said to me, " The best working committee is a committee of twenty-one, which entrusts all business to a sub-committee of three, of which one member is sick and another is out of town ; then you get something done ! " And he added, " Have you never noticed that you may take seven men, any one of whom will give you a wise and prompt decision if you consult him alone, but when you constitute them into a committee or board, they act unwisely, afraid to decide, sluggish to move, even where all hangs on quick work ? " Sometimes in a great emergency a church board has delayed, waited to discuss, and finally adjourned without doing anything, all seemingly afraid of doing too much or doing something unwise, when anything was better and wiser than to do nothing ! Or, how often again, when old methods fail and a new way promises well, has a board clung to the old with its failure, instead of giving the new a chance, where at the worst it could only *fail?* Of all fetters what are more rasping to a divinely quickened soul than the iron bonds of ecclesiasticism, that, by undue jealousy for churchly traditions hinder the success of the work of God ? There are some people who would hesitate to throw a plank to a drowning man, unless they first knew to whose ecclesiastical lumber-pile it properly belonged, or in what theological planing-mill it had been smoothed down ; people who would let millions die without a hearing of the Gospel message, rather than that they should hear it at the lips of one who was not in the " apostolic succession," or had not been trained in some peculiar denominational shibboleth.

Sometimes church boards are arbitrary and even despotic, full as much so as any one man who keeps matters unduly in his own hands. Has there never been an autocrat at the secretary's table, who has dictated unreasonably and unrighteously to missionaries thousands of miles away in matters about which they had far more knowledge and capacity than himself? In one case, known to the writer, a secretary demanded of missionaries a course of conduct that, if followed, would have been disloyal to Christ and dishonorable to man, and he made compliance a condition of continuance and maintenance on the field! Missionaries on the ground should be far more independent of home control than they often are, and far more of the actual administration of the work and distributing of money in the work should be left to them, who are actually in the very center of the activities of missions, and are more competent wisely to settle many such matters.

There are also both advantages and disadvantages in independent, individual, and undenominational mission enterprises. Their main justification is this, that they supply a channel for putting at work many who will not in any other way come in active contact with the field, and that they enlist the sympathy and cooperation of many who for some reason or other do not approve of the ordinary methods or do not work through them.

The reluctance of some people to send their money through the boards, they explain by the fact that they do not believe in the *expense* attending administration, even when economically conducted. They maintain (unreasonably, perhaps), that all secretarial work may be done and should be done gratuitously, and that there are men and women who would gladly serve God in this sphere at their own cost, like that prominent secretary of one of the greatest missionary societies who never received a penny for his services, preferring to do his work gratuitously. Another man who is the actual conductor of a great missionary enterprise, has never used a farthing, given for missions, for personal purposes. A poor servant maid, who saved twenty-five dollars to send the Gospel abroad, learned that it took a thousand such gifts as hers to pay the salaries of the good men who supervise the work, and in her ignorance she failed to see that her savings had done any good to the lost souls that she gave her money to help. It takes a mind more philosophical than hers to trace the gift, and see that what helps to maintain the pilot at the wheel, speeds the vessel and its cargo towards the haven, and so, in the long run, it pays to have salaried agents.

Others conscientiously feel that the ordinary missions of the Church are not conducted on apostolic principles, and they crave a new way that is in their opinion really the older way. Rev. J. Hudson Taylor is a deeply taught disciple, and we have seen how he felt convinced, in 1865, that God wanted a new enterprise begun for Inland China, on lines more primitive than those in general use. He especially felt that there was lacking *a spirit of believing prayer, of dependence on the Holy Ghost, and of direct looking to God both for men and money;* and he undertook the China Inland Mission especially to emphasize these *three* principles. Dares any one who has been watching its history for these thirty-five years now dispute that God's broad seal is upon his work?

Independent missions have greatly multiplied, and are still multiplying. The philosophy underlying them we are now seeking to learn. No doubt one reason in God's mind for introducing these methods into His all-embracing plan may be that they afford opportunity for *experimental trials* of methods hitherto comparatively unused, as, for instance, *industrial* missions and colonization schemes, so that whatever is valuable in them may be proven such, and introduced as features into older schemes. Wise men never stop learning, nor pursue their way in such blind con-

fidence in their own infallibility, as to be unwilling to mod-
ify and improve their methods.

At a meeting held in connection with missions at Northfield in 1897—speaking of a missionary fund which it was
proposed to raise to help volunteers into the field whom
ordinary contributions might not suffice to send—Mr.
Moody said:

> "I am in sympathy with the boards, and have no sympathy
> with the croakers. You cannot find a better set of men on this
> continent than those in the American board, or in the Presby-
> terian Board. We are in hearty sympathy with these regular
> boards. I think it is a great mistake to send any money outside
> of the regular hannels."

Mr. Moody, however fully in sympathy with the
Boards, no doubt believed there are many organizations
" outside of the regular channels " that God is greatly using, and he certainly could not have meant that all who
differ from the established methods, or encourage these
outside agencies, are to be put down as " croakers ". There
is one man whose heart was so moved by the needs of Korea, that he sent out and supported at his own cost several
missionaries to the Hermit Nation; yet he also recently
gave liberal help to lift the enormous debt of the Baptist
Board. Pastor Harms was so moved by the appalling destitution of a dying world, that he turned his own church of
poor peasants into a missionary society, sent out hundreds
of missionaries, and set up scores of stations in unoccupied
territory. Was his work illegitimate? Yet he not only
had his own society and missions, but his own mission ship,
mission magazine, and mission training-school. The
eighteen Christian centuries furnish no more startling example of the Spirit's leading, and of the possibilities of
service, than this Hermannsburg Missionary Society,
working entirely outside the previously used channels.

Henry Grattan Guinness represents an independent society, which has for more than a quarter century been carrying on a grand missionary training-school, has founded the Livingstone Inland, and Kongo Balolo missions in Africa on a very extensive scale, and is now undertaking to evangelize the neglected continent of South America. Mr. Moody himself encountered some little criticism by his independent working outside the regular channels. The Training Institute at Chicago was regarded by some as diverting students from the theological seminaries, and hurrying into the field at home and abroad, some who have never had full training. Yet this grand work at Chicago is only another proof that God has room for many forms of working in His plan, that may not be perfectly regular according to man's notions.

But we cannot afford to sanction any undue irregularities. If mission work is carried on independently of the ordinary denominational methods let it be carefully guarded from all abuses and perversions, lest it forfeit public confidence and the right of continuance. And it is in no censorious spirit that we now calmly but candidly state some of the defects or disadvantages of these independent ways of working.

(1) The fundamental risk is that such enterprise shall *center unduly in one man,* and revolve about his personality.

Human nature is not yet sanctified enough to risk putting too much power in one man's hands. What modestly begins as a private venture of faith and prayer, may, when it grows to unexpected proportions, become a public calamity by the autocratic and despotic way in which it is conducted. While its originator was almost its sole supporter it might be allowable that he should be its sole director. But as others become active participators in the work and its support, they should have a voice in its conduct. This is God's corrective for the peril of the despotism possible even to the religious autocrat.

(2) Workers should not be *hurried into the mission field* without any proper preparation. But the standards of fitness are not always scripturally chosen. There is a natural demand for *educated* preachers and teachers, and they are needed nowhere more urgently than in foreign lands. But two things must not be forgotten: first, that there is much work that can be done by comparatively uneducated people, as in a war effective fighting is often done by raw recruits as well as trained veterans. Many a man can follow who can not lead. And again, we must not forget that God's standard of education is different from man's. He has His own school, and some are deeply taught in God's university who never were graduated at an earthly college. To be taught of the Holy Ghost makes up even for bad grammar, and poor logic is more than compensated by the demonstration of the Spirit. The history of missions shows some ignominious failures on the part of some of the most conspicuous scholars, and as glorious successes on the part of some others, who knew little Latin and less Greek.

(3) Another danger quite as obvious, is that of *giving money impulsively* and wastefully to irresponsible, incapable, or even fraudulent parties. A letter has been received from a most intelligent and devoted missionary, lamenting that, notwithstanding repeated cautions, good Christian people in England and America continued to send money to a man who pretended to be doing mission work in the East, but whose whole career was suspicious. He says:

" I lived in the same place with this man, off and on, for three years, and during that time frequently saw him and his family, and my connection with the field and people gives me opportunity of judging. Our opinion, and the opinion, I believe, of all the resident English in that field is that the work of this man is *most unsatisfactory,* and not by any means what he professes it to be. I have passed his house constantly, not only daily, but often many times in a day, and I have never seen his much-talked of *inquirers* entering and leaving his house. He has undoubtedly linguistic gifts, which ought to make him a most useful missionary, but, to speak candidly, I believe he makes practically no use of them. (1) If a man repeatedly tries to become connected with evangelical missionary societies —a man who has many gifts which should make him a valuable agent—and after inquiry these societies refuse to employ him, must there not be something wrong? (2) If a man tries to run a mission on his own account, collecting all the money, not responsible to any committee, ' *can he possibly carry on satisfactory mission work?* ' I have not the slightest grudge, but I honestly believe his presence here is rather a hindrance than a help to mission work."

Apropos of irresponsible missions, we extract from *The Missionary Herald* a letter, with the brief comments upon it. The whole matter is one of such gravity, and so bearing upon Christian work, both at home and abroad, that it should receive most careful attention.

" There has recently appeared in several papers of India and Great Britain a letter addressed to the Christian churches of Great Britain, Australasia, and America, prepared by members of the Madras Missionary Conference, calling attention to a matter which seems to them most serious. It is signed by a large number of members of various missionary societies, and also by a number of native Christians in the Madras district. The letter will explain itself, and we give it entire, commending it heartily to the attention of all Christians in the United States.

" DEAR BRETHREN :—Of recent years several Indian Christians from South India and Ceylon have either visited your churches in person or have issued appeals by letter, and by these means have collected considerable sums of money for the purpose of carrying on different forms of mission work in this country.

These persons were for the most part workers in connection with the various churches or missionary societies, but in most cases their actual connection has ceased. They have issued their appeals in their own name, and the work which they have initiated and profess to be now carrying on is not under the control or oversight of any one except themselves. The actual work carried on in most cases bears but a small proportion to that set forth in their appeals as what they propose to do.

"The interests of truth and righteousness demand that these facts should be stated, and in view of the injury they have already done, and the still greater injury they are calculated to do to the cause of Christ in this land, we can no longer keep silent.

"These appeals are a source of grave moral danger to those who make them, for they have to administer large funds without the safeguard of the control of others, and are thus exposed to a strong temptation to employ for private purposes money intended for public use. They are injurious to the cause of missions in those countries from whence the funds come, for certainly sooner or later the contributors will find out that their gifts are either not being used for the purposes for which they were made, or that the work carried on is very disproportionate to the funds expended. Distrust will thus be excited, which will extend even to undertakings where the proper use of the funds is adequately guaranteed. With some of the evils which these appeals produce in this country we are already too familiar. One of these is their tendency to demoralize the Indian community. The idea is abroad among a certain section of that community that an Indian Christian has only to go with a specious plea to Great Britain, Australasia, or America to obtain large sums of money from persons who will not inquire too closely as to how their gifts are to be used, and who, if they see their contributions acknowledged in a printed subscription list, will be satisfied that they are being properly spent.

"In order to check such evils, resulting from appeals by irresponsible individuals, we would respectfully suggest that contributions should only be given to those who are able to give guarantees, *first,* that they are the accredited agents of a responsible committee of persons who reside in the immediate neighborhood where the proposed work is to be done; *secondly,* that the special object for which money is solicited is distinctly approved by that committee; *thirdly,* that accounts will be rendered to all subscribers, giving not simply lists of subscriptions and donations received, but also a balance-sheet duly audited, showing that the moneys received have actually been spent upon the objects for which they were given. We are convinced that no cause which is really good will suffer by the exercise of these precautions, as those who plead for such causes will have no difficulty in giving the guarantees required."

Signed by T. P. Dudley, Secretary of the Madras Christian Conference; by N. Subrahmanyam, barrister, and by seventeen others.

It is possible that there might be a *combination* of several of the now existing independent missions in one organization. Some such plan has been proposed in London, and may be put into execution. It is suggested that a general society be formed, having in charge various unoccupied fields, such as Tibet, South America, the Sudan, etc., and that all undenominational and independent missionary enterprises be invited to enter into this united organization, without interference with the special methods and principles of each, but as a guarantee to the public that there is proper supervision, fidelity in management, and integrity in the use of funds. Rev. F. B. Meyer, James E. Mathieson, Esq., and other prominent men have been proposed as the committee to represent this united society. Could such a method be adopted, might it not greatly relieve the present situation?

What is here written would be misinterpreted if construed, as, directly or indirectly, an attack on the " boards," or established agencies which represent the various churches of Christ in the work of missions. It is sufficient proof that no such motive actuates the writer, that he has always both advocated, and cooperated with, the regular church methods, so long in operation. The object in view is, not to criticise or to condemn any existing system, whether denominational or independent; but calmly to consider, and carefully to weigh, both the advantages and defects of all methods, so that whatever is good may be conserved, and whatever is undesirable may be avoided. If we have indicated any dangers that threaten the working plans of the Church, it is only in hopes to increase their efficiency. Infallibility pertains only to God, and men often learn quite as much from errors and failures, as from their best endeavors and most triumphant successes. We invoke blessing on all who honestly seek to advance the cause of missions.

CHAPTER XXI

WENDELL PHILLIPS was recognized as one of the foremost of American orators. There was especially noticeable about him a marked *ethical momentum.* No other phrase so well expresses it. Momentum is the product of the mass of matter by the velocity of movement. When he spoke on great moral questions, he carried his auditor with him by an oratorical force, into which entered two grand elements: first, a noble, strong, weighty manhood, back of the speech; and second, a rapid, onward movement in forcible argument, intense earnestness of emotion, and lofty purpose, all facilitated by simplicity of diction and aptness of illustration.

This American Demosthenes had gone through the temptations to early dissipation which a rich young man confronts, and developed a great moral character, which constitutes him one of the noblest figures in the history of New England.

An interesting fact is related of his youth.

One day, after hearing Lyman Beecher preach, he repaired to his room, threw himself on the floor, and cried: " *O God, I belong to Thee! * Take what is Thine own. I ask this, that whenever a thing be wrong it may have no power of temptation over me, and whenever a thing be right it may take no courage to do it." " And," observed Mr. Phillips in later years, " I have never found anything that impressed me as being wrong, exerting any temptation over me, nor has it required any courage on my part to do whatever I believed to be right."

What a key to a human life! In that supreme hour his higher moral nature, with God's help, subjugated his lower self; and for him, henceforth, there was no compromise with animal passion, carnal ambition, selfishness, cupidity, or any other debasing inclination; they were " suppliants at the feet of his soul."

The supreme motive both to holiness and service is found when any man or woman can say from the heart, " O God, I belong to Thee!" and no other impulse is proof against all worldly argument and temporary discouragement.

We are now to look still further at some of those undertakings which aim at the rapid evangelization of the world, but for some reason have cut loose from the ordinary denominational and corporate methods. Some of these are operating in North Africa, South America, Korea, etc.—but one—the China Inland Mission—stands out conspicuous, and may be taken as an example of all, as it is, perhaps, entitled to outrank the rest, both from priority in time and scriptural simplicity of method. Its history, now put into a printed record, deserves careful perusal by those who would more minutely look into one of the most romantic, heroic, and inspiring chapters which modern missions has added to the unfinished " Acts of the Apostles."*

When the history of this enterprise covered little more than a quarter century, already its stations were scattered over an area continental in extent; its missionary force numbered nearly 700, with about 350 native helpers,—a total working force of about 1,000—reporting about 250 stations and outstations, over 5,200 communicants, and 18,000 adherents, having added 850 in the year;

* " Story of the China Inland Mission." Geraldine Guinness. F. H. Revell Co.

66 schools, with 880 pupils, and an income for the year of nearly 170,000 dollars. Interdenominational from the first, and now international, it has given such ample scope for testing the practibility of the principles which underlie it and the methods which it advocates, that there is a certain obligation to examine candidly and carefully into its annals, that we may see how far God may be behind it, teaching us all some great lessons.

Its founder, Rev. J. Hudson Taylor, himself asserts that " the firm belief in the plenary and verbal inspiration of GOD'S WORD lies behind the whole work; it is assumed that His promises mean exactly what they say, and that His commands are to be obeyed in the confidence that 'all things are possible to him that believeth.'" He adds: " a personal experience of more than forty years has growingly confirmed this confidence, and has shown us ever new directions in which to apply it. We were early led to trust the LORD to supply *pecuniary* needs in answer to prayer, and then to obtain, in the same way, *fellow workers* and *open doors;* but we did not learn, till later, what it is to 'abide in' CHRIST, and to find *spiritual need* all met, and *keeping power* through faith in Him. More recently the infilling and refilling with the HOLY SPIRIT has taken a place among us, as a mission, that it had not before; and we feel that we are still only beginning to apprehend what God can do through little bands of fully yielded, fully trusting, overflowingly filled believers.

" Thus we have come to value missionary work, not merely for the sake of the heathen, but also as a spiritual education for the missionary, who, in the field learns, as never at home, to find CHRIST a living, bright reality; nor is the education confined to the missionary, but blesses also the beloved ones at home, who, having 'nothing too precious for the LORD JESUS,' have given up their dearest and best, and who share in their hundred-fold reward. Such prove that it is indeed 'more blessed to give than to receive,' and the whole church at home is not less blessed than the heathen abroad."*

This testimony of the founder of the China Inland Mission we give thus fully, because he is entitled to be heard in explanation of his own course, and in interpretation of the history inseparable from his personal convictions and endeavors. It will thus be seen at the outset, how emphatically the brief sentence which opens this chapter may be written over this whole work: " O, God, I belong to Thee!"

God demands on the part of His true servants, a perfect and perpetual surrender unto Him, without reservation or limitation. We take Him, as He takes us, once and for all, or not at all. He will not consent to be made a liar by our disbelief, to be dishonored by our distrustful experiments, or to accept our self-offerings under any conditions as to service or suffering, sphere of labor or length of time. We are to give ourselves to him beyond recall, and bear the self-surrender in constant remembrance. These conditions are not arbitrary or unreasonable, but are the necessary and indispensable requisites to a true consecration. God can not receive us, we can not become His, in any other way or on any other terms; and above all must such surrender prepare us for any large, spiritual, successful mission to a dying world. We may well afford to study the history of any work which is conspicuously blessed of God, and discover if possible the secrets of such blessing and success.

In the autumn of 1860, Mr. Taylor came back to England, after seven years of absence in China, years of strange providential preparation for the great enterprise he was to launch. At this time no definite thought of attempting any such stupendous work as the evangelization

---

* The italics and capitals are Mr. Taylor's.

of Inland China had yet entered his mind. To go even one hundred miles inland implied a long and perilous journey; and, with notable exception of Rev. Griffith John and Mr. A. Wylie, the far interior had never yet been penetrated with the Gospel.

But on the wall of Mr. Taylor's room hung a large map of China, and when his eye fell upon it, *eighteen populous provinces* stood out, in deep black, as all enveloped in a darkness that might be felt. And from that map he turned to the Book, which said " *Ye are the Light of the world;* " and the question would recur constantly: There a midnight; here the Sun of Righteousness; how may that Sun be made to shine in that night? Mr. Taylor and his colleague, Mr. Gough, could not rest without laying this whole matter before the Lord, and they found themselves on their knees pleading that somehow God would drive away that awful darkness by sending forth His light and His truth. In two of God's choice saints, Mr. and Mrs. Berger, a symphony of desire and prayer was found; Mr. Taylor's pen began to burn with his message, and by degrees the zeal of God more and more controlled him.

On the other hand, he could not but see that the church as a whole was slumbering while the world was dying. Dr. Duff's sentence: "We are playing at missions," seemed to describe only too aptly and awfully that trifling with the great problem of a world's redemption, which allows fifteen hundred millions of people to perish, three times a century, and two-thirds of the whole number without even knowing that Christ died for them! At that time, after 1,800 years of Christian history, *eleven vast interior provinces of the Celestial Empire, had not one resident Protestant missionary.* In China alone, at least one-tenth of the whole race were dying without Christ, or even the opportunity of hearing the Gospel. He felt the conviction grow that some *new and special agency* for the evangelization of Inland China was needful, which should dare to trust God for both the open door into the heart of the Kingdom and for the men and money to do the work.

A question now arose in his mind: God has given me light, and light means responsibility. I see the need clearly; why not go ahead and trust God to work out His designs through me? The thought had a grip on him and would not let go. It was early in the year 1865, when this conflict began to be intense in his soul, and unbelief was battling with faith, and self-distrust with confidence in God for the victory. Sleep almost fled from his eyes. The sense of bloodguiltiness for the million a month who were dying in China, was both a load on his heart and a goad to his conscience. And, on June 1st, at Mr. Berger's chapel, he appealed for intercession with God, that suitable men and means might be furnished for the evangelization of these destitute eleven provinces. But at this time Hudson Taylor had not got to the point of self-surrender as himself one of this new band—not to say as the leader.

An invitation to rest for a few days at Brighton, brought him to an unexpected crisis of decision. It was Sunday, June 25, 1865, and the church bells rang. But Mr. Taylor could not go to the place of public prayer, for the overwhelming shadow of China's need rested on him also, and he could not forget that, while these assemblies of disciples were gathered in their superb sanctuaries, rejoicing in their ample privileges, and heedless of the heathen, more than one thousand souls in China would pass into the unseen world, Christless. His agony of soul drove him to the beach, where he could walk and talk with God, looking out on that wide sea—the fitting symbol of the awful ocean of eternity, which was swallowing up all these vast millions while its unrippled calm was undisturbed by their doom.

On those sands, this humble man, alone with God met *the crisis of his life*. " God can *give* the men to go to China, and God can *keep* them there; " this was the voice that spoke to him. The decision was made: " Thou LORD shalt be responsible for them, and *for me, too*." The burden was gone. Hudson Taylor first gave himself to the Lord for China, and then asked for those who should go *with him:* twenty-four in all—two for each of the eleven provinces, and two more for Mongolia. On the margin of his Bible he at once wrote down this brief sentence, which remains the simple record of that momentous transaction with the God of the covenant:

" *Prayed for twenty-four willing, skillful laborers, at Brighton, June 25, 1865.*"

Mr. Taylor was at this time thirty-three years old—as his Lord was, when He went to the Calvary where He bore our sins. The plan of the China Inland Mission slowly took shape. It must be wholly *according to the mind of God,* for otherwise *prayer* would lose its power to claim blessing. The mission must therefore be:

1. *Interdenominational.*—Catholic, evangelical, and so both inviting and embracing all sympathetic disciples who were willing to cooperate.

2. *Spiritual.*—No intellectual, social or personal accomplishments; no wealth, rank or position, could atone for the lack of a thoroughly spiritual type of character in the workers and the administrators. Educational advantages, tho not to be despised, must be supplemented by gifts and graces of the Spirit.

3. *Scriptural.*—Debt must never be incurred. No regular salaries could be pledged, for this implies an assured and definite income. Whatever God gave, would be used as given, for the work and the workers, and only those who were prepared to accept this basis would be accepted.

4. *Voluntary.*—The supply both of men and women,

and of means, must be through free-hearted self-offering and offerings of substance. Appeals to be avoided as tending first to undue dependence on human effort; second, to impulsive and unconsecrated giving; third, to diversion of attention from God as the supplier of all need. Appeals to men dishonor God, and mislead men, for they imply that God is unduly dependent on human gifts. Hence it was determined to make no collections in connection with the mission meetings, but leave the hearer to contribute afterward as mature thought and prayer might dictate.

5. *Prayerful.*—Literally full of prayer. The noontide hour, then given up to a household meeting, at the throne of grace, for China, and the Saturday afternoon larger meeting for the same purpose, set the key to the concert of prayer that for a quarter of a century has never failed.

A short sentence of twenty-four words expresses what was felt to be the supreme need: "*to get God's man, in God's place, doing God's work in God's way, for God's glory.*" "*God alone is sufficient for God's own work.*"

Another twenty-four words embody what God seemed to say to Mr. Taylor as in an audible voice: "*I am going to open Inland China to the Gospel: if you will enter into My plea, I will use you for this work.*"

These were the days when conventions were beginning to be held for promotion of spiritual life, but the missionary appeal was seldom heard in them; and just then Mr. Taylor found himself in Perth at the annual conference. He himself had been a beloved fellow-worker of William Burns, and this happy link gave him access to the leaders of the conference; and he asked that he might say a few words for the Middle Kingdom and its needy provinces. This was the surprising response: "It is quite out of the question; you surely misunderstand; *these meetings are for* EDIFICATION!" Persistence again prevailed, and Mr. Taylor got a chance—twenty minutes only—at the morning meeting. Doubly shy, because his native timidity was intensified by the reluctance of the permission given, he rose, stood silent a moment, unable to begin, and then quietly said: *"Let us pray."* Five minutes of his twenty were taken up in getting boldness from God to use the other fifteen for China and China's Savior. That lifted the load, and he first told of a drowning Chinaman and the indifference of bystanders to his fate; then, like Nathan, applied his parable, and said: "Thou art the man!" And so Hudson Taylor began his convention work. And where is the conference that now would not welcome him?

As the days came when the actual bearing of the burdens of this new mission began to bow down the backs of those who had undertaken it, at times it seemed as tho a horror of deep darkness was upon them. What if, after all, money were not forthcoming, and workers should be starving in Inland China, and the whole work become a by-word of derision and reproach! The last day of the year, 1865, was set apart as a day of fasting and prayer. Each one of that little band of praying souls sought to keep in such close harmony with God, that the symphony of prayer might be music in His ear as well as in their own. And, as of Jacob at Peniel, it may be written: " AND HE BLESSED THEM THERE." So conspicuous was the blessing received *that day*, that December 31st has been for twenty-five years the annual prayer and praise feast of the mission both abroad and at home.

From this point on, also the history of the China Inland Mission seems to those who have watched its whole course, like the footsteps of God. On February 6, 1866, special prayer was offered at noon that the Lord would graciously incline His people to send in from £1,500 to £2,000 to meet the expenses of the outgoing party of ten brethren and sisters who had offered to accompany Hudson Taylor. On March 12th following, before the first printed statement of the work was in circulation, *over 1,970 pounds had come in unasked, save of God.* The need was more than met before the want had been made known to the Christian public.

Thus early in the mission this lesson was taught and learned, that if there were *less pleading with man and reliance on man, for money,* and *more pleading with God, and dependence on His Spirit,* to guide in the work and to deepen the spiritual life of God's people, the problem of missions might find its solution. During this whole subsequent history it has been found that God has met every special need by a special supply, and that when the special need ceased, so did the supply. The whole party that first sailed May 26, 1866, numbered twenty-one, including children.

On May 2, before sailing, Hudson Taylor spoke on China at Totteridge near London, and it was thought to be a mistake that he declined to have any collection taken at the meeting. His host, the chairman, had remonstrated against his not striking while the iron was hot, but Mr. Taylor quietly assured him that he wished to avoid the impression that the main thing wanted was money, and added that, if there was a true self-surrender, all else would follow. His host next morning acknowledged that he had passed a restless night; that if he had had his way, the collection would have been taken, and he would have put in a few guineas; but that further reflection and prayer had satisfied him that such gift would have been only an evasion of duty, whereupon he handed Mr. Taylor a check for 500 pounds sterling.

The voyage to China on the *Lammermuir* was itself a *mission* to the unsaved; *twenty of the crew* found the Savior, and among them, some of the most unlikely at the first; in fact, the opposers all came over. But the voyage was not without trials. Two typhoons struck the vessel, even the sailors gave up hope, and the life-belts were gotten out in readiness for the worst. But God wrought deliverance from shipwreck—a type of many other deliverances, all His own. A subscription of more than 120 dollars from the officers and crew was a sufficient witness to the fact that God had been with this mission party on the outgoing voyage.

These pages are not the place for extended accounts. It was marvellous, however, how needs and supplies exactly corresponded, in amounts of money and fitness of time, so that another motto was suggested: " GOD's *clocks keep perfect time.*"

The year 1867 opened with united prayer, that God would extend and advance the work, and closed with the opening of the great city of Wan-chow to the Gospel, Siao-shan, Tai-chau, and Nan-King, having also been occupied. The number of stations had doubled, and the border had been crossed into Kiang-su province.

The little band had to face the risk of death in the Yang-Chow riot, but God kept them in the midst of great perils, and showed himself their avenger also; for *all those who were concerned in that outbreak,* singularly fell into trouble. The prefect and his son lost their lives, their property was pillaged, and the family reduced to beggary; the district magistrate, the whole family of one of the chief inciters of the riot, and the leader in ruffianism became infamous; so that the people feared to join in any further violence against those whom God so defended.

When Mrs. Taylor died in 1891, and his partner in prayers was no more on earth, Mr. Taylor said to the LORD: " Be Thou my partner in supplication, as well as my High Priestly intercessor," and another step was taken in fellowship with the Great Friend, who said: " Lo, I am with you alway."

The gradual opening of Inland China to the Gospel, and the growth and influence of woman's work in the far interior; the itinerary preaching that covered 30,000 miles in two years, through regions beyond, hitherto almost unvisited; and especially that most memorable prayer-meeting *for seventy new workers within three years;* the faith that took God at His word and turned that prayer-meeting into one of praise in anticipation of answered prayer, and the glorious answer that followed long before the three years expired—the story of " the *hundred* " given in the year when the mission reached its majority—all this, and far more, we have to pass by without further reference. The work has now included America, Europe, Australia in its scope, and embraces councils in five lands, which send out and support their own representatives.

To only one more thing we tarry to call attention: It is to the *careful and admirable financial system* of the China Inland Mission. More than one promising scheme has been wrecked, losing public confidence by mismanagement or arbitrary and irresponsible use of its funds. Those who sustain a work have a right, first to *know* what is done with the money given, and then to some *voice* in the conduct of the work. There is a great risk of *autocracy* in the Lord's affairs. Sometimes a man with whom a new benevolent enterprise originates, either determines to keep the whole matter in his own hands, or does it without deliberate design. His head becomes its office and his pocket its treasury. The work enlarges and the constituency of supporters grows correspondingly, but he continues to be the *factotum.* His judgment is the final court, perhaps the only court of appeal. He gives no account to anybody, and, even without the loss of faith·in his *honesty,* faith is lost in his wisdom, charity, and respect for the rights of his brethren; until, by and by, the work itself can longer prosper only as it cuts loose from connection with him. We have seen at least seven such forms of good service split on this rock of autocratic management.

Geo. Müller, Hudson Taylor, and others like them, have had the sanctified common sense to see that, when a work develops, its management should broaden also—and so they have associated with themselves a competent council of sympathetic advisers. But especially is it noticeable how transparent the *financial methods* of the China Inland Mission are. Every penny given is first acknowledged to the donor or the parties through whom it comes, by a *numbered receipt;* then, in the published report, the amount is again acknowledged and can be *distinguished by its number,* so that every gift, large or small can be traced. There is no chance either for misappropriation of funds, or for their appropriation by the autocratic and independent head of the whole work who does as he pleases. Such transparent conduct of money matters inspires the full faith of the Christian public, and is partly the secret of this remarkable and unprecedented growth.

The China Inland Mission is fallible and imperfect, and no doubt makes mistakes, but there are about it great attractions.

Its founder has sought to impress on all connected with it, the need of *humility.* Spurgeon used to tell of a certain alchemist who waited upon Leo X. declaring that he had discovered how to transmute the baser metals into gold, expecting to receive a sum of money for his discovery. Leo was no such simpleton; he merely gave him a huge purse in which to keep the gold which he would make. There was wisdom as well as sarcasm in the present. That is precisely what God often does with proud men: He lets them have the opportunity to do what they boast of being able to do. Not a solitary gold piece was dropped into that purse, and we shall never be spiritually rich by what we can do in our own strength. Be stripped of self confidence and be clothed with humility; and then God may be pleased to clothe you with honor; but not till then.

Dr. Payson said: "The most of my sufferings and sorrows were occasioned by my unwillingness to be nothing, which I am, and by struggling to be something."

Another fundamental principle constantly impressed on all these mission workers is absolute *absorption* in God, without which there is no real dependence on Him or confidence in Him. How often one recalls the sublimity of that quiet resolution of President Edwards: "*Resolved, that I will do whatsoever I think to be most for God's glory and my own good, profit and pleasure, on the whole, without any consideration of the time, whether now, or never so many myriads of ages hence?*" This is surveying and laying out a track through eternity! And the deeper and more quiet the solitude, the better it will be done. Such absorption in God is the only basis of an unchanging *fixedness of purpose,* our will being both lost and saved in union with His, losing its own carnal wilfulness and gaining His divine energy. Hear Sir Thomas Fowell Bulton: "The longer I live, the more I am certain that the great difference between men—between the feeble and the powerful, the great and the insignificant—is energy, invincible determination, a purpose once fixed on, and then death or victory. This quality will do anything that can be done in the world; and no talents, no circumstances, no opportunities, will make a two-legged creature a man without it."

Once more the China Inland Mission seeks to impress the great law of *fellowship* with God in His work. Hence comes the confidence that He will supply both men and means. Let the *old story* of "A Loan to the Lord," teach us a lesson in its quaint way. A poor man with an empty purse came one day to Michael Feneberg, the godly pastor of Seeg, in Bavaria, and begged three crowns that he might finish his journey. It was all the money Feneberg had, but as he besought him so earnestly in the name of

Jesus, he gave it. Immediately after, he found himself in great outward need, and, seeing no way of relief he prayed, saying: " Lord, I lent Thee three crowns; Thou hast not yet returned them, and Thou knowest how I need them. Lord, I pray Thee, give them back." The same day a messenger brought a money-letter, which Gossner, his assistant, reached over to Feneberg, saying: " Here, father, is what you expended." The letter contained about 200 thalers, or about $150, which the poor traveler had begged from a rich man for the vicar; and the childlike old man, in joyful amusement, cried out: *" Ah, dear Lord, one dare ask nothing of Thee, for straightway Thou makest one feel so much ashamed!"*

CHAPTER XXII

INDIVIDUAL LINKS BETWEEN GIVERS AND THE MISSION FIELD

A PRACTICAL problem now occupying the wisest and best minds, is, how to secure, from cheerful givers at home, a hearty and unfailing support for workers abroad, or on the borders of civilization in the home land. Great as is the need of sending a larger force to the field, the question pressing just now, with tremendous weight, is how to *keep* the laborers already in the field, and prevent disastrous retrenchment. On every side, and in every direction, grand undertakings are at risk. Debts, so enormous as almost to wreck boards representing home and foreign missions, and deficiencies so crippling to all aggressive action as to compel retrenchment instead of advance, have caused a chronic alarm and apprehension that are paralyzing to all hopeful enterprise. It is only great faith in God that dares take one step forward and onward when the work presents such an aspect and prospect.

Devout souls stand in the presence of such a crisis with the deep conviction that it is both needless and shameful. There are both money and piety enough to remedy all these evils and supply all these deficiencies, were the money and the piety only made available. In nature, power and energy have always been present, but not always properly applied. And so the connecting links seem somehow wanting between Christians at home and the work and workers abroad. Dr. Thomas C. Upham has said, * that there is in

* Life of Faith. 300 p.

every commonwealth, " a conservative body of men who, in their freedom from passion, can estimate the just claims of truth, and, in the strength of moral and religious principle, will at all hazards do what is right." And hence, " when great constitutional and moral questions are at stake, the results have generally been favorable to law and truth, in consequence of the accession, at the precise moment of danger, of those of all denominations of persons, who, in their devotion to rectitude of principle, have declined to recognize the coercions of party discipline, and who constitute the genuine ' Imperial Guard ' or ' Macedonian Phalanx,' who strike only at the moment of imminent hazard, and whose moral strength renders them invincible."

The Church of God is the hope of all good enterprises, and within its sacred inclosure is the very " Body-guard of the King "—a company of prayerful, intelligent, consecrated men and women, sufficient in number, efficient in faculty, and withal not deficient in either sympathy for holy activity or in self-sacrifice for its promotion ; and, if this body of saints could be brought into vital touch with the work of missions, money and workers would be continually forthcoming ; there would be alike men in the field and " meat in God's house." It is *the link of connection that is lacking.* The majority of disciples *know* little of the wants of the field, and so *feel* little the needs and claims of the work. Their minds and hearts, consciences and sympathies, have not yet been really enlisted. If any impression has been made, it has been occasional and incidental, and hence the response has been spasmodic and impulsive. But in them lie the latent possibilities of vast increase in all that aids the best enterprises of the Church—the *motor* which needs only proper *machinery* to connect it with the work.

When any temporal disaster, like plague or famine,

makes its appeal, money flows in streams, and sometimes in floods. The difference lies here: the appeal in the latter case is loud and strong, echoed by every newspaper, emphasized in every sermon and public meeting for relief. The calamity that is present or threatening becomes everywhere the current topic of conversation. There is no eluding its clamorous demand for help, and knowledge of facts kindles sympathy and sympathy loosens purse-strings and heart-strings. Can not the perishing millions who know not the Gospel, be so brought practically into proximity with the millions of disciples who really love the Master, and are ready to respond to His command and to their claims, as that a constant stream of consecrated gifts may be secured beyond the risk of all this uncertainty?

It is our deliberate, prayerful, and mature judgment, that *no one thing would do more to secure a prompt, permanent, and altogether unprecedented advance in missions*, than the plan, now steadily growing in favor and in success—*of supporting individual missionaries in the field by individual contributions.*

Nothing is more needed in all missionary aggressive enterprise than three grand conditions: *Knowledge of the field, sympathy with the worker,* and *prayerful interest in the work.* When these are secured, gifts pour in without special appeals and without cessation. One method of supplying all these conditions readily suggests itself. Any man or woman of a family that is immediately linked to the missionary cause by the support of a missionary, will naturally come to know the field, to feel oneness with the worker, and to pray interestedly for the work and its progress. In Britain, hundreds of families, *as such,* support one or more missionaries, in some cases one of their own number, and in others, of the church or denomination to which they belong. And in such cases there are uniformly found an intelligence as to missions, a deep personal sympathy with missionaries, an absorbing interest in the work and in the people among whom it is done, a high standard of giving, and a high level of praying, not commonly met with *under any other circumstances.*

For example a Scottish family—a poor family—gave one, two, three sons to missions. One of them became disabled, and his sister went and took his place, and two of the grandchildren followed—six from one house. Need it be said that in that household the standard of knowledge, zeal, prayer and giving, was very high? Another family—that of a Scottish knight—sent a daughter to India as a fully equipped medical missionary; the effect on the whole family life was uplifting, and that family became itself a little missionary society, with all the conditions of success. Again a family—comparatively wealthy —resolved to give, pound for pound, and shilling for shilling, to the support of missionaries, the amount spent on *home* expenses. That house is the gathering-place of missionaries and a school of missionary information. Both the husband and wife can discourse of missions in any part of the world with intelligence and power. There is a family in Liverpool, whose son is in India in the Civil Service, but himself practically a missionary. Letters pass to and fro, and in that home the condition, especially of Indian missions is known, and a habitual giving is found, which shows a world-wide sympathy. A family in London supports not one but many mission workers, wholly or in part, in various fields. A *framed list* of subjects for daily prayer is hung up in plain sight, and, as each new day comes, the subject for that day is conspicuous. Of course, giving is bound to go with such praying, and the husband and wife, each one the independent possessor of a fortune, have given up all hoarding of money that they may enrich others, and frugally avoid needless expense that they may have more to bestow. That home is another missionary training-school. Another family of eleven sons and daughters are all engaged in mission work of some sort; the city of London is their field. One of them is training for the foreign field and has offered himself; and there again all the conditions are met, high intelligence, earnest prayer, fervent sympathy, and habitual giving. Such examples might be multiplied without limit. But these justify and illustrate the principle, which is all that is needed.

Before being confronted with such examples, the writer, in the year 1870, proposed to a church, of which he was then pastor, that the *young men* should form themselves into a missionary circle, and undertake to support a young man abroad. The proposal proved a seed in a congenial soil and took root. A number of the young men thus associated undertook the support of a young missionary just going to Japan and who spent years there as a missionary and educator. Need it be said that the standard of knowledge, praying, and giving in that church rose to an uncommon level? In 1869 the sum total of benevolent and missionary offerings reached about $1,800; in 1879 they reached about $18,000, for that church was one of the best organized in the country in the matter of its mission bands and societies, from the " Rhea Band " of the Sunday-school up to the adult organizations.

In 1883 the writer settled in Philadelphia, as pastor of a large body of people, numbering in all from 3,000 to 4,000, more or less closely identified with Bethany church and its great Sunday-school. After some few years of education in missions, taking up country after country and missionary heroes and heroines, etc., a band of several young people proposed to go out to some foreign field as a colony, and Hon. John Wanamaker offered a thousand dollars for the pastor to go and prospect and locate the field for the colony. It was then probable that the entire support of this mission band would have been attempted by the church, as in Pastor Harms' church in Hermannsburg, so long before. The head of this proposed mission band was a young Welsh licentiate and his wife, others who offered being simple artizans and tradesmen. At that time there was presented to the presbytery a printed statement covering all the facts, and asking only for encouragement. It was most graciously received, and referred to a committee to confer with the board; and the result was that it was deemed by the board unwise to encourage any such innovation, and so the whole matter fell through. On calmly reveiwing the whole matter, there is no doubt that there would have been a large shrinkage had the theory been reduced to practice. Some of this proposing mission band would probably have " gone back " when the actual work was undertaken. No doubt much of the glamor of enthusiasm would have faded away, like Ephraim's goodness, the morning cloud, and early dew. No doubt the conservative policy of presbytery and the board had much worldly wisdom back of it. But, after all reductions and deductions have been made, it still remains true that, had that church sent one or more missionaries *direct to the field* it might have become, with the generous and enterprising business man who has from the beginning been practically at its head, one of the main feeders of missions!

Take the Presbyterian Church as one example of what could be done by the *individual missionary plan.* The board needs annually, let us say, $1,000,000 for the proper prosecution of its existing missions. It has all it can do to get this sum, tho it has a membership of as many souls as it asks dollars annually. Of course, if this amount could be equally and proportionately divided; if each member would give one dollar a year, one-third of a cent a day, the whole amount would be raised without any self-denial—tho that would be a damage rather than an advantage. But this result, simple as it is, can not be secured,

The bulk even of Presbyterian church-members give nothing! What if out of the whole denomination *five hundred* churches could be found from Maine to California that would give $2,000 each to the support of a missionary abroad, keeping in touch with him by letters, studying his field, and praying habitually for his work? We should have the $1,000,000, with all the rest of the denomination left to work on for surplus amounts. Or, if 1,000 churches give $1,000 each, the same result is accomplished.

In this vast membership of about 1,000,000 there are believed to be not less than twenty thousand millionaires. There are no less than *two hundred and fifty* men in this one denomination that represent an average of ten million each, or an aggregate sum of $2,500,000,000. How few of us know what that sum means! If piled up, in five dollar gold-pieces, that aggregate wealth would reach *three thousand five hundred miles into space!* But, of course, millionaires are not always or generally self-denying givers. But can not there be found 1,000 men or women in this whole Church that will *each* undertake, at the cost annually of $1,000, to support a missionary in the field? And what unspeakable advantage to the *givers!* What increase of knowledge of the field of work! What increasingly sympathetic touch with the missionary and through him or her with all other fields and workers; and what a stimulus to prayer, to giving, to personal consecration! What has been shown to be possible in this one denomination is only an example of general possibilities if the Church of God were in dead earnest.

Eighteen centuries have sped since our Lord gave his final commission. To-day there remain at least 800,000,-000 of human beings to be reached with the Gospel message. And of these 25,000,000 will die during each year, over 2,000,000 a month! At the *present rate* of mission progress the world will *never be overtaken.* In fact, at a time when every condition of the field demanded *advance* and every condition of the Church justified it, in seven out of ten missionary societies the decree went forth for *retrenchment from twenty to twenty-five per cent!* In other words, with the population increasing at the rate of 2,000,000 a month, and proportionately dying, the Church of Christ, that aggregates at least fifty million Protestant members with hoarded wealth that defies computation, instead of sounding the silver trumpet for the assembling of the camps and the forward march around the ark of the covenant, bids the drum of a worldly selfishness to beat an ignominious retreat; and we retire from positions, gained at the cost of blood and of treasure, and of lives given for Christ; we actually surrender from one-fourth to one-fifth of our outposts and captured fortresses, and bid the foe once more sweep back upon the territory claimed and possessed for God!

And if one nowadays raises the cry of alarm, and thunders out a remonstrance; if one declares that missions have never been in *greater danger of utter collapse through this lack of adequate giving,* the answer, from some fellow-believers, is ridicule, rebuke, stigmatizing epithets, such as " pessimist," " croaker," etc.

One grave consideration should be before us as to individual responsibility. Untold disaster to Church-work has been entailed by the withdrawing and withholding of offerings on the part of those to whom the local church and the denomination have a right to look for financial support. A church-member should have very solid reasons—reasons that would stand not only the scrutiny of an enlightened conscience, but the searching inquiry of omniscience—who treats with neglect, indifference, or contempt the mission work of the church and denomination to which such individual member belongs. A board, or other representative committee, is but an administrative body. It sends missionaries to the field under the implied pledge of the church it represents, to stand behind it and to support them there; and to this implied covenant every church-member is a necessary party. To allow the missionary agency to be crippled by an empty treasury and half wrecked by debt, is something for which, therefore, every church-member is responsible, and will be held accountable by the Master of us all.

This plan of thus directly connecting home churches, families, and individual givers with the mission field by these living and personal links, has been growing in favor, and having increasing proof of God's blessing, of late years. In connection with the Church Missionary Society of Britain, there are about 300 missionaries maintained by special gifts of individual donors, *without prejudice to the general work,* which is a very important fact. Other boards in this country are just now advocating a similar policy, encouraging individuals to give to the support of special missions and missionaries, while they carefully caution such donors that they deem it unwise for such gifts to be *limited to special objects* in the mission field, as it has been found that interest is apt to decline, and support to be withdrawn, when such special object is no longer deemed advisable or practicable. * Of course, when gifts to missions are prompted by a truly Christ-like spirit, they

---

* A pertinent example of this method of supporting a missionary, and of enlisting the sympathies of a church is furnished in the case of the late Dr. A. C. Good, who was sustained in his arduous work in Africa by the contributions of Trinity Presbyterian Church in Montclair, N. J. This church asked the board that they might assume his entire support and salary, and regard him as their special representative abroad. The arrangement resulted most happily. His relation to the board was unaltered thereby, and a particular benefit accrued, not only to that church, but to the Church at large; for never before had he allowed himself to write such full, leisurely letters. The pastor, Rev. Orville Reed, testifies to the blessed influence of these letters on the church, in the real interest awakened in foreign missions, the warm attachment to the missionary, and the increase of prayerful giving. It was as tho the church had a second "*pastor* in Africa."—"A Life for Africa," pp. 148, 149.

will never be limited by too narrow a range of personal sympathies or individual preferences. The work is cosmopolitan, and demands a cosmopolitan soul behind it—catholic, impartial love, universal sympathy and support. When it ceases to be wise to pursue any particular line of work, or to occupy any particular sphere of service, or when any form of effort obviously lacks the divine sanction, consecrated gifts will not be withheld altogether, but only diverted to some wiser, better channel; the work at large must never suffer because any local work fails to commend itself to our further approval and cooperation: otherwise we are moved by self-will and not the will of God.

We commend for consideration the following suggestions:

1. That every *local congregation* shall at once organize with reference to the support of at least *one foreign missionary,* to be associated with its own church life and work. Some congregations can do more than maintain one; others may not feel equal to the support of even one, and such may associate with themselves one or more smaller churches.

2. Let each *family* ask the question: Can we as a household support a missionary abroad? Many a family that has never yet thought of such a thing as possible, will at once see that, by a small reduction of family outlay or by consecrating a certain percentage of family income, a missionary could represent them abroad.

3. Let every *individual* Christian solemnly ask and answer this question: Could I not this year *support a missionary?* There is a man—known to the writer—who is alone in the world and spends at least $10,000 a year for his own keeping; another believer who pays $10,000 a year rent and has not a child or dependent; another who spent

$25,000 in one year's travel; another whose personal expenses are at least $15,000 exclusive of house rent; another who, with one child, spends $10,000 annually. There are others who retrench in every direction, cheerfully and habitually, in order to give, like that man who supports an *entire mission* with its six workers, paying outfit, transportation, salary, etc., out of his own pocket; yet that man is *not* a rich man, but one of very moderate means, but who does business and makes money for Christ.

Alas! the Church of God as a body is still asleep, or, if awake, criminally apathetic and lethargic. And the Master of us all will have some day an awful reckoning with us for wasting His goods, and neglecting His scattered sheep, and disobeying His command. There is bloodguiltiness to be required of this generation. Let us abandon the work of missions altogether if it be not *God's work and ours by His appointment.* But if it *be* His work, then in the name of God and of Christ, and of the Gospel, and of Humanity let us *do it,* and do it with some such enthusiasm, prayerfulness, generosity, sacrifice, giving of money, and giving of self, as the magnitude of the trust and the field, and the magnificence of the work and the reward, and the majesty of the Divine King and Captain demand!

The one thing which the Master is now pressing upon the attention of all His disciples who have ears to hear is the absolute necessity of remembering, as before God, their individual duty and privilege. He solemnly challenges every disciple to face three great questions, as one who alone is to give account of himself unto God. However we may hide here behind the mass, or lose ourselves in the crowd, at the judgment-seat of Christ every one of us, in awful aloneness, must confront these tremendous questions: " Hast thou wasted my goods?" "Hast thou neglected a dying world?" "Hast thou shut thine hand and purse against thy needy and perishing brother man?" And we need to meet these questions, now, with a practical answer which will stand this scrutiny, if we are not to be "ashamed before Him at His coming."

CHAPTER XXIII

MEDICAL MISSIONS: SAMUEL FISK GREEN, M.D. *

EXAMPLE incarnates argument; it is the word made flesh and dwelling among us. The theory and philosophy of medical missions are illustrated in the lives of medical missionaries, whose careers have silenced all objections and supplied irrefutable reasons for enlarged service along the same lines. We give one such example out of many, namely, Samuel Fisk Green, who from 1847 to 1873, a period of twenty-six years, was identified with work in Ceylon.

In his eighteenth year he found Christ and became a member of the Mercer Street Presbyterian church in New York. He inherited a leaning toward the medical profession, and sundry influences swayed his choice, so that at the age of nineteen, he was studying medicine, and entered the college of physicians and surgeons.

The experience of the dissecting-room was very repulsive to his sensitive nature, but he endured all that was necessary to his fitness for his life-work; and the familiarity with the human body, which often leads to materialism, only called forth in him more reverence as it revealed the two grand arguments for a Divine design: First, the mechanism of every part, and second, the adaptation of all parts to the whole. Familiarity with suffering also, instead of hardening, softened him, and made him more sympathetic and tender.

---

* See Life and Letters of Samuel Fisk Green, M. D. Compiled by Ebenezer Cutler, D.D.

In March, 1846, he asked himself: "Why is it not better for me to go where I can be very useful, as well in my profession as otherwise, at once—go to a land of darkness, and heal the bodies and enlighten the minds of some error-bound people?" That question led to his self-offering for the field, and he was soon after under appointment to Ceylon, as a missionary of the American Board, and landed at Ceylon in October, reaching Battecotta shortly after, at the completion of his first quarter century.

It was not a fortnight, before success in a surgical operation established him at once in the confidence of the Tamils. With insight, born of a thorough knowledge of the healing art, he discovered an abscess in the abdomen, and removed it. The patient was cured, and the fame of the new doctor spread through the peninsula. The natives began to talk about the miracle of this cure; the new English doctor "had taken out the bowels, adjusted them, and refixed them." He was a demigod at once, and, of course, people flocked to him from all parts. He remembered the deeper sickness that needed a divine physician, and, as he healed the sick, he preached the Gospel, seeking to apply to every patient the spiritual remedies of the Gospel. Even while yet using an interpreter he explained how all sickness is the ultimate fruit of sin, and often the immediate penalty of violating God's laws. He distributed well-selected tracts, and so began his two-fold work for body and soul.

In February, 1848, he was removed to Manepy, and there again "the people thronged him." At the temple of Puliar, a great festival begins about March 25th, and holds for three weeks.

Dr. Green writes:

On the second Sabbath of the festival, I saw, in the midst of the throng, a man rolling along on the ground, holding in his hands an offering—a little brass vessel of milk—under an arch trimmed with peacock feathers and painting; behind him an old religious beggar ringing a bell; before him another bearing some incense burning. The poor fellow rolled over and over, his black body whitened by the dust, for about half a mile and then around the temple. He had been sick and made a vow to do this. He got medicine, I understand, of me; but if mine did him any good he ascribes the virtue to Puliar; so I have been an instrument, perhaps, of leading this man to serve the devil.

This is an example both of the opportunities and difficulties which heathenism presented. To uproot growths of superstition, tradition, caste, and custom, which had rooted themselves for centuries, was a hard task, but Christ long since said: "Every plant which my heavenly Father hath not planted shall be rooted up." Nothing was more disheartening than the spiritual apathy about him. The people would assent to almost anything, and yet remain unmoved. Prayer must call down fire from heaven if such moral stagnation and self-complaisance were to be changed.

By the autumn of his first year Dr. Green had two young Tamils as students of medicine, for he felt the need of a native force of helpers. After eight months he began to speak the Tamil, and a few months later could understand a sermon in the vernacular. He saw that his main business was to spread knowledge of salvation, and gave out tickets on which were printed not only health-rules, but Gospel truths—a synopsis of truths touching soul-health.

Dr. Green was no idler. In thirteen months previous to January 1, 1848, 2,544 native cases had been treated, one-third or more of them surgical, including tumors, cancers, cataracts, strangulated hernia, amputations, fractures, etc., and not a few of these were major operations in point of critical and dangerous character, as when the left upper jaw and cheek bones were removed for a cancerous fungus in the antrum filling the whole mouth and left nostril.

Some of the worst phases of heathenism were inwoven with the notions concerning the nature, causes, and treatment of bodily ills. Superstitions about the "evil eye" and evil tongue are numerous and deep-rooted. Fires were lit at junction of two roads to counteract the evil tongue. Praise might cause the party praised to be ill, and mango leaves, salt, red peppers, and the dust from the tracks of him who did the praising, must be used to undo the harm; the leaves waved thrice about the head, the salt, etc., rubbed on the body, then all these burned at evening. Cows were daubed with soot to keep off the evil eye, etc. Akusteer, a fabulous dwarf, a cubit high, is the famous medical authority, whose prescriptions are servilely followed. A famous practitioner in Manepy had been in practice forty-two years, yet had never known the difference between arterial and venous blood, did not know that there was black blood as well as red, nor had he ever seen a vital organ. He thought the *pulse* to be the *motion of air* in the body.

A sort of *scapegoat* idea was sometimes found prevailing, as when a mud image represents a sick child, and a ceremony about that image is supposed to cause the sickness to leave the child and enter the image. Horses' teeth and rhinoceros' horns are used as remedies. From a goldsmith's arm, who was down with fever, was taken a charm, a gold tube, with which was a sheet of lead ruled off into forty-nine squares, and in this diagram were written several muntras, and under them a prayer to Siva. The swami (idol) is supposed to reside in this mystic seat, which is tied above the right elbow to chase away intruding demons.

These and kindred superstitions Dr. Green felt it to be his mission, by a truly scientific treatment, to uproot, destroying the very basis of the native system of dealing with disease, and so delivering the people from the deceptions, delusions and cruelties of native doctors.

Difficulties there were in treating disease. Even cholera patients would not always accept a physician's aid.

Some fear to take medicine lest it offend their gods; refusing medicine and taking only the juice of the leaf of the sacred tree over Genesa's temple, mixed with water. They would rather die without medicine and take their chances with their gods in the unseen world than recover by the use of medicine, and encounter the malice of their gods in this world.

He was sometimes asked to feel one's pulse through silk, so as not to impart pollution by his touch. A Brahman wished him to examine his wife's case without putting his fingers or instruments into her mouth. He met such demands sometimes by refusal to comply, and sometimes by a droll facetiousness which disarmed prejudice.

A wealthy Moorman called to consult about his wife, who has apparently a mammary abscess. I suggested that he take a Lalimer (a Tamil), and let him examine, and, if necessary, use the lancet. He could not consent; no one could be allowed to *see his wife*. I proposed that she be seated *behind a curtain,* through which the doctor could do the needful, but he would not agree.

In Syria an American doctor insisted on at least examining tongue and pulse, in order to prescribe for a pasha's wife; and so a slit in the curtain was made, and a tongue and a hand successively thrust through, which, being normal, he found to be the hand and tongue of a *maid*. He was expected to examine his patient by proxy!

Early in the fourth year Dr. Green was recalled to Batticotta. He was having an average of 2,000 patients a year, and was giving religious instruction to nearly thrice that number annually. All his work as a medical man was anointed with the fragrance of prayer, and he sought to impress upon his patients that this was all *religious* work. He said of the removal of a cataract:

This is, perhaps, the most delicate operation in surgery. Completely successful. I scarce expected aught but failure; but the Great Physician guided my hand.

When subsequently he undertook an operation which he thought too trifling to pray over, he failed in it; and accepted the failure as a lesson to show that, without God he could do nothing.

To get any fair command of the Tamil tongue was to Dr. Green a preparation for providing a *medical literature* for the people in their vernacular—another hard task, for in science as in religion, the very mold of a heathen language is often so cramped and distorted as to make it well nigh impossible to express normal conceptions.

He started a vocabulary, defining English and Latin terms in Tamil, as the basis, and planned some pamphlets on the more important branches of the healing art, with the Gospel on the reverse of every leaf—" a good *backing* " —for gratuitous circulation. These primers he carefully prepared, beginning with the most needful. He inspired and directed his students, so that they should both do good work and aid his own.

In 1851, a complete glossary for anatomy was made, and the Tamil medical dictionary was begun. The first work selected for translation was Dr. Calvin Cutter's work on " Anatomy, Physiology, and Hygiene," with cuts. And so the work was fairly on the way, which was to make European medical practice indigenous and ultimately displace the native system. In June, 1852, this first work on anatomy, etc., was ready for the press. It took three months of close attention to get the book out with its illustrations, and in a week a quarter of the edition was disposed of and being eagerly read by the native doctors.

From a census of *readers* among his patients, taken in 1852, he estimated that, of the 432,000 inhabitants of the province, 132,000 were readers, of whom about 2,600 were women. In 1816 but one Tamil woman in the province could read, and this large increase of women readers was a prophecy of a time coming when female education would be nearly as universal in Ceylon as in England.

At this time, as he had help in teaching, Dr. Green was able to meet the demand for practice at the homes of patients more than before. He studied and loved the people, and avoided no labor or sacrifice that would help him meet their needs.

In 1854-5 cholera visited Ceylon, and the people fled before it. A day of fasting was kept by all the missions in December. In the Jaffna district alone were reported for the year 8,000 cases, besides 2,500 of smallpox. But Dr. Green, tho never strong himself, was ever ready to help others, and was himself violently prostrated, causing intense anxiety. He took " medicine enough for a horse," and his recovery was like rising from the dead.

During six months, in 1856, 1,032 patients were registered, and his literary labors were vigorously prosecuted. With aid from his munshi and Rev. Mr. Webb, of the Madura mission, he completed vocabularies for chemistry and natural philosophy, revised his work on obstetrics, etc.

In 1857, ten years of service being completed, he took a respite from labor, leaving Ceylon for America. In a decade of years, he had so mastered the hard tongue as to preach in it directly from his English manuscript; he had published tracts, laid the basis of a Tamil medical literature, published two important works—translations from Cutter and Maunsell; he had been connected with the treatment of over 20,000 patients, to whom, and as many more of their attendants, he had made known the Gospel remedies for soul-sickness. Twenty young men he had qualified for medicine and surgery, and some of them were teaching others.

En route to America, he visited Edinburgh by invitation of the Medical Missionary Society, and drew up an outline of his views on medical missions, which is one of the best pleas for the combination of the healing art with Gospel work. In May, 1862, he again set sail, having married Miss Margaret Phelps Williams, in every way worthy of her husband; and in October they were welcomed in Manepy, where he gladly resumed his manifold activities as medical teacher and practitioner, evangelist, expositor, translator, editor, counselor and friend.

Soon after he was asked to take the superintendence of the hospital connected with the " Friend in Need Society," and consented to make a trial of it for three months. He at once reorganized the work for greater efficiency and economy. Some idea of the surgery made necessary may be seen from one record of August 7th, 1863.

Two Chank gatherers severely bitten by a huge shark. One has four bad, deep, large bites in his right thigh, and the other his right thigh bitten off, leaving as stump the upper third. We sawed off a bit of the bone which projected about three inches. Performed Simm's operation on an unhappy woman, and tapped a Moorman, making out a pretty good clinic for the thirteen students and three doctors present.

Here, beside his other work, 8,000 patients were annually treated, the worst cases being attended to by himself, and all under his oversight. After three months' trial, he concluded God had opened before him this new and effectual door of service, and he continued as its superintendent.

Meanwhile light so increased in Jaffna that the head place of Siva was seen to be a den of infamy, and even the heathen began to demand reforms. All the Brahmans about that shrine were reported licentious and the temple was but partner to the brothel.

He wrote of the Hindu religion:

It is dovetailed into the whole social system. Astrologers must fix the day to build a house, and the propitious time for the thatching must come before the first leaf is tied on. In Batticotta women will, but men will not kill a centipede; for once a woman tried to poison her husband by soup, but a centipede falling into it stopped his eating it, and so defeated her malice and saved his life.

What can be viler than the revered, sacred books! He who would faithfully translate Koo-rul into English would become infamously famous; and sensual corruption pervades the very sanctum of idolatry. When heathenism sinks the Brahmans will sink with it, from deities to men.

Dr. Green compares Indian false religion to a huge banyan with ten thousand branches, far-reaching and rooting themselves anew in every direction, and the missionary force that is sent forth to fell it, he likens to a few puny white boys with playing hatchets!

During the deputation's visit, and while they were about to ordain and install the first native pastor, the mission adopted, as part of the church covenant, a solemn renunciation of caste. Within a month there were nearly one hundred signatures; and Dr. Green's personal influence over his medical class led the members not only to Christ, but into His church, at cost of everything.

During the ravages of cholera in 1866-7, he found his hands full. Health handbills were issued, and tracts on cholera, and the commissioners of government publicly commended his tireless endeavors to abate the scourge. But he never lost sight of his greater work to save souls from the second death.

In the summer of 1868, he summed up the results of the six years, since his return. He had led a class through two-thirds of their remaining course of medical study in English, graduating eight physicians; and carried as many more through their whole course in the vernacular; he had trained three dispensers wholly in Tamil, and three more partially. He had made out six vocabularies, and completed four others; carried one large volume through the press, and prepared another; secured three volumes in manuscript, soon to be printed, and five more in crude stage, besides all his guidance of work which others had done.

Before the close of this year he was compelled to resign his hospital superintendency, in face of all pressure to remain. The term of service begun for three months as an experiment had continued to twenty-two times that period.

In the spring of 1869, Dr. Green was busy on the revision of the *Physician's Vade Mecum*, the hardest revision work he ever undertook, the " translation being bad, and the subject obstinate," and not until fifteen months later was the work completed. His health was very frail, and disease threatened, but the impossibility of creating a pure literature for the Tamils without Western aid kept him at work, and he was already a leader in the creation of science in the Tamil tongue. His works, printed in that language, covered nearly 4,500 octavo pages.

The place of *medical literature* in missions he both testified and tested. For instance, he says of the use of certain cuts in Dr. Smith's anatomical atlas, in connection with his own work on anatomy:

I regard a volume of this kind as most distinctively aggressive on Hinduism. There is a radical antagonism between the truths it will spread and the prevalent ideas here concerning the body. It should be shown that the body is the Lord's wondrous mechanism, and not the lodgment of divers gods, nor its various parts controlled by the constellations. With plenty and good illustrations the book will be doubly useful. It will be as different from a non-illustrated volume as daylight from dawn. These will advance one item at least of missionary work far toward that desired state in which " the light of the sun shall be as the light of seven days."

A prominent authority on medical missions, in Edin-

burgh, wrote of Dr. Green that no then living missionary "had had such lengthened experience, or done so
much to extend the benefits of European skill, by transla-
ting and publishing a comprehensive medical and surgical
literature in the South India vernacular, and by training
native medical evangelists."

His medical labors are not easily tabulated. Thousands
first heard the Gospel at his lips, and who shall tell the
outcome? He found at the seaside, and by seeming accident, a blind woman who recognized his voice, and told
him that, fifteen years before, she had fever and was healed
at his dispensary, and that he told her about Jesus Christ;
and she added, " I have prayed to Him ever since, and have
not worshipped idols."

As another ten years since his resumption of work in
Ceylon approached completion, his return to America
seemed inevitable. During his two terms sixty-four had
been trained in medicine (whereas only seven or eight had
been, before his advent), and over half of these sixty-four
in the vernacular; and a class of twenty were well started
before he left. He had produced eight larger works, besides the smaller, and four were yet in manuscript. His
graduates were filling important positions, " studding the
province," and the hospital he had conducted for five years
and a half was now manned by them, and had more patients than all the hospitals in the other provinces.

When in September, 1873, Dr. Green and his wife and
children reached the family home at Worcester, he did not
cease to be a missionary. Translations and new composi-
tions, correspondence, conversation, public addresses, and
the constant persuasive fragrance of his personality, kept
up the " apostolic succession."

To Dr. Green had been born, between 1864 and 1871,
four children—three daughters and a son, and he did not
forget these " olive plants " at home, but took untiring in-

terest in their training, using as his helpers books and the world of nature, fauna and flora, with microscope and lancet, and above all the Bible, with rare fidelity to God's ideal, putting first what belongs first, not the mental or physical, but the moral and spiritual.

Home rest slowly brought recuperation, and he hoped to return to work, and said, " Altho powerfully weak, we multiply half strength by tenfold demand, and get the result of fivefold usefulness."

In 1880, he took whooping-cough from his own children, which probably gave strength to a constitutional malady long preying on him; and, at noonday of May 28, 1884, with hope at its meridian, he passed into the life that knows no end. His last words were a benediction, and his last legacy a self-oblivious decree:

I wish that my funeral may be conducted as inexpensively as may consist with decency and order. Let the exercises be simply to edification; and of the dead speak neither blame nor praise. Should I ever have a gravestone, let it be plain and simple, and bear the following inscription, viz.:

SAMUEL FISK GREEN,

1822-1884,*

MEDICAL EVANGELIST TO THE TAMILS.

JESUS MY ALL.

---

* The last date, left blank, is supplied to complete the inscription.

CHAPTER XXIV

THE name of Florence Nightingale is inseparably connected with a new form of woman's ministry to man generally, in a wide-spread movement for the *reform of sanitary conditions in the camp and campaign, of soldiers and sailors.*

She was an Italian by birth, being born in Florence, Italy, in 1823, of English parents. Highly educated, brilliantly accomplished, of refined sensibility, every inch a woman, and with none of the masculine traits, often associated with women of public action, God prepared in her a mighty force for the relief, and in fact reconstruction of unhealthy and abnormal conditions in the British Army, and, through her success there, inspiring similar movements elsewhere.

She early showed intense interest in the alleviation of suffering which, in 1844, at the early age of twenty-one, led her to give close attention to the condition of hospitals, so that, like John Howard, and Elizabeth Fry, who was called the Female Howard, she undertook a personal visitation and inspection of the civil and military hospitals all over Europe. She studied, with the sisters of charity of Paris, the system of nursing and of management in the hospitals, and in 1851, at twenty-eight, herself went into training as a nurse in the institution of Protestant Deaconesses, at Kaiserwerth on the Rhine. Thus qualified, on her return to her own land, England, she put into thorough working order, the Sanitorium for Governesses in connection with the London Institution. All unconscious of the wide work for the world and the ages for which God was thus fitting her, she had thus served a ten years' term of apprenticeship for the sublime and self-sacrificing career that lay just before her.

In the spring of 1854, when she was in her thirty-second year, war was declared by Britain against Russia, and a force of 25,000 British soldiery embarked for the Golden Horn. The battle of Alma was fought on September 20, and the wounded with the sick were sent down to the hastily improvised hospitals, made ready to receive them on the banks of the Bosphorus. Crowds of men in every stage of sickness and suffering from wounds, unskillfully treated and still worse, neglected, were thus huddled together. How unsanitary the conditions were, may be inferred from the average rate of mortality. The hospitals were more fatal than the battle field, the ordinary casualties of the fiercest battle being insignificant in comparison to the death rate in the wards.

Dr. Hamlin well remarks that the Crimean war brought out both the noblest and basest attributes of human character. There were Hedley Vicars among the officers and Dr. Blackwood among the chaplains, and his noble wife, Lady Alicia, and Florence Nightingale in the hospitals, who will forever stand out as exhibiting the glory of our common humanity and Christianity. But the same events gave opportunity to exhibit the meanest selfishness and sordidness.

In the great hospital at Scutari, the severest sufferings were in the night. At ten o'clock P. M. the lights were put out and no one came near the sufferers until the morning. The night was made hideous and horrible by agonizing cries for water, groans of the dying, and ravings of the delirious. Dr. Hamlin offered Dr. Menzies, the chief physician, his own help and that of a dozen or fifteen of his most trustworthy students, as night-watchers, but the proposal was not only rejected, but rejected with asperity. He went further and applied to Gen. Posgaiter, commissary general, offering to organize a relief force of volunteer night watchers, from American and English residents, who would obey all the rules, subject to Dr. Menzies' orders, undertaking simply to relieve the awful and needless suffering of the sick and wounded soldiers. When the commissary general forwarded Dr. Hamlin's note with his own, the only result was another repulse, the Doctor replying curtly, " We cannot admit any outside interference; " and so thousands of brave sufferers were cruelly left to agony of thirst, torture of pain and even to death, in the darkness of a doubly unrelieved night.

Of course, in such a hospital the conditions were all horribly unsanitary. The smell was like that of a dissecting chamber, where corpses lie in all stages of putrefaction, nauseous in the extreme, and showing not only neglect, but downright incapacity on the part of medical attendants. Dr. Menzies was finally removed and removed in disgrace.

Dr. Hamlin tells also of the condition of things in the Kulelie hospital. The battle of Inkerman was fought in November, 1855, and a week or so later, the *Himalaya,* the huge English iron merchant steamer, was lying at Kulelie and two hundred and fifty wounded were in the cavalry barracks and some Russian wounded on the float wharf. Both the English and Russian soldiers' blankets were full of lice, and Dr. Hamlin says, " I picked off eleven of the most atrocious beasts I ever saw, from my woollen gloves." The English wounded had had no washing done for five months, for lack of wood and water; and their under flannels were such nests of vermin that they wore none, preferring to suffer from the cold. There was plenty of clothing but it could not be worn. Dr. Hamlin ap-

pealed to the chief physician about the washing, but met
only another surly reply, " it could not be done ;" and, when
a way to do it was suggested, he damned Dr. Hamlin as
an intruder, his dirty meerschaum hanging in the corner
of his dirtier mouth. Dr. Hamlin then found the " sar-
geant " of the clothing, who showed him a great hall where
were piled up garments for a thousand men. The place
was a plague breeder, unventilated, with beds and bedding
and clothing, taken from the wounded and the dead, filthy
and full of vermin, and such looking animals, overgrown,
flat, hellish looking, their bite like that of a scorpion, irritating and maddening, producing fever heat and burning
itch. Dr. Hamlin says that these vermin killed more men
than the bullets.

In despair of cleansing such clothing, a furnace was
built to burn it.

Florence Nightingale, with her nurses, appeared on the
scene of the Crimean conflict and all was changed in these
hospitals. She had many coadjutors and evinced large capacity to deal with the conditions she found. One improvement followed another in rapid and glorious succession,
until the hospitals became models of sympathetic care and
sanitary provisions. The hideous nights of suffering were
relieved and shortened by the tender sympathetic hand and
heart of woman—all presided over by one woman, who
combined in herself marvelous common sense, sound judgment, and intelligent Christian capacity.

The crisis in the Crimea which led Florence Nightingale
to offer herself as a missionary to the sick and suffering at
Scutari, was one of what Dr. Croly called the " Birth
hours of history." The reorganization of that nursing department at Scutari meant a reform in all the treatment of
sick and wounded soldiers and sailors in war times, and a
permanent and world-wide advance in this department,
even among semi-civilized peoples.

Lord Herbert, then at the War Office, gladly accepted her offer, and within a week after, Miss Nightingale was on the way with her nursing corps. She reached Constantinople in November, 1854, just before the battle of Inkerman, and the beginning of the terrific winter campaign, in time to receive from that second battle the wounded, though the wards already had in them 2,300 patients.

History, poetry, and art have vied with each other fitly to represent the heroic devotion of that woman of thirty-one, to the sufferers from that cruel war. She was known to stand on her feet twenty hours at a time, without once sitting down, that she might personally see sufferers provided with such accommodation and care as their condition called for. The following spring, while in the Crimea organizing the nursing departments of the camp hospitals, she herself paid the penalty of her untiring toil and unsparing self-sacrifice, in a prostrating fever. Yet she refused to desert her post of duty, recovered, and remained at Scutari until the British evacuated Turkey in July, 1856.

How many soldiers owed to her life and health we know not, for of some facts no history has ever been adequately written. But the mental and physical strain told upon her naturally frail constitution. She, like her Master, saved others, but herself she could not save. She yet lives, but an invalid, withdrawn from public life into the quiet of her rural home—modestly shrinking, especially from the visits of the curious who would like to see the heroine of the Crimean hospitals; but still devising means for the improvement of the health of the soldier.

In 1857, when a commission was created to inquire into " the regulations affecting the sanitary condition of the British Army," she supplied a paper of written evidence in which, with peculiar force, she emphasized the many lessons learned in the Crimean war which were char-

acterized as a " sanitary experiment on a colossal scale."
During her experience there, the results which accumulated under her own eyes, proved that, with proper provision for food, clothing, cleanliness, nursing, and various
sanitary conditions, the rate of mortality among soldiers
may be reduced to *one half of the average death rate in
time of peace and at home!*

Such discoveries naturally fixed her mind on the general question of sanitary reform in the army, and first of
all the army hospitals. In 1858, she contributed other
papers, on Hospital construction and arrangement, to the
National Association for the promotion of social science.
Her *Notes on Hospitals,* clear in arrangement and minute
in detail, are alike valuable to the architect, engineer and
medical man. Her *Notes on Nursing* is a text book in
many a household.

The results of her work in the Crimean war, prompted
a fund to enable her to form an institution for training
nurses—a fund which yields an annual interest of 1,400
pounds sterling. No separate Institution has been formed,
but the revenue is applied to training a superior order of
nurses in connection with existing hospitals.

How highly Miss Nightingale's opinions are held in esteem even by the British government is evinced for example by one fact. When in 1863, the Report of the Commission on the Sanitary Condition of the Army in India
was made in two folios of a thousand pages each, the
manuscripts were forwarded to her for her examination,
and her observations are inserted with the published report. In these observations and comments, there is such a
masterly array of facts, such clearness of statement and
such incisive force as render it one of the most remarkable papers ever reduced to written form, and it
marks a new era in the government of India.

As already hinted, the study of Miss Nightingale's

career naturally suggests a comparison with the singularly parallel career of John Howard, who attempted his "circumnavigation of charity" in the interests of the prison reform, and with that of Elizabeth Fry who, born ten years before Howard's death, in a remarkable manner took up and carried on at Newgate and other prisons of Britain, the work he began. It is another curious coincidence that each lived about the same period—sixty-five years.

The labors of Miss Nightingale have led to the formation of the *Red Cross Association,* which had its origin, nine years after the Crimean war called her to the scenes of oriental conflict, in a proposal made in February 1863, at a meeting of the *Society Genévoise* by Henry Dumant, who had witnessed the horrors of Italian battlefields, " whether it would not be possible in time of peace to form societies for the relief of the wounded when war should again break out "? A committee appointed to examine into the matter called an International Congress at Geneva, in the autumn of the same year, and another general congress convened in Geneva in 1864, at which sixteen European powers were represented, and the terms of a treaty were signed by twelve delegates and later by four others. The principal terms of this convention, were that in time of war the hospitals and all pertaining to them be considered as on neutral ground and wounded and sick soldiers shall be cared for, to whatever side they belong in the conflict.*

---

*ARTICLE I. Ambulances and military hospitals shall be acknowledged to be neutral, and, as such, shall be protected and respected by belligerents so long as any sick or wounded may be therein. Such neutrality shall cease if the ambulances or hospitals shall be held by military force.

ARTICLE II. Persons employed in hospitals and ambulances, comprising the staff for superintendence, medical service, administration, transport of wounded, as well as chaplain, shall participate in the benefit of neutrality while so employed, and so long as there remain any wounded to bring in or to succor.

ARTICLE III. The persons designated in the preceding article may, even

It was necessary, according to Article VII, to have a flag or sign to distinguish those laboring under the direction of this organization. A red cross upon a white background was chosen. This choice was for the purpose of honoring Switzerland. It shows the flag of that country reversed.

In 1867, at Paris, the rules of the convention were extended to naval conflicts also. The beneficence of the Red Cross Association was soon and very grandly proven, in the wars of 1864 and 1866 and subsequently in the Franco-Prussian, Russo-Turkish, American Civil War, America-Spanish War, &c. In the war of 1866, nearly 14,000 Austrian wounded were cared for by the Prussian Society of the Red Cross, at a total expense of over a million and a half of dollars, and in the Franco-Prussian war the Red Cross had 25,000 beds in towns between Dusseldorf and Baden alone.

----

after occupation by the enemy, continue to fulfil their duties in the hospital or ambulance which they serve, or may withdraw to join the corps to which they belong. Under such circumstances, when these persons shall cease from these functions, they shall be delivered by the occupying army to the outposts of the enemy. They shall have the special right of sending a representative to the headquarters of their respective armies.

ARTICLE IV. As the equipment of military hospitals remains subject to the laws of war, persons attached to such hospitals can not, in withdrawing, carry away articles which are not their private property. Under the same circumstances an ambulance shall, on the contrary, retain its equipment.

ARTICLE V. Inhabitants of the country who may bring help to the wounded shall be respected and remain free. The generals of the belligerent powers shall make it their care to inform the inhabitants of this appeal addressed to their humanity, and of the neutrality which will be the consequence of it. Any wounded man entertained and taken care of in a house shall be considered as a protection thereto. Any inhabitant who shall have entertained wounded men in his house shall be exempted from the quartering of troops, as well as from the contributions of war which may be imposed.

ARTICLE VI. Wounded or sick soldiers, whatever their nationality, shall be cared for.

Commanders-in-chief shall have the power to deliver immediately to the outposts of the enemy, soldiers who have been wounded in an engagment. when circumstances permit this to be done, with the consent of both parties, Those who are recognized as incapable of serving, after they are healed,

In 1883, Queen Victoria instituted the Red Cross order in behalf of the British Army, with a fitting decoration.

Every country in Europe and almost every nation on the globe has signed this treaty, the United States being almost the last formally to accept its humane principles.

During the late wars, among women were many who followed the American armies and cared for the wounded upon the battle field and in the hospital. One of the very best of these nurses was Miss Clara Barton. With untiring zeal she worked, with her heart of love, through all those years of the Civil war. Her labor for others did not close when the war was at an end. Many an anxious parent or friend had sons or loved ones who were asleep in nameless graves. Miss Barton began the great task of marking the graves of those who fell in that war, and for three years she labored and toiled, until success beyond all expectation crowned her efforts.

With the Red Cross movement in America, the name of Miss Barton is henceforth conspicuously linked.

---

shall be sent back to their country. The others also may be sent back on condition of not again bearing arms during the continuance of the war. Evacuations, together with the persons under whose direction they take place, shall be protected by an absolute neutrality.

ARTICLE VII. A distinctive and uniform flag shall be adopted for hospitals, ambulances, and evacuated places. It must on every occasion be accompanied by the National flag. An arm-badge shall also be allowed for individuals neutralized, but the delivery of it shall be left to military authority. The flag and arm-badge shall bear a red cross on a white ground.

ARTICLE VIII. It is the duty of the conquering army to supervise, as far as circumstances permit, the soldiers, who have fallen on the field of battle, to preserve them from pillage and bad treatment, and to bury the dead in conformity with strict sanitary rules. The contracting powers will take care that in time of war every soldier is furnished with a compulsory and uniform token, appropriate for establishing his identity. This token shall indicate his name, place of birth, as well as the army corps, regiment, and company to which he belongs. In case of death, this document shall be withdrawn before his burial, and remitted to the civil or military authorities of the place of enlistment or home. Lists of dead, wounded, sick, and prisoners, shall be communicated, as far as possible, immediately after an action to the commander of the opposing army by diplomatic or military means.

The contents of this article, so far as they are applicable to the maxim, and capable of execution, shall be observed by victorious naval forces.

The close of this task found her, like Miss Nightingale, broken in health, and her physicians urged her to go to Europe, for a change of air and rest. Not long after the Franco-Prussian war broke out, and the sufferings incident to war led her again to enter the battle field to alleviate them, and made her acquainted with the workings of the Red Cross. She saw how incomplete was her labor in the American Civil war, through inadequate organization. The Red Cross supplied the lack. The child bearing a cup of cold water to a wounded soldier was absolutely safe in the enemy's ranks, with the Red Cross on the arm.

Miss Barton returned to America resolved to have the principles of the Red Cross adopted by the United States. She visited President Garfield, who had been a soldier, and knew how much suffering might be alleviated by proper means, and he promised to do all in his power for the new movement. He brought it before his cabinet, and had it brought before Congress, and through his labors it passed both houses. Laws regulating the action of the nation in times of war were changed to conform with the regulations of the Red Cross. Just as the treaty was ready for his signature, the assassin's bullet took his life.

This treaty of the Red Cross is one of the missionary movements of our century. It has caused all nations to see more fully the cruelty and horrors of war, and has tended towards the settlement of national difficulties by arbitration, rather than by arms, thus, indirectly, furthering peace and unity among nations. Even outside of the miseries of war, this organization has for its prime object the relief of suffering. Muskets and cannon may be silent for a while, but the warring elements, fire, water, and wind, may cause suffering at any time. With this in view, there has been added to the original scheme what is called the American amendment. At Washington, D. C., is stationed a field agent, who visits in person every place where aid is rendered. In 1881, it relieved those who suffered from the effects of the forest fires of Michigan; in 1882, the suffering incident to the Mississippi overflow; in 1883, from the disaster of the Ohio River, etc., and the Louisiana cyclone.

War will never again be attended with the nameless and needless terrors and horrors of the Crimean hospitals. Christianity has indirect as well as direct effects; and her mission in the world is not only Glory to God in the Highest, but on Earth, Peace, Good Will toward men.

CHAPTER XXV

SYSTEMATIC CHRISTIAN WORK AMONG SOLDIERS

No work done among soldiers has more fascinating interest than that of the late Cav. Luigi Capellini in Rome, Italy, the "Evangelical Military Church," founded in 1872 by this earnest man of God.

He who was thus at the head of this enterprise for twenty-five years—and whose work so strangely synchronized with that of McAll in Paris—was characterized as "the soldiers' friend," as his fellow-worker in France was known as "the friend of *les œuvriers.*" From its inception this project was essentially Italian, and both in its promptings and methods intensely personal. Signor Capellini "lived, moved, breathed, and had his being" in his work for the soldiers. To help, teach, and in every way befriend them; above all, to introduce them to the true knowledge of the Captain of their salvation, was his master passion. His fitness for the service for which he had such a consuming passion showed that he had been raised up of God for it; that it was his divine mission, and he, an apostle—one sent of God. Many young men of the Italian army have through him become good soldiers of Jesus Christ, and have endured hardness for His sake.

Little has been published as to Capellini's great mission, but the brief "memorials" are doubly interesting and suggestive to such as have been at the chapel services in the Eternal City, and have seen the ardor of this consecrated teacher and the responsive fervor of the absorbed audience which gave such eager ear to his appeals.

Capellini was born of popish parents and bred in Romish errors. His father died when he was a boy of ten, and his mother sent him to school under priestly control, where he stayed till he was eighteen, when he was strangely led to enlist in the army. A short time after, in strolling through the streets, he picked up some leaves of the New Testament. They proved to him light in darkness, liberty from bondage, and life from the dead. A new proof of the power of the living Word and of the use God makes of His own book. Capellini from that day knew that justification and salvation come by faith alone, without human merit or priestly mediation, and at once he became a free man in Christ Jesus.

Of course, he had to meet opposition. His companions tried ridicule and threat. They sneered at him as a fool, and railed at him as " a Protestant." They warned him that the Bible is a bad book and is forbidden; but this drove him to study it the more that he might find out why it was a proscribed book. He longed for evangelical tracts, something, " some man, to guide " him in his inquiry after truth. One day he came upon a man who was giving away just what he wanted. This man was Angelo Castioni, Miss Burton's Bible colporteur. He won his confidence, and that very evening Capellini and Castioni were together, like Philip and the eunuch, and the Italian soldier went on his way rejoicing that he had enlisted in the army, since that was God's way of bringing him to the light of life.

Pity for his comrades led him to seek to bring them out into larger place of faith in the great sacrifice, and soon he saw them taking from their necks the medallion images of the Virgin, worn as a charm, and studying the forbidden book; and not a few were converted. Miss Burton furnished him with Testaments and tracts, and he used all his available time in opening up the treasures of God's Word to as many of his comrades as he could gather about him in the barracks. Soon after, the command of a detachment, sent in pursuit of the brigands, made him his own master, and Capellini had religious conferences with his men unhindered. Morning and evening they had readings and prayers in common, and those who at first were only hearers of the Word, became doers of the Word, and then distributors of the Scriptures among the scattered peasantry on mountains, plains, and lowlands about Puglia and the Abruzzi. Then came the war with Austria, in 1866, and then the men went forth, all having Bibles in their knapsacks, and, as opportunity afforded, the commander and his regiment read the Scriptures and prayed together.

The thought was thus born in Capellini's mind that, by the agency of converted soldiers, God's Word might be borne into every city, village, hut, and hovel, and from this came in a little time the wider conception realized in the military church.

While at Parma, Capellini was attacked by cholera. His soldiers never left him. They repaid his ministries, reading and praying at his bedside, and interceding with God for his restoration. As strength returned to him, he felt that he must learn more of the Gospel that he might do more for men, and he sought the help of Rev. Henry Piggott, at Padua, at the same time enlarging his own holy effort in behalf of soldiers. Then, as Rome became free, he felt that there his headquarters must be, because there was the main rendezvous for the military class.

Difficulties and dangers found him undaunted. Turned out of doors, he made the street corners his meeting-places. Crowds hung upon his words, but his money was exhausted. But God stood by him. Rev. Mr. Waite, minister of the American Union church, and later, Rev. Leroy Vernon, of the American M. E. church, came to his help, until the Wesleyan Methodists assumed the support of the work, provided a meeting-place, and paid Capellini's salary.

Easter, 1873, witnessed the first celebration of the Lord's Supper, and Whitsuntide the second, when of the 200 persons present, forty-five were communicants. The *Roman Observer*, chief organ of the Vatican, now thundered against this " proselytizing of the soldiers." Persecution began to lay bare her red right arm, and soldiers were deprived of their " Protestant " books, and there were even arrests and imprisonments. Certain converts were arraigned, but refused to renounce their faith, and were dismissed with warnings to let alone evangelical meetings and Protestant books. A report was sent to Prince Umberto—since King of Italy—giving names of converted soldiers, and a council was called to consider how this work could be stopped. Prince Umberto concluded the council with these memorable words: *" See that no political plotting goes on under a religious garb, but do not hinder the men from fulfilling the duties of their religion."*

This story has a charm seldom rivaled in any tale of Christian heroism. On Christmas day, in 1873, Admiral Fishbourne presented, in behalf of English soldiers, two chalices and accompanying vessels for the eucharist, and the flagon bears the inscription: " From the soldiers of England to the evangelical soldiers of Italy." And such was the eagerness of the men to be present at the Lord's Supper that they stayed in Rome at their own cost, paid for substitutes, if on duty, or slept on benches in the chapel, if too poor to hire lodgings.

For the conduct of the military church, a deacon was chosen from every corps and from the hospital attendants —the latter to look after sick soldiers. It is interesting to notice how this hospital deacon, Basato, met the priests and nuns bearing the consecrated host and wafer to a dying man. They bade him remove his cap and bow his knee, but he calmly answered: " I worship God alone, and *not a god made of flour.*" This exposed him to persecution, but he bore it meekly.

From time to time classes are discharged, having served their time, and those who have received evangelical truth are sent home with ample supplies of good books to give away, and so this military church is a recruiting office for the ranks of the soldiers of the Cross. During the legal period of service the troops have been brought under the teaching of Capellini, and then have returned home to disseminate the precious truths they have learned, and become an evangelizing power in the entire country of their birth. The chapel at Rome is a receiving and distributing reservoir through which the Italian soldiery pass.

In 1875 the meetings were transferred to a larger chapel in Via Bottighi Oscure, where a library was started, etc. When the same year the military church kept its second anniversary, 250 soldiers and 105 communicants were present, and, as on former occasions, every participant took away a Bible as a memento.

The soldiers, who as converts return to their homes, have to meet persecution. Some have to leave their homes, and even the neighborhood, and flee to some other place, stripped of everything except their faith. Yet conversions go on at Rome, and the work of witness everywhere where the " elect dispersion " are scattered.

On one occasion the church was much disturbed by the colonel of the Bersaglieri, who, by pretenses of various sorts, found out who were evangelicals, and took all their books from them. Capellini complained to the general in command, and the result was again a vindication, for it was found that these Protestant " perverts " were *in no way transgressing their duties as soldiers of Italy;* and a religion that makes better men and more loyal soldiers may find toleration even in the Italian army. As a colonel said, when told that the whole regiment was turning Protestant: " Better the evangelical meeting than the tavern or brothel."

The whole history of these twenty-seven years is full of romantic reality, but abounds with examples of the power of the Word of God, and of the God whose Word it is. How often have officers, who have forced the men to give up their testaments, read a few pages, out of curiosity, and found salvation! Once a soldier, who had frequented the meetings and accepted the books gathered his comrades by the Tiber and threw the books into the river. Many fell short, however, and were picked up on the bank, and again led to the knowledge of God. The name and address of the military church being on the cover, this also drew the men to come to the meetings, so that some of them witnessed that they had " become disciples of Christ by means of a New Testament saved from the water." Again a host at a tavern found on the dead body of a victim of accident a Capellini Testament, which he stole glances at and begged he might keep.

The heroism of Capellini could be learned only at the Cross. In the army of Italy all shades of opinion are found, from atheism to ultramontanism, and acts of intolerance are inevitable from those who, because they believe nothing, persecute believers, or from those who, because they believe something, will allow no one to hold any other doctrine. And so the poor soldiers run a perpetual gauntlet between two rows of enemies, the infidels and the bigots, both armed with clubs that are as merciless as the iron flail of Talus.

Again, the convert is in constant danger of imposition as well as opposition from some officer, as when a private, Luigi Fares, for a month was kept on duty so constantly that he had *not a night's rest in bed.*

Perhaps the greatest discouragement of Capellini was the constant depletion of his church membership by the return of soldiers to their homes. In the autumn of 1880 the soldiers' church had but twenty left in Rome, and six regiments, with 7,200 men, had not among them one Protestant. In 1881, 400 registered hearers of the previous year were transferred, and only 37 communicants remained. Yet the same untiring, persistent evangelism! Capellini and his evangelists and colporteurs stationed themselves at the fountains where all have to go for water, and there led thirsty souls to the well of living waters; or they went away to more distant encampments to gather in recruits for the army of the Lord. And, when the soldiers leave Rome, as active a correspondence as is possible is kept up with these scattered members of the flock, who are often as sheep among wolves. Tracts, Testaments, and books are diligently and at all times scattered in every direction, and blessed are they who, like Mr. Hawke and Mrs. Robertson, have the privilege of supplying the seed for such wide sowing.

The results of this work can not be tabulated, but the first eight years' labor showed an aggregate of 730 registered converts. What could be shown if all the fruits of the work of the subsequent seventeen years could be presented also! And what of the unhistoried distribution of the Word of God and of the living epistles!

Cav. Luigi Capellini was a minister of the Wesleyan Methodists, who supported his work in the main, but the soldiers of the military church are not reckoned as Wesleyans, but are encouraged to join the evangelical body nearest their homes, and all evangelical communities are gainers by the undenominational work done in Rome. Let Christian visitors go and see for themselves the noble work done in Via delle Coppelle No. 28, and Christian givers send help in the Lord's name, and so become sharers in this noble work.

In 1879, Leo XIII. took alarm and ordered the monks and nuns in the military hospitals to carry out among the soldiers a more aggressive propaganda, and the Bibles were stolen from under the pillows, and every effort was made by threat and bribe to induce them to return to popish books and priests, but in vain.

In his report for 1897, Cav. Luigi Capellini wrote:

" In one of the meetings, among the young men attentively listening to the preaching of the Word, I noticed a young corporal of cavalry who made a strong impression upon me by his intelligent air and the attention which he paid to the sermon. My second son, Alfred, a student at the University, who goes to the services, and sometimes takes my place when I am absent, went up to him and invited him to come up to the house. Here we found that he is the nephew of the pope—Count Pecci. His open countenance, his loyal and frank way of speaking, convinced us that he was really seeking the truth, and I gave him a Bible and some books. His uncle, the pope, had made him one of his ' Guardia Nobile,'— but he had to serve under the king as an Italian subject. He not only continued to attend the services as long as he was in Rome, but he also brought with him many of the men under him, thus becoming himself a propagator of the truth."

Later on in his report, Signor Capellini said that in order to stop or neutralize his work, the priests instituted organizations called Catholic Military Clubs, providing for the soldiers amusement, cigars, and tobacco, and Catholic books. Among these books was one called " Errors and Heresies of the Protestants," in which ridicule was cast upon the services of the military church. It was important that something should be done to meet this dangerous innovation, so Cav. Capellini opened schools in which the uneducated soldiers might be taught to read and write, and provided rooms with books and writing materials for the use of the better instructed. This provision has been highly appreciated by the men, and the work has gone forward all along the line.

WORK AMONG THE SOLDIERS OF INDIA.

The " Prayer Room " movement and Soldiers' Christian Association in India is another of the comparatively unknown forms of Christian service among those who follow the profession of arms. W. B. Harington is the founder of this really great enterprise, that has been so singularly owned and sealed of God.

If anything has been a public scandal it has been the British soldier in the land of the Hindus. His life, character, and environment have to a surprising extent been the theme of private and public comment for twenty-five years. So dark, so sad has been the picture drawn that there have been not a few who have contended that there was a fatality about his evil-doing, and that the combined influences of climate, diet, army life, separation from home influence, and the contagion of a vicious atmosphere, both perpetuate and extenuate a low type of morals. The Christian sentiment of the world has been shocked—nay the worst of it is that so much so-called Christian sentiment has *not* been shocked—when a life of shameless debauchery has been defended, and unlawful lust been provided for as tho lechery were a necessity! and even a conspicuous Christian woman has been found to justify the sacrifice of her own sex on the altar of this modern unchastity.

We are glad to be able to paint a very different picture, and show how much has been already done to help British soldiers to learn the victorious power of the Christ-life, and so to walk in the Spirit as not to fulfil the lusts of the flesh. We do not designedly pass by any other good work done in promoting sobriety and chastity, by the army Temperance Association and army guilds, etc., when we refer somewhat at length to the noble effort of Mr. Harington, which was first begun in 1859 in Oudh, and has for more than forty years been spreading throughout India, and even to Cairo, Mauritius, and Singapore.

For many years Mr. Harington has met the British soldiers five times a week, in barracks, camp, or on the line of march. Forty years ago, three soldiers of the 54th Regiment, quartered in Oudh, came over from camp to the tent of Mr. Harington, where he was occupied with the matter of hutting British troops, and asked that they might use for devotional meetings, every evening, a small building he had just completed for an office. And now Mr. Harington has, with government sanction and aid, secured, and in fact, *erected*, in nearly every military center throughout India, a *Soldiers' Prayer-Room*. So manifest were the blessed results attending his earlier efforts that, as a matter of the " Department of Public Works," with which he was connected, it was deemed the most economical use of the public funds to provide at least one place in every British cantonment, where the soldiers may find a reading-room, writing-room, and a meeting-place for Sunday and week-day assemblies for prayer and praise. Mr. Harington has planned these buildings, their size, shape, and fittings, and they are places which the soldiers may call their own. In 1868, the governor-general in council declared that such rooms " shall be considered one of the recognized requirements in the barracks of every British regiment or considerable detachment of troops ; " and thenceforth the government undertook the provision and maintenance of these prayer-room buildings with fittings, furniture, lighting, warming, cooling, etc.

Mr. Harington has also formed in every cavalry regiment, infantry battalion, and nearly every battery of royal artillery, in service in India, a branch of the Soldiers' Christian Association. The diminution of vice and crime has been remarkable. The loss of good conduct badges, the trials by court martial with imprisonment and other penalties, have comparatively ceased, and the physical and moral health of the whole army has been vastly improved. The governors, judges, magistrates, and statesmen, who have been most eminent in Indian affairs, have been the foremost in their testimony to Mr. Harington's work and given their aid in it; and from officers, chaplains, and men, he has had warm and enthusiastic support in his self-denying and successful labors. Government aid did not cover such items as Bibles, hymn-books, libraries, papers and magazines, wall texts, and table covers and table lamps, clocks, musical instruments, etc., so that for the proper prosecution of the work donations are constantly needful, and the more as the work rapidly expands. Printing, stationery, postage, traveling expenses, etc., need also to be met by special gifts.

In 1895 the number of prayer-rooms was 89, of which 30 were garrison or depot, 5 cavalry, 19 artillery, 35 infantry, and the average expenditure was but ten pounds annually for each room. Up to the end of 1889 Mr. Harington met to a very large extent out of his own purse the needs of the work. Since retiring from service—having reached the age limit—he has given his entire time and attention to *this* work, and hence has been unable to bear the financial burdens as he did when in government employ.

The work which is before Mr. Harington and his helpers is nothing less than winning soldiers to Christ. The Word of God, prayer, praise, personal contact, all wholesome restraints and loving constraints, are the weapons which have proved not carnal indeed, but mighty to the pulling down of the strongholds. The motto which is to be found conspicuous in the prayer-rooms, " Jesus only," well defines the basis of trust and the object of effort. " Joined

in prayer—joined in the Word—joined in His work,"—
this is the practical bond and secret of unity. The work
is carried on as under the eye of the great Commander.
Knowing Mr. Harington personally, we have no hesitancy
in commending this work to the sympathy, prayer, and pecuniary aid of every true lover of the soldier and his welfare. The Soldiers' Bible and Prayer Union (with the
Soldiers' Magazine as the common organ) was started in
1886, and is now therefore in its fourteenth year.*

THE SOLDIERS' CHURCH IN ADEN.

Of the work among the soldiers in Aden there is not
space to treat. Under the charge of Dr. John C. Young
it progresses promisingly. Dr. Young, who went to
Arabia under the Keith Falconer mission to work for
Arabs, writes:

" When I came here five years ago, I found that the non-
Anglican soldiers were without a place of worship, and that no
services of any kind were carried on. . . . Having obtained
liberty from the home committee, services were started, and continued for four years, in the largest room of the principal hotel
in Aden. On the fifth anniversary, however, we entered our new
church. Since then we have never had a smaller congregation at
the evening service than 100 soldiers, and last Sabbath there were
twice as many soldiers as the government return declared there
are of non-Anglican soldiers in the whole garrison.

" Many have declared that they have been spiritually helped.
One man, who had been promoted through bribing his senior
non-commissioned officer, after conversion handed me £10 to send
anonymously to the man he had wronged, and, having given up
his stripes, declared that he never felt more happy in his life.
Nearly a year after he wrote, telling me of the real joy he felt,
and how now he could speak to his fellows with a clear conscience.

" At the prayer-meetings on Wednesday nights there are some-

---

* Address, W. B. Harington, Gen. Hon. Secretary, S. C. A., Totland Bay,
Isle of Wight, England.

times more soldiers present than at 'parade service,' when the men are forced to attend. The vestry of the church is used by the soldiers' Christian association, 'and there is a meeting of some sort every night.' "

CHAPTER XXVI

WORK AMONG DEEP SEA FISHERMEN

How seldom do we ponder over the fact that, as the Scotch ballad puts it, " the price of fish is the lives of men ! "

" Nor'ard of the Dogger " is the story of " Deep Sea Trials and Gospel Triumphs," or the work among the deep sea fishermen. E. J. Mather was the founder and for some years the director of the mission, which belongs conspicuously among the marked movements which we are now tracing as parts of God's providential plan.

The support of these mission ships in the northern seas is a many sided benefaction. It looks to the physical, mental, moral and spiritual uplifting of a numerous and hitherto much neglected class, scattering wholesome reading, giving surgical and medical aid, offsetting the wretched grogships; but above all the mission ship becomes to multitudes a lifeboat indeed, in which they find salvation from the second death.

A simple question—as in so many other cases—was the starting point in this new mission. In the autumn of 1881,—now nearly twenty years since—a man, interested in those who sail the sea, said to Mr. Mather, " Don't you think something might be done for our men in the North Sea ? " Ignorant of all the real conditions of these fishermen, and scarcely knowing of their existence, the answer was one of those ready replies whereby even Christian workers evade such approaches : " O, yes, I might send them some parcels of tracts." The questioner, with a hearty laugh, replied: "You can't have much notion of who and what our men are, if you think that sending a bundle of tracts would be '*doing*' anything in the sense intended."

How many of us know much more than Mr. Mather then did, of that floating population,—upwards of twelve thousand—that go down to the sea in ships and do business in the great waters, between lat. 54 degrees and 56 degrees N., forced to fight the winds and waves, because too far from the shore to find shelter? Voyages of two months, with only a few days on land in the intervals, occupy the deep sea trawler, with whom *this* life is so hard that the "life to come" has little thought or care. The Dogger Bank reaches about 170 miles north and south by 65 east and west, and it is a harvest field whose annual average yield is 400,000 tons of fish. Mr. Mather, with his companion, Rev. R. B. Thompson, on their experimental trip, came up with the "Short Blues" about 300 miles from the Thames, and beheld 220 fishing-smacks, of from 50 to 80 tons burden, extending for miles each way from the admiral's vessel. Among the 1,500 men in the fleet, there might have been *one in fifty* that was a professing Christian; but the rest were heedless, godless, universally profane, and quarrelsome. The visitors had with them 1,000 portions of the New Testament and sundry illustrated periodicals—furnished free by the Bible and Tract societies of Britain—and these they gave away to men hungry for anything to relieve the monotony of their life.

Of course difficulties were to be grappled with among such a class of men—stormy opposition there was sure to be where Satan had so long had a supreme control, and the worse antagonism of indifference—the dead calm or apathy and lethargy. A few men were found longing for some stated "means of grace"—hungry for a prayer meeting, a testimony meeting, a time to hear God's word and to offer worship: but the most of them and conspicuously godless captains were rather ready to curse the men who came to turn the fishing smack into a gospelship, and some were so hardened that they would rather have a floating ginshop or brothel than a floating chapel or Bethel.

Away in that North sea sin may be seen in its awful nakedness, with all its fascinations stripped off. The greatest foe of the fishermen was the *coper* or grogshop, the curse of the fleet. For more than fifty years these foreign vessels hung about the British trawling ships. They seem first to have come from Dutch ports bordering the fishing banks, and to have originally been trading shops for clothing, etc.; but they rapidly degenerated into grogshops. The Dutch copers made a pretense of selling tobacco, which on these boats escaped the heavy duty, and could be bought for less than half what it cost on shore; but once on board the fisherman found himself within the clutch of the drink temptation; and many a total abstainer, beginning with " von leetle drop " by and by would trade sails, ropes, nets or even the clothes on his back, as well as fish, for drink. The coper has been well called the " Devil's mission ship." And grog worked ruin on the sea as everywhere—only worse; for what must become of a fleet in a gale when skipper and crew were dead drunk on the cabin floor! or when a drunken steersman had hold on the helm, or men, crazed by whiskey, would leap overboard! Where Dutchmen set the example, even Englishmen were found to follow; vessels sailed from British harbors, disguised as trawlers, and steered straight for Nieudiep, took in grog and tobacco and joined the fleet to make one hundred per cent profit, in a voyage that took but a few weeks or months. Action against the copers was first taken by the insurance companies that refused applications unless the abandonment of the whiskey trade was a condition.

Here, then, these two visitors to the Nor'ard fleet saw in their five days on board a promising—certainly a needy—field for a mission. In a village of 1,500 souls, which was the population of the floating village—there would be four churches or chapels, as many doctors, a dispensary, library, town hall and mechanics' institute: should not the cruisers have at least some of these advantages? The purpose slowly took form: these fishermen must have a mission vessel—which should be at once church, temperance hall, library and dispensary.

Like every true work for God, prayer was its baptism into Christ, and its chrism of power; and prayer brought an offer of 1,000 pounds, to rig up and send out a fishing smack, to be used to start the mission: the fish taken would cover expenses and the *Ensign* was within three weeks ready for sea. A small cabin was partitioned off in the hold for the misisonaries' quarters; grants of Bibles and other books, woollen mufflers and mittens, and a ship's medicine chest, were supplied without charge, and a Christian skipper put in charge; and on that unlucky day, " Friday," was launched " one of the most remarkable social revolutions of modern times." The *Ensign* shook out her twenty-foot mission flag to the breeze—some shouting in derision and others bidding it godspeed; but amid the jeering and the cheering, away she sailed, four months later to run in between the piers, amid the welcome that even foes are glad to join in when " success "—that great vindicator of all enterprises—puts her crown on a new scheme.

The history of the Nor'ard mission has its funny features, as when one smacksman, having a bottle, labelled " for external use only," not knowing what " *external* " meant, poured it down the throat of a poor fellow who had a " powerful " attack of bronchitis. But the fun is the exception. Think of a man trying to work in a tremendous storm with a bad attack of measles; of another, scalped by a piece of spar and the frost so intense that the wound stopped bleeding because the blood turned to ice before he could be carried below deck; think of salt water irritating cuts and wounds; of a broken leg, getting stiff before any doctor could be got to set it. That first mission ship encountered a gale of derision when she came near to the fleet and her mission was known; but again prayer was her armor and artillery: and the first who ridiculed was the first who learned to pray. The meetings began, and the total abstinence pledge was signed by a few, and the loving message of the Gospel was heard, and there was nothing to pay for medicine or the balm of Gilead. No man came to get healing or nursing who did not hear of the Great Physician. In one morning and within a few minutes, ten boats boarded the *Ensign* for medical and surgical aid, and lips, unaccustomed to such words, invoked " blessings on this 'ere vessel." From the first voyage, victory was assured. God and man had both set seal of approbation on the deep sea mission. Ship owners offered their congratulations and donations; families ashore joined in praise for the saving of life and health and time and wages; and one smackowner who had little care for the souls of men, gave his guineas yearly to a work that kept the men from *bartering his nets to the coper for brandy!*—conversion valued from a business point of view. Some conversions meant a different attitude for a whole vessel and its crew, as when the "creagan" would no more be hoisted as a signal to the coper, and the patronage of a whole ship's company was lost to the foreign grogshop.

Every day the mission vessel had a " service; " and the worst and wildest men were often the first to be reached. On one lovely summer's day, ten vessels were lashed side by side, the mission ship in the center; fifty-two men and boys were in one group on the deck and there was an eight hour service, which concluded only when the clock struck eleven P. M.! and even then an inquiry meeting followed till 1:30 A. M.! Three skippers and a cabin boy had found their way to a life of temperance and of piety. No wonder if an Ostend skipper as long ago as 1884 said: "Those cursed mission ships are ruining our trade, and if many more of them come there'll soon be no *copers!*"

In the spring of 1883, one fearful storm, "the great March gale," sacrificed over 360 men and boys. The dangers which these northern fishermen meet are many and grave. "We lose on an average thirty-five yearly in boarding fish, or transferring the heavy trunks of fish from small boats to the vessels," said the owner of one large fleet. The lives of men might be saved, but they think it cowardly to wear life belts, and this introduction of life jackets as a condition of small-boat work was one of the first reforms. At the best this is hard work. The trunks have hand holes at each end, and it needs a strong lift and a heavy heave to land them on the rail of the carrier and to time the movement to the swing of the waves. If the man that heaves, or the man that is to catch, is an instant too slow, overboard goes the trunk, if not the heaver or the catcher, and accidents are constant and well nigh inevitable; and when injured, the poor fellows, three hundred miles from all medical and surgical help, had to toss about for days before proper treatment could be had at the London hospital. It seemed, at first, impracticable to have a doctor in the fleet, and even if there were one, one day's round of visits through the small boats would be enough to wear him out.

Mr. Mather saw that dispensary work at least must be done on the fleet, and this was the next item that entered into his plans.

It is really beautiful to find beneath the roughest, coarsest exterior, the signs of the soft heart. And the smacksmen, with all their wrong-doing often manifest toward a fellow-tar in his distress, a tenderness and generosity that prove the survival of humanity within them, as when poverty and bereavement strike the fisher's home circle, or there is permanent disablement through injury. When one of them sees others in peril he becomes oblivious of personal risk and plunges into the work of rescue. But when these fellows find Christ, they find also their own true self with its latent possibilities, that has been hidden beneath the wickedness of a godless life. How manly and courageous and unselfish they often become! Lord Northbrook found in the North Sea trawling fleet such a recruiting ground for the Royal navy that 4,000 smacksmen were at one time enrolled in the naval reserve. But how many faithful followers has He enrolled who found in Galilean fishermen apostles that left boats and nets and all behind and went to fishing for men.

When, in 1882, the *Ensign* was rigged out as a mission vessel, it was found that she maintained herself by trawling. This emboldened the leaders of this mission to secure three more vessels, the whole being the property of men who invested in the matter as a Christian business enterprise, appointing Mr. Mather managing owner, and lending the vessels for the purposes of the mission, looking to the profit of fishing for a reasonable interest on their outlay. But the decline of the fishing trade caused a change of plans, and led to the purchase of these three additional vessels, for the mission, and not long after the *Ensign* likewise was bought and renamed the *Thomas Gray* in recognition of many acts of kindness from the head of the main department of the Board of Trade. In answer to prayer for additional ships, a letter from the Duchess of Grafton brought another gift of 2,150 for a new mission ship, to be named the *Eustin* and this gift opened a new era in the matter of the mission ships—as it proved that of the Lord directly might be obtained vessels for His work without the worry of caring for property, lent by business men as a commercial venture; and it became more and more evident that the command to " go into all the world " meant the world of waters, too, and the promise " Lo I am with you alway," covered the trackless highways of sea as well as of land.

The fisherman seems to find in his pipe a necessity, and even the Christian sailors felt tobacco to be an essential, not only to comfort but to warmth and endurance. But if tobacco was to be supplied it must be through some agency that would rid the fleet of the standing menace of the coper. Some felt it to be a mistake, but the mission conductor undertook to remove out of the way temptation to visit the copers, by supplying cheap tobacco to those who felt it a *sine quâ non*. After a careful and we doubt not a prayerful consideration of the whole matter, it was determined to make this effort to neutralize the traffic of the floating grogshops, and such was the actual result, so that the copers' business was not " regulated but relegated to their native shores." The government at last allowed tobacco to be sold in the fleet, free of customs duty, thus facilitating the work of antagonizing the copers.

The good wrought by this mission to the deep-sea fishermen no statistical column could exhibit. One vessel that left Hull without two men aboard that feared God, returned with all but five rejoicing in Him.

The work among the fishermen became known, and every summer witnessed volunteer missionaries electing to pass their vacation among the trawlers: and with constantly increasing interest and enlarging success. The returns for such work proved comparatively quick, obvious and abundant, more fruitful than work on shore. Eleven clergymen were afloat in the mission ships in 1886, twelve in 1889, and in one case the evangelistic efforts proved so blessed that seventeen out of nineteen skippers who had attended the valedictory prayer-meeting when the mission smack was leaving for port, had learned to trust in the Lord Jesus on board the " Bethelship."

It is now thirteen years since the mission to deep-sea fishermen was duly recognized, registered and certified by the Board of Trade, with a council of fifteen members and various subcommittees. The work still goes on, and the copers find their office gone and the amount of their trade not worth the expenditure.

Note.—Mr. Mortimer Sladen of Windermere, England, has lately given a Pioneer Hospital Steam Trawler to the Deep Sea Fishermen. It is a superb vessel, 154 feet long, by 22 feet broad. Its tonnage over 93 tons, and its total value, with fittings and furnishings, is nearly $80,000. Her name is *Alpha,* and her speed over 11 knots. She is fitted with four water-tight bulkheads, and a collision bulkhead in addition, at each end. Mr. Sladen has left nothing undone to make his splendid gift as perfect as possible.

The hospital is supplied with a hot water heating installation, ventilation and sanitation provisions, swing cots for fracture cases, the best surgical appliances, including a Röntgen Ray apparatus, etc.

At the same time more than fifty other unique features contribute to the completeness of this as a *mission* ship, also—bookcase, library, harmonium, electric lights, communicating cabins and saloons that can be used for public services—whatever could help to make this more adapted for its various service, Mr. Sladen's fertility of resources, and generosity of heart have assured.

We have the pleasure of knowing the donor, who himself, with his brother Alfred, has designed their own steam launches, and so has a special fitness for the planning of such a ship for the deep sea work.

CHAPTER XXVII

MISSION WORK AMONG LEPERS

WHEN Spirit-moved men and women undertake mission work among lepers, they reach and touch the lowest depths of human degradation, wretchedness, and hopeless misery.

Of all human maladies, leprosy is the one, unique, solitary disease, that has borne, throughout all time, the brand of peculiar curse, as "*the scourge of God.*" Technically, it is a chronic skin disease, whose main characteristics are two: ulcerous eruptions, and successive desquamations of dead skin. The name is now usually restricted to *elephantiasis.* It is clearly hereditary, and overwhelming facts seem to show that under some circumstances it is contagious; that, at least, where there is habitual contact and association, as between parents and children, it is communicated, whereas separation prevents its development even where there is a leprous parentage.*

A leper is a walking parable of guilt and death. To the Jew especially, leprosy was the sign and seal of sin, already bearing its visible judgment. A leper was unclean, and he was obliged to proclaim his own uncleanness. His touch was defilement, his garments were spotted by the flesh, and he lived apart from others, and could not even come

---

* There are believed to be 500,000 lepers in India, 100,000 in China, as many more in Japan, 1,200 in the Hawaiian Isles, 27,000 in Colombia, South America, 500 in the United States, as many more in Cuba, 2,000 in Norway, etc. Isolation is the only known means of eradication. There is a growing sentiment in favor also of the separation of the sexes, that there may be no propagation of offspring that have predisposition to the taint of this horrible disease. It seems as tho no measures were too drastic to stamp out this malady.

near to the altar where sin was expiated by blood. Miriam, tho the sister of Moses and Aaron, was shut out of the camp when the leprous brand appeared on her brow, and King Uzziah was shut out from his palace, and " lived in a separate house until the day of his death." Trench, in one awful sentence, sums up the matter: " Leprosy is nothing short of a living death, a poisoning of the springs, a corrupting of all the humors of life; a dissolution little by little of the whole body." No language can describe the horror and terror inspired by the sight of a crowd of abject leprous beggars, as they are seen thronging the Jaffa gate of the sacred city, and reaching out the stumps of handless arms, their faces ghastly, with sockets from which the eyes have dropped out, perhaps without ears, and their bodies in every state and stage of actual physical defect. The leper is the slow, sure victim of a death that kills one member at a time, and severs it from the body, like a dead limb that drops off from a tree by its own rottenness. Dante, in his visits to the *Inferno*, never beheld any sight that so suggests the awful curse that follows sin to the third and fourth generation, if not the fortieth, or compares with this in indescribable repulsiveness. Surely it is no accident that, in that eighth chapter of Matthew—*Scriptura Miraculosa*, as Ambrose called it—the first recorded miracle is one in which the great Healer not only made the leper clean, but by touching him, thus identifying himself with his uncleanness and becoming ceremonially himself a leper! No wonder Isaiah, foreseeing His glory and speaking of Him declares, " Himself took our infirmities and *bare our sicknesses.*"

We can not appreciate the Christlike self-sacrifice and passion for souls that must have moved holy men and women to approach a leprous community, and even become permanently identified with their relief and salvation, unless we first get a true glimpse of the actual condition in which lepers were found. And here again words fail. There are no terms quite equal to the description. For example, when, some years since, investigation was made of matters in Viliusk, in Siberia, the frightful state of the lepers in the province was found to be worse even than as set forth in the report of the medical inspector. They were found driven into exile in vast forests, almost nude, and closely packed in dirty yourtas. So great is the dread of this disease that people suffering from other ailments are often exiled with the lepers and forced to abide with them, through mistakes of the natives when defining leprosy; and awful brutality is practised, under plea of banishing a leper from society, where greed is the motive—some small fortune left by a relative being thus seized by the persecutors, a leper being treated as one civilly dead, and having no right to property. A supposed child-leper was starved to death, for the sake of a few cows left him by his parents. An uncle, whose ward he was, first murdered his sister, and then persuading his neighbors that the boy was a leper, drove him into a forest in the depths of a Siberian winter, and there, with no shelter but a sort of kennel, a few sticks lightly covered with cow dung and snow, starved, half-frozen, and on the verge of madness, the boy was left to die. When found the body was but skin and bones, with a little clay in the stomach which had been devoured in the pangs of hunger, and there was not a sign of leprosy or any other disease!

The crowding together of these outcasts in the same filthy yourta, makes physical cleanliness and moral purity alike impossible. The yourta or yurt, is often only a pen in which human beings and cattle herd together, men, women, and children, all alike. It is made of logs, covered with earth and moss, and partly sunk in the ground, one of the most primitive human habitations, and having none of the qualities of a comfortable or decent dwelling.

Certain visitors found the Siberian lepers clad in cast-off garments of the Yakuts (members of the Turkish race, of the basin of the Lena, E. Siberia), these garments being generally fur-skins filled with vermin, filthy beyond words, and at best a mass of tatters.

The leper is so accustomed to being avoided and shunned that, even when approached by the messengers of love and pity, he shrinks as in terror, or as tho some violence or insult were intended. He feels himself an outcast, doomed to be an exile from all clean society. One visit to the vile and small huts where lepers dwell is enough to fix itself forever on the mind of the visitor. There is almost no light, a door so low that one can not enter without bowing, and the air, which even the fire can not purify, foul to suffocation with the leprous exhalations and the odors of rotten fish that are their chief diet. No beds or linen, but benches, and no robes but rags, and all this for years at a time. In a small hovel, six men and three women were often found huddled together. Of course, such abodes are absolutely without sanitary provisions and swarm with vermin, and often the only places to sleep are rude trunks of trees covered with planks, on which these outcasts lie, packed together, the head of one opposite the feet of the next. And in such abodes they eat, cook, sleep, live, and die. It is customary for a dead body to be kept in the hovel for three days, and in a visitation of smallpox, four dead bodies were thus kept during such time in the same room with the living!

Mr. Guilford gives a similar account* of his own visit to the leper asylum at Tarn Táran (India) with its 234 wretched inmates. There he met a surging crowd of deformed, mutilated human beings, in whom all the dire effects of sin ever wrought on the human frame seemed presented in one mass before his eyes. To stay long in such

* "The Lepers in Our Indian Empire."   W. C. Bailey.

a scene was impossible, but he said that until death the sight would haunt him. It was a living charnel house.

Various efforts have been made in behalf of the lepers, in which we are not surprised again to find the Moravians leading. Always ready to dare the worst climates and the most hopeless conditions, before the first quarter of the century had passed, in 1822, they began work at Himel en Aarde (Heaven and Earth), in South Africa. Four years before, the colonial government, fearing the spread of leprosy, had built a temporary asylum in this valley, whose weird name suggests its isolation, far from human abodes, and so hemmed in by rocks as to be opened only to the sky. The hospital having been enlarged, Governor Somerset sought for a Moravian to manage the institution and to teach the inmates Christian truth. Rev. Mr. Leitner and wife took up this work, and supposing it to involve risk of contagion, they entered this asylum, thenceforth to be themselves virtually ranked as lepers.

The transformations were marvelous. Industry and intelligence and cleanliness proved to be the handmaids of piety, and neat gardens surrounded the hospital, and an aqueduct was built to supply water. During six years Mr. Leitner baptized 95 adults, and on Easter-day, 1829, while baptizing a convert, he suddenly passed to his reward. For ten years more the Moravians were in charge; and in 1846 the hospital was enlarged, improved, and removed to Robben Island, near Cape Town. The duties of the missionaries were henceforth restricted to the educational and spiritual, government officials being in general charge. A school was begun, whose first teacher was a young Englishman, John Taylor, who after five years of earnest work died in 1866. The Moravians continued identified with this hospital at Robben Island until 1867, when a chaplain of the Church of England was appointed to the religious oversight of the institution.

The Moravians have been similarly connected with the leper Home at Jerusalem, erected outside the Jaffa gate, and which owed its suggestion to Baron Von Keffenbrinck-Ascheraden's visit to the Holy Land. He and his wife saw these wretched outcasts, dependent on the alms of passers-by, lodging amid abject poverty, and dying in unsoothed agony. And again, when a small home was provided, the United Brethren gave Mr. and Mrs. F. Tappe to become father and mother to the loathsome and incurable lepers. This asylum, opened in 1867, was enlarged in 1875 and 1877, and a new and larger building erected on a new site in 1887, at cost of $20,000. In 1884 Mr. Tappe's health having compelled his retirement, Fritz Muller and wife took charge. Out of about twenty Moravians who gave themselves to this sacred ministry not one has taken the disease. The leper-home at Jerusalem has issued its twenty-ninth report. Since 1891 Mr. and Mrs. Schubert have been in charge. The year 1896 began with 19 patients, ten of them being men and nine women; and during the year, fifteen more were admitted, and one died. Diligent study and effort are now directed to the medical treatment of leprosy.

We can not within such limited space give the complete history of missions to lepers; but, in this great work, Wellesley C. Bailey, of Edinburgh, the well-known secretary of the Mission to Lepers in India, must have a conspicuous mention. It is now twenty-six years since, returning from mission work in India, he told Dublin friends of his efforts to help and save lepers. His tracts on the subject, half a million of which were circulated, united with his personal appeals, kindled such interest, that in 1878 a committee was formed in Dublin, and the work reorganized and enlarged, nine years later. No one who has been at all familiar with this grand work needs to be told that from 1875 onward, in Chamba, in the

Sabathu asylum at Ambala, in the Punjab, in Almora, at Dehra, at Calcutta, at Lohardugga, and Purulia, Chota Nagpore, at Travancore, at Rurki, at Pithora, at Allahabad, at Rawal Pindi, at Madras, in Neyoor, etc., etc., this society has either built or aided asylums. About twelve years ago the work of separating untainted children from their parents was begun, and retreats were provided for such children at Almora, Pithora, Lohardugga, Purulia, etc. The aim of this organization is twofold, philanthropic and evangelistic, its supreme aim being not only to better the temporal condition of the lepers but to save their souls.

One of the most humane results of the mission to the lepers, has been the *separation of children,* born of leper parents, from their original surroundings. Most medical men are now agreed that the disease *is* undoubtedly contagious,* and that the worst condition of such contagion is where children continue to live in the leprous homes where they were born. Before reaching majority it has been found that the great bulk of such offspring develop the loathsome disease, so that of all who were born in the

---

* This seems to be a good point at which to refer to the recent Leprosy Conference at Berlin. It was called by the foremost Leprologists in the world, and the following conclusions were reached :

1. The disease is communicated by the bacillus, but its condition of life and methods of penetrating the human organism are unknown. Probably it gains entrance through the mouth or mucous membranes.

2. It is certain that mankind alone is liable to the bacillus.

3. Leprosy is contagious but not hereditary.

4. The disease has hitherto resisted all efforts to cure it.

Observe, that in affirming the contagiousness of the disease, it is probably meant that it is contagious by some form of inoculation only, such as receiving into a cut or abraded surface some particle from a sore or ulcer of a leper. We must not confuse *contagion* and *infection.* Medical missionaries and others freely handle lepers and dress their wounds, yet no one has ever been known to contract the disease. Children of lepers probably have a hereditary predisposition to the disease, and if left to live in the same huts, sleep in the same beds, and eat out of the same vessels, run great risk.

asylum at Tarn Táran, during thirty years, and who were left there, *only two did not become* confirmed lepers. At Almora, however, for years past children have been separated from their parents, and only *one child* has shown signs of leprosy, * proving how much can be done to stop the spread of this scourge. No wonder Mr. Guilford pronounced it the saddest of sights to see a bright, innocent, untainted child fondled by a leper mother, and fed from hands that are a mass of corruption; and yet in India thousands of sights like this may be seen daily.

Can the souls of such wretched outcasts be reached? Let Mr. Guilford again testify. † At one time the asylum at Tarn Táran was in charge of a native doctor, whose hatred of Christianity was proverbial, and when some converted lepers sought a home in the asylum, in a rage he drove them away until they should renounce their faith. Hear their answer: " If you refuse us admission unless we deny our Lord and Master, we are content to go and sit on the highway and die." And there they sat for eight long days, with no shield from the intense sun save the trees, and with scarce a morsel of food, and this inhuman native doctor would not even allow the asylum shop to *sell* them food! In the asylum at Purulia, Mr. Bailey met a bright, happy audience of lepers, where only five out of 116 were even nominally heathen, and nineteen came forward for baptism in one service. What a sight to see these lepers bowing at the communion of the Lord's supper, where the bread had to be dropped into their hands, or put into their mouths because they had no hands, and the ' cup ' served to them by a spoon! "

Without the Camp states that the Mission to Lepers in India and the East works in connection with 18 so-

* " The Lepers in Our Indian Empire." Bailey, p. 107.
† *Ibid.* Bailey, p. 103.

cieties or denominations and 40 stations in India, Burma and Ceylon, and 7 in China and Japan. Of asylums and hospitals *of their own* they have 14 in India and Burma; 5 in China and Japan; with 14 homes for untainted children; they aid 11 other institutions and have 15 places open to them for Christian instruction. In all, 2,700 persons receive help.

Were the history of missions to the lepers fully written, it would supply some of the most pathetic tales of heroism ever recorded even in missionary history. We all remember the interest which centered about " Father Damien's " work among the lepers on the island of Molokai. Tho there was thought to be some false glamor or halo about this man, especially after his death, the Prince of Wales presided over the committee formed to raise a monument to this departed worker, to establish leper wards in hospitals, and to send out physicians to cope with the terrible evil and study its cure or relief.

Leprosy was brought to the Sandwich Islands by a traveler from Asia early in this century, and spread so fast that the government, in 1865, decreed the banishment of every tainted man, woman, and child to the island of Molokai, and in thirty years more than 3,000 have thus been exiled to await death in this lonely seagirt home. When, in 1873, Father Damien went there he found these lepers given over to every form of sloth, lawlessness, and vice. Before his death he saw very great improvement, and aroused not only the Hawaiian government to a sense of shame and duty, but awakened all civilized peoples to active sympathy for these outcasts. His own hands became so crippled by the disease that at the last he could only sign letters that he could no more write. Father Damien was wont to speak to the unhappy inmates of the island as " *we* lepers; " and when he took the disease, he told them it was God's way of bringing him and them closer together. Through his work miserable huts were exchanged for clean cabins; there is a hospital, costing $10,000, with skilled physicians.*

Those who have read the heroic story of Miss Mary Reed, will not need to be reminded of its indescribable pathos. She is an American missionary of the Methodist Episcopal Church in India, and, her health giving way, she came home, but for a year had no suspicion of the real nature of her illness, which baffled all the science and art of medicine. God himself, in midnight vision, revealed to her that it was leprosy, and made plain to her that she was henceforth to be a messenger of mercy to a leper community in the mountains of India. A specialist subsequently confirmed the impression of the vision, and all her suspense was over. To lessen the pain of parting, she left her father, mother, brothers, and sisters without revealing her secret, save to one sister, and on her way wrote home the terrible news. Then she went on to Pithora, in the Himalayas, and has been finding in those mountain heights —what they mean—" heavenly halls." Here is a refined, cultured young woman, smitten with this awful malady, exiling herself for the sake of these outcasts. She went among them, and, with hot tears, said, but without a tremor in her voice, and with a heavenborn smile: " *I am now one of you.*" There on the heavenly heights of Chandag, 6,000 feet above the sea, she is pointing outcast lepers to the Friend of outcasts, and her heart finds joy never known before in her Christlike work. She may be found daily binding up with her own hands the wounds and sores of lepers, while she pours the oil of God's consolation into their souls. She was found with 73 inmates

---

* An interesting description of this settlement is found in Jno. R. Musick's " Hawaii: Our New Possessions." Funk & Wagnalls Co.

in the asylum, and 500 within ten miles radius, whom she aims to get under the same blessed shelter.*

---

* Those who would read more fully on this terrible yet fascinating theme, may find in the following books more ample information: " The Lepers in Our Indian Empire," " Mission to Lepers in India and the East," and " A Glimpse at the Indian Mission-Field and Leper Asylums," etc. W. C. Bailey. John F. Shaw, London. " On Sledge and Horseback to Outcast Siberian Lepers." Kate Marsden. Cassel Pub. Co. "The Story of the Mission to Lepers in India." H. S. Carson, London. " European Lepers in India." Miss Lila Watt. " Without the Camp." Magazine, Lombard Street, Toronto, Canada, and Edinburgh, Scotland. " Encyclopedia of Missions." Funk & Wagnalls Co. " Picket Line of Missions." Eaton & Mains, New York.

CHAPTER XXVIII

RESCUE MISSIONS

THIS name has come to stand for organized effort to reach and save those most desperately lost—lost not to God only but to man; sunk to the lowest level, and beyond the ordinary touch of Christian benevolence and beneficence. They do not go to church, and the church does not go to them. They are in a pit so deep that the common means of grace do not avail; a special " life-line " let down to their level, and fitted to grapple them fast—a special message and mission, with peculiar love for the lost and passion for souls, seem needful for this sort of work. The Church has often been charged with *indifference* where, perhaps, the real difficulty is *inadequacy*. Many a pastor or earnest Christian stands and looks on the dying thousands of drunkards, harlots, criminals, paupers, about them, and simply turns away, sick at heart, as a helpless observer, standing on a sea-beach, beholds others hopelessly carried beyond reach of any available life-saving apparatus, to drown.

This half century has witnessed rescue work on a scale of magnitude, both as to the effort and its results, probably beyond any other period of history. A few forms of this philanthropy deserve special mention, while others which may have only a mention, are no less deserving of sympathy and aid. The Salvation Army and American Volunteers,* The Mission to the Deep-Sea Fishermen, The

---

* Mrs. Ballington Booth's work for the prisoners.

Jerry McAuley Mission, The Florence-Crittenton Midnight Mission may stand as representative movements. The first two are directed toward the poor and outcast classes generally; the third, toward the fishermen off the British Isles; the fourth is planted amid the drunkards, thieves, and worthless scamps of Water Street, New York; and the last is sacredly limited to the street-walkers and lost women who have sacrificed chastity on the altars of passion, poverty, and ignorance of the value of womanhood and virtue.

As to the Salvation Army, the one personality about whom this gigantic scheme revolved, and from whom it took its real character, was perhaps Catherine Booth, more than even her husband. She will ever be remembered as " the mother of the Salvation Army." Her memorials, in two great volumes, octavo, of about 700 pages each, are before the public, written in sympathetic ink by her son-in-law, Mr. Booth-Tucker. They show how far-reaching and deep-reaching her influence was, and are more fascinating than any fiction. Mrs. Booth was one of the greatest and best women of her century. A daughter who was one of the rarest gifts God ever gave to a parent; a wife that stood by her husband at risk of everything, and stirred him up to as much good as Jezebel stirred Ahab to evil; and a mother who swore a solemn oath before high heaven that she never would have a godless child!

Upon her heart lay like a nightmare the awful woe and wickedness of the " submerged " populations that are sunk out of ordinary reach, and almost out of sight, in their own wantonness and wretchedness. And when little by little the plans grew whereby it was proposed to get a hold upon these neglected and neglecting millions, she became the cherishing mother of the whole movement. She nursed it from the full breasts of her consolations; she bore it in the tireless arms of her faith; she fostered it by her prayers; she bathed it in her tears; she wrapped it in the mantle of her love; she patiently forebore with its follies and wants; she as patiently counseled and cautioned, while she passionately pleaded and urged. When she died it seemed to "General" Booth himself as tho this world-embracing scheme had lost its head and heart, and was in a state of widowhood and orphanhood, both at once.

The Salvation Army, with all its extravagances and serious defects has been on the whole a great success. Two great errors mar its record thus far; it has not sufficiently *exalted the Word of God,* and it is virtually *a church without sacraments.* There is an undue emphasis upon a subjective experience and a personal testimony, while the objective truth and the inspired Book of Witness fall into the background. In the Salvation Army halls the Bible is rarely lifted to prominence, as the acknowledged centre of all testimony and teaching; nor are Baptism and the Lord's Supper observed in connection with this organization. True, Mr. Booth disclaims all churchly character for the organization; it is not a church, but an army. Yet it remains true that he gathers in converts, and teaches them to make the army their church—for he says they can not serve in the army and at the same time be active members in any church—and yet he makes no provision for obedience to the only two *specific* ordinances ever enjoined by our Lord.

Nevertheless, the army has achieved great things. It has planted everywhere its halls, its refuges, its homes, its hundred-fold methods,* and they have proved effective beyond anything of the sort, in actually uplifting, saving, and transforming men and women. And, altho the head

---

* The latest enterprise in America is the Farm Colony established in California, and intended to provide homes for the poor of our great cities who are willing to work. This colony is not "cooperative," but has certain rules and restrictions calculated to contribute to the well-being of the community. Thirty-one houses had already been built in the first colony in 1898.

of this vast organization is one of the most autocratic of autocrats, he has handled immense sums of money and given a good account of his stewardship. Even his enemies and detractors have failed to find any fatal flaw in his business-like, economical, honest, and judicious use of money. He seems to live for the work he has undertaken, and to have laid himself on the altar of his service.

The work of Jerry McAuley, the apostle to the outcasts, recently commanded special public attention by the observance of its twenty-fifth anniversary, in Carnegie Hall, New York, of which ample notice was taken by the press.

In nothing does God's hand more strikingly appear than in the fitness of workers for their work. Times, places, forms of service, and adaptation of means to ends, all show intelligent design and a personal control. In the character and career of this founder of the " Water Street " and " Cremorne " missions for the reclamation of the worst and most dangerous classes, there may be seen a convergence of many marked providential lines of preparation.

Well known as are this man and his work by name, it is very doubtful whether one in ten, even of the church-goers in the great metropolis, knows much of the actual inception and growth of this enterprise, still less of the way in which it is carried on. Yet it is certain that no true disciple could doubt, after personal observation, that if anywhere in this vortex of crime our Divine Master is closely imitated it is in the Jerry McAuley work.

No 316 Water Street, New York, is almost exactly underneath the western approach to the great suspension bridge which spans the East River. Any night of the year a good-sized room may there be found, full of men, who for the most part, are obviously poor, given to drink and other vices; and many faces bear the marks of crime. A few seem to have the black brand of Cain. The tramp and pauper, the pickpocket and river thief, the besotted sailor and highway robber, the procurer to lust and the blatant blasphemer—every class of the worst men and women find their way there, and one may there speak to from two hundred to three hundred of these victims of want, woe, and vice. On one night of the week these hundreds are freely fed with good bread and coffee, as well as with the Bread of Life. The Gospel is sung with rousing effect, brief and simple Gospel talks interspersed, and an after-meeting always follows for prayer and testimony, and hand-to-hand touch with inquirers.

For over a quarter of a century, night after night in hot and cold weather, in wet and dry, with no dependence but faith in God, with no recompense but the wages of soul winners, his work has gone on, at times scarce surviving for want of funds and popular sympathy, yet always outliving any threatened danger of collapse, because God is behind it. It is no slight upon any other true work of God among the lowest classes, to record the calm conviction that, beyond any other one agency in the great metropolis, the Lord has used this Water Street Mission to reach, reclaim, and restore the very outcasts, and particularly *men*. Tho there has been no jealous care to count up converts and tabulate tangible results in statistics, during the quarter century, this mission and the Cremorne Mission in Thirty-second Street, which is its later outgrowth, have, without doubt, caused a million outcasts to hear the Gospel, and at least fifteen thousand men and women have found their way to a sober, honest, virtuous life by these means.

Such a work, going on quietly, on such a scale, demands attention and assistance from those who would help to save the lost. While others *talk* and *write* about the problem of reaching the outcasts, this mission is *doing* it, doing it so scripturally as to defy criticsm, and so efficiently as to merit imitation. After frequent visits to both the Water

Street and Cremorne missions, we bear witness that no feature of the work has left an unfavorable impression. Economy and simplicity of management, directness of appeal, evangelical tone, a prayerful spirit, dependence on God, hearty sympathy for man as man, and a divine passion for souls, seem to mark the whole history of the work which Jerry McAuley founded, and which Mr. S. H. Hadley and others carry on in the same spirit. If any doubt whether any good thing can come out of Nazareth, the old remedy is still at hand, " Come and see."

As this mission of Jerry McAuley has completed its first quarter century, it may be well to give a brief resumé of the rescue work.

Its beginning was unique. John Allen—" the wickedest man in New York "—kept a saloon and dance-house in Water Street, two doors from the site of this mission. In a dare-devil spirit he asked some missionaries, as they passed along one Sunday afternoon in 1868, to come in and hold a prayer-meeting in his saloon. They consented, if he would shut up his bar, which he did, and in this strange place for a Gospel service, praise and prayer and testimony for a little time displaced drunkenness, profanity, and lust. Allen's drunken fun led to serious business, for the invitation was soberly repeated, and the saloon was packed the next Sunday, and many could not get inside. New Yorkers will not forget the wild excitement which is forever linked with John Allen's name, from this remarkable· invasion of his premises by the Gospel of grace. Up to this time the Water Street neighborhood was a gateway of hell, nay, one long row of " dives " and " dance-halls," where almost every door led down to the devil's headquarters. Kit Burns' ratpit was but a block away, where " Jack, the rat," bit off rats' heads for the entertainment of sightseers!

This open door at Allen's saloon led to further attempts to enter this highway to perdition. A missionary, Mr. Little by name, while mounting a stairway found a gigantic amazon disputing his advance. " Madam," said he, offering a tract, " do you know Jesus? " " Faith, and who is *He?* " was the answer. A few feet away, and within a door that stood ajar, lay Jerry McAuley—drunk. He had been converted at Sing Sing prison by hearing " Awful " (Orville) Gardner, the famous prize-fighter, give his testimony in the prison chapel. Jerry had known him well before the grace of God touched him, and he could not resist such witness to the power of God. It resulted in such a change of life in himself that Governor Dix pardoned him and set him free. But the ex-convict found even divine pardon was not social restoration, and for lack of a helping hand, he fell back into evil ways. The mention of that magic name, " Jesus," even in a drunkard's ear, proved mighty to recover the backslider, whom it had saved as the outcast sinner. Jerry leaped to his feet, and his whole attire and appearance helping to render him frightful, he ran after the fleeing missionary, asking: " What name was that you mentioned to that woman? " The missionary thought he was confronting another belligerent fellow worse than the amazon; but Jerry continued: " I used to love that name in prison long ago, but I lost Him. I wish I knew where to find Him again! "

Mr. Little got him to sign the pledge, but he soon broke it, and was again on the road to crime when again he met the missionary. " Jerry, where are you going? " " I can't starve," was the sullen answer. " I will pawn my coat for you, Jerry, before I will see you steal." A glance at the coat, which would not have brought a half dollar at a pawn shop, gave Jerry McAuley a glimpse into the unselfishness of love, and he said, " If you love me that way,

I'll die before I steal." Mr. Little gave him that promise of
God to live by and live on, which has sustained many a
sinking soul: " Seek ye first the Kingdom of God and His
righteousness, and all these things shall be added unto
you." He said, " I'll take it," and that very night he
parted from his companion in thievery. Even yet, his
backsliding was only in part arrested, until he sacrificed
his last idol, tobacco, and after that he never fell again.
Four years later, he began the Water Street work.

The Lord gave Jerry a grand helper in his faithful wife,
who became at this time a convert to grace. The beginnings of their mission work were small and humble, but
the work was of God. The methods were novel in their
very simplicity. There was no rant or cant, no icy for-
mality or fashionable rigidity. It was a hand-to-hand
contact for soul saving. Any and every man and woman
who wanted salvation, or was willing to hear the good
news, was welcome, but cranks, impostors, disturbers of
the peace found the atmosphere uncongenial. Jerry,
sometimes, had desperate fellows to deal with, who were
the devil's own agents to break up his meetings, but in
God's name he grappled with them, and seemed to have
the strength of Samson and the courage of Joshua. Persecution was not lacking. Coals of fire were literally
flung on McAuley and his wife when they ventured into
the street. They were arraigned in court as disturbers of
the peace they were seeking to *make*, and but for friendly
intervention would more than once have got—where Paul
and Silas did at Philippi—into jail. The work went on,
though human malice and Satanic might united to crush
it. The old building was torn down in 1876, and the
present one took its place. Then, six years later, the Cremorne McAuley Mission, 104 W. 32d street, was begun,
and there he finished his course, leaving both missions to
other hands, by whom they are carried on in like manner.

Those who feel an interest may find in two books the outline of this history of a quarter century rescue work.* Better still, let any who can, *visit* the mission, where a warm welcome will await them. There the convict is as much at home as the most respectable citizen, and as sure of a handshake, with Gospel love behind it. There he will find food, clothing, lodging, if he needs them, and better still, hope for a new life. He will not be put through a catechism, nor bored with a homily, nor placed under espionage. He will be *trusted*—a strange experience for one who has always been suspected. He will find a Christian atmosphere, but not a pious hot-house where religious life is forced upon him. Many a criminal and outcast has found there a home—and felt the touch of a fraternal hand, an unvarying and indiscriminate kindness. Are not this kindness and confidence abused sometimes? Certainly, often. But love is not discouraged. It " beareth all things, believeth all things, hopeth all things, endureth all things. Love never faileth." The poor thief steals, and then steals away—but he comes back—there is no other resting place. Perhaps hunger and want drive him back, but he meets no reproaches, or upbraidings. He may sin seventy times seven times, but the forgiveness that awaits him has no limit, because it is patterned after the model shown in the Mount. And so the same results follow as have ever followed where Calvary is reflected— Christ draws all unto Him. Hard hearts are broken, habits of vice and crime are abandoned, wrecked lives— and worse, wrecked characters—are not put in dry-dock for caulking and painting and remodeling, but forsaken, like a sinking old hulk, for a new life and character in

* Read "Jerry McAuley, His Life and Work." Edited by Rev. R. M. Offord. Published by *The N. Y. Observer*, Fifth Avenue. Also, " Down in Water-Street for Twenty-five Years," by S. H. Hadley, Supt. Apply to Mr. Hadley, 316 Water Street, N. Y.

Christ. In two weeks a man or woman is sometimes transformed beyond recognition, even in the *face,* and tempters and seducers and procurers become soul winners.

Water Street Mission early learned that methods commonly in use will not suffice there. The work of saving drunkards and thieves and harlots was undertaken, not as a bit of polite philanthropy, nor even of Christian duty, but under the divine impulse of *passion for souls.* No kid gloves there to act as non-conductors—but a bare hand with holy love to give a sympathetic grasp. Front seats and best seats reserved, not for the gold ring and goodly apparel, but for the vile raiment and sin-scarred face. The fundamental law of soul saving there is that you *must be in close touch with those whom you would reach.* And the history of these twenty-five years proves that some men and women, who were apparently not worth the effort to save, who were like the dog and the sow that return to their own vices and wallowings, have, by grace, become the most heroic and successful evangelists and missionaries and soul savers, because they *knew* and *felt* what it was to be hopelessly. and helplessly lost and know and feel what it is to be both saved and kept.

The superintendent of the Water Street Mission is himself a man gloriously saved from the lowest hell of drunkenness. No wonder he can sympathize. He glories in a " Sinners' Club House," where the doors are always open and the work never stops. The devil's castaways are welcome there. When a man is kicked out of all the dens of infamy and iniquity, because he is of no more use, and nothing more can be got out of him, he is received with open arms. The mission belongs to no church or denomination ; its field is the world, especially the worst part of it, and its working force the whole Church of Christ, especially the best part of it. Those who visit that mission see how the cross is still the hope for the dying thief and the seven-demoned Magdalen; and how the Pentecostal fire is the secret still of all holy witness and work of God. Would you like to speak to such men and women? No rhetoric or eloquence is demanded—it would be out of place. Go and tell what Jesus has done for you, and let there be a *grip* in your testimony. You will find men and women who will come and kneel down by those " tear-stained benches," and give themselves up to the Gospel of grace to be created anew in Christ Jesus. Every night in the year you may find some one over whom heaven is set ringing with new praises and songs of joy.

And yet this mission has to struggle with debt! Are there none among the children of God, whose eyes read these pages, who will send offerings of love in money or clothing to Mr. Hadley for the men who, in destitution, are seeking to be clothed in respectable garments, befitting the newly-clothed soul?

Mr. F. N. Charrington was born in Bow Road, in the East End of London, February 4, 1850. The great brewery of Charrington, Head & Co., is situated in the Mile End Road, and covers an immense space of ground. To a share in this lucrative concern he was born.

At an early age he was placed in a school in Brighton, and at Brighton College, finished his curriculum of education, and after leaving school, went on a continental tour. His father offered to send him either to Oxford or Cambridge University, but this he declined, and commenced learning the business at once by becoming a pupil of Neville, Reed & Co., brewers to the Queen, at Windsor.

After remaining at Windsor for twelve months, Mr. Charrington entered his father's brewery. Soon after this he accompanied his parents on another tour on the Continent, and on this occasion he met with Mr. William Rainsford, son of the Rev. Marcus Rainsford, of Belgrave Chapel. They traveled in company on the return journey, during which Mr. Charrington invited his young friend to visit him at his father's house at Wimbledon.

During this visit Mr. Rainsford spoke to Mr. Charrington about his soul, and plainly asked him if he knew whether he was saved. Mr. Charrington protested against such a subject being brought up, especially after such a pleasant time spent on the Continent. Mr. Rainsford, however, pressed home the question, and made Mr. Charrington promise he would read the third of John when alone. The next night he fulfilled his promise, and while thinking over the passage, he recalled the following incident:

On one occasion while staying at Hastings, he met with a young friend, Mr. Manning, who was visiting that watering place with his tutor, and who at the moment of meeting, had just been hearing Lord Radstock preach. Mr. Canning related how he had been converted at the meeting, and was now a saved man. To Mr. Charrington all this was simply a riddle, and he thought it was at least indecorous for a youthful aristocrat to go and hear a Dissenter, even though that Dissenter was himself an aristocrat. When thus, two years later, he sat down to read the Gospel in the solitude of his own room, this came back fresh into his mind, for he thought it was strange that two of his friends of a similar age should agree in giving a certain passage the same singular interpretation. As he read, however, the light came: and he now looks back to this hour as the one when he received the truth and became a believer in the Lord Jesus.

Mr. Charrington at once became possessed with new desires and ideas. He first spoke to an old school-fellow, a young lawyer, who was converted at school. " Christ died for us," argued Mr. Charrington; " and we ought to do something for Him." Soon afterwards he waited upon the Rector and Rural Dean of Stepney, who, while encouraging his application for work, could think of nothing more effective than a night school.

The young convert was glad in any way to make a beginning. His days were occupied in the great brewery, while his evenings were spent in the night school. At this time he became acquainted with two men who were carrying on in the immediate neighborhood a work of a more evangelistic character among the rough boys in a hay-loft.

Mr. Charrington thought, as he stood and listened: "This is far more like real work for the Lord than my own more secular night-school work." At the close of the service the singing made such an impression upon him that he again sought an opportunity of visiting the work in the hay-loft, and at once proposed that they should join forces.

Up to this time Mr. Charrington had remained in the brewery, but momentous changes were at hand. He was now heart and soul in his new work, but his conscience was not at rest. Wherever he went, he saw his father's name in connection with the firm, printed on large signboards over the various public houses. He began to witness sights that touched his heart. He saw drunken fathers, gin-drinking mothers, ill-used children whose worst enemies were those whom God designed to be their natural protectors. There might seem to be light, warmth and cordials within; but brawls and fights spoiled the glitter; and then above all he read, " Charrington, Head & Co., Entire."

In addition to this, the lads were continually asking him questions about the drink, that were not at all likely to make his conscience more at ease; his visitations to the homes of the poor revealed a state of things that he had never dreamed of; and he began to feel that, as a brewer, he was pulling down with one hand what, as a Christian worker, he was building up with the other.

The crisis came. Mr. Charrington told his father that he could have nothing more to do with the business of the brewery. The decision came so unexpectedly that it was a great blow to the family. He renounced his trade with its golden prospects, without asking about the consequences, and was allowed to retire in quietness. On his death-bed the father expressed his approval of the course his son had taken, altho in his will (which had previously been made) the share in his father's brewery was offered for his acceptance, with an alternative of a sum of money sufficient to produce an income to maintain him for life.

Mr. Charrington's withdrawal from the brewery created considerable commotion. His temperance friends invited him to take the chair at the Annual Meeting of the Band of Hope Union at Exeter Hall. On the night of the meeting (February 18, 1873) the streets outside were crowded; the crush within was very great, the cheering was deafening, and the waving of hats and handkerchiefs was to be seen all over the hall, while many hearts were uplifted in earnest prayer that the young man might be kept true to the profession he had made, and become pre-eminently useful in the service of Christ.

Street preaching was a means greatly used of God from the outset. The work now began to get known, and the parents of several boys, seeing the change in their children's lives, came to the Mission Hall to see this young converted brewer, as Mr. Charrington was called. Then they asked permission to stay to the service themselves, till they came in such numbers that a separate meeting had to be held for them. Soon after this, an iron building, to seat 500 persons, was erected by the late Mr. Pemberton Barnes, in Carleton Sq., Globe Road, and given over to

Mr. Charrington for adult work. This effort succeeded so well that Mr. Charrington hired a tent, and placed it upon a site in the main thoroughfare of the Mile End Road, and here a great work for God was done, and many souls saved.

A still better site was afterwards purchased, and in order to lose no time, a large circular tent was put up and opened in May, 1876.

In 1877 a temporary building of brick, wood, and corrugated iron—being part of the Hall in which Messrs. Moody and Sankey held their services on their first visit to London—was substituted for the tent, and formed one of the most noteworthy features in the Mile End Road; not on account of its beauty, for utility supplanted all such considerations; but principally by reason of its size, and of the great eagerness displayed by the crowds of East London to obtain admission.

The great Assembly Hall has always had one distinguishing characteristic,—a characteristic which it shares with no other public building of the kind in the Metropolis. Since its erection it has been open every night, all the year round.

The work had now grown so much that a larger building was needed. The regular attendants at the Hall—poor as they are—feeling this great need, contributed in small sums upwards of $1,500 to the Building Fund; $45,000 was laid out in the erection of frontage buildings, covering a site 90 feet in width and 43 feet in depth. They comprise a spacious Coffee Palace, which is self-supporting, and supplies all the attractions of the public house without the intoxicating drink; a Book Saloon, where pure literature is sold, counteracting the pernicious influences of the well-named " penny horribles ; " and, on three upper floors, various club rooms and offices, Young Men's Christian Association and Young Women's Christian Association Rooms, Building Societies, Coal Club, Provident Club, Phœnix Order, Temperance Society, Singing and Violin Classes, Benefit Club, etc., etc. Three fine entrances, one on either side and the third in the center, lead into a vestibule of octagonal shape, and of what is considered a perfect design for the purpose, the number of exits being great. Behind the vestibule stands the New Hall, holding nearly 5,000 persons. On Sunday nights its accommodation is none too ample, hundreds often being unable to get in.

The Hall has a height of nearly 50 feet in the clear; and a depth of 154 feet, the width being 70 feet. There are three galleries, with double platforms, and space for organ and choirs. The ceiling is nearly flat, for sound, with covered sides. This Hall, apart from the frontage, has cost $100,000.

CHAPTER XXIX

OF the efforts made in this direction we give two notable examples, both of them described in the language of others: first the Little Republic at Freeville, N. Y., and the other the Orphan Colony at Bridge of Weir, Scotland.

Of the former, Mr. Delavan L. Pierson has written:

Mr. William R. George, a New York business man, who for years had taken a deep interest in the boys of the slums, devised a plan whereby they could be taken out of their degrading surroundings and placed where they might have every opportunity for learning the art of self-control, and be taught Christian ideals of life and service.

Mr. George had studied the boys from their social and industrial side, and in the boys' clubs had come to understand and love them. Requesting appointment as special detective, he studied them also from their criminal side. Moved by their poverty and the degraded character of their surroundings, he planned to give some of them a summer outing on a country farm in Freeville, Tompkins County, N. Y., near his boyhood home. The first year he "aired" fifty and the second year two hundred of them, but physical vigor seemed to be gained without corresponding advance in moral character, and it soon became clear that they came merely for what they could get, and felt justified in claiming as their due whatever they might wish to ask for. The result was that they were being pauperized. Incorrigible at home, they were as bad

under their changed conditions, and all rules and requirements were deliberately broken. Neither corporal nor
any other form of punishment availed to prevent evil-
doing. Mr. George had recourse even to substitutionary
punishment, himself taking the lashes deserved by the
boys. But swearing, gambling, stealing, and other vices
continued to flourish.

Much of the pauperizing evil was done away with during the fourth summer, when the children were obliged
to work for the clothes or gifts which they wished to carry
back to the city. Most of them, however, chose to go
without rather than sacrifice their leisure. One day the
adult overseer, being obliged to absent himself for a time,
Mr. George hesitatingly placed in charge one of the older
boys, a leader among his mates. To his amazement, the
discipline and order was markedly better. To these boys
the law, and its most familiar exponent, the " cop," are
institutions to be outwitted, evaded and duped, as are all
superiors and supervisors. But when one of their own
number assumed command, all this was changed. There
was no glory to be had from outwitting an equal, but a
great deal of ignominy in suffering punishment at his
hands. This experience led Mr. George to inaugurate
trial by jury for all offenses, with a penalty of fines to
be paid by a certain number of hours of work. He found
among the boys a spirit of justice, tempered by mercy,
which was a revelation to him. He, however, still kept
tight grasp of the helm, appointing the jurors himself,
and often personally superintending the penal labor. In
1895 he gave up his business in New York, deciding that
no permanent good could be done when the boys were
with him so short a time. He, therefore, resolved to keep
as many as would stay through the winter. The success
of the boys in administering their laws led to the idea of
allowing them to make their own laws as well. Thus, as

by an inspiration, the whole scheme of the Junior Republic, with its bread-earning, law-making, and law-executing citizens, was born July 10, 1895.

The government of the Republic is a democracy of the citizens, by the citizens, and for the citizens, even more truly than is our greater republic, since the extremes of poverty and wealth are not present to deflect the course of righteous government. The constitution is modeled after that of the United States, the laws are those of the State of New York, and the form of local government contains many features of municipalities. At present Mr. George acts as president. Cabinet officers are elected by the citizens, good, moral standing in the commuunity being a prime requisite in candidates for office. The chief of police draws the highest salary, but candidates for this and all other appointive positions are required to pass a civil service examination. There is at present rather a rapid rotation in office, but as the number of citizens increases, the term of office may more safely be lengthened.*

All tenure of office is dependent upon upright behavior. It is the ambition of every boy to attain to the distinction of the vertically striped trousers. Most of them would rather be " cop " than president. In 1896 a force of fourteen policemen were necessary to preserve order, but now the state is encumbered with the support of but two. The positions of chief justice, civil service commissioner, board of health commissioner, sheriff—in short, nearly every office connected with our complicated city and state organizations—has its counterpart in this Junior Republic, excepting that of coroner. There is even an officer detailed in the early fall to compel lazy truants to attend school.

---

* According to the constitution, adopted March 8, 1898, representatives held office one month, senators three months, and president one year. Since Jan. 1, 1899, a town meeting has taken the place of the two houses of congress as the legislative body.

The number of citizens is necessarily limited. In June, 1898, there were forty-four boys and seven girls; eight of the number were minors. The regulation of the summer citizens, who formerly came for July and August, was a difficult problem, and this feature of the work has now been abandoned. They came in great numbers from haunts of unrestrained evil, and they did not stay long enough to become imbued with the spirit of honorable self-support, nor to acquire love for the institutions of their adopted state, yet, because of their superior numbers, they often ran the legislature, or at least had great influence in that body. But to deny them the rights of citizenship would have been to set aside the very foundation principles of the republic. To remedy this evil, Mr. George proposed to found another state, to be composed almost entirely of summer citizens, with a few all-year residents for ballast. The farm is a large one, containing fifty acres, and there would be ample room for such division, if the additional expense could be met.

A new citizen generally spends much of his first month in jail for offenses of one sort or another, after which it takes a month of exemplary conduct to qualify him to hold any office; thus, if his stay is only three months long, he leaves just as he and the state are beginning to reap the rewards of his well-doing.

The citizens of the Republic are largely New Yorkers, as Mr. George's previous work was with the boys of the East Side of that city, but there are numerous sources of supply. Parents whose children are wayward and disobedient, police whose lives are made miserable by little incorrigibles, heads of reformatories who acknowledge their inability to restrain or improve their vicious young charges, and judges of county courts, who, after a boy has served a sentence or two without improvement, turn him over to Mr. George that he may be checked in his career of crime—these, together with the Society for Prevention of Cruelty to Children, send to the Junior Republic material, which, altho most unpromising at first, is developed in a year or two into upright, steady, and usually Christian citizens, who often go out to assume positions of trust in the business world. As is usual with such successful enterprises, there are about four hundred more applicants than can be accommodated, one great difficulty usually being the regular supply of funds to carry on the work.*

Twelve years is accounted the age of majority, all under twelve being minors without full citizenship. These latter are under guardians appointed by the state from among the older boys and girls, who must render account to the state for their stewardship. Many of these guardians have shown themselves to be wise, tactful, and loving caretakers of the little ones entrusted to their charge. When the minors can not fully support themselves, their guardians must look out for them, so that the state is not encumbered with their support. This fact alone bespeaks unselfishness in the citizens who assume the care of minors.

One little fellow only nine years old, who had already been found guilty in five cases of arson, and two of theft, was sent to Freeville, and given into the care of a lad of thirteen with fatherly instincts. This lad took the boy into his room, and spoke to him lovingly of the past, and of his desire to make a man of him, and then knelt at his side and prayed for help. The little chap is still at the Republic, and is now one of the most active Christians there. In prayer meeting his childlike testimony or prayer is seldom wanting. Last winter he confided to Mrs.

---

* The Republic is supported by voluntary contributions, five dollars a year constituting a member of the association, $25 yearly a sustaining member, and $250 a life member. Mr. A. G. Agnew, 7 Nassau street, New York, is the treasurer, to whom donations of clothing, books, or money should be sent.

George a little struggle which he had had with himself. It was zero weather, and he had undressed and crawled into bed under the warm blankets as quickly as possible. " I remembered," said the boy, " that I had not said my prayers. It was so awful cold, I thought I wouldn't get up. Then the old devil began to jolly me and tell me I was a good boy, and hadn't done anything much that was bad that day. He kept on talking that way, till he almost talked me to sleep. Then I roused up like, and I prayed the Lord to help me down the old devil, and I got strength, and just jumped out of bed and made my prayer, and then I knew that I had downed the old devil."

As has already been mentioned, a small portion of the citizens are girls. This will undoubtedly seem to some to be radically opposed to all established reformatory principles. Yet the results without exception have been more than satisfactory. One girl who had been dismissed from an institution on account of her frequent night escapades with boys is now a trusted industrious helper in the Republic. Mr. George has no hesitation in giving her permission to attend the midweek services at the village church a mile away, and one of the boys is despatched at nine o'clock to bring her safely home. When she first arrived her actions were so uncouth and vulgar as to attract the notice of all. The boys shunned her, and one and another came to Mr. George in confidence to say that they did not like the new girl's actions and would have to keep an eye on her. Shortly after, one of the girls came expressing the same opinion, but added, " I am going to try and win her, and make her see that her life is all wrong." Under the influence of this little friend, letters written to boys were never sent, and an honest shame and penitence filled her and she was saved from physical and spiritual ruin.

Another girl, whose mother had died, was sent to the

Republic by her father, who had no control over her. At the time of our visit she had just returned home to nurse her father through an illness and most encouraging letters had been received from her, full of loving solicitude for her father and a desire to atone for her years of wilfulness and disobedience.

The woman suffrage question at the Republic is essentially one of taxation without representation, since the girls have no husbands, fathers, or brothers to represent them and protect their interests in the legislature, and the question has had varying fortunes. On the first of July all amendments which were not reenacted were formally declared null and void, so that the woman suffrage law, being necessarily an amendment of a state law, passed through a yearly crisis and struggle for existence. The unfair apportionment of an imposed tax two years ago made the girls petition for the ballot once more, and at the next meeting of the legislature woman suffrage prevailed.

The latest improved ballot is used at all their elections. Boys who have learned the value of the ballot at the Republic will not lightly give up their privilege of casting their personal vote, and the tactics of the ward politician will be much better understood by those young citizens than by their ignorant parents. One boy gave expression to these thoughts when he said, " I tell youse, I've been a citizen meself, an' Jimmy O'Brien won't never lead me around by de nose like he leads me fadder. I knows a ting or two about politics meself, see ! "

Laws wise and otherwise find their way into the statute book of the Junior Republic; but as each law is strictly enforced, it takes but a short time to test the wisdom or folly of a new measure. At first very lenient pauper laws were passed. The paupers were fed at the expense of the state, altho in a humiliating manner, at a second table from which the cloth and other accessories had been removed, and portions were served like prison rations. But there were some boys who had but little self-respect, and as long as the food was plentiful, they preferred to idle away their time and be dependent upon the state. Having no income they were practically tax free except the insignificant poll-tax which is levied upon all. It was not long before the industrious citizens and taxpayers began to realize the expense which idlers incurred to the state. Finally a senator, *whose own parents at home were wholly dependent upon city charity*, submitted a bill to the legislature to the effect that those who would not work should not eat. The lazy poor were thus deprived of support, but those who through illness were unable to work were provided with meal tickets.

An amusing incident happened in connection with the enforcement of this law. There were three restaurants at the time in the Republic, one furnishing meals for fifteen cents, another for twenty-five cents, and a third an elaborate· fifty-cent dinner.* When the meal tickets were distributed, they simply read, " Good for one meal," not designating the restaurant. Of course, the fifty-cent restaurant was uniformly patronized, and when the hotel-keeper's bill was rendered to the government, there was hardly money enough to pay, and the state was in sore straits for a time. It is needless to say that this happened but once.

Since the laws of New York State are their models, they may not exceed the state fines for any offense. In one case the legislature passed a law that swearing, or the use of any improper language, should be fined $5. But a prisoner arrested on this charge contested the validity

---

* In all references to money in this article the coin of the George Junior Republic is the standard of value. These coins are made of tin, and, of course, have only a local and nominal value.

of the law, since the laws of New York State place the fine at $1, and the law was revised.

A heavy fine was imposed on cigarette smoking; but nevertheless boys would often steal away beyond the policeman's beat, and indulge this lawless habit. Consequently an amendment was passed, which made a citizen liable to arrest and punishment if the *smell* of smoke could be detected in his breath. The penalty is a fine from $1 to $3, or from one to three days in the workhouse.

Gambling of any sort receives no quarter from the officials. The first boy caught " shooting craps " was a senator, and even tho he pleaded guilty, the judge fined him $25. He refused to pay. He lost not only his state position, but also his rights of citizenship, and was obliged to don the striped suit and break stone at five cents an hour. One night as Mr. George was passing down the prison corridor, he spoke to the boy, kindly and earnestly, and advised him to pay up and get out of prison. " No, I won't do it," the boy answered; and then with the ready wit of the street urchin, he added: " I guess I'll take the smallpox and break out." Some days later, as he was breaking stone, he threw down his hammer, threw up his hands in a tragic manner, and exclaimed: " I surrender ! March me to me bank account."

When we reflect that these laws against swearing, impurity, gambling, and smoking—vices which are the very life of the criminal classes—with their heavy penalties attached, are of the boys' own making, and are enforced with a rigor which bespeaks a strong public sentiment against this evil, we gain some idea of the success which has attended this effort at self-government.

The laws in no way curtail the liberty of the citizens. Times for retiring at night or rising in the morning, are not matters of law. Early bed hours are in vogue, however, because of the healthy weariness following a day of hard work. Early rising is practiced because of the requirements of employers, and because the hotel proprietor objects to having his beds occupied at the expense of an airing. The frequent visits from the board of health make him apprehensive of a fine.

The George Junior Republic is in many respects a model reformatory, and yet it has few of the failings and disadvantages which characterize the ordinary reformatory system. Everything is as unlike an institution as possible, and the citizens resent very much the application of that term to their enterprise. The laws being enacted and enforced by the boys themselves, the punishment of the culprit is never laid at Mr. George's door.

To the casual visitor this system might seem like playing at law-making; but it is far from play to the boys. It must be remembered that they are forced to abide by their laws, and feel their responsibility of legislating for their individual interest and for the welfare of their Republic. Valuable lessons in parliamentary procedure and in debating, and in caution and in forethought, are learned in the Town Meeting, which has now displaced the more cumbersome Congress.

It is instructive as well as interesting to notice how the questions which confront our greater republic come up for discussion and settlement in the smaller. Women's suffrage, free-trade or protection, tariff, trusts, income tax, free "tin," pauper labor, all have presented themselves. On returning from the village some boys brought candies, fruit, etc., which had been purchased at cheap rates, or had been presented to them by some kind-hearted farmer's wife. These they sold to their fellows at lower prices than the government licensed store could afford to furnish them. The storekeeper appealed to the government, and a tariff of thirty-five per cent. was laid on all imports.

The Republic has its own currency, made of flat pieces of tin, stamped, George Junior Republic, and in denominations from one dollar down. Silver, nickel, or copper can purchase nothing within the Republic. The Republic maintains the bank, and all official payments are made by means of drafts upon it. Two per cent. interest is paid on all deposits, and any citizen who has accumulated a little sum, may, on leaving the Republic, have it redeemed in U. S. coin at one-fifth its face value.

The financial system of the Republic is based upon wages for work. Its motto is " Nothing without labor." The government lets out contracts of all sorts,—farming, road construction, landscape gardening, hotel keeping, etc., etc., and the contractors hire labor, paying different prices, according to the skill of the workmen, from fifty cents to one dollar and fifty a day. Wages are paid once a week, and no favors are shown to those workmen or government officials who recklessly spend their earnings the first few days of the week. A coarse diet and a harder bed await such until next pay day.

An excellent little paper, *The Junior Republic Citizen,* is published by the boys. They write freely for it, using their own language and spelling, and are not held to account for the opinions they express. It is issued monthly and contains reports of census and " police blotter." This is one of the marked features of the Republic.

The problem of a congested labor market has never had to be grappled with in the Republic. There is work for every boy who will work. Some boys, preferring their own independent enterprises, have started barber-shops and tailoring establishments. One boy, only thirteen years old, being hard pressed by the hotel proprietor, announced a course of lectures on " The Minor Lights of History," Miles Standish, Captain John Smith, and John Brown, and altho he set his prices high (single lecture, fifty cents;

course tickets, one dollar), the hotel corridor was filled all three lecture nights.

Another boy, much interested in natural history, made a collection of insects, cocoons, nests, nymphs, etc., but his companions would not deign to notice his collection. One day he announced the opening of a " Dime Museum," and at the appointed hour there was a line of boys reaching clear to the police station, each with his dime in his hand waiting for admittance. When the doors were opened, the show was found to consist of this same entomological collection; but the boys had paid their money, and so they listened attentively to the interesting explanations of the museum proprietor, and afterwards voted it a " huge success."

The buildings of the Republic include: (1) The " Republic," containing a kitchen and two restaurants, a library, hotel, and " garroot "; (2) the school-house, bank, and store; (3) the court-house, jail, capitol, post-office, store, and Waldorf Hotel; (4) Carter cottage for boys; (5) Rockefeller cottage for girls; (6) business offices; (7) hospital; (8) barn; (9) tool-house and work-shop; (10) laundry and bath; (11) dairy; (12) shoe shop; (13) a chapel has also been promised. Everything is exceedingly plain. It is to be hoped that this feature of the Republic will never be altered, for finer surroundings would only breed dissatisfaction with their city homes and teach lessons of extravagance. Cleanliness is carefully taught as a habit to be practised by all classes, and a neglect of this virtue may bring about a fine from the Board of Health.

The jail is no play house, but has small cells with veritable bars and high windows, hard slat beds, and prison meals. A formidable constable's desk stands in a recess at the entrance, while almost opposite in a niche is a little melodeon for use in the religious services held weekly in the prison corridor. Upstairs is the court room, containing, among other things, a trap door for the entrance of the prisoner, an imposing high desk for the judge, and a juror's bench. There is a small space railed off for the witness stand, and rows of seats for interested listeners. The sessions of the court are most orderly and impressive. The pros and cons are carefully weighed; evidence is called for in its proper place, and most heartstirring appeals are made to the jury. One judge walked ten miles to Ithaca and back again that he might attend a court session and learn how to conduct those of the Republic with proper decorum. Only one case of bribery has ever been discovered, and the guilty officer was immediately deposed and suffered disgrace as well as legal penalties. The rear of the court room is partitioned off into " lawyers' offices," and bears this prohibitory sign, " Citizens not allowed to climb over this partition."

It is, perhaps, to be deplored that the court and legal proceedings have such a prominent place in the Junior Republic, but the fairness of the judgments, and the submission of the guilty to the punishments imposed, counteract, to some degree, this unfortunate feature. The police court must, inevitably, play a large part in the lives of such children, and how much better to have justice and equity demonstrated than bribery and harshness.

Most of the citizens of the Junior Republic live in boarding-houses or hotels. These latter are two in number, the " Republic Hotel " and the " Waldorf," (which is the second class hotel). The accommodations at the " Republic " are of two grades; pies and cakes, and linen tablecloths and individual chairs go with the twenty-five cent meals. The " garroot " boarders are served in a separate dining-room, with less elaborate, altho none the less clean surroundings. The sleeping rooms range from those hung with curtains and store-framed pictures to those whose only charms are light and air. "The garroot" has no individual rooms, but one long gabled loft, with a chest by the side of each fellow's bed to hold his wardrobe. Here lodge the impecunious, brought to this pass either by the love of play or by fondness for candy and other luxuries. Board must be paid in advance, and prices are higher, of course, for transients.

A new plan has recently been put into operation. Two simple cottages have been built, each to accommodate twelve boys or girls, who constitute a family, with a motherly woman as "house mother." All work toward the support of the homes, the girls doing the mending and housework, the boys, like older brothers, supplying the needful money. The householders pay Mr George a nominal rent. One cottage has recently been sold to eight boys for $1,200. They paid $200 down, and Mr. George holds a mortgage for the remainder.

There is a library, a memorial gift, and the shelves contain over 1,200 volumes: fiction, history, science, poetry, essays, and reference and religious books, with some juvenile books and many leading periodicals. The most thumbed books of all are those which treat of the penal and civil code of New York State.

The problem of book study for the winter residents has given Mr. George some difficulty. It goes without saying that all the citizens are in need of education, and the Republic school is now a part of the country school system of the State. Attendance upon this school is obligatory by the law of the Republic, and a truant officer gathers in any who "play hookey." Several members of the Republic attend the high school of a neighboring village, and three have now entered Cornell. The civil service examinations, which cover all the ordinary branches, debar the ignorant and the inattentive from holding the coveted position of the police or judge, health commissioner, sheriff, or any other appointive office. This gives importance and attractiveness to " education," which the street gamin has never before conceived possible. He learns that education means power.

Church and State are separate in the Junior Republic, and there is no legislation bearing directly on religious matters, but the founder being a man of strong religious convictions, such an atmosphere of godliness emanates from " the capitol " that the citizens are unconsciously affected by it. Roman Catholics attend a little Catholic church near by, and Protestants go to the village Methodist church and Sunday-school. The citizens have also organized among themselves a Christian Endeavor Society, and it would be hard to find a more earnest little band, altho of opposing creeds and diverse beliefs. Little Roman Catholic children attend mass in the morning, and, perhaps, lead or take part in a regular Christian Endeavor prayer-meeting in the afternoon. A falling off in church attendance was noticed at one time, and the legislature provided that a missionary should be appointed, whose duty it should be to visit delinquents, urge upon them the duty and privilege of church worship, and to warn the erring.

Especially solemn and impressive are the meetings held in the jail corridor for the prisoners. In the midst of one meeting a little girl was seen to slip out quietly, and in a few moments returned with her arms full of Bibles and prayer-books. Going to each cell, she discriminated between the Protestant and the Roman Catholic prisoners, giving the former a Bible and the latter a prayer-book, with a tender word of encouragement to read it.

Family prayers are daily held, led sometimes by one of the older helpers, but as often by a citizen. God's blessing is also asked at table, usually by one of their own number.

We believe that Mr. George has taken a wise course in the religious conduct of his miniature republic. His helpers are all Christians, who have entered upon the work with the missionary spirit—an earnest desire to win these boys and girls for Christ. Six days in the week, at the carpenter bench, or on the farm, or over the stove, or at the machine, they patiently help to solve the knotty problems of manufacture or cultivation, and on the seventh set an example of restful worship and meditation which is not lost on their young charges. Quiet heart to heart talks are continually bearing fruit in the little Republic, unto life eternal. If attendance upon church service were a matter of compulsion, when everything else is free, or if the church were given prominence through being constituted a State church, the present well-balanced condition of things could not exist.

Mr. George has expressed the conviction that any one of his several older citizens, who have spent two or three years with him, would be thoroughly competent to superintend another republic, and make it in every way as great a success as Freeville. If in making this statement he has carefully taken into account the far-reaching religious influences of the leader, the confidence and esteem in which he holds these boys must be very great.

Mr. George says that there has never been a boy, who has stayed at the Republic as long as he (Mr. George) felt he should, who has not left a thoroughly upright, self-dependent citizen, having learned lessons of obedience to law and respect for the rights of others. Of course, some are taken away by their parents or guardians before they are ripe for dismissal, and a few become rebellious and return of their own free will to their idle city life. Who can estimate the work this one little Republic is doing, in converting paupers and criminals into citizens who make for righteousness and peace, and girls whose feet were already turned toward hell, into women of chaste, industrious lives?

Two years ago Mr. George took one of the younger citizens to Brooklyn to speak in behalf of the Republic. The boy communicated his enthusiasm to his audience in a wonderful way. At the close a lady, with purse in hand, pressed up to him and offered it to the little speaker. Mr. George, from his position in the audience, noticed her turn away chagrined. In a few moments she came to him, saying, " Won't you take this money and use it for that boy." " Wouldn't he accept it? " asked Mr. George. " I never received such a rebuke in my life," replied the lady; " when I offered it to him, he said, ' I can not take it, Madam, I have done nothing to earn it.' "

When the previous history of some of the boys is known, the visitor's most natural question is: Have you ever had to expel any because of incorrigibility? The question always calls forth the same reply: " The worse the boy, the more his need of the Republic and its influences. No; we never willingly let go of our *bad* boys."

It will be seen from the foregoing account that the Junior Republic is indeed a *model reformatory*. Amid wholesome surroundings, and under judicious Christian management, the boys and girls are taught self-control, self-help, obedience to law, the blessing of service to others, and are given every opportunity to become honorable Christian citizens in our larger republic.

The principles upon which the Junior Republic are founded are sound, and are the outcome of years of study of the city street gamin; but even with such a complete system, not every one could successfully carry on such a republic. The principles of self-help and self-government among the boys must be wisely recognized by a

Christian governor, and a consistent course of non-interference practised at the same time that a vigilant outlook is kept.

Some minor phases of the Republic's life are still in their experimental stage, but the Republic itself has passed beyond that stage and has clearly vindicated its right to exist, and to be supported by the interest and prayers and gifts of the Christian people of our land. It is philanthropic work without any of the pauperizing tendencies of ordinary philanthropy, and, on the other hand, it does away with the opportunity of self-gratulation, which mars so much of our charitable work. The sense of personal responsibility for law and order, is visible in each sunburned freckled face of the citizens, and boys who have had a common education in dodging police, will legislate and oversee with a sharpness in which the ordinary adult is pitifully deficient.

If the Republic stopped short of being a Christian enterprise, there would be no opportunity for the highest forms of altruism. With pauper laws that are inexorable, with competition that is sharp, altho friendly, with a decided spirit of self-interest and preservation, there would be developed only a high sense of justice and a healthy regard for the rights of others. But, lifted to the plane of Christianity, the opportunities of visiting the sick and the imprisoned, the faithful exercise of guardianship and the repression of covetousness and jealousy, all give opportunity for the exercise of the highest altruism in accordance with the teaching of Christ.

It is very evident that the love which Mr. George has for his boys and girls is heartily reciprocated. No thief ever steals from him. The tender accent they give to the word " Daddy " when they speak of him, and the confident manner in which they approach him to ask a question, to tell him of some loss, or inquire for a missing companion ;

the alacrity with which they run on little errands for him, and the stream of evening callers to bid him good-night before retiring, all speak loudly of the love which they bear toward him. As the last one bade him good-night and left him, with a look of satisfaction, Mr. George turned to us a beaming face and said, " I wouldn't change places with any one in the world; I believe I'm the happiest man alive."

We subjoin an interesting letter published in *The Christian,* Jan. 4, 1900, on a visit to Scotland's orphans, at Mr. Quarrier's village, Bridge-of-Weir.

A group of little ones passed the house, their happy faces turning radiant at the sight of Mrs. Findlay, who threw hand-kisses to them, saying, " These are some of our infant orphans." " Why, you have no uniforms, then?" said I. " No, father does not believe in uniform dressing. It puts the stamp of pauperism upon the children whom we wish to save for society. We do not like them to think that they are different from the others. Each child is dealt with individually, watched and observed, and when the time comes for choosing a trade or a profession, we know something of the proclivities of each."

Anxious that no individuality should be lost sight of, Mr. Quarrier avoids uniformity even in buildings. Of the fifty-seven Homes which form this " City of the Young," each presents the aspect of a residential villa, with distinct architectural features of its own, and a garden-plot adjoining it. Prizes are given to the Homes that have the best-kept gardens. This system was first objected to on the ground that it involved expenditure; but in the course of time the founder was able to show that taste and beauty, as well as variety, could be effected within the limits of a strict and true economy. For £12 a year, on an average, an orphan is housed, fed, and educated.

The ten-roomed Homes are occupied by thirty inmates or less. Girls are under the supervision of a mother. A married couple has the charge of the boys, who, in their spare time, are taught a trade by the father.

As this was the usual half-holiday, we missed seeing the children at work in the Homes; but, being shown round, could easily imagine their beehive-life during the week. From *James Arthur,* an iron brig of over 120 ft. in length, the generous gift of a widow lady in memory of her husband, we saw some of the juvenile crew playing football by the banks of the river Gryffe. They reside with their captain on board the brig, erected on a firm bed of concrete, and are taught navigation, as far as it can be taught, on dry land. Mr. Quarrier hopes thus to raise up some missionary seamen.

In passing some ruins we learned that, owing to the break-out of fire on October 19, all the workshops had been destroyed, including the laundry, bakery, joiner's, shoemaker's, printer's, and tailor's shops.

At the great store—where, as everywhere, cleanliness, neatness, and order are observed—forty-eight dozen loaves of bread pass over the counter every day, and the total per month is about eight tons of flour, two and a-half tons of meal, and one ton of sugar. Much of the wearing apparel is sent in by kind friends, but the largest part is manufactured on the premises. " The Lord will provide " is the motto carved in stone over the entrance to the building.

With Mr. Quarrier it was trusting in the Lord all the way through. Without ever applying directly to anybody, or asking help from bazaars or entertainments, he always had his needs provided in due season. Here is his testimony:—

" We passed through many a sore trial. We were often short of money, but never needed to stint food to our children for lack of provisions," said he, as we sat down by the fireside. " This work is a standing rebuke to those who deny a prayer-hearing and a prayer-answering God."

Yes, truth is stranger than fiction. There is much more romance in the life of a child of God than there is in the most exotic imagination of a novelist. Let us listen to him as he recalls the principal points in his career.

He knew what property was, and what it meant to lose a father in early life. Feeling keenly in his own experience the lot of others, he made, like Abraham Lincoln, only much earlier in life, a resolution which he never forgot: " Mother, when I am a big man I shall build a home for orphans just like me." This was said one day in the High Street of Glasgow fifty-eight years ago. Years rolled by, and the little boy was becoming a successful business man, when he took the first step towards the accomplishment of his childish desire, by establishing, in 1864, the Glasgow Shoe-black Brigade, which had for its object the gathering in and assisting of the little street arabs of Glasgow.

The work grew, and seven years later the Lord sent him, in answer to prayer, £2,000, which enabled him to open the first Orphan's Home in Renfew Lane. It was an old workshop, where some thirty orphans were gathered in and cared for. "How many did you get in the first day?" asked my husband, at this juncture of the story. "Only one; and he was hesitating as to whether he should come or not. We had to coax him in. After giving him a bath and something to eat, we put him to bed, and then he said: 'Oh, that's grand, sir!'"

The City Home soon became too narrow for many applicants. Mr. Quarrier, wishing to find a place for building a series of Homes—not farther than three miles out of Glasgow—made arrangements for the purchase of twenty acres, which were to cost £6,000; but something happened by which the negotiations were set aside. A friend mentioned the present site, but was met with the objection that it was too far out from Glasgow. Yet, on visiting it, he could see at once that it answered his own ideal of what was needed, far more than the other. He lifted up his heart and voice and said: "Lord, this will do. Thy will is far better than mine, and I accept it thankfully." He purchased forty acres at a cost of £3,560 and the change to Bridge of Weir was made in 1876. In 1878 the first building in which were combined home, church, and school, was finished. The present area consists of 106 acres, and during the past year there were over 1,300 children at the Homes.

As the work became more and more known, people ceased to call Mr. Quarrier an Utopian. Friends were raised for his schemes, and contributions came in from all parts of the world, varying in amount from the widow's mite to the merchant prince's thousands. One day Mr. Quarrier found an old envelope containing bank-notes to the value of £1,700, with anonymous request to build a home called Sagittarius. Another time he received a donation of £500 saved in pennies by a poor widow.

Then, again, one day a Glasgow washerwoman sent for him to tell him that she wished to give him her fortune. She had been a hard-working woman all her life, spending most of her time at the wash-tub. Of an economical turn of mind, she put penny to penny and shilling to shilling for a rainy day. Long years of saving and compound interest accumulated her earnings to the handsome sum of over £1,400. She was an unconverted woman. God moved her heart at the right time for the Homes to be provided with pure water by means of her money, and for her to receive the Water of Life through the instrumentality of Mr. Quarrier. She died a few days after the donation act, with the words trembling upon her lips, " Just as I am, without one plea."

These are only a few instances of the wonderful ways in which funds came in just at the very moment they were needed. If they were not coming in, the servant of God would understand that he was not called to do the work that lay on his heart. He never undertakes anything without the necessary amount in hand; consequently there is not a penny of debt upon any of the Homes.

Until recently Mr. Quarrier sent bands of boys to Canada; but, owing to an act passed by the Ontario Government, which came into force in September, 1897, the outlet to the Dominion has for the present been closed. This law prohibits children from being taken into the province without a descriptive licence, which is degrading to the children, as it reminds them and others of their antecedents. Under these circumstances Mr. Quarrier has resolved to make provision for a longer residence in the Homes, thus securing for them a more thorough training for trades and domestic service at home. This will require the erection of ten additional Homes, which will cost £2,000 each.

Since our visit the twenty-eighth annual meeting was held, on November 22, at the Christian Institute, Glasgow, under the presidency of the Hon. the Lord Provost, Mr. Samuel Chisholm, and attended by a large and influential company of friends.

W. M.

CHAPTER XXX

THE GROWTH OF BELIEF IN "DIVINE HEALING"

FOR about half a century, the inquiry has excited increasing interest, "How far may we carry to the Lord bodily ailments, in prayer and faith for healing?" A body of believers, both numerous and respectable, affirm belief in divine healing as a truth taught in the Word, and as a fact of their own experience.

There are those who sympathize with such views; others who either doubt or deny and reject all such notions and experiences as illusive and delusive; and others who feel neither sympathy nor antipathy, but *apathy;* hesitating to dispute such testimony, yet ready to take no definite position.

Is it possible to find a firm standing-place, and form an opinion, clear, reasonable and scriptural?

There is a Scriptural basis for the doctrine of divine healing, in answer to prayer. The doubt concerns its *present application.* That the "prayer of faith shall save the sick," admits no more question than the incarnation, atonement, or any other truth, explicitly taught in the Word. But, we need to guard this admission by a few careful limitations, such as the following:

1. Disease is treated in the Bible as one of the consequences of sin, and one of those "works of the devil" which Christ came to destroy. (Job ii, 7; Luke xiii, 16; I John iii, 8.)

2. Disease is commonly represented as a judicial infliction from God in consequence of sin; the promise of,

at least, comparative immunity from it is attached to obedience; and its removal is conditional upon repentance and reformation. (Ex. xv, 25, 26; Deut. vii, 15; xxviii, 27-35; Psalm xci, 5-8; cv, 37; Isaiah xxxiii, 24; 2 Chron. vi, 28-30.)

3. Healing power is not ascribed to remedial agencies, but always primarily to God. Remedies may conduce to the result, but are inadequate without His blessing. Hence, Asa is disapproved because his primary reliance was on the physicians, and not on God. (2 Chron. xvi, 12-13; Ex. xv, 26; Psalm ciii, 3; 2 Chron. xxxvi, 16 [margin]; Jer. xxx, 17; Deut. xxxii, 39.)

4. The power to forgive sins and the power to heal disease are so associated that one is used to confirm and establish the other. (Psalm ciii, 2, 3, 4; Mark ii, 5-10.)

5. Miracles of healing were, next to his teaching, the conspicuous feature of our Lord's earthly life, inseparably linked with His atoning work. Isa. liii, 4-5, is quoted in Matt. viii, 16, 17. The circumstances are specially significant. In this " Scriptura " Miraculosa of Matthew, a comprehensive array of miracles of healing is presented; and, in the midst of the account, no reference being made to the typical character of disease or the spiritual application of Christ's atoning work, the quotation occurs: " That it might be fulfilled which was spoken by Isaiah the prophet: Himself took our infirmities, and bore our sicknesses." The previous verse contains an epitome of Christ's healing works, and thus connects them with this prediction. If the quotation has no reference to bodily infirmity and sickness, what is its pertinence or connection? These miracles of bodily healing are treated as a fulfilment of that prophecy, as though He, who " bare our sins " somehow also bare our sickness.

6. Miracles of healing were among the signs which

were to follow those that believe, as part of the witness of the gospel's power, and of the glory of its triumph. (Mark xvi, 15, 18; John xiv, 12, etc.)

7. Divine healing continued to be wrought through the apostolic age; nor is there a hint of any purpose of our Lord that these displays of divine energy should ever cease; and, as the New Testament nears completion, prayer for the sick is enjoined as a means of divine healing. (John xiv, 12; Mark x, 51, 52; vi, 13; Acts ii, 43; iii, 6, 7; iv, 30; v, 15; ix, 40, 41; xiv, 8-10; xix, 12, and James v, 14.)

8. It can not be proven that such healing has ever wholly ceased. It may have declined, in proportion to the decline of evangelical faith, evangelistic activity, unworldliness of life and power in prayer; but competent witnesses testify that healing, in answer to prayer has, to some degree, been found in every age. Especially do "signs", similar to those of primitive days appear to have been wrought by devoted missionaries and their simple converts, where the gospel has been brought into contact with a people rude, unimpressible, ignorant and in conditions, similar to those which prevailed when it was first preached and which seemed to justify the expectation that God would give "boldness" to His servants in preaching, "by stretching forth His hand to heal." These statements were not generally doubted by believers, until zeal to overthrow the "faith-cure delusion" led to rash attempts to prove that all supernatural signs long since answered their purpose and entirely ceased; and so, classed with miracles, they have been treated as impossible, on whatsoever testimony supported. Such a position is almost identical with that of the deist, Hume, whose name is linked with Gibbon, Bolingbroke, Rousseau and Voltaire, as a deadly foe of our faith.

This is a question, first, of scripture testimony, and, secondly, of trustworthy evidence; on such grounds the issue should be tried.

Who are the witnesses? Christlieb writes, in his volume on " Modern Infidelity," p. 332, " In the history of modern missions, we find many wonderful occurrences, which unmistakably remind us of the apostolic age. * * In both periods, there are similar hindrances to be overcome in the heathen world, and similar palpable confirmations of the Word are needed to convince the dull sense of men." He instances Hans Egede, pioneer in Greenland, who, finding that his hearers, like many in the time of Christ, had a perception only for bodily relief, sought with prayers and tears the gift of healing to prove to them the power of the Redeemer whom he preached; then ventured in the name of Christ, to lay his hands upon the sick, and scores of them were made whole. Similar facts are recorded of the Moravian missionaries, Spangenberg and Zeisberger; of the Rhenish Mission in South Africa in 1858, in the memoir of Kleinschmidt, and of Nommensen in Sumatra.

Luther, after wrestling in prayer at the bedside of the dying Melancthon, said " Philip, be of good cheer, thou shalt not die," and, from that hour, Melancthon revived. Bengel records the case of a girl in Leonberg, immediately healed by the prayer of faith, whose case was examined and publicly certified as genuine. Spurgeon, in review of the testimony to supernatural power in the institutions, founded by Frankè, Falk, Stilling, Gossner, Müller, Fleidner, Harms, Wichern, Dorothea Trudell, etc., designated these believers as " modern workers of miracles." He declared that he had seen unquestionable instances of divine healing in answer to prayer, but had not given them publicity, " lest the minds of men should be unduly turned from spiritual healing to the relief of bodily disease."

Rev. Dr. Burr, in " Ad Fidem," discussing " Modern Signs," says to unbelievers who clamor for present examples of supernatural power, " I am able to present to you substantially just such examples of the personal intervention of God among men as you ask. You shall have examples belonging to your own time and sphere." Then giving thirteen pages to answers to prayer, he says, " they are divine actions, as truly such as any which under the great name of miracles are attributed to the world's early ages. We do not choose to call them ' miracles,' But, for all that, they are direct divine interpositions, and can no more, in accordance with the scientific principles of evidence, be ascribed to any natural source, than could the sundering of the Red Sea under the outstretched arm of Moses."

C. K. Studd, Stanley Smith and others, of the famous " Cambridge Band," were peculiarly anointed of God, and great power attended their prayers. In Pekin, an epileptic, regarded as incurable, was by the physicians themselves indicated as a good subject for the experiment of what prayer can do, where medicine fails. Mr. Stanley Smith and Dr. MacKenzie anointed him and prayed over him, and he was perfectly restored.

Dr. A. J. Gordon, of Boston, became personally acquainted with unquestionable cases of God's healing in answer to prayer; as for instance, a slave to opium, who, in 1876, during Mr. Moody's meetings in Boston, in great mental distress, begged Christians to pray for his deliverance, believing that, without the direct power of God, his case was hopeless. A few gathered round him, and earnestly besought God for him. He never afterward felt the least craving for opium, and became a prominent Y. M. C. A. secretary. Dr. Gordon had a friend, a returned missionary, whose son had a cancer in the lower jaw, and the removal of the jaw was the only hope of saving his life.

He was at the hospital, and the next day was set for the operation. The evening previous, fervent prayer was offered. Dr. Gordon's mind was impressed that the Lord might be expected to interpose in behalf of this young believer, the son of a devoted missionary; he invited the afflicted father to his house, and sat up with him till midnight, conversing and praying over this matter. The father then resolved to cast himself and his boy wholly on God, and the next morning the lad was brought to Dr. Gordon's house and was pointed to Christ as his healer. His mind became imbued with the conviction that God was able and willing to heal him, and the directions in James v, 14, 15 were literally followed. The jaw entirely healed, not a trace of the cancer could, after a few weeks, be found; and even the teeth, which had been loosened, were again held tightly in the jaw. In Pastor Blumhardt's Prayer cure, a few hours from Tübingen in Germany, both body and soul are restored to wholeness in answer to prayer, and the only remedy applied is that divine panacea, the Gospel.

9. Sickness being obviously included among what the Bible calls " God's chastenings " (Hebrew xii), it is plain that, so far as this fatherly discipline has in view the correction of faults and the rebuke of sin, the only remedy must be, repentance and reformation.

Physical suffering may be classed under three heads:

1. Organic penalty, due to violation of natural laws, including hereditary infirmity or diseased tendency.

2. Physical retribution, or punishment for violations of moral law.

3. Divine chastisement or fatherly correction, not for judgment, but for weaning us from this world and all other idols. This is limited to children of God by faith.

4. Educative suffering, to ripen such virtues as implicit

faith, patience, unmurmuring submission, and sympathy with sorrow.

So far as bodily disease or infirmity is the organic result of sin, a judgment on sin, or a correction for faults, resort to medicine, instead of repentance, evades the whole issue. If natural laws have been transgressed by excesses, over-eating, intemperate drinking, overworking, reckless exposure, irregular habits, neglect of sleep and of Sabbath rest, God uses the scourge of nature to whip us into obedience to the laws of health. Medicine may bring temporary relief; but, if the violation of physical law continues, we only invite a more violent scourging which no medicine can even relieve.

A friend asked Mr. Moody to make a certain minister a subject of special prayer, who had suffered for years from insomnia, nervous depression, indigestion, and symptoms of approaching paralysis. " There's no use praying for that man," abruptly answered Moody, " unless he is going to obey the laws of nature. He has been sitting up half the night to write editorials, and worked for years without regard to proper rest or sleep. I don't believe in praying for the recovery of any man who doesn't obey the laws of health."

Even where disorders are hereditary, rigid attention to cleanliness, pure air, good food, regular habits; careful avoidance of the excesses and exposures to which, in the parent, the hereditary taint was due, may relieve, and in many cases remove, the evil. Sometimes the scourge is God's reminder, to induce such care and caution as may prevent the further transmission of similar morbid tendencies. Combe, in his " Constitution of Man," writing only as a scientific infidel, vindicates this law of nature as, on the whole, wise, just and good, notwithstanding the suffering it often causes; and he invents a fable to illustrate this.

A young heir complains to Jupiter because, in consequence of his father's debaucheries, he is pierced with pangs, for sins not his own. Jupiter replies that, by the very law of which he complains, he also receives from his father delicate nerves, vigorous muscles, keen senses and many noble capacities and faculties of mind and heart; he offers in his case to suspend the offensive organic law, but warns him that, in losing his pain, he will also lose all advantages and benefits coming to him through hereditary descent. He further reminds him that even his pain is a kindly monitor, to warn him from the paths of vice, trodden by his father. The sufferer withdraws complaint, resigns himself to his sufferings, and resolves, by obedience to all bodily laws, to reduce his pains, and, if possible, bring back his body to a normal and healthy estate.

So far as disease is a direct divine judgment on moral offences, we can hope for its removal, if at all, only as we repent and reform. This was continually illustrated in the history of Israel. Idolatry, rebellion, profanity, sensuality provoked God's judgments, in pestilence, plague, and calamity of every form. Imagine the Hebrews, when that great plague smote them at Kibroth Hattaavah, for their angry murmurings, sending to Egypt for medicine men, holding consultations about herbs and poultices, applying sinapisms and cataplasms to heal a plague that only sorrow for sin could even soothe! Or, when Miriam's jealousy led her to rebel against Moses, and God smote her with leprosy, imagine Aaron calling together the skilful doctors of Israel and of surrounding countries to treat her case, using curious prescriptions of drugs; allopathic doses, homœopathic dilutions, or hydropathic packs and washings, as remedies for God's own judgment on her sin! Pharaoh might as well have tried to rid himself of the plagues by medicating the Nile, by frog-traps and fly-traps, and fine-toothcombs, by fumigations and salves and patent medicines. Had Miriam attempted any such remedial treatment, it would have been fresh insult to the Lord who was dealing with her. She consented to be shut out of the camp as unclean, for seven days, until fasting, humiliation and prayer removed the leprous scourge.

When sin against moral law—intoxication, sensuality, debauchery, deliberate abandonment to crime,—has brought a stroke of judgment, it is aggravated rebellion virtually to deny God's connection with the bodily curse; and, instead of turning to Him in repentance, turn away from Him and undertake to undo His work of judgment by the aid of drugs! To permit such devices to succeed, would be striking a blow at His own authority,—entering into competition with man, and allowing man to circumvent Him!

The third class of ailments are corrections in love. We have some fault, that the Father would chasten away; some wrong temper or disposition, that He would transform; we have wandered, and He seeks to reclaim; we are unduly attached to some idol, and He seeks to wean; some lack of conformity to His will He would correct! In such cases, the discipline ought not to cease, until the wrong is purged away, or the result attained! The very word, " chastisement," has a lesson. A parent chastises for a fault; the object of correction is to correct; as soon as the child becomes obedient, and the fault is corrected, the chastisement is of course abated; for, from that moment, if chastisement continued, malice would displace mercy, and hate, love. But, until then, to abate chastisement would be sparing the rod but spoiling the child.

God dealeth with us as a father with the son in whom he delights, and, so far as bodily suffering is His chastisement, we should seek its removal only so far as its end is attained. The first step, therefore, should be to the Physician, not of the body but of the soul; not the poultice of figs, but the face to the wall; not the decoction of herbs, but the panacea of the gospel. We are to inquire what the Lord seeks to rebuke, change, correct, or remove. One ounce of holy reflection, penitence, prayer, is worth a pound of drugs. One drop of Jesus' blood or the oil of the Spirit, is worth all Neptune's ocean, or all the essences and extracts in the world. It is not the balm of the apothecary, but the " balm of Gilead," that is needed. This would not be disputed, had not materialism and practical atheism so tainted Christian life, that we practically shut God out from our affairs. In modern notions the universe is a clock work, wound up somehow, and somehow never running down; the wheels move regularly, and nothing can stop them; there is no intelligence guiding them; blind " natural law " is the mechanical mainspring. If you get caught and half crushed between the cogs, it is an accident; and all you can hope to do is to get the doctor to bind up your wounds with bandage and healing salves and ointments and set your broken bones. You have come into collision with a machine, which has neither intelligence nor will, love nor mercy. All you can do is, if possible, to repair the damage by some other machine or mechanical appliance, and for the future be more careful. Medical science drifts, nowadays, towards this materialistic, mechanical theory. God is excluded from the domain of bodily ailments, and uniform, inexorable laws control health and disease. The physician has investigated the machine, and can tell you how to keep out of its way; or, if you have got hurt, he has his machinery of bandage and poultice, knife and battery, drug and salve, to make you over, good as new. If you have sinned by overwork, dose yourself with quinine; if you are sleepless from excessive study, court artificial sleep by soporifics and anodynes; if you have disordered your stomach, " use for your stomach's sake," a little wine or more powerful stim- ulants; if you have been guilty of sensual excesses, resort to patent medicines. No recognition of God or con- science! no injunction to obey God's law, keep the Sabbath holy, cease mad pursuit of gain and fame, fast instead of feasting, give brain and stomach rest, and cut off all sins of the flesh. Thank God! all physicians have not been swept along upon this current of practical atheism! The mention of Sir James Y. Simpson of Edinburgh and Al- fred Post of New York reminds of the illustrious host of Christian physicians, who have both believed and taught a Scriptural theory of disease: that man sins against God when he transgresses a moral or physical law; that repentance is therefore the first step toward a true re- covery, and obedience the true preventive of similar ills; that, behind physical laws and their uniformity, is an in- telligent, benevolent Sovereign, whose ways of working they are, and right relations with whom are the primary secrets of all normal conditions of body or soul. Some of the most skilful doctors never wrote a prescription or administered a remedy without a prayer for guidance. One such, who stood at the head of his profession, would in the sick-room, seek, first, to lead his patient to repent- ance toward God, and faith in our Lord Jesus Christ; and he said that remedies proved practically ineffectual, where the patient was rebellious and disobedient toward God; and that, " where there was a right spirit toward God, all his remedies wrought far more rapidly and effectually; and that, in many cases, a change in the spiritual life became the basis of physical cure." He would therefore counsel the sick, show them their disobedience toward God, guide them to Christ and pray at their bedside; and, where all remedies failed, point the dying to the Physician of souls.

As to bodily afflictions designed for the education of

character, God may have lessons for His saints which can be learned only in the school of suffering; and this may account for the fact that some who have so learned patience and submission that their faces shine with the solar light, and their bed-chambers are the vestibule of heaven, abide for long years in a suffering body.

Just here, the " Faith Cure " school often runs to an extreme. Some say that all sickness is the result of sin; that, as the atonement of Christ avails for sin and all its consequences, of which sickness is one, faith will enable us to escape sickness, and they conclude that all sick persons are sinners, or if not unsaved sinners, unbelieving saints. The fallacy and sophistry of such reasoning are not hard to trace. Sickness is the fruit of sin, but not necessarily of the sin of the *individual sufferer.* As parts of a social organism, none of us are independent of others; and when, at any point, the organism suffers injury, the shock is felt throughout; suffering is entailed not only by heredity, but by society; nor shall we be wholly delivered from partnership in the sorrows and sufferings of humanity till we are no longer part of an unredeemed society, and we must all " travail in pain together," until the " day of redemption."

10. There is a Redemption for the body and, while its consummation is found only in the resurrection, bodily health in its anticipation. (3 John, 2; 1 Thess. v, 23; 1 Cor. vi, 19; Ephes. v, 30; Rom. viii, 11; 2 Cor. iv, 10, 11.)

The drift of such passages is that, by faith, we become so identified with Christ, that our bodies become the temple of the Holy Spirit, and the life of Jesus is manifested in them. Surely, a body in which the Spirit dwells ought, by virtue of that fact, to be a better body, and feel the thrill of that divine life in better blood, brain, brawn, bone and nerves! The divine indwelling should have both a purifying and healing effect on even the material temple.

11. As " Jesus Christ " is the " same yesterday and to-day, and forever," the measure of blessing we receive from Him depends on the appropriating power of our faith. Perhaps the notion that healing power is no longer exercised, hinders asking in faith, and touching the hem of His garment, so as to be made whole. " The blood of Jesus Christ cleanseth from all sin." Yet we are not cleansed from all sin so long as feeble faith does not grasp the fulness of this promise. And so, while He has still the same divine healing power, believers may not receive the fulness of healing virtue, because faith does not lay hold on His power. Increase of faith may make larger blessings possible. " Far more people are humbugged by believing too little, than by believing too much," said Barnum. And in our relations with God, a faith whose boldness and largeness of expectation border on presumption, is far better than the unbelief that dares neither to ask nor hope for blessings which He only waits for our asking, to bestow.

12. If, therefore, supernatural signs have disappeared in consequence of the loss of primitive faith and holiness, a revival of these latter may bring new manifestations of the former. Supernatural signs appear to have survived the apostolic age; but we cannot trace them beyond the period of Constantine, when the church lost its separateness, merged with and into the state; when evangelistic activity declined and evangelical faith decayed; and so the conditions of God's special presence among His people no longer existed. If in these degenerate days, a new Pentecost should restore primitive faith, worship, unity and activity, new displays of divine power might surpass those of any previous period.

In conclusion we set up a few landmarks of limitation and qualification.

1. There is in the Old Testament an emphasis on tem-

poral blessings, not found in the New. Hence Francis Bacon wrote: " Prosperity is the blessing of the Old Testament; adversity, the blessing of the New." Before Christ came, the future state was more imperfectly revealed, and the life that now is was correspondingly prominent. The definite promise of long life, immunity from disease, and outward well-being, is not, for some reason, repeated in the New Testament. When Christ brought life and immortality to light, the emphasis passed from things temporal to things eternal, and the need of incitements to duty and obedience, drawn from this life, does not exist to the same degree. In the New Testament, there is a conspicuous absence of such incentives—no promise of long life, but only of abundant life; not of barns filled with plenty, but only of necessary food and raiment; not of freedom from disease, but only of blessing through discipline. Those who hold opposite views must go back to the older Scriptures for their primary warrant.

2. No use of natural means can be proven improper, provided dependence be on God. The most marked cases of healing have been, like that of the " woman with the issue of blood," where ordinary means have failed. If some rush to extreme positions, neglecting even common precautions and abandoning even harmless remedies, using prayer as the only antidote to poison, the only healer of broken bones, the only preventive of small pox, the only substitute even for vitiated air, there are others who, free from such fanaticism, hold the truth within spiritual and rational and sensible limits.

Faith in God's healing power is not to be put on a level with the presumption of the fanatic who, finding his wife suffocating with charcoal gas, instead of opening the window to let in fresh air, leaves her shut in, while he runs for the elders with their anointing pot. A witty editor who stigmatizes the advocates of faith-cure as those who " neither use a fig-poultice nor care a fig for a poultice," raised a smile of derision, but convinced nobody. " A light word is the devil's keenest sword," and such weapons are easily turned by him against the truth and its defenders. No doctrine is so fundamental, no fact so unmistakable, that it has not been robed in satire—" The blood " sneered at, the Lord's table caricatured, the inspiration of the Bible travestied: but all these are like the attempts of the smart boy to excite laughter by charcoaling the clown's features over the alabaster face of a Minerva or a Madonna.

In weighing truth or falsity we need calmness, fairness, courtesy, charity, sound argument and a Scriptural spirit. Yet how seldom do we find such a spirit in the examination of the question, as is found in Dr. Gordon's " Ministry of Healing." " Faith-cure " is the butt of so much satire that one can scarce write on it, without risk of being made a blind Samson " to grind in the mill, while the Philistines look on and make sport."

As we should not carelessly resort to ridicule, so ought we not to be blinded by prejudice. Bacon classed the barriers to progress,as the idols of the tribe,or race prejudice; idols of the den or cave, or individual prejudice; idols of the forum, or contagious prejudice, and idols of the theater, or prejudice imbibed from influential men or teachers. There is plenty of this fourfold idolatry. When intelligent believers affirm their conviction, founded on experience and observation, that God directly, in answer to prayer, heals otherwise incurable disease, they are met, not with impartial and courteous investigation; but with prejudices that spring from violent hostility to everything supernatural, from professional bigotry, from obstinate conservatism, or from virtual idolatry of a few prominent leaders or teachers who know everything, and whose dictum settles all questions at once.   It is our duty neither to be biased by previous judgments, nor borne down by the weight of mere human authority, though a Daniel come to judgment, or an "infallible" Pope issue his "bull." Every question is to be examined in the light, first of Scripture teaching, and then of competent testimony.   No shafts of ridicule, no bolts of denunciation need alarm, for he who is on the side of truth and God, may dare to stand alone, for " one, with God, is a majority."

3. Fanatical extremes are no argument against essential truth.   Coleridge said that fanaticism is often only "the refraction of a truth yet below the horizon;" and consequent discoloration.   Much fanaticism is the result of convictions of truth, embraced amid opposition.   Behind the " vagaries of faith-healing," may be hidden a precious truth which the mass of professing Christians live in too worldly a state to recognize or accept.   Hence, those who do, driven by antagonism and ridicule, into separation and isolation, run to extremes ; but such has been the history of every reform in morals or religion.

Some earnest Christians who believe in Divine Healing hesitate to avow it.   A godly and conservative minister who is at the farthest remove from fanaticism, constitutionally calm, discreet, judicious, declared to me his belief in healing in answer to prayer ; accounting it a gift never wholly withdrawn from the church, varying in extent with the conditions of spiritual life ; but he does not think the use of proper means excluded, or that all sickness implies in the individual a low state of piety or faith.

4. There is no necessary antagonism between divine healing and human healing.   The discoveries, achievements and advances of medical science are wonderful, especially in anæsthetics, antiseptics, febrifugal and kindred

remedies and appliances. But such science is neither omniscient nor omnipotent; at best, in many things uncertain and experimental, if not blind and powerless, even by the confession of experts.*

Idolatry of medical science, on the part of doctor or patient, is wicked and absurd. While using lawful means, we are to remember that only He who made this body, understands its healthy or morbid conditions, and the causes and cure of its diseases, and no remedy can even relieve without His blessing!

5. Divine Healing has been brought into contempt by the rash claim that, if authentic, it belongs to the *miraculous*. The broad distinction between *miraculous* and *supernatural*, even Horace Bushnell failed to recognize. The *supernatural* moves *above nature;* the *miraculous* moves *contrary to nature,* as where the dead are made to live or a lost limb is restored. The supernatural may move in the same direction as nature, adding the impulse of a divine energy. Conversion is not miraculous, but it is supernatural. In the mind it produces convictions; in the heart it awakens affections; in the will, it stirs resolves, beyond the power of the natural man. A wind may blow against a running stream so as to *arrest* its flow; or in the direction of its current, so as to *quicken* its flow; the former illustrates the miraculous; the latter, the supernatural. When God needed to accredit His messengers,

---

* Prof. N. Chapman says: "Medical conclusions differ widely from every other species of evidence; we cheat ourselves with a thousand illusions and have imposed on us still more deceptions. Dark and perplexed, our devious career resembles the blind gropings of Homer's cyclops round his cave." Sir Astley Cooper says, "The science of medicine is founded upon conjecture and improved by murder." Oliver W. Holmes said that "it were better for mankind, but bad for the fishes, if all drugs were cast into the sea." Prof. Armour wrote: "Drugs are administered, patients recover and we suppose we have cured them, whereas our remedies may have had little or nothing to do with their recovery; very likely it took place in spite of our drugs."

He wrought miracles, which were in contrast with all natural modes of working; as when fire burned up a sacrifice soaked with water, and even licked up the water, or an impotent man suddenly got not only strength to walk, but acquired the art of walking; bread is added to as it is subtracted from and multiplied as it is divided; water, that nature takes a season to transform into grape juice, is turned instantly into wine in water-pots; and a man, dead four days, is called forth by a voice. There may be no more need of such miracles, and it may be best that they should not be wrought, that they may stand as God's special seal of authority upon certain inspired teachers. If a seal becomes common, it loses value; if any believer may work a miracle, and even fanatics, extremists and heretics, what becomes of God's attestation of his prophets, his apostles, his Son?

But it by no means follows that God is not always supernaturally working. Every believer who receives from God strength to do what otherwise he could not do; to see a truth to which the natural man is blind; to love the holiness to which the carnal heart is hostile; whose will is divinely enabled to break the bonds of a life habit; who feels the thrill of conscious contact with God in the closet, and goes forth in His might, to speak for Him and battle with evil—is wrought upon by a supernatural energy: it may use his natural powers and work in the lines of his ordinary work and life; there may be nothing sudden, startling and appealing to the grosser senses; but a divine Spirit is moving the man with a new and strange energy.

Every true disciple begins to be such by a supernatural act called regeneration, advances by a supernatural work, called sanctification, is qualified for service by a supernatural anointing, known as unction, and with literal truth can say, " it is no more I that do it, but Christ that dwelleth in me." Who shall dare say that supernatural working is confined to the spiritual nature, and does not touch the physical? If, inhabiting the believer, the Spirit of God works in him to will and to do, so that his spiritual life is essentially a supernatural life, on what authority can any one declare that the body can feel no effect of that divine indwelling? John Knox, George Whitefield, John Wesley, Edward Irving and many other such saints have risen from the sick bed to undertake for God work that demanded the full strength of body; or, in the midst of incessant strain and tension of work, have not even known fatigue! They found it true that there may be *exertion without exhaustion;* they renewed their strength, waiting on God; they walked and fainted not; ran and were not weary; and, when every natural power seemed to fail, mounted up on tireless wings as eagles.

6. As to anointing, various views are held, which may be classed as medical, symbolical, sacramental. The symbolical seems most sensible—that it was a symbol of the anointing of the Holy Spirit. So regarded, it may be used or not, as the believer prefers, as one of those matters of which every man is to "be fully persuaded in his own mind."

Some decline to anoint, for fear of unduly magnifying a mere outward form; but it is possible to elevate it to undue importance, by making an issue upon it. Why not yield to honest preference in things "not essential?" If ministers of Christ would use this harmless form, where desired, it would at least withdraw one comparatively trifling matter from the arena of controversy.

Worldliness and carnality are so overrunning the church, that the breath of believing prayer is stifled by a godless atmosphere. Much of the connection between sin and sickness is thus overlooked; chastisements, meant to scourge us for violations of natural laws and divine commands, are accepted as inevitable; and, instead of leading to repentance and reformation, foster a mistaken martyr-dom. Hundreds of cases of bodily infirmity which might be remedied by prayer, holy living and laying hold on God, get no relief, because relief is sought in medical expedients: the cause lying deeper, the remedy fails to reach the seat of the disease.

One thing is sure: prayers for the sick often do not avail. To say that God's promise is limited to the " *prayer of faith*," and that such faith is not simply a *grace*, but a *gift*, not to be exercised by all and at all times, may be only an apology for the lack both of the gift and the grace! The more of the *grace* we cultivate, the more of the *gift* is likely to be conferred. The one need of our day is a higher type of piety—a closer walk with God. The carnally-minded disciple can not have the contact with God which conveys to our impotence the energy of omnipotence. To live for the treasures or pleasures of this world is to be dead while we live; and a dead Christian is a powerless Christian. A new hold on God might prove a new revelation of a faith that removes mountains, and wrenches sycamores from their rock-bed! a faith to which nothing is impossible!

CHAPTER XXXI

THE study of questions of *eschatology*, or " the last things," particularly the approaching " end of the age," has taken on new interest of late.

Many think such studies unpractical, and that to determine anything, as to the future, with certainty, is impossible; and yet, among those who have investigated along these lines, and claim to have reached positive conclusions, are many, whose scholarship is of a high order, ard who have both large acquaintance with Scripture, and intense devotion to the person of Christ. There is also among such a general consensus of opinion that we are now on the threshold of that crisis, unparalleled in the history of the Church and of the world, concerning which Christ bade us to " watch and pray."

In view of all this, it may be well to consider some of the main arguments urged for the conclusion and conviction that the time of the end is drawing near.

We select *twelve* of the more conspicuous, presenting these positions, rather as the historian or annalist than as the advocate. These opinions are not always mutually consistent, not all starting from the same point of departure, nor based upon the same systems of interpretation and calculation; yet they are of value as illustrating one common trend of opinion toward the one common conclusion which, like the golden mile-stone at Rome, is thus reached by many roads from diverse starting points.

Six of these methods of computation have a *numerical*

basis, and to appreciate the argument, at whatever be its
worth, one must understand and recognize a NUMERICAL
SYSTEM as manifestly pervading the whole Word of God
from Genesis to Revelation, and which constitutes a sort of
mathematical framework upon which the entire structure
of written Revelation is built. This will not surprise those
who have already found such a numerical structure pervading all the *works* of God in creation, and have traced
the curious mathematical correspondences in historic
periods. In astronomy, chemistry, biology, mineralogy,
botany, anatomy, there are mathematical laws of dimen-
sion and proportion, geometrical ratios, and numerical
systems, that the scientific observer is compelled to admit
and admire.* There are signs of one mathematical Mind
which astonish and overwhelm us. The orbits, periods of
rotation and revolution of the planets, and their respective distances from the sun; the spiral course and regular
recurrence of leaf-buds on the trees and plants, the proportions and dimensions of crystals, the chemical ratios—
all these and similar facts found among the thousand
forms of life and myriad operations of nature, reveal conformity to strict mathematical laws. There are octaves
of color as well as of sound, and from Sirius down to the
invisible atom, the uniformity of order tells of one Creator
and Designer. This fact being once admitted, it becomes
less a novelty to find evidence of a like mathematical precision in the structure of Scripture and the events of history.

Thus prepared, we may glance at the various positions
taken by devout students of prophecy and history, as to

---

* Thomas A. Edison has the insight to see through mechanism into the
Mind behind it. "Chemistry," he says, "undoubtedly proves the existence
of a supreme Intelligence. No one can study that science and see the wonderful way in which certain elements combine with the nicety of the most
tdelicate machine ever devised, and not come to the inevitable conclusion
hat there is a big Engineer who is running this universe."

the time of the end, and seek to get the outlook from *their* points of survey, noting in advance that, by at least twelve independent methods of calculation and computation, they all reach a common conclusion that *some great crisis lies between the years* 1880 *and* 1920, *or thereabouts.*

I. THE MILLENARY BASIS.—We are told that " One day is with the Lord as a thousand years, and a thousand years as one day." (2 Peter iii, 8.) This is taken as a hint, by no means obscure, of God's chronology, and is construed as favoring the old Jewish tradition that there are to be six millenniums, or days of a thousand years each, and then a grand seventh millennial day—a thousand years of rest—the true millennium. If so, this thousand years of Sabbatic rest, crowning the six long days of a world's toil, can not be far off. According to the current chronology, but one more century would be needed to complete the six millenary periods; but reckoning Joshua's " long day " as the turning point when the longer *solar* year gave place to the shortened *lunar* year as the standard of reckoning, the year, 1899, would complete the sixth millenary since creation (2,555 + long and 3,444 + short years). This method of construing Scripture and computing time has gained many adherents of late, both in Britain and in America, and it has at least the merit of symmetry and simplicity. It divides human history into seven equal periods of a thousand years each, making it all one great week of millenniums, whose vanity and vexation of spirit end in one grand final seventh period of Sabbatic triumph and rest.

II. " THE TIMES OF THE GENTILES."—Our Lord uses this phrase (Luke xxi, 24), making their fulfilment the boundary limit of Jerusalem's desolation, and Paul (Rom. xi, 25) uses a similar phrase, " the fulness of the Gentiles," as limiting the period of Israel's judicial blindness. It is, therefore, a natural and legitimate inquiry what period the times of the Gentiles span.

There is general agreement that Nebuchadnezzar, as the "head of gold" (Dan. ii, 38), and representative of the first of the world kingdoms (Dan. vii, 3, 4) is the typical world power from whom these times are to be reckoned, and that the "seven times" or years that "passed over him in his strange insanity" typify seven longer years or periods, each composed of 360 year-days,* or a total of 2,520 years, as covering the times of the Gentiles, to be fulfilled before the end. Reckoning from Nebuchadnezzar's first incursion into Judah, when Daniel was made captive (606 B. C.), the twenty-five hundred and twenty years would be complete about 1914 A. D. If the leading of the British Chronological Association be followed, and we reckon from Nabopolassar's assumption of the crown of Babylon, in the year 3377 A. M., the seven full "times" would expire in 5897 A. M., which is believed to coincide again with the year 1899. By a second road, therefore, the time of the great crisis is identified with the current period of human history.

III. The "Historical" Method.—Closely connected with this is a third mode of computation. "The times of the Gentiles" (2,520 years) apparently fall into two equal divisions of 1,260 year year-days or "forty and two months," "a time, times, and half a time" (3½ years). This division is conspicuous both in Daniel and the Apocalypse,† and the desolation of Jerusalem in the seventh century seems to be the dividing line. Advocates of the "historical" interpretation of the Apocalypse generally hold

---

* The prophetic year seems to be one of twelve equal months of 30 days each.

† Rev. xi, 2, xii, 6-14, Dan. vii, 25.

the " beast " and " the false prophet " to represent respectively the papal and Moslem world powers, the Crucifix and the Crescent. They find a curious coincidence at least in the fact that both these systems date from the point where the first 1,260 years end, a period lying between 606 and 620 A. D. approximately, these being the dates of the " decree of Phocas " and of the " first Hegira."* Taking these dates as the terminus *a quo,* and adding 1,260 they come again to a terminus *ad quem,* lying somewhere between 1866 and 1886, as the beginning of the end of these systems as world powers. Moreover, in Rev. xi, 2, the treading down of Jerusalem by the Gentiles is the starting point of the second period of 42 months. If this be reckoned from 637 A. D. when, after centuries of nominally Christian rule, Jerusalem yielded to the victorious Omar, and he entered the city seated on a red camel, without guards or any precaution, the 1,260 days from that date bring us to about 1897 A. D.†

---

* If there were space for a fuller presentation of this subject, we should give more of the conjectures as to dates. For example, Elliott put the beginning of the 1,260 years at 529 or 533 A. D., when Justinian's edicts acknowledged John II. as the head of the church. Luther put it at 606, when Phocas confirmed Justinian's grant. Fausset thinks 752 the likeliest date when temporal dominion began by Pepin's grant to Stephen II.

† A writer in *The Biblical Scholar* says : Whenever Jerusalem gets into the enemy's hand she loses in a sense her glorious name of Jerusalem, " The Foundation of Peace," and becomes " Jebus," trodden down (see Judges xix, 10, 11). But this is not an everlasting condition ; it has an end. Once more shall Jerusalem be called " the city of righteousness " (Is. i, 27), which is equivalent to the *foundation of peace.* The times of the Gentiles seem even now hastening to their close in the utter failure of the Gentiles in government. The exact date of that end none can tell. It synchronizes with the restoration of the kingdom to Israel in her true Messiah ; but we remember that when the disciples asked the risen Lord as to this, He replied, " It is not for you to know the times, or the seasons, *which the Father hath put in His own power* " (Acts i, 7). " The Day," to which Scripture so often refers as " The Day of the Lord," has, like the natural day, its preceding evidences or signs, its streaks of dawn along the east, so that we may *see* the Day approaching " (Heb. x, 25), but the moment when the true Sun shall throw His glorious beams across this turbulent scene is hidden. Assuming the times of the Gentiles to have begun at the first capture of Jerusalem, B. C. 606, at the date of which the book of Daniel opens, then have

IV. The Sabbatic System.—The septenary division impressed upon the whole face of Scripture history is to many Bible students the key to unlock God's chronology. This Sabbatic system reaches back to Eden, and characterizes the annals of the race. First, God consecrated the seventh *day;* to this, in the Mosaic era, were added a seventh *week,* a seventh *month,* a seventh *year,* a seventh *seven of years* (the interval between the Jubilees), and a seventh *seventy* (490), introducing the Grand Jubilee. In at least two conspicuous places this last sacred number appears (1 Kings vi, 1; Daniel ix, 24). It covers first the years from the Exodus to the *completion* of the Temple, and again from the New Exodus from Captivity to the building of the New Spiritual Temple under the Messiah.

This number, 490, is a double type of completeness, being the product of seven times seventy, and of seven sevens (the Jubilee interval), multiplied by another sacred number, ten. The Jubilee periods reckon, of course, from Moses, under whom the first law of the Jubilee is announced. Counting the Exodus from 2515, A. M., the full seven periods of 490, or 3,430 years, would bring us to 5945 A. M., or 1943 A. D., as their extreme limit. But if reckoned by the *prophetic* year of 360 days, twelve equal months of 30 days—the limit will fall at about the present time.

V. The Antichrist Number.—This suggests a fifth mode or computation. This mystic number, " six hundred three score and six," is taken by some as a key to God's reckoning of time—or the Divine Calendar. (Rev. xiii, 18.)

This is the Divinely given mark of the Lawless One, who is to be revealed in the last year-week, and it is thus

they already lasted two thousand five hundred and four years, a period in itself of sufficient length to make us anticipate that its end must be drawing near.

inseparably linked with the Man of Sin in whom, personally, are to "head up" all the antichristian systems of history. This number is thought by not a few to be the symbolic number of perpetual unrest and incompleteness, being a repeating decimal, 666, ever approaching but never reaching seven, the number of completeness and rest. If this number be again multiplied by six—its conspicuous and characteristic factor—we get 3,996, a number having singular prominence in history. It measures the period of years between the creation of Adam, and the grand crisis, the *Birth of Christ.* Or again, reckoning from the Birth of Abraham, the Father of the Faithful,—a conspicuous epoch in sacred history,—we come to the close of this century as marking a new grand crisis, the Messiah's reappearing. This mode of computation will be at once rejected by many as fanciful, yet it has its value as another thread in the rope of many strands, which seems to unite the age in which we are now living with the grand consummation, and as such we give it a place in this array of argument.

VI. "THE ELEVENTH HOUR" MODE.—This method of computation is suggested by the parable of the laborers in the vineyard (Matt. xxi, 6), and has at least the merit of ingenuity. According to this view the world age, from the time of Christ, is to be divided into twelve "hours," marked off and separated by events of supreme significance, as the striking of God's clock. Of this mode of computation, Lieutenant Totten is an exponent. He makes the hours to be one hundred and fifty-three years each, this odd number being apparently suggested by the strange exactness and particularity with which the number of fish is recorded in John xxi, 11, the first miracle after Christ's resurrection, and connected with the labor of His apostles.

According to this reckoning, and counting from 3991 A. M., the beginning of the fifty-eighth generation of seventy years, and about the period of the birth of Christ, the hours would respectively end as follows: A. M., 4143, 4296, 4449, 4602, 4755, 4908, 5061, 5214, 5367, 5520, 5673, 5826, corresponding to A. D. 147, 300, 453, 606, 759, 912, 1065, 1218, 1371, 1524, 1677, 1840. Then would follow another generation of seventy years, to cover the calling of the laborers and giving them their hire—a series of judicial visitations, bringing us again to the same approximate limit, A. D., 1910.

The six other methods are not numerical but historical in their basis, and have reference to conditions existing among the three great divisions—the Jew, the Gentile, and the Church of God. (1 Cor. x, 32.)

VII. THE WORLD-WIDE WITNESS.—Our Lord Himself distinctly gave this intimation that the Gospel must first be published among all nations, and preached as a witness to all nations, and " *Then* shall the END come." Compare Matt. xxiv, 14; Mark xiii, 10.

With no little force many argue that there was never a period of such world-wide evangelism as now. Over three hundred missionary societies have spread their network over the earth, and more than ten thousand missionary workers, with a force of five times as many native Christian helpers. The Bible, translated into some four hundred languages and dialects, publishes by its printed pages the Gospel message, which living tongues proclaim. A few countries like Tibet remain to be entered, but even in these the iron doors seem about to open, and the time may be very near at hand when to every nation the witness shall have been proclaimed. Certainly, never at any previous period in human history has the " witness " been so generally borne to the various nations of the fallen race as

ion. Even the peoples among whom no missionary dwells have more or less come into contact with the testimony of the Bible and the missionary to the facts of Christianity.

VIII. THE LAODICEAN STATE.—This mode of estimating our present place in the world's history, is of course drawn from the hints found in Rev. iii, 14-22. But the argument is especially strengthened and confirmed by a comparison with Matt. xiii, 47-50. The latter gives a glimpse of the last state of the *Kingdom* as the end draws near, and the former, of the *Church* at the same period. In Matthew we have the world-wide evangelism, already referred to, symbolized in the *Dragnet,* cast into the world sea, and gathering of every kind; and, in Revelation, we have the Laodicean church, with Christ shut out, and self-satisfaction and offensive lukewarmness reigning within; and these two apparently contradictory conditions, coinciding and coexisting in the last days. With awful emphasis do some devout souls point us to the startling fact that just now, and never before, this strange paradox is realized: the Church engaged on the one hand in the most extensive and world-wide evangelization, and yet involved on the other hand in the most hopeless deterioration, rich, increased with goods, in need of nothing, but virtually shutting out Christ. This is called the paradox of history, and it is maintained that these seemingly conflicting states are to be realized in the days immediately preceding the coming of the Son of Man—as a like paradox existed in the Jewish state at His first coming.

IX. THE APOSTASY.—Another basis of computation, similar to the foregoing, but not identical with it, is found in a much broader exposition of the Scriptures. We are plainly told of a falling away (*Αποστασια*), to precede the Son of Perdition, and the Parousia of the Son of Man.

2 Thess. ii, 3. This apostasy has a full portraiture in the Pastoral Epistles, in Second Peter, First John, and Jude. The features in the portrait are marked. They are such as these: a colossal development of selfishness, a generation of *heretical teachers*, iniquitous practises even among believers, the love of many waxing cold, the Church of God becoming Satan's synagog and seat, the Word of God and His doctrine blasphemed, the Church wedded to the world, having the form without the power of godliness, and the Lord's coming, the blessed Hope, scorned and scoffed at, etc.

To these and similar features, many prayerful disciples call attention, and ask whether we are not even now in the age of the apostasy, iniquity abounding and the love of many waxing cold; the authority and inspiration of the Word undermined even by professedly Christian teachers and preachers, and a wave of worldliness and materialism, sweeping over the Church, and carrying away every distinctive mark of an apostolic assembly. Similar conditions have existed before, but, it is said, never in the face of such light, privilege, and opportunity, nor to a similar extent.

X. THE ANARCHISTIC AGE.—Side by side with the prophetic hints of an *apostasy in the Church* stands the portrait of *anarchy in the world,* and in the same writings. And again the features are very marked: gigantic selfishness, covetousness, pride, self-glory, blasphemy, false accusation, idolatry of pleasure, etc., but mainly the lawless spirit—ANARCHY. Lawlessness in the family, in marital incontinence, and disobedience to parents; lawlessness in society, in truce breaking, and false accusation; lawlessness in the state, in despising those that are good and being traitors to those in authority; lawlessness toward man, without natural affection, and toward God in scoffers that

mock His warnings; wandering stars refusing wholly the
orbit of obedience and moving further into the blackness
of darkness.   Behold, say many, the lawless spirit now
prevailing, the uprising of organized resistance to all lawful authority, magisterial or ecclesiastical—the combination of forces to supplant all government; and at the same
time the arbitrary attempt to compel men to limit even
trade and commerce by a certain " mark," which alone
shall authorize one to " buy and sell " (Rev. xii, 16, 17).
For the first time in history these two signs of the last
times of anarchy have had simultaneous development;
the recent growth of communism, socialism, and nihilism,
wholly unprecedented, and side by side the growth of
monopolies, trusts, trades unions, and protective organizations, restricting even buying and selling by their " mark."

XI. THE JEWISH SIGN.—Many regard as another sign
of the end, the obvious drift of the Jews toward their own
land and the rehabilitation of their national life, not to
speak of the conversion of so many under Rabinowitz and
other evangelical leaders, etc.   This is believed to be the
putting forth of the leaves of the " fig tree," which our
Lord gave as a sign that the end is " near, even at the
doors " (Matt. xxiv, 32, 33).   There is something startling about the rapidly increasing Jewish element in Palestine and the movement known as " Zionism " that has developed within a few years, and summoned four great conferences in European centers, where leading Jews have met
to discuss the very problems of Jewish colonization and
national revival.   Has the patriotic and national spirit of
the Jewish remnant had any such time of reawakening
since Christ ascended?   Is this the fulfilling of Ezekiel's
vision of the dry bones (Ezek. xxxvii.) ? If so, what events
are " at the very doors? "   A missionary in Palestine calls
attention to the fact that ten times as many Jews reside

there as forty years ago, and that their social status is becoming more influential and commanding. Hundreds of converted Jews are already in the Church of England, and thousands in the Church at large, and there are unmistakable signs of Jewish reawakening.

XII. THE SPIRIT'S RESTRAINT.—The last of all these signs of the end to which space allows reference is that which concerns the mysterious prediction concerning Him who continues to " let " or act as the Hinderer of Evil, and whose self-removal is to leave the mystery of iniquity to find full revelation (2 Thess. ii, 7).

Some hold that, as Satan is the hinderer restraining all good, so the Holy Spirit is the Hinderer, restraining all evil; and that the good Spirit will be withdrawn in effect as an active administrator in the Church and resisting force in the world, before the crisis of lawlessness comes, and the end of the man of sin in the second Advent. Those who maintain this view contend that every sign shows that the Spirit either has withdrawn or is withdrawing even from the Church, *as a whole;* that as a cause or a consequence of such withdrawal there is left so little spiritual worship or work, spiritual faith or life; that, while these all exist in the elect few, they characterize individuals rather than the Church as a body. Especially is this fact made prominent by the advocates of this view, that in the matter of *administration,*—the specific office of the Spirit, —He is displaced by the spirit of the age, as evinced by the worldly men, maxims, methods, the secular spirit, artistic music, worldly oratory, entertainments, etc., everywhere prevalent. And those who sound this note of warning, this midnight cry, feel constrained to bear witness that no sign remains in the Church at large that the Spirit of God retains His seat in His own temple, and that the Shekinah glory is already departed.

All this should at least stir up thoughtful readers to search for themselves into the warnings of the Word, to watch the signs of the times, and to ask what are the indications above the prophetic and historic horizon.   " Daniel understood by books the number of the years," and hence knew that the seventy years of desolation were about accomplished (Dan. ix, 2).   If the signs of the near end of a longer period of desolation are to be found in the books, and read as in the sky, it may well incite us all to be among the searchers and the watchers, who, while others sleep, are awake and looking for the dawn.

APPENDIX

Circular of the Adult Bible Class

or

Superintendent's Guild of Bethany Church,
Philadelphia, Penna.

APPLICATION FOR MEMBERSHIP

My name is...

I live at...

Occupation and where employed:

...

My family consists of.............................

If a member of any Church, please state what Church:

...

I AGREE

FIRST.—To attend every Sabbath afternoon, Providence permitting, excepting the....................Sabbath of the month.

SECOND.—I will faithfully endeavor to live up to the rules of the Class, and do whatever I can in making the Class useful.

Signed, full name:

....

The
Articles of Association
of the
Superintendent's Bible Guild.

We agree to associate ourselves together, mainly for an hour's conference on religious subjects, on Sunday afternoons, and for such other means of improvement and usefulness as are herein set forth or may from time to time be adopted.

Agreement of the Teacher

The teacher binds himself to be present, to give a twenty-minute talk, every Sunday, unless sick or absent from home.

Members' Agreement

The members agree to attend each Sunday, as stated by each one at time of making application, unless sick or away from home.

Members' Bibles

Each member agrees to own a moderate-sized Bible and bring it to the study meeting every Sunday.

Members' Weekly Gifts

Each member agrees to give the fixed sum of not less than either two or three cents a week, to make ten cents a month, for the purposes stated further on.

Members' Pledge

If a Christian, to engage with the teacher and put *conscience* in such work as he may propose.

If not a Christian, to spend a little time each day, alone, with the question, " Why am I not a Christian?"

Members' Duty

To make it a point to attend:

1. A monthly Vesper Service, from 7 to 8, on the first Sabbath evening of each month.

2. The Quarterly Conference, to be held the fourth Monday night of March, June, September, December.

3. The Anniversary Meeting, during the month of February.

Members' Promise

a. To read over during the week the Scriptures to be studied on the Sabbath.

b. To do all fault-finding with each other and the teacher privately, and only with the person at fault.

c. To try each week to find some one to invite to the Sunday meeting of the Guild.

d. If not able to attend, to send a written resignation, and, if removing, to take a Certificate of Dismission.

Form of Organization

Each ten members shall constitute a Club or Band, and shall have as its captain, or leader, a head, to be known as the Titheman. They shall sit together, in seats specified by the teacher.

Each nine Clubs (9 x 11—99 persons) shall have a Governor or Centurion.

The Centurions and Tithemen and the membership of each of the Bands shall be appointed by the Teacher.

Each corps of one hundred shall have a name and each company of ten shall have its own name.

Certificate

Each member will receive a Certificate of Membership when admitted, and an annual statement of the number of times attending during the year.

Accounting Steward

There shall be one Accounting Steward, who shall sit at the Treasury table and receive the collections and the moneys to be paid over by the Tithemen, keeping proper accounts, and reporting each Sabbath the collection of the previous Sabbath.

Attending Stewards

There shall be four Attending Stewards, who shall be at the doors when members are entering, and give out the envelopes. They shall also attend to all distributions, and take up the basket collections.

Secretary

There shall be one Secretary, who will keep the Roll-books, and have charge of all the blanks and printed matter.

Duties of the Centurions

They shall sit at a desk provided, keep a record of the attendance of the Tithemen and see that they attend to their duties, receive the contributions of their respective Guilds, count the same, keep a record, or pay over each Sabbath to the Accounting Steward.

They will maintain, by their personal diligence and the aid of their Tithemen, a kindly watch and care over the hundred souls committed to them, advance their welfare, wherever possible, by good counsel and helpfulness, and see that the teacher is apprised of anything that can be done by him to be useful to the flock. The Centurions will take turns in conducting the opening worship of the Sabbath meeting.

Duties of the Tithemen

To be present each Sabbath ten minutes before meeting begins; to see their members seated, receive the tithes and mark the attendance in Band book. To pay over each Sabbath the gifts to the Centurions, and to make out and give to the Secretary at the closing of each session, for the teacher, the daily statement of the class present, etc., on blank furnished by Secretary. It will also be their duty to visit the absentees, or state that they cannot do so.

Fortnightly Conference

A conference of the Centurions and Tithemen with the Teacher will be held the first and third Sundays of each month, at 2 p. m.

Honorable Mention

The Band showing the most regular attendance during the year shall be mentioned at the Annual Meeting, and shall be known as the " King's Guard " and shall be entitled to first rank and special honor on all occasions.

THE SPECIFIC AIM OF THE GUILD SHALL BE:

FIRST. To study and practice the Bible and encourage each other in the business of life.

SECOND. For each one to find something to do (if ever so little) for the good of those around us.

SOME OF THE METHODS TO BE EMPLOYED ARE THESE:

FIRST. To help the poor, sick and unfortunate.

SECOND. To maintain a Bible Woman and Colporteur to visit and circulate books.

THIRD. To maintain one child in the Orphanage.

FOURTH. To educate a deserving boy or girl in the Northfield Schools.

FIFTH. To maintain a weekly house prayer-meeting.

SIXTH. To maintain a mother's meeting.

SEVENTH. To actively engage in the temperance work.

EIGHTH. To engage in such other work as the teacher may from time to time suggest.

TEXT OF THE CLASS:

For the Son of Man came not to be ministered unto, but to minister and to give His life a ransom for many.

MOTTO VERSE OF THE CLASS:

> I live for those who love me,
>   For those who know me true;
> For the heaven that smiles above me,
>   And awaits my spirit too;
> For the cause that lacks assistance,
>   For the wrong that needs resistance,
> For the future in the distance—
>   For the good that I can do.

The Lord's Day, March 4, 1888.

TITLES in THIS SERIES

geles, 1925), *AROUND THE WORLD BY FAITH, WITH SIX WEEKS IN THE HOLY LAND* (Los Angeles, n. d.), *TWO YEARS MISSION WORK IN EUROPE JUST BEFORE THE WORLD WAR, 1912-14* (Los Angeles, [1926])

6. Boardman, W. E., *THE HIGHER CHRISTIAN LIFE* (Boston, 1858)

7. Girvin, E. A., *PHINEAS F. BRESEE: A PRINCE IN ISRAEL* (Kansas City, Mo., [1916])

8. Brooks, John P., *THE DIVINE CHURCH* (Columbia, Mo., 1891)

9. RUSSELL KELSO CARTER ON "FAITH HEALING." R. Kelso Carter, *THE ATONEMENT FOR SIN AND SICKNESS* (Boston, 1884) *"FAITH HEALING" REVIEWED AFTER TWENTY YEARS* (Boston, 1897)

10. Daniels, W. H., *DR. CULLIS AND HIS WORK* (Boston, [1885])

11. HOLINESS TRACTS DEFENDING THE MINISTRY OF WOMEN. Luther Lee, *"WOMAN'S RIGHT TO PREACH THE GOSPEL; A SERMON, AT THE ORDINATION OF REV. MISS ANTOINETTE L. BROWN, AT SOUTH BUTLER, WAYNE COUNTY, N. Y., SEPT. 15, 1853"* (Syracuse, 1853) *bound with* B. T. Roberts, *ORDAINING WOMEN* (Rochester, 1891) *bound with* Catherine (Mumford) Booth, *"FEMALE MINISTRY; OR, WOMAN'S RIGHT TO PREACH THE GOSPEL . . ."* (London, n. d.) *bound with* Fannie (McDowell) Hunter, *WOMEN PREACHERS* (Dallas, 1905)

12. LATE NINETEENTH CENTURY REVIVALIST TEACHINGS ON THE HOLY SPIRIT. D. L. Moody, *SECRET POWER OR THE SECRET OF SUCCESS IN CHRISTIAN LIFE AND*

WORK (New York, [1881]) *bound with* J. Wilbur Chapman, RECEIVED YE THE HOLY GHOST? (New York, [1894]) *bound with* R. A. Torrey, THE BAPTISM WITH THE HOLY SPIRIT (New York, 1895 & 1897)

13. SEVEN "JESUS ONLY" TRACTS. Andrew D. Urshan, THE DOCTRINE OF THE NEW BIRTH, OR, THE PERFECT WAY TO ETERNAL LIFE (Cochrane, Wis., 1921) *bound with* Andrew Urshan, THE ALMIGHTY GOD IN THE LORD JESUS CHRIST (Los Angeles, 1919) *bound with* Frank J. Ewart, THE REVELATION OF JESUS CHRIST (St. Louis, n. d.) *bound with* G. T. Haywood, THE BIRTH OF THE SPIRIT IN THE DAYS OF THE APOSTLES (Indianapolis, n. d.) DIVINE NAMES AND TITLES OF JEHOVAH (Indianapolis, n. d.) THE FINEST OF THE WHEAT (Indianapolis, n. d.) THE VICTIM OF THE FLAMING SWORD (Indianapolis, n. d.)

14. THREE EARLY PENTECOSTAL TRACTS. D. Wesley Myland, THE LATTER RAIN COVENANT AND PENTECOSTAL POWER (Chicago, 1910) *bound with* G. F. Taylor, THE SPIRIT AND THE BRIDE (n. p., [1907?]) *bound with* B. F. Laurence, THE APOSTOLIC FAITH RESTORED (St. Louis, 1916)

15. Fairchild, James H., OBERLIN: THE COLONY AND THE COLLEGE, 1833-1883 (Oberlin, 1883)

16. Figgis, John B., KESWICK FROM WITHIN (London, [1914])

17. Finney, Charles G., LECTURES TO PROFESSING CHRISTIANS (New York, 1837)

18. Fleisch, Paul, DIE MODERNE GEMEINSCHAFTSBEWEGUNG IN DEUTSCHLAND (Leipzig, 1912)

19. SIX TRACTS BY W. B. GODBEY. *SPIRITUAL GIFTS AND GRACES* (Cincinnati, [1895]) *THE RETURN OF JESUS* (Cincinnati, [1899?]) *WORK OF THE HOLY SPIRIT* (Louisville, [1902]) *CHURCH—BRIDE—KINGDOM* (Cincinnati, [1905]) *DIVINE HEALING* (Greensboro, [1909]) *TONGUE MOVEMENT, SATANIC* (Zarephath, N. J., 1918)

20. Gordon, Earnest B., *ADONIRAM JUDSON GORDON* (New York, [1896])

21. Hills, A. M., *HOLINESS AND POWER FOR THE CHURCH AND THE MINISTRY* (Cincinnati, [1897])

22. Horner, Ralph C., *FROM THE ALTAR TO THE UPPER ROOM* (Toronto, [1891])

23. McDonald, William and John E. Searles, *THE LIFE OF REV. JOHN S. INSKIP* (Boston, [1885])

24. LaBerge, Agnes N. O., *WHAT GOD HATH WROUGHT* (Chicago, n. d.)

25. Lee, Luther, *AUTOBIOGRAPHY OF THE REV. LUTHER LEE* (New York, 1882)

26. McLean, A. and J. W. Easton, *PENUEL; OR, FACE TO FACE WITH GOD* (New York, 1869)

27. McPherson, Aimee Semple, *THIS IS THAT: PERSONAL EXPERIENCES SERMONS AND WRITINGS* (Los Angeles, [1919])

28. Mahan, Asa, *OUT OF DARKNESS INTO LIGHT* (London, 1877)

29. THE LIFE AND TEACHING OF CARRIE JUDD MONTGOMERY Carrie Judd Montgomery, *"UNDER HIS WINGS": THE STORY OF MY LIFE* (Oakland,

[1936]) Carrie F. Judd, *THE PRAYER OF FAITH* (New York, 1880)

30. THE DEVOTIONAL WRITINGS OF PHOEBE PALMER Phoebe Palmer, *THE WAY OF HOLINESS* (52nd ed., New York, 1867) *FAITH AND ITS EFFECTS* (27th ed., New York, n. d., orig. pub. 1854)

31. Wheatley, Richard, *THE LIFE AND LETTERS OF MRS. PHOEBE PALMER* (New York, 1881)

32. Palmer, Phoebe, ed., *PIONEER EXPERIENCES* (New York, 1868)

33. Palmer, Phoebe, *THE PROMISE OF THE FATHER* (Boston, 1859)

34. Pardington, G. P., *TWENTY-FIVE WONDERFUL YEARS, 1889-1914: A POPULAR SKETCH OF THE CHRISTIAN AND MISSIONARY ALLIANCE* (New York, [1914])

35. Parham, Sarah E., *THE LIFE OF CHARLES F. PARHAM, FOUNDER OF THE APOSTOLIC FAITH MOVEMENT* (Joplin, [1930])

36. THE SERMONS OF CHARLES F. PARHAM. Charles F. Parham, *A VOICE CRYING IN THE WILDERNESS* (4th ed., Baxter Springs, Kan., 1944, orig. pub. 1902) *THE EVERLASTING GOSPEL* (n.p., n.d., orig. pub. 1911)

37. Pierson, Arthur Tappan, *FORWARD MOVEMENTS OF THE LAST HALF CENTURY* (New York, 1905)

38. *PROCEEDINGS OF HOLINESS CONFERENCES, HELD AT CINCINNATI, NOVEMBER 26TH, 1877, AND AT NEW YORK, DECEMBER 17TH, 1877* (Philadelphia, 1878)

39. *RECORD OF THE CONVENTION FOR THE PROMOTION OF*

Scriptural Holiness Held at Brighton, May 29th, to June 7th, 1875 (Brighton, [1896?])

40. Rees, Seth Cook, *Miracles in the Slums* (Chicago, [1905?])

41. Roberts, B. T., *Why Another Sect* (Rochester, 1879)

42. Shaw, S. B., ed., *Echoes of the General Holiness Assembly* (Chicago, [1901])

43. *The Devotional Writings of Robert Pearsall Smith and Hannah Whitall Smith.* [R]obert [P]earsall [S]mith, *Holiness Through Faith: Light on the Way of Holiness* (New York, [1870]) [H]annah [W]hitall [S]mith, *The Christian's Secret of a Happy Life,* (Boston and Chicago, [1885])

44. [S]mith, [H]annah [W]hitall, *The Unselfishness of God and How I Discovered It* (New York, [1903])

45. Steele, Daniel, *A Substitute for Holiness; or, Antinomianism Revived* (Chicago and Boston, [1899])

46. Tomlinson, A. J., *The Last Great Conflict* (Cleveland, 1913)

47. Upham, Thomas C., *The Life of Faith* (Boston, 1845)

48. Washburn, Josephine M., *History and Reminiscences of the Holiness Church Work in Southern California and Arizona* (South Pasadena, [1912?])